The Performance of Self

THE MIDDLE AGES SERIES

Ruth Mazo Karras, Series Editor
Edward Peters, Founding Editor

A complete list of books in the series
is available from the publisher.

The Performance of Self

Ritual, Clothing, and Identity During the Hundred Years War

Susan Crane

PENN

University of Pennsylvania Press

Philadelphia

10 9 8 7 6 5 4 3 2 1

Published by
University of Pennsylvania Press
Philadelphia, Pennsylvania 19104-4011

Library of Congress Cataloging-in-Publication Data

Crane, Susan.
    The performance of self : ritual, clothing, and identity during the Hundred Years War /
Susan Crane.
       p. cm. — (Middle ages series)
    Includes bibliographical references (p.) and index.
    ISBN 0-8122-3658-0 (cloth : alk. paper)
    ISBN 0-8122-1806-X (paper : alk. paper)
       1. Hundred Years' War, 1339–1453 — Social aspects — Great Britain.   2. Identity
(Psychology) — Great Britain — History — To 1500.   3. Hundred Years' War, 1339–1453 —
Social aspects — France.   4. Costume — Great Britain — History — Medieval, 500–1500.
5. Identity (Psychology) — France — History — to 1500.   6. Costume — France — History —
Medieval, 500–1500.   6. Ritual — Great Britain — History — To 1500.   7. Ritual — France —
History — To 1500.   8. Great Britain — Social life and customs — 1066–1485.   9. Great
Britain — Court and courtiers — History — To 1500.   10. France — Court and courtiers —
History — To 1500.   11. France — Social life and customs — 1328–1600.
DA185 .C89   2002
306'.0941 21   2002018727

Contents

Illustrations

Figures

Plates (follow p. 106)

A Note on Citations

English translations are provided for all citations from other languages. Translations from medieval texts are my own unless otherwise noted. In quotations from medieval texts, I have followed the modern distinctions between *i* and *j* and between *u* and *v*. Where they have become conventional, I use English forms for some French names, such as John the Fearless and Joan of Arc. I cite scholarly works' published translations in English whenever I am aware of them. Where the original publication of a scholarly work preceded its translation into English by more than ten years, the original date is provided in brackets in the bibliography.

Introduction

My target is a medieval courtier who is behaving strangely. What can she mean by dressing in leaves and flowers on the first of May? Why does he disguise himself as a wild man to interrupt a wedding feast? At such moments, self-conception intersects with self-presentation, and behavior conveys something of how courtiers inhabited their social identities. What these courtiers say about themselves could be seen as extraneous to their behavior, but I take their words as a functional part of their behavior, a component of their performances that should not be isolated from the material register. Conjoining these registers brings out complexities in medieval self-conception that may seem alien now, complexities that tend to be ignored in histories of self-consciousness.[1] Yet scholars, except perhaps for the most traditional Cartesians, are in agreement that self-conception is profoundly shaped by cultural and material conditions. We should expect people to understand and perform themselves differently from place to place and time to time. By attending to place, time, and performance together, I mean to apprehend secular identities in their specifically courtly and medieval aspects.

My premise that identity is both material and conceptual dictates a range of sources from lyric poetry to household accounts to chronicles and beyond. It might be objected that my evidence recovers not vanished performances but merely their textual vestiges. A chronicle's account of a courtier's disguising offers only mediated access to a historical moment, but its very mediations—its explanations of the behavior, its economy of representation, its judgments—constitute a generically shaped discourse of identity. Similarly, a lyric poem about May cannot record whether historical women accepted the poetic trope that they were daisies, but it can demonstrate the trope's place in a complex of ideas about courtly identity that Maying was said to enact. Wardrobe accounts provide another kind of information about the purposes of Maying, as they detail which emblems are embroidered on May garments and who wears a lord's livery for the festival. All these texts are at some remove from historical performance

itself, but they do articulate contemporary understandings of courtly performance and its meanings. Moreover, the very distinction between performance and texts is specious, insofar as performance is itself grounded in
conventions. Literary characters express chivalric commitment through the
poetics of a genre; historical knights are similarly engaged in a rhetoric of
appearances. It is on this citational plane of performance that historical and
literary instances of chivalric behavior meet and influence one another.

Late medieval courts are architectural spaces, institutions, and social
groups that assert their separateness and superiority to the wider world,
and claim in consequence an array of privileges and powers that further set
them apart. Castle building was an important form of social display, and
licenses to crenellate were eagerly sought, even in peacetime, because of
the tradition that aristocratic power derives from armed might. In provin-
cial castles and halls, the term "court" is generally less appropriate than
the term "household" to describe the institutional nature of a relatively
small assembly of people in varied ranks who serve a gentle family and
maintain its property; even in the large courts of kings and lords from
which my examples tend to be drawn, the household is a more visible
and documented institutional formation than the group of social peers I
call courtiers.[2] Late medieval courtiers constitute themselves especially by
staging their distinctiveness: their feasts, tournaments, entries, and weddings define their peculiarly elite splendor, generosity, power, and lineage.
The value of the term "court" for my study, which concentrates on social
relations, is that the term encompasses architectural and organizational
meanings as well, recalling that the successful court event mobilizes an
appropriate setting and a specialized administration, as well as its elite
participants. One of the courts I discuss, the ecclesiastical court of Rouen
that tried Joan of Arc for heresy, differs from the others in its religious
agenda but shares with the others a group of peers, a locus, and an admin-
istrative arm that together ritualize an important moment, soliciting a
public performance of identity and recording it with care.

I concentrate on courts in part because of the wealth of documen-
tation that is available about them, but also in order to extend the perspectives of cultural studies from the familiar terrain of how power speaks
to the oppressed to the less familiar question of how power speaks to itself:
how elites understand ideologies that are intrinsic to their authority, and
how they manage or fail to manage their intramural conflicts. These elites
wrote relatively little about their secular self-conception, and scholars have
followed their lead. Michel Foucault is not at his most revisionist in declaring the discourse of penance to be the medieval "technology of the

self," excluding any secular discourse from consideration. Caroline Bynum follows John Benton in concluding that the medieval "individual" exists only insofar as "the development of the self was toward God. . . . The goal of development is likeness to God." Brian Stock finds self-awareness beyond religious circles in the learned humanists of the late Middle Ages, but stresses that among them "a precondition of self-understanding is withdrawal from the world."[3] The artful personas of court poets have received important attention from literary scholars,[4] but their focus on written articulations does not tend to encompass the richly significant performances that accompany courtiers' assertions about identity.

To uncover these socially engaged selves, I concentrate on performances that supplement verbal with material self-presentation. By "performances" I mean heightened and deliberately communicative behaviors, public displays that use visual as well as rhetorical resources. My first chapter treats the wearing of elaborate court dress as a sort of synchronic performance, but most of the examples I consider are framed segments of time in which material appearance is as significant as verbalization. In these events ceremony, spectacle, ritual, festival, and celebration overlap, requiring the flexible, locally sensitive approaches to such events in recent anthropology and performance studies. Rather than seeking a definitive taxonomy, I concentrate on the specifics of each event and the place of self-assertion in it. Not that each event can be perceived in isolation: theorists of performance have complicated the apparent uniqueness of verbal assertions by pointing out that they are not purely under the control of their speakers but are instead complexly revoiced citations. "I do" marries people not because it is a totally self-generated assertion of will but because it reiterates a convention within a ritual framework that people generally accept as accomplishing marriage. The relation of one performer to her own words and gestures is embedded in prior performances and contingent on how others understand her. Performance studies take this troubling of agency as a productive link between individuals and their social situation: reiterative behavior recreates social identity, alters social relations, even reshapes beliefs and institutions.[5] "Performance" emerges in postmodern scholarship as an immensely compelling act at the intersection of agency and prescription, innovation and memory, self and social group.

Looking to performance for information on self-conception is appropriate to the particular shapes identity takes for secular elites.[6] The identity a knight displays in a tournament is radically performed; Maying, betrothal, and masking similarly intensify gesture and dress in order to articulate valued aspects of identity. The courtiers I study perform extensively

not only in specially framed moments but in their most routine encounters. Charles Taylor posits a dual source for contemporary selfhood, the
classical "honour ethic" of the warrior and leader, which is based in performance, and Plato's counterproposal that life should be guided by reason
and reflection. According to Taylor, both ethics, the performative and the
contemplative, persist in contemporary identity, but we no longer tend to
credit honor with its own rationales for making decisions.[7] For late medieval courtiers, the category of honor is large and central, encompassing not
just courage for men and chasteness for women, but many behaviors rela-
tive to personal comportment and social standing, everything indeed that
distinguishes courtly status from vulgar. Measures of honor most fully
define secular elites to themselves, although contemplation and faith may
occupy a subdominant role. Living in the externally oriented honor ethic,
secular elites understand themselves to be constantly on display, subject to
the judgment of others, and continually reinvented in performance.

    Their understanding resists associating performance with pretense and
falsification. Specifically, it rejects the broadly modern dichotomy between
an inner self that preexists social interaction, and a subsequent outer self
that conceals a more genuine inner nature. Sarah Beckwith argues that
asserting this dichotomy was crucial to the Reformation's attack on medieval theater, but was inaccurate to that theater's practice: the modern
claim that theatrical representations of God were blasphemous pretense
did not perceive, or willfully forgot, that medieval acting was a matter of
signifying rather than falsifying. In the cycle plays, Beckwith argues, "a
mask is not a disguise but a sign," a formal expression of the actor's willing participation in the communal, sacramental experience of the festival
of Corpus Christi. Stephen Jaeger argues analogously, in the context of
courtiers' professions of love, that medieval societies considered public,
conventional, calculated declarations of passion to be reliable and honorable, before this way of behaving became suspect in the Renaissance.[8]
Beckwith's and Jaeger's perceptions press against wider claims that the
social performances I examine are without substance, just "illusion and
dream" in Johan Huizinga's terms, "only style and ceremony, a beautiful
and insincere play."[9] My chapters will argue that, in several medieval contexts, public appearance and behavior are thought not to falsify personal
identity but, on the contrary, to establish and maintain it. A striking con-
gruence, though hardly an equivalence, links this medieval understanding
of identity to the postmodern perception that the ongoing gestures of
self-presentation amount to the very constitution of the self, not just its
secondary modeling.

The conviction of medieval elites that identity exists in social performance invites the analytical approaches of practice theory. Pierre Bourdieu's objection to "the biographical illusion," the misconception that one life can be narrated independently of other lives and their social nexus, has a lineage reaching at least to Norbert Elias's *History of Manners* and Erving Goffman's *Presentation of Self in Everyday Life*.[10] These early resistances to dichotomizing self and society insisted on their founding interdependence and the necessity of comprehending a social system in order to understand any single act within it. More recently, Michel de Certeau and Marshall Sahlins as well as Bourdieu have developed particularly influential versions of practice theory that articulate social insertion in terms of deeply ingrained behaviors which, by force of repetition, move from constructed to natural status in the understanding of practitioners. The "habitus" (Bourdieu's term adopted from Marcel Mauss) shapes consciousness from the outside in, pressing people to identify with their learned but profoundly habitual ways of conducting their lives.[11] Practice theory counters mentalist explanations of culture and cultural change; thoughts and intentions are themselves grounded in the repetitive practices of the habitus. Still, practice theorists make room for change within a sequence of repetitions: these can be nuanced, partly forgotten, varied in their timing, and assigned new meanings.[12]

The social performances on which I concentrate gain heightened significance from their formal, festive, and most often ritual contexts. Jack Goody argues that the term "ritual," like the term "intelligence," is too protean to be trenchant unless it can be specified in each new instantiation.[13] My chapters works over the category in relation to their diverse cases, but a few generalizations can be made here. For practice theorists, ritual is a powerful behavior because of its strongly reiterative quality. Understanding ritual as a repeatable performance, a "restored behavior" or "twice-behaved behavior" in Richard Schechner's terminology, unites ritual to the citational aspect of social performance in general.[14] Rituals resemble other performances not only in their repeatability but also in their tendency to use symbolic strategies and to assert a connection between the framed event and the wider world. At the same time, I am committed to a few of the venerable distinctions between rituals and performance in general. Rituals seek to draw all the members of a group into performance; even apparently passive onlookers have a stake in the rituals' operations. These are quite formal occasions that assert prominent cultural values, occasions that accomplish their work by invoking the power of shared commitments and beliefs. What that work is—what rituals mean to accomplish—is the most difficult question for my cases. They have less transcendent goals than (for example) baptism, but even secular rituals sometimes work to transform participants. A dominant concern of my chosen cases is to mediate tensions between persons and groups, in part through ambiguities and concessions that grant a certain latitude to any one participant's experience. Other events stage elite superiority precisely by framing and enhancing individual performances, producing an apparently seamless consonance within power.

Most clearly unifying all these court rituals is that they solicit intensified performances of secular identity. Because these performances rely on material as well as verbal resources, clothing is pushed forward to peculiar significance. For example, in a poetic version of charivari in the *Roman de Fauvel*, courtiers wear masks of peasants, fools, and animals but also take care to remain recognizable to each other. Rather than concealing a prior identity, they seek a dynamic simultaneity between that prior self and the supplementary identity of the costume. Their new hybridity licenses their disruptive response to a royal marriage by claiming the counterhegemonic position of marginal figures without entirely giving up the authority of courtiers.

For my concern with self-performance, clothing offers a more productive focus of attention than the body beneath it. Scholarship that focuses on the body owes much to practice theory's insistence that identity cannot float free from materiality. Historical, psychoanalytic, and anthropological work converges around arguments that body and consciousness are intimately related and that they express one another reciprocally. Scholars' reembodied consciousness rejects the possibility of a "natural" body preexisting acculturation in favor of a culturally constituted body rich in symbolic meaning.[15] This cultural body is necessarily clothed, but the specific mechanisms and meanings of clothing have received little attention. In the performances I examine, restricting the material register to the body is insufficient: the body is costumed, and clothing, not skin, is the frontier of the self. Theories of sexuality have tended to absorb the body into self-consciousness, stressing that consciousness produces and shapes embodiment. I want to push this perception that consciousness and physicality are interdependent in the opposite direction, outward, to stress the materiality of self-presentation, including every strategy of dress and gesture that a given event mobilizes.

The symbolic use of clothing in rituals is salient, but clothing is charged with meaning in all circumstances. Perhaps the most obvious function of clothing is to express and enforce standards of appropriateness, for example to mark social position, age, gender, season, and even time of day. Where luxury elaborates garments far beyond the norm, aesthetic considerations may seem to dominate semiotic ones, but the dichotomy is false; Bourdieu's work on aesthetic choices amply demonstrates that "the 'eye' is a product of history reproduced by education."[16] Aesthetic value is one aspect of social meaningfulness, an aspect that has peculiar stratifying potential because it is more susceptible to redefinition (in fashion trends, for example) than other meanings clothing can express (such as income and office). Clothing bears many further kinds of meaning as well. Sumptuary legislation restricts certain materials to certain statuses; liveries ally household members with one another and assert their lord's generosity but also his dominance; and rhetorics of austerity, immodesty, exoticism, or humility can permeate particular ways of dressing.[17] Only a few of the multifarious meanings for clothing will fall within the purview of this study. I have felt some frustration at exploring the extraordinary symbolic importance of clothing in late medieval practice while excluding most manifestations of that importance from these chapters. Clothing could provide the stuff for several books on "the social life of things" and "the cultural biography of objects," the ways crafted and manufactured products operate in people's daily lives.[18]

My examples are drawn primarily from the English and French fourteenth and earlier fifteenth centuries, the "long" Hundred Years War that Christopher Allmand sets at circa 1300 to circa 1450.[19] Although I am not investigating the Hundred Years War itself, it is more than a chronological frame for this study: it designates the paradoxical closeness of English and French speakers during this time. Not simply conflict but much negotiating, tourneying, hostage holding, intermarrying, gift exchanging, feasting, and celebrating brought the elites of England and France into close contact over these hundred and fifty years. The English claim to French territory depended on lineal claims to French titles that implied cultural ties as well. Until at least 1400, French was the identifying language of the English aristocracy, and throughout the wars, French manuscripts moved persistently across the channel to England, in patronage as well as in plunder. French aristocrats compounded their hostility with substantially less desire, but they did participate in English culture as captives: Charles d'Orléans wrote poetry in English; his brother Jean d'Angoulême took his manuscript of the *Canterbury Tales* home to France and continued to use it there. More generally, French and English elites subscribed to the notion of a transnational "order of chivalry" that gave them common ground. John II's Order of the Star imitated Edward III's Order of the Garter, and

English and French courts vied productively with one another in staging their public events.

My first chapter begins by tracing the exceptional importance of court clothing as a symbolic medium in the later Middle Ages, both within and beyond ritual. Expansively and expensively marked with mottos, heraldic signs, occulted signatures, symbolic colors, and allegorical messages, the courtier's dress was a visual manifesto for its wearer. The strongly rhetorical quality of court clothing helps explain its prominence in ritual articulations of identity. Using the Griselda story and the ceremony of alliance held at Ardres in 1396, this chapter argues that secular rituals facilitate self-definition by interrelating material and rhetorical performance.

Around the turn of the fourteenth century, courts celebrate the first of May by figuring women metaphorically as flowers, dividing participants into parties of Flower and Leaf, and in further ways elaborating contiguities between court and nature. My second chapter argues that wearing and becoming plants in this ritual shapes participants' sexuality and offers them the pleasures of fetishization. Courtly Maying draws on the popular festival but shifts it in just a few strategic ways to celebrate elite difference and superiority. A final section on the persona of Maying poetry finds analogies between poetic and ritual personas: both enjoy an identity poised between authenticity and dissimulation that enables them to comment on as well as profit from the ritual process.

My chapter on cross-dressed women focuses on Joan of Arc's performance for the ecclesiastical court that declared her a heretic. During her mission and even after her capture, Joan wore men's clothing (an embroidered blue silk hat survived for several centuries; she was captured in cloth of gold). During her long trial, her judges urged her repeatedly to give up her male dress. Joan first argued that cross-dressing was simply instrumental to resisting the English, but her argument failed as she refused to take women's clothing even in order to receive the sacraments. Joan's secular piety and the meaning of her dress become clearer in relation to a large vernacular literature of cross-dressing women. In relation to this literature, I argue that Joan is attempting to redefine her sexuality as well as her social standing.

Chivalric selfhood, the topic of Chapter 4, is intensely visible, gestural, and ritually performed. For lineal marks of identity, such as coats of arms, heraldic beasts, and ancestor myths, I argue for a totemic sensibility that locates selfhood beyond the confines of an individual body. Founded in honor as well as in blood, a titled knight's identity is impressively magnified in tournaments and other performances submitted to public judgment.

The Order of the Garter provides another ritual scene for knighthood, one that both resists and sustains individuation. A knight augments his stature by performing it so overtly, but the risk of misjudgment complicates his relation to the community of peers who certify his identity.

My last chapter treats wildness in courts. In January of 1393, Charles VI and several courtiers dressed as wild men for a wedding feast. One chronicle treats the performance as a charivari, a noisy protest against an irregular marriage; another declares it was only a festive interlude designed to entertain the wedding guests. I frame the chronicles' accounts with the charivari in *Le Roman de Fauvel* and the Christmas interlude in *Sir Gawain and the Green Knight*, exploring the motives for wild disguises and the compatibilities of wildness and courtliness.

The rituals I have chosen to examine differ widely in the kind of performance they solicit, from the rhetorical elaboration required in Joan of Arc's testimony about her clothes to the noisy spectacle of wild men dancing. These rituals concur nonetheless in assuming that identity can be performed, and that its performance makes it meaningful. In contrast to much postmedieval thought, and to strands of medieval religious thought as well, these rituals assert that the concretely visible—the courtier variously costumed, masked, liveried, cross-dressed, and disguised—is crucial to establishing identity and asserting its worth.

I

Talking Garments

CLOTHING WAS A SYMBOLIC MEDIUM for personal, lineal, social, and political messages in the courts of the Hundred Years War. Charles d'Orléans, as a young poet not yet in English captivity, had song lyrics embroidered along the two sleeves of a robe, with 568 pearls making up the musical notes to accompany the words "madame, je suis plus joueulx" [my lady, I am more happy].[1] Charles and his contemporaries covered their clothing with mottos such as "le droit chemin," "y me tarde," and "syker as þe wodebynd." Often the embroidered motto accompanied an appropriate visual sign: leafy branches for "the right road," a slow-growing oak for "I tarry here," and twining vines for "tenacious as the honeysuckle."[2] Motto and sign together were called a badge, a *devise* in French, and on occasion these badges spoke to each other: Louis d'Orléans's belligerent "Je l'envie" [I challenge him] with its knotty stick inspired his rival John the Fearless to reply with "Ik houd" [I hold firm] and a carpenter's plane.[3] Poets articulated symbolic associations for colors in clothing: black for austerity and mourning, blue for constancy, white for joy.[4] Most stable of all, though still subject to innovations, were heraldic marks of identity. Knights wore their coats of arms for combat but also on ceremonial cloaks and robes, and women's robes impaled their husbands' arms with those of their families of birth. Arms themselves could talk (*armes parlantes*, canting arms): Roger de Trumpington bore trumpets, the Wingfield family bore wings, and the memorial brass of Robert de Setvans is designed to show seven winnowing baskets (*sept vans*) scattered across his shield and battle dress.[5]

The very garments that make such assertions also convey enigmas. Who is "my lady," what is the "right road," where is it that "I tarry?" Personal signs tend to articulate a bearer they simultaneously mystify. One could trace this doubleness to the function of dress itself, which both presents and conceals a body. One could trace it to the nature of language itself, which never quite closes the gap between words and meanings. This chapter passes over the problem of origins to argue more narrowly that, in the later Middle Ages, personal identity and secular ceremony make substantial use of the talking garment. Its interplay of assertion and enigma sustains the courtly self and the court ritual alike. The ceremonies of alliance this chapter investigates (between kings and countries, at Ardres in 1396, and between husband and wife, in the Griselda story) transform participants by engaging them in elusive metaphors for their altered status. Badges deploy elusiveness to enlarge personal prestige and facilitate political alliances. My claim that ritual and self-performance depend on enigma as well as assertion meets its limit case in wifehood: Chaucer's version of the Griselda story assumes that she is capable of hidden thoughts and secret desires, but locates her virtue as a wife in her perfect visibility. The pivotal role of clothing in all these expressions of selfhood requires a quick summary of the social functions of clothing in late medieval courts.

Luxury Consumption and Fashion

Clothing is literally superficial (above the body's surface), but neither moralists nor legists of the period took it to be trivial or insignificant. A pervasive topic for moralists was the sinfulness of extravagant dress, whether too luxurious or too revealing.[6] A common understanding that dress should fit vocation informed the carefully chosen habits of different religious orders, whose colors, fabrics, belts, and sandals could all be glossed spiritually. In the secular realm, sumptuary legislation assigned clothing significant social weight. This legislation, which flourished throughout Europe from the later thirteenth century through the seventeenth, restricted various fabrics, furs, and ornaments to the use of specified ranks and income levels. Sumptuary regulation mixes conservative resistance to social climbing with a more pragmatic awareness that dress was becoming an important system of recognition in urban and mobile populations.[7] Clothing figured in interpersonal transactions as well: it was willed, resold, and recut, in part because the cloth itself was worth about ten times the tailor's charge for ordinary as well as luxury garments.[8] In wealthy households and in guilds, wearing liveries obligated the wearers to sustain their masters and companions but also licensed their independent actions by associating them with the superior power of the household or guild as a whole. Both the obligation and the license that liveries conferred were subject to abuses that worried moralists and parliaments.[9] In short, dress had moral, legal, and class significance throughout English and French culture, and regulating dress was understood to facilitate projects as vital as salvation, civic integration, and interpersonal harmony.

My focus, however, will not be on regulation but on its contraries—consumption, luxury, and self-assertion, where late medieval clothing works as substantially as in the realms of regulation.

A court "robe" of this period was made up of two to six pieces, such as tunic, supertunic, cloak, mantlet, and hood. Fine wool from Brussels, cloth of gold, satin, and velvet were sometimes brocaded and often decorated with embroidery, edgings, buttons, gems, pearls, appliques, beads, glass disks, and metal ornaments. Dress historian Kay Staniland points out that the manuscript illuminations and monumental brasses of the period do not adequately reproduce the complexity of luxury garments. Staniland locates several garments in a Great Wardrobe roll for the years 1350–52 that took from 300 to over 800 working days to produce because of their elaborately figured and trimmed surfaces.[10] A fine example of such decoration is a Christmas dancing doublet and "hancelyn" (loose outer garment) made for Roger Mortimer, fourth earl of March, in 1393. They were cut from nine yards of white satin; the doublet was embroidered with gold orange trees from which were suspended a hundred silver gilt oranges. The outer garment was embroidered all over with leeches, water, and rocks ["ove leches tout le garnement ove ewe et rokkes"] and further adorned with fifteen gilded whelks, fifteen gilded mussels, and fifteen cockles of white silver, weighing in sum more than 12 Troy ounces. Five suppliers were paid separately for the cloth, tailoring, embroidery, metal ornaments, and linings.[11] At a total cost of £24, this dancing outfit was worth more than twice Geoffrey Chaucer's annual salary as controller of customs, but it was only half as extravagant as Queen Philippa's five-piece robe for Easter 1332. At £54, this green outfit lined with miniver and edged with ermine was worth Chaucer's annual salary as clerk of the king's works plus many years' rent on his house and garden at Westminster.[12]

Luxury consumption tends to look aberrant in supply-and-demand terms, which take demand to be a universal driving force that responds to need. Luxury consumption as a way of life, that is, the apparently unnecessary consumption of fine goods at a persistently high volume, makes little sense in economic models where demand arises rationally from pragmatic needs for shelter and subsistence.[13] The 3,412 miniver skins (trimmed northern red squirrel bellies) used in just one of Charles VI's robes certainly respond to a desire for warmth, but exceed by several factors the actual bodily surface that needs protection.[14] But in a real social economy as opposed to a model, consumption is driven by a constellation of considerations in which managing and displaying status can be more compelling than keeping warm. Jean Baudrillard attacks "the myth of primary

needs" by arguing that consumption is always laden with symbolic importance, so fundamentally laden that utility is a subordinate concern in any
exchange. Marshall Sahlins similarly redefines the economic realm to encompass symbolic as well as material registers of value, using dress as his
example of how fully social meanings infuse the desire for goods. "Cloth is
a total social fact, at once material and conceptual," he concludes, urging a
revised model of production and consumption based in "cultural intention" rather than the "need satisfaction" model.[15]

As one "cultural intention" among many, the production and consumption of luxury clothing urged expansion in foreign trade and capital-
ization in cloth production during the later Middle Ages.[16] By the mid-
fourteenth century, technological advances in cloth making together with
tailoring techniques made possible by these advances brought about an
explosion of social meaning around clothing. Not that clothing dominated
production in general or that people spent most of their income on it, but
the innovations around fine clothing gave it a social importance comparable
to the high profile of coffee and chocolate in the late seventeenth century,
or television sets in the mid-twentieth century. A similar aura of cutting-
edge consumption based on new technologies unites these instances. The
changes that prepared for clothing to become such a highly charged product by the mid-fourteenth century were the establishment of an Italian
silk industry, long-distance trade in furs and oriental fabrics, and tighter,
more flexible weaving in northern European fabrics that made possible
form-fitting garments, such as long stockings, decoratively cut or "dagged"
edges, narrow hems, and precise tailoring.[17]

These advances amount to the origin of "fashion," which arises first of
all from the virtually infinite combinations of tight and loose elements that
can be achieved in one garment by precise tailoring, as opposed to merely
draping and gathering fabric. Until the fourteenth century, garments for all
social levels used simple, geometric cuts that might conceal or reveal the
body, but did not aspire to revise the body's contours. To be sure, earlier
centuries found ways to shape garments to the body: for example, lacing
and stitching after a garment was donned could tighten it. "Cutting-to-fit"
emerges only in the fourteenth century.[18] More significantly for the birth
of fashion, fourteenth-century tailoring commingles precise fitting with
artificial exaggerations and emphases. Fine tailoring allows silhouettes to be
endlessly reshaped, making change itself an aspect of consumption, alongside the more stable qualities of the fabric and its decoration. A salient
example of simultaneously fitting and revising the body is the short jacket
for men that appeared in the 1340s, worn with full-length stockings that

took advantage of the increased elasticity in fine wool weaves. The shaped torso with sleeves cut separately and fitted snugly into armholes announces "the definitive end of the totally rectangular cut" characteristic of earlier men's tunics, but in addition this new jacket is cut to enlarge the chest, padded there but nipped in at the waist.[19] The gentlemen serving at a feast of 1378, as illustrated soon thereafter in the *Chronique de Charles V*, wear this striking masculine silhouette, equally puffed in the middle and tightened at the extremities (see Figure 11). Chaucer's *Parson's Tale* objects to such garments' "inordinat scantnesse," but also to the waste of cloth in dagged, pierced, and trailing garments.[20] English chronicles blame the arrival of fashion's rapidly changing silhouettes on the Hainaulters who accompanied Queen Philippa to England, and who for the ensuing eighteen years

ordeyned and chaungyd ham every ȝere divers schappis of disgyngeȝ of cloþing, of long large and wyde cloþis, destitu and desert fram al old honeste and good usage; & anoþer tyme schorte cloþis & stret-wasted, dagged & ket, & on every side desslatered & boned, wiþ sleves & tapets of sircotys, & hodeȝ overe longe & large, & overmuche hangynde. . . . And þe wemmen more myseli ȝet pasted þe men in array, and cureslicher; for þey were so strete cloþed þat þey lete hange fox tailes sawyd beneþe with-inforþ hire cloþis, forto hele and heyde hire ars. . . .

[have ordained and changed every year diverse disguising shapes of clothing, from long, large, and wide clothes that abandon all old propriety and good usage; and at other times short narrow-waisted clothes, dagged and cut and on every side slitted and boned. The sleeves of their surcoats like their hoods have tappets, long and wide, which hang down too far. . . . And the women surpassed the men in the curiousness of their clothing, which was so tight that they had fox-tails sewn under their dresses at the back to hide their arses.][21]

This conjunction of diverse shapes and rapid change is the origin of fashion. The chronicler exaggerates the rate of change at once a year, but the very exaggeration stresses the importance of change, and its close relation to expert tailoring, in the fashion system. Hainault was not to blame; throughout Europe in these years the cut of garments began to emphasize and revise bodily contours and to change frequently.[22]

Scholars tend to see fashion and sumptuary regulation as contradictory forces driving incompatible economies (modern/traditional or capitalist/feudal). Fashion is said to speed up consumption by rushing ahead of all but the wealthiest, and sumptuary laws are said to slow down consumption by resisting change.[23] But the two forces coexisted from the late medieval into the early modern centuries, they cannot characterize entirely conflicting economic systems where they are so persistently in company. Since sumptuary regulations were largely unenforced in England and

France, Alan Hunt may be correct that they are more "declaratory" than proscriptive, aiming at "ensuring recognizability" rather than at constraining consumption.[24] In that case, sumptuary regulations and fashion trends would be hand-in-glove assertions that clothing expresses social standing; rather than exerting contradictory pressures on consumption, they could both be seen as urging the importance of consumption. For example, the distant origins of ermine, the expense of importing it, its heraldic use on coats of arms, and its sumptuary restriction to high ranks combine to produce and perpetuate ermine's exceptional status, whether or not the sumptuary restriction was obeyed and enforced. Ermine is already so enclaved by its scarcity, cost, and heraldic cachet that sumptuary law is but a belated contribution to its value. Far more than the law determines that ermine will be trimming Queen Philippa's Easter outfit, and not Philippa Chaucer's.

I have been heading toward two claims in this brief overview of the kinds of meaning attributed to clothing in late medieval milieux, the place of luxury consumption in the wider economy, and the exceptional importance that clothing acquired with the convergence of special markers such as exotic provenance, fine quality, tailoring, and the use of personal badges. The first claim, to be developed with regard to badges and other personal signs, is that courtiers thought of their clothing as a representational space for making personal assertions. One ground for this claim is the cultural prominence of luxury clothing: it had exceptional status even within luxury consumption. The second claim, to be developed in this chapter's third and fourth sections, is that clothing acquired special expressiveness in ceremonial situations. Coronation regalia would be an extreme example of clothing that has metaphoric meaning: these are signifying garments, often with a deep history of association to royalty, that take "investiture" back to its etymological roots. Another familiar example is the persistent importance of the bride's wedding dress. Throughout this chapter, I seek to demonstrate the importance of material self-presentation in social performance. I begin with the apparently synchronic case of badges in court dress, but I soon turn to two ceremonial cases, the marriage negotiation of 1396 between Richard II and Charles VI and the marriage represented in the tale of Griselda.

Personal Signs

A quite literal instance of the talking garment is the hundred-year vogue for using personal mottos, signs, and colors in clothing. These three media of representation could be closely associated, as were black, ostrich feathers, and the motto "Ich dien" [I serve] for the Black Prince, but often color, image, and motto were less firmly linked together. The practice of wearing such personal signs grew out of heraldic representation and is complexly related to it. From about 1350, self-chosen signs could supplement the comparatively fixed system of heraldry, which was becoming a closely regulated science of identification. Some of these personal devices, such as the Black Prince's ostrich feathers and the Bohun family's swan, pass down the generations and back into the province of heraldry; freshly invented devices cease to appear around 1450.[25] During most of the Hundred Years War, aristocratic clothing as well as furnishings and personal objects were pervasively marked with these self-generated signs. The practice is worthy of more attention than it has received. Perhaps the profound scorn of Johan Huizinga for this and all medieval "forms of thought in practice" has deflected scholarly energy toward less sullied ground.[26] The meanings of this curious practice begin to emerge where there is evidence for how personal signs were mobilized in specific encounters.

These are transient signs that can be advanced, withdrawn, and recombined over time. An illumination in *Les Demandes faites par le roi Charles VI* can begin to illustrate this fluidity (Plate 1). Charles's secretary and ambassador Pierre Salmon composed this book of advice and reports on his diplomatic missions in 1409, and a lavishly illuminated manuscript (Paris, BNF, MS fr. 23279) was complete within a few years of that date.[27] Pierre kneels next to the king's bed, his subordinate posture excusing his superior knowledge, while three other courtiers converse nearby. One of these is apparently John the Fearless, with his device of hops embroidered on his sleeve.[28] The king's superior authority is indicated not only by his half-reclining position but also by the multiplicity of his signs, which extend from his houppelande to cover also the bed and its hangings.[29] Five are depicted in all: the motto "jamais" [never] on the houppelande and the bed's canopy, the four colors of the canopy's fringe, the branches of broom and may on the bed's cover and curtains, and the animal on the curtains and the sleeve of Charles's houppelande. The illuminator mixes devices from various periods of Charles's life, as if to provide a historicized representation of him; Charles's wardrobe records indicate that his actual garments also evidence this ongoing reassemblage. More mobile and layered than identification by a coat of arms, this complex of ever-shifting personal signs asserts identity richly but also enigmatically.

The motto "jamais" appears in Charles's youth, in association with a winged white hart and the three colors green, red, and white; Colette

Beaune has shown that Charles drew on an episode from the *Queste del saint Graal*, which he had on loan from the royal library at the time, to transform a peculiar collared hart captured on a real hunt of 17 September 1382 into a royal badge reflecting sovereignty's transcendent power. In the *Queste*, a white hart enthroned, then flying upward, proves to be a figure for resurrection that was itself prefigured in a green, red, and white boat made of wood from paradise. "Jamais désormais nul autre ne le verra" [never again will anyone see this], says the inevitable hermit explicator as the hart vanishes.[30] "Jamais," the winged hart, and the three colors together make a powerful claim, as Beaune explains in detail, for the supreme authority of Charles VI. After 1394, however, the winged hart and the three colors almost disappear.[31] The four colors of the Salmon illumination (green, red, white, and black) appear from 1393 on, sometimes in association with the motto "jamais" and often in association with broom (*geneste* in the wardrobe accounts). Branches and pods of broom are among the most durable of Charles's devices; they appear on his clothing, beds, and personal objects, with the motto "esperance" as well as "jamais."[32] Branches of "may" (honeysuckle or other twining vines suitable for May chaplets) appear on garments for the first of May and occasionally elsewhere.[33] The animal on Charles's sleeve and bed curtains has been variously identified as a dog, tiger, wolf, and civet cat.[34] A tiger is most likely, since gold tigers figure elsewhere on Charles's clothing and manuscripts. There and in heraldic representation generally, tigers have no stripes, a tail ending in a brush, and "the curious head which it is so difficult to describe, but which appears to be more like the wolf than any other animal we know."[35]

From three to four colors, from winged hart to tiger to greenery, the carefully assembled coherence that Beaune finds in the early device ("never again will there be such a transcendent king") disperses in apparent confusion. The disappearance of some signs implies changes in Charles's commitments, but the persistence of other signs represents him in terms of constancy rather than change. And even as they express a dynamic personal history, Charles's devices shroud this layered self in mysteries. Is the 1393 addition of black to Charles's original three colors related to his first episodes of madness?[36] Do the tiger and its motto of 1394, "j'aime la plus belle" [I love the most beautiful one], have any ground in Charles's experience, as did the winged hart?[37] Some stories may be lost, but the enigmatic quality of most mottos suggests that personal devices were often deliberately occulted. Rather than simply proclaiming the bearer's identity, enigmatic signs work to mystify the aristocratic self by enlarging its signature but at the same time resisting close scrutiny.

One source of such enlargement is that personal devices, in principle at least, were not only self-chosen, but were unique to oneself. Jean Froissart relates an angry encounter between two young knights, Sir John Chandos of the English side and Jean de Clermont, marshal of France, on the eve of the Battle of Poitiers (1356). While churchmen attempted to negotiate a pause in the hostilities, the two knights discovered that each had independently adopted "une meysme devise sus son senestre bras dessus ses parures; c'estoit ouvré de brodure une bleue dame en un ray d'un soleil bien perlée et bien arréée" [an identical badge on his left arm above his garments; it was a blue lady embroidered in a ray of sun, well laid out and trimmed with pearls]. Each man contests the other's right to the badge and offers to fight to defend it. Froissart conjectures in his later version of the *Chroniques* that the badge had its origin in courtship: "cil doi chevalier . . . estoient jone et amoureus, on le doit et poet entendre ensi" [these two knights were young and in love, one can and should understand it thus]. Froissart acknowledges his interpretive leap in the phrase "one can and should," but his conjecture that each man adopted the badge as a result of experiencing love is not at all the conjecture of Jean de Clermont. Jean instead accuses Chandos of a dishonorable larceny that typifies the English in general: "Camdos, Camdos, che sont bien des ponnées de vos Englès; il sèvent à leur honneur faire peu de cose de nouviel" [Chandos, Chandos, this is so typical of you Englishmen; they can do very little that is new to accrue honor].[38] Jean's accusation is that Chandos shamefully purloined the badge from somewhere other than his personal experience and invention. Heraldic disputes make an instructive contrast with this dispute: in a case such as *Scrope v. Grosvenor*, the right to a coat of arms depends on proving the absence of innovation and the persistence instead of an unmodified coat through as many generations as possible.[39] Quite differently, honor accrues to the wearer of a badge insofar as it is his unique and independent self-expression.

This very uniqueness, paradoxically, makes badges a valuable currency for distribution to others. Even hidden origins and meanings contribute to negotiability when they imply a personal commitment. Well designed to this effect are the devices of Philip the Good, "aultre n'auray" [I will have none other], and his sister Marie de Clèves, "rien ne m'est plus" [nothing means more to me]. These assertions of profound devotion give a confessional weight to the device, inviting its recipients to share in the donor's occulted desire.[40] More often, the devices deemed appropriate for distribution have veiled political implications. "Ic houd" [I hold firm] of John the Fearless gets some focus from the carpenter's plane, which responds as if in a game of scissors-paper-rock to Charles d'Orléans's knotty stick. Yet John's verbal motto is cast as a general principle instead of an agenda, stopping just shy of pointed belligerence. The chronicler Enguerrand de Monstrelet interprets another of John's devices, the mason's level, in the same principled terms: recording John's distribution of tiny gold and silver mason's levels as New Year's gifts, he explains, "laquelle chose estoit en significacion, comme on povoit croire et penser, que ce qui estoit fait par aspre et indirecte voie, seroit aplanyé et mis à son reigle, et le feroit mectre et mectroit à droicte ligne" [this meant, one might believe and think, that what was made in a rough and crooked way, would be leveled and put to measure, and he would align it and set it right].[41] John's audacious claim to the power to "right" his world gains authority as it is shared among followers, while protecting itself from critique through its framing as an unimpeachable moral generality. The negotiability of badges explains in part their enigmatic turn; they invoke ideals, generalities, and vague desires as the common ground that can unite a giver and receiver.

Not every personal sign gets distribution, but many are deemed appropriate for household liveries, for gifts to small elites, and for striking alliances with adversaries. Charles VI commissioned robes with the tiger badge in 1394 for just himself and his brother Louis, whereas John the Fearless distributed 226 silver carpenter's planes to the "gentilshommes" of his household.[42] Charles VI used broom on widely distributed liveries, but at the same time he severely restricted its use in his "ordre de la cosse de genêt," really a pseudo-order in that it had no statutes, chivalric component, or assemblies. Its gold collar of broom cods, leaves, or flowers was a special mark of the king's favor, granted to only about twenty men and women per year.[43] Individual gifts could also bear personal signs: for example, Charles d'Orléans gave Joan of Arc a robe in his house colors, embroidered with his badge of nettle leaves, to thank her for liberating his city of Orleans.[44] These distributions are not identical in their implications; they are variously embedded in wider traditions of maintenance, chivalric alliances, diplomatic relations, and festive generosity. Distributions do share a presumption that a personal device draws its significance from being integral to the giver, yet also that its significance can be dispersed outward to those who receive the device.

The Salmon manuscript's representation of Charles VI conveys something of this paradoxical integrity and dispersion in personal devices (Plate 1). Charles's signs and colors circle around him, perhaps centrifugally such that he is embedded securely in his representations, but perhaps centripetally as well, in a visual attempt to represent the distributive, outward-flowing energy of personal signs as they were actually used. What kind of performance is implicated in signs so oddly poised between expressing a unique identity and distributing that uniqueness to others?

The evolutionary answer is that a significant "development" takes place between self-representation in coats of arms and in badges: the latter are personal rather than lineal; they instantiate "the developing opposition between a consciousness of birth and inheritance on the one hand and of individual subjectivity on the other."[45] That is, coats of arms value lineal identity, whereas badges value a unique interiority—distinctiveness from others rather than relation to them. The quotation is from Jonathan Alexander, but it could as well be from many other scholars for whom a teleology of growth divides medieval identification with groups from modern individuality, which resides in private thoughts and feelings.[46] My fourth chapter confronts at length this familiar story of growth, but it should be noted here how poorly personal signs match up with it. Far from indicating that aristocrats were coming to identify with isolated interiority, badges value alliances and communications. They situate identity in visible signs and audible mottos. To describe the distinctive identity expressed in badges, a term such as "negotiable self" or "self in circulation" would be preferable to "individual subjectivity." Nor does it make sense to think of coats of arms and badges in "opposition" to each other. Badges more accurately expand on heraldry than rebel against it. Badges can modulate an inherited coat of arms and they can be distributed, whereas coats of arms are inalienable. At the same time, badges perpetuate heraldry's bright symbolization, its compact and esoteric communication of identity.[47] Badges then push heraldic communicativeness beyond its bounds: they take signs of a self-chosen, distinctive identity to be negotiable and transferable.

The interplay of assertion and enigma in badges makes especially clear that celebrating interiority is not their purpose. Where a badge posits a hidden desire, it does so precisely *to make public use* of that desire. What is "individual" is most of all what one can put into circulation. Rather than expressing a "developing opposition" between familial and private selves, badges expand the repertoire of self-performance from the lineal to the individual register. Each of the signs and colors swirling around Charles in the Salmon manuscript is a personal assertion of some kind, an assertion the illuminator has chosen from Charles's own repertoire. Together they constitute his portrait more tellingly, for his time, than would a perfect depiction of his lineaments.

Personal Signs in Secular Ritual

An English observer has left a detailed account of one exchange of personal
signs that illustrates their use on a specific ritualized occasion. Anthropologists have long noted that gifting can produce subordination or alliance,
it can stratify parties or bind them up, depending on the nuances of its
deployment. In the negotiations for Richard II's marriage to Charles
VI's daughter Isabel, exchanging personal signs had an important place in
striking an alliance, together with the dowry and dower arrangements,
diplomatic agreements for a twenty-eight-year truce, and the church wedding. The marriage process stretched over many months. Official negotiations began in July 1395; once the most important terms were established,
a proxy marriage took place in Paris in March 1396. Preparations for the
ceremonial encounter of the French and English parties took several more
months. This three-day ceremony, held in late October on a hillside
between Richard's city of Calais and Charles's city of Ardres, was far more
extensive and expensive than the wedding ceremony itself. It was the
occasion for Richard and Charles to meet in person, seal their alliance, and
transfer the seven-year-old Isabel from her father's care to her new husband's. The church wedding followed on November 4 in Calais.[48] Richard's
and Charles's meeting near Ardres invents and plays out a secular ritual
designed to incorporate their personal interests and histories into the state
occasion of allying England and France.

The most complete account of the ceremony near Ardres is that of
an English participant, writing in Anglo-Norman; a shorter eyewitness
account appears in Michel Pintoin's *Chronique du Religieux de Saint-Denys*.
The latter version carefully details the written diplomatic agreements of the
meeting, but hardly mentions the ceremonial work of gifts and dress. Similarly, the *Annales Ricardi Secundi* translates much of the Anglo-Norman
account, but omits big chunks of the narrative having to do with Richard's
and Charles's most personal interactions.[49] From perspectives beyond and
outside the courts of Richard and Charles, it is understandable that the
event's salient outlines would be found in its signed agreements and long-
term implications, but the English participant's account insists that the
agreement between states depends on a transformed relationship between
the two rival courts and their respective leaders.

The English account of this event is particularly sensitive to ways in
which the setting, encounters, and gestures of the meeting near Ardres
aspire to transform aristocratic rivalry into alliance. On an unsettled hillside, the tents of French and English parties were divided by a road on

which stakes marked "le lyeu lymittee pur l'assemble des rois," the liminal meeting point at which the kings would cross into each other's camps. Two concerns govern these crossings: to knit the French and English spaces together, while also asserting their perfect parity. On the first day, for example, the two kings process to their separate tents, guided by emissaries from the other side; then each king sends a noble messenger of his own to the other side, confirming the time for their meeting. From the meeting point, the two kings walk up to a viewpoint, then down among the French tents, then over among the English tents, then to the French council tent where they take spices and wine and Charles presents gifts, and then to the English council tent where they take spices and wine and Richard presents gifts. Parting finally at the "lyeu lymitee," they agree to share in building a chapel on the spot to "Nostre Dame de Pees" (Peace).[50]

Secular rituals such as this one face the challenge of accomplishing a specific transformation without the reassuring support of long-established forms that most religious rituals enjoy. The distinction between secular and religious rituals, however, should not be sharp, despite its important role in the early ritual studies of Emile Durkheim and Arnold van Gennep. Neither religion nor ritual should be conceived as original and stable in contrast to the turmoil of daily life; rather, all rituals as well as much of the rest of human endeavor involve innovation as well as repetition, timely calculations as well as appeals to longstanding values and beliefs. What sets both religious and secular rituals apart from other social behavior is their mission of "fixing public meanings": they need to consolidate and clarify that a crucial moment of change has been accomplished and worked into the participants' understanding.[51] Often the best way to ritualize a trans-formation (such as a peace, marriage, death, inauguration, investiture, graduation) is by performing a traditional ceremony, but the absence of tradition does not obviate ritual. Just establishing a distinctive space and time for formal recognition of the moment can prepare for innovative gestures that manage to seal it.[52] Thus the plan to build a chapel to Our Lady of Peace calls prospectively on the divine sanction that a religious ritual could invoke by means of its long tradition. The further innovations at Ardres draw particularly on two familiar ritual strategies, long lavish outlay and mimesis, that express the commitment of England and France, as personified in their kings, to shifting from enmity to alliance through truce and marriage.

The long lavish outlay needs little explanation; a universal premise of ritual is that "the *longer* a rite is staged and the grander the scale of the ritual's outlay and adornment, the more important, the more efficacious the ceremony is deemed to be."[53] Ardres was a staggeringly expensive operation, costing the English side at least £10,000.[54] Each king was accompanied by four hundred armed "gentieux" [gentlemen] and a smaller retinue of nobles; the Anglo-Norman account lists the names of sixty-four "seignours" who accompanied Charles VI and twenty-two "dames et damoiselles" who accompanied Isabel when she arrived on the final day of the meeting.[55] The lesser attendees spent a great deal of time arrayed in ranks and kneeling in respect, marking the occasion's importance and its peacefulness; the nobility participated in some of the gift exchanges and served as attendants, stressing from their more privileged position the exceptional status of the occasion and its central figures. As well as endorsing royal power and ritual formality, these many followers are also participants, members of the two nations, armies, and courts whose reverent attentiveness dramatizes that they too have a stake in the success of the ceremony.

Mimesis is another fundamental means of ritualization. Most obviously, the kings' gestures play out their desire in the miniature world of the encampment. When they cross and recross the boundary between English and French tents, they intend a transformation of English and French relations encompassing their whole kingdoms. This kind of metaphorical mimesis can seem superstitious, as if the physical gesture could itself produce the desired transformation: joining hands to marry, dancing a successful hunt before undertaking a real one, burying a hatchet to end a war, seem to assume that concrete physical gestures can manage a complex, unforeseeable future. But Jonathan Z. Smith's careful reconstruction of hunting rituals concludes that ritual mimesis is not meant to compel events; instead it is *"a means of performing the way things ought to be in conscious tension to the way things are."*[56] A difficult transformation demands ritual behavior by the very incongruence between what is desired (say, a perfectly harmonious marriage) and what is likely to ensue (something more tumultuous). Joining hands to marry makes a metaphor of harmonious union that gets reinforcement from the words, gestures, time, expense, and witnessing of the ceremony. The hope of ritual is that by asserting the metaphor "we two are one" in these many registers, the transformation already inherent in the metaphor will implant itself in the understanding and behavior of the participants, better enabling them to produce the desired future.

Another mimetic shape for the Ardres ceremony is the wearing and exchanging of personal signs. The two kings perform their alliance not only by walking together but by holding hands, wearing each other's devices, and presenting each other with gifts, including these devices. On the first day of the ceremony, Richard wears "un riche coler entour le col, de la livrée le roi franczois, ovec un graunt cerf en son arme" [a rich collar around his neck of the livery of the French king, with a great hart on his arm]. Charles wears "un coler de soun propre liverée et un cerf en l'arme" [a collar of his own livery and a hart on his arm].[57] Charles's livery collar, worn by both kings, was sent from Charles to Richard in March 1396, on the occasion of the proxy marriage. Made by the Parisian jeweler Jehan Compère, these matching collars for Ardres were formed of gold branches, flowers, and seed pods of broom, trimmed with pearls, green and white enamel, a ruby, and fifty pendent gold letters spelling out the motto "Jamès" ten times.[58] Broom is simultaneously Charles's most dispersed sign during the 1390s and his most exclusive one: chaplets of broom are embroidered around the neck and on the sleeves of livery for Isabel's cortege, but only a few participants wear the gold collars of "son liverée de broincoddes."[59] This prestigious sign is well balanced by the badge of a hart that each king wears on his arm. The *Annales Ricardi Secundi*, which tends to abbreviate the eyewitness account, here specifies that the hart worn by both men is "de liberata Regis Angliae," Richard's badge of the white hart, not the winged hart Charles used until 1394.[60] Richard distributed his badge of the white hart widely from about 1390, but the costliness of its exemplars served to calibrate the favor: badges made for eight squires in 1398 cost less than 4 shillings each, but in the same year a gold badge for the archbishop of Cologne cost £36.[61] If we accept the expansion in the *Annales*, it would seem that Richard gave a suitable version of his badge to Charles in anticipation of this meeting, perhaps in return for Charles's collar of broom. Beaune asserts that in 1396 Richard wore his badge of a white hart with the motto "Pax," adapting the badge to the purposes of this ceremony and the wider attempt at a lasting peace between England and France.[62]

On this first day of the ceremony, Richard and Charles mirror each other's social identity as expressed in their signs and mottos. The full potential in their badges to make a personal bond is being invoked. In addition, each king has chosen to share a sign that has unusually deep familial roots: broom appears on the clothing and personal objects of other Valois figures, including Charles V and Louis d'Orléans, brother of Charles VI; and Richard probably took his white hart not only from his mother, Joan of Kent, but through her from her guardian and his grandmother, Philippa of Hainault.[63] The familial aspect of each device is appropriate to negotiating a lineal realignment through marriage as well as a personal realignment of Charles's and Richard's relations. It is intriguing that both the broom and the hart have already overlapped in Charles's and Richard's use: the latter's lodged white hart may imitate or pay homage to the winged white hart; and broom appeared in Richard's and Anne's use around 1392, presaging its long importance as a canting representation for the family name Plantagenet (*planta genista*).[64] Thus the devices Richard and Charles exchange and wear for the Ardres ceremony's first day are complexly their most longstanding and lineal signs, yet also signs already favored by their counterparts. Since, as M. V. Clarke puts it, "Richard's subjects could read a coat more easily than they could read a letter," it is likely that all these nuances were in play as Richard and Charles met.[65] If they were, the exchanged devices metaphorically unite the two kings in personal allegiance but also unite their families and even imply a prior contiguity between families through the overlapping use of harts and broom that, in earlier uses, may have been competitive.

This exchange of signifying devices illustrates an important feature of the ceremony's gift exchanges in general. An enormous array of jewelry, serving plate, ewers, paintings, even a horse with a silver saddle, change hands among Charles, Richard, and the lords in attendance. Often the English observer as well as other chroniclers note the cost of these gifts, but their excessive cost signifies that cost is beside the point ("money is no object" in making this personal and national alliance). Cash settlements did characterize the dowry and dower negotiated earlier in Paris, but passing ingots back and forth at the Ardres ceremony would have been completely inappropriate. This distinction between cash value and gift value grounds Annette Weiner's reconsideration of gift exchanges across cultures.[66] She argues that gifting has been wrongly described in terms of "reciprocity," the idea that gifting binds social groups because every gift requires a return gift of equivalent value, however deferred and refigured it may be. Instead, she locates the meaningfulness of gifting in the permeable boundary between persons and the objects they own. Objects acquire something of the nature of their owners, and confer a personal connection on recipients—but at the same time, in the typical case, much of the owner's integrity, authority, status, and so on is withheld from the gift. This paradox of "keeping-while-giving," which Weiner traces in a variety of exchange relationships, urges that the gifts exchanged near Ardres both bind the givers and receivers in personal alliance, and establish that they are powerful men who are retaining status in the very act of giving. Weiner plausibly suggests that self-withholding, rather than surrendering goods, "generates the thrust of the exchange."[67] Self-withholding is particularly evident in the distribution of badges, where the value of the badge resides partly in its ongoing connection to the giver's experience and personal use.

The ritual of alliance again moves outward to Richard's and Charles's families in its uses of Anne of Bohemia's livery. On the first day of the Ardres ceremony, Richard's followers dress in red gowns with white bends "de la livrée du roigne que derrein murrust" [in the livery of the queen who lately died]. Queen Anne's death two years earlier was painful for Richard, so painful that J. H. Harvey surmises that Richard's obsession with her loss inspires the use of her livery at Ardres.[68] Mourning is not, however, appropriate to celebrating a truce and second marriage; Anne's livery is easily readable in other ways, such as a representation of Richard's widowed condition, a way of honoring his first queen within the context of taking a second one, and a status-enhancing reference to his prior alliance with the house of Emperor Charles IV. Anne takes a more engaged position at the end of the ceremony's second day, a day given to extending and signing the prior agreements concerning the truce and mutual aid. Richard and Charles again walk hand in hand toward their meeting point, where "our lord the king gave to the French king a collar of pearls and other precious stones of the livery of the queen who lately died, worth around 5,000 marks; the French king put this collar around his own neck, and the king of England fastened it" ["le roy n. s. donna au roi franceois un coler des perles et autres preciouses perres de la liverée de la roigne que derrein murrust, près de vm. marcz; luyquel coler le roi franceois mist entour son propre cole, et le roi d'Engleterre le ferma"].[69] As Anne's livery moves from Richard's followers on the first day to Charles's neck on the second, her enigmatic trace shifts the ceremony from its opening concern with sealing a diplomatic alliance to its ultimate concern with marriage.

Charles wears "ycelluy coler entour soun col quel le roi n. s. luy donna le samady" [that same collar around his neck that our lord the king gave him on Saturday] for the third and final day of the ceremony, the day on which Isabel is transferred to Richard's care.[70] Anne's collar exemplifies both a ritual drive to act out the desired transformation and a ritual tendency to shroud metaphoric representations in ambiguity. I might hazard that, in wearing Anne's collar, Charles is endorsing Richard's identification of Anne with ideal womanhood, or that Charles is invoking Anne's history as an auspicious precedent for his daughter's married life, or that Charles is recognizing the pivotal role of women in the wider attempt to make peace with England. But it is easier to acknowledge, in relation to any concrete formulations, that "meaning is everywhere, but supremely vague," as Catherine Bell observes of ritual's gestures; or as Bourdieu puts it, "the

gymnastics of ritual, like dreams, always seem richer than the verbal translations, at once unilateral and arbitrary, that may be given of them. Words,
however charged with connotation, limit the range of choices and render
difficult or impossible, and in any case explicit and therefore 'falsifiable,' the
relations which the language of the body suggest."[71] Here the uncertainty
in all metaphoric connections adds to their appropriateness in ritual: at the
same time that placing Anne's collar around Charles's neck asserts a transformed relationship between Richard, Charles, and Anne, the metaphoric
gesture also conserves a certain indeterminacy around the relationship.

The "language of the body" involves women in several ways as the
Ardres ceremony draws to its close. Isabel's uncles carry her in a procession from the French council tent to the assembly point and then to the
English council tent, preceded and followed by women of the two courts.
Isabel is dressed heraldically in blue velvet embroidered with fleurs-de-lis,
and wears an adumbration of her English crown, "une cornal d'or et peres
preciouses en manere d'une coronne" [a coronet of gold and precious
stones in the style of a crown].[72] At their departure for Calais, Charles
kisses Isabel and the English and French women accompanying her, and
gives them all rings. He blesses Isabel and they weep together. Wearing
Anne's livery collar, Charles places his own collar of broom around the
necks of four English noblewomen who will accompany Isabel to Calais.
The dead queen's livery, drawn into the ceremony from two years gone,
argues the more clearly that the ceremony seeks to integrate women and
men, the affective and the political, into its reorientation of English and
French relations generally. Anne's livery suitably clothes Charles's kissing
and tears, not only by licensing an emotional intensity that is generally
associated with women, but also by representing the perpetual loss of
loving relationships that Anne's death exemplified, and Isabel's departure
now repeats.

Do these gestures also elaborate a dehumanizing traffic in women between
Valois and Plantagenet males? Isabel certainly resembles one of the expensive gifts the two parties have been all along exchanging, presented as she
is in the arms of her uncles and silent as she is while Charles offers her to
Richard and Richard accepts "son graciouse et honourable doun" [his gracious and honorable gift].[73] Drawing on the work of Claude Lévi-Strauss
in particular, scholars in many fields have accepted a close relation between
the exchange of gifts, which Lévi-Strauss argued was fundamental to the
formation of societies, and the exchange of women, which treats women
as objects in making alliances among families or larger affiliations.[74] For

Lévi-Strauss, marriage is a prime instance of gift exchange between men that sustains their peaceful coexistence.

Medieval European marriage alliances do subordinate women to men, just as medieval lineages subordinate the female to the male line, but subordination is not identical to commodification or dehumanization. While Isabel's subordination, as a woman and a child, is evident in her ceremonial positioning, at the same time her heraldic dress recalls Jack Goody's important observation that European kinship is bilateral at its core, although it also has patrilineal features.[75] Goody points out that maternal blood and alliances by marriage count heavily for medieval aristocracies. Primogeniture restricts inheritance, but women do inherit in a number of ways, and dowries become an alternate "patrimonium" that women and their heirs retain at the end of a marriage.[76] It might seem that linking brides with transfers of wealth would commodify them and diminish their humanity in the view of their culture, but instead a large dowry was understood to confer honor on the bride, as did the dower that brides' families exacted from their husbands.[77]

Annette Weiner could well have used Isabel's case in her argument against Lévi-Strauss's position that marriage is an exchange of women among men. Her counterproposal derives from her more general point that gifts and persons interpenetrate for givers and receivers. In the ceremony at Ardres, gifts take significance not so much from their financial value as from their personal associations with Richard, Anne, and Charles. A principle of reciprocity and equal exchange is not what motivates gifting, Weiner concludes, but really a reverse principle of strategic withholding and self-assertion. The gifts' personal component is "inalienable" from the givers, still conveying the givers' independent authority even in the process of making alliances. Weiner proposes that we should see marriage in these terms as well. Wives are "inalienable" from their families of birth; they are given in marriage only within a context of "reclaiming actions" that maintain the connection between the wife and her own family.[78] Isabel's heraldic robe asserts that she conveys access to relationships and status that come to Richard through her family. At the same time, her very bearing of those enhancements into the marriage trails streamers of attachment back to her family by which they continue to claim her. To be sure, Isabel is urged to align herself with her husband. Her peculiar subordination is most evident in her father's instruction that she should be loyal and pleasing to "his English son," as if Richard's new kinship with Charles weighed as heavily as her own blood.[79] Yet the written marriage agreement stipulates that her consent must be won when she reaches the age of twelve, with provisions for the event of her refusal; the agreement thus recognizes that she will maintain commitments and desires that could ally her more tellingly with her family of birth than with Richard.[80]

The Griselda story, circulating in several versions at the time of this marriage, imagines that women can undertake marital subordination intentionally and even powerfully. Particularly in the French and English versions, Griselda narratives comment on contemporary marital norms. Griselda's case may seem remote from Isabel's except in their radical subordination: Isabel's youth redoubles her feminine subjection, and Griselda's oath of subordination compounds the inferiority of her sex and birth. Despite other differences, Griselda's imagined performance of marriage articulates social understandings of wifehood that are implicit in the Ardres narrative, providing a complement to its emphasis on masculine negotiations.

Griselda's Performance

In all the fourteenth- and fifteenth-century versions of the Griselda story, Walter has Griselda reclothed by women of his retinue in the course of marrying her. This reclothing elevates Griselda's social status but also depends on her oath of submission to Walter. Like Isabel's heraldic blue and gold dress and the exchanges of livery between Richard and Charles at the Ardres ceremony, Griselda's reclothing illustrates Grant McCracken's observation that, "charged with semiotic effect and potential, clothing is one of the chief opportunities for exercising the metaphoric and performative powers of ritual."[81] To be sure, the tale's Italian, Latin, French, and English redactors use clothing to sustain diverse strands of moral, political, allegorical, and historical meaning in their narratives; these meanings have attracted more critical attention than the marriage rite and Griselda's wifehood.[82] Yet Chaucer's version sharply interrogates women's place in marriage. Chaucer took that cue from the French versions of the tale, which are particularly concerned to model conduct for women.

The unprecedented interest in the Griselda story at the end of the fourteenth century touches Richard's marriage to Isabel both specifically and generally. Philippe de Mézières, earlier a tutor of Charles VI and a member of his father's royal council, wrote from his retirement in the Convent of the Celestines to Richard II in 1395, urging him to remarry "for the furtherance of peace in Christendom and the comfort of your royal person," and praying that God "grant you a wife such as Griselda, the wife

of the Marquis of Saluzzo."[83] Philippe refers to the version of the tale by
"the learned doctor and sovereign poet, Master Francis Petrarch," perhaps
to authenticate the tale's merit but perhaps also with false modesty, since
Richard would have been less able to read Petrarch's Latin than Philippe's
recently completed French version.[84] Chaucer drew on another French
translation of Petrarch, together with Petrarch's text of 1374, for his *Clerk's
Tale* in the early 1390s.[85] A third French version, a verse drama based on
Philippe's translation, may have been written and performed to celebrate
the proxy marriage of Richard and Isabel in March 1396.[86]

Chaucer's concern with wifehood, already developing in his French
source, is an important reorientation from Petrarch's Latin, which he
directs to a male readership and applies to the human relation to God
rather than wives' relations to their husbands. As a model of wifehood,
Petrarch concludes, Griselda is "scarcely imitable," but his male readers
may be stirred to "perform for God what this woman performed for her
husband."[87] In contrast to Petrarch's interpretive address to "constantibus
viris" [steadfast men], the several translations into French are sharply
aware of their vernacular feminine audience, and tend to address the tale
specifically to wives and women.[88] Most prolix on the exemplary value of
the story for women, and least concerned to hedge and qualify that exemplarity, is Philippe's *Livre de la vertu du sacrement de mariage*. He at first
resists Petrarch's conclusion on wives' incapacity only hypothetically, claiming that *if* any woman *were* able to behave as Griselda did, she would be
able to do so only with God's help, but soon he is working Griselda into
the exemplary scheme of his "miroir des dames mariées" by comparing her
to heroic women of antiquity and urging contemporary women "to imitate
the Marquise of Saluce by pleasing first their immortal spouse, and then
their mortal husband" ["d'ensuir la marquese de Saluce et de plaire pre-
mierement à leur espous immortel, et aprés à leur mari mortel"]. Remarkable as the story may be, it is held true ["reputée pour vraye"] in Lombardy
and Piedmont.[89]

This reorientation toward exemplarity for women is most nuanced
in Chaucer's *Clerk's Tale* and the French translation he used alongside
Petrarch's Latin version of 1374.[90] Chaucer's French source, *Le Livre
Griseldis*, translates Petrarch's closing allegorical application faithfully, but
it opens by offering the tale "a l'exemplaire des femmes mariees et toutes
autres" [as an example for wives and all other women].[91] Throughout,
Chaucer's French source refocuses Petrarch's narration on the literal, material events of Griselda's experience.[92] Chaucer immensely complicates his
version by intensifying both the literal cruelty of Walter and the spiritual

references to Job, Christ, and pious acceptance of God's will.[93] I do some violence to these complexities by speaking little of them and more of Chaucer's expansions around marriage.

Chaucer alters the earlier accounts of Griselda's oath by uniting it to the marriage oath she exchanges with Walter. In classical and folk analogues such as the Cupid and Psyche myth, the oath of obedience is the single preoccupation of the plot, and marriage is either unrepresented or unproblematic.[94] Similarly, Petrarch's Walter has Janicula's permission to marry and simply assumes Griselda will be pleased; her promise to be subject to him is a separate issue from their marriage: "when that [marriage] is done which shortly shall take place, will you be prepared, with consenting mind, to agree with me in all things. . . ?"[95] In Chaucer's tale, Griselda's consent to marriage is part of the choice Walter presents to her, and her promise to subject herself becomes a marriage vow:

> "Grisilde," he seyde, "ye shal wel understonde
> It liketh to youre fader and to me
> That I yow wedde, and eek it may so stonde,
> As I suppose, ye wol that it so be.
> But thise demandes axe I first," quod he,
> "That, sith it shal be doon in hastif wyse,
> Wol ye assente, or elles yow avyse?
>
> I seye this: be ye redy with good herte
> To al my lust, and that I frely may,
> As me best thynketh, do yow laughe or smerte,
> And nevere ye to grucche it, nyght ne day? . . .
> Swere this, and heere I swere oure alliance." (CT 4.344–54, 357) [96]

Walter's plural "demandes" are so closely linked that the transition between them, "I seye this," makes the second seem a restatement of the first: "will you consent to marriage" is equivalent to "will you consent to perfect obedience." Walter's final line, unique to Chaucer's version, again fuses Griselda's consent to obedience with her consent to marriage and the ceremony's vows: "Swere this, and heere I swere oure alliance." In response, Griselda articulates her consent to marriage as the first instance of her submission and promises to continue in that mode:

> She seyde, "Lord, undigne and unworthy
> Am I to thilke honour that ye me beede,
> But as ye wole youreself, right so wol I.
> And heere I swere that nevere willyngly,
> In werk ne thoght, I nyl yow disobeye,
> For to be deed, though me were looth to deye." (CT 4.359–64)

Griselda's deeply subordinate relation to Walter, already inherent in her father's consent and her social inferiority, is at the same time a relation she must affirm for herself. The need for her affirmation takes for granted that she has a will of her own ("right so wol I," I want it thus) but it simultaneously requires her to "nevere willyngly" have a will other than Walter's. This paradoxical surrender and persistence of Griselda's will prepares for conflicting formulations later in the tale. For example, "as I lefte at hoom al my clothyng . . . lefte I my wyl and al my libertee" pictures a lost or discarded will, in contrast to "I wol no thyng, ne nyl no thyng, certayn, / But as yow list," which figures a perfect consonance of two wills, and "I desire no thyng for to have . . . save oonly yee. / This wyl is in myn herte, and ay shal be," which asserts a powerful effort of will on Griselda's part (*CT* 4.507–9, 646–47, 654–56).[97]

This paradoxically erased and powerful will could illustrate Marilyn Strathern's revision to the "exchange-of-women" model in which marriage is a foundational instance of gift exchange among men. She argues instead that marriage is one kind of personal exchange among many (such as indentures, oaths of fealty, taking holy orders) that "objectify" persons, but by this term she does not mean that persons become inert, dehumanized things such as gifts and commodities. Instead, people "objectify" themselves when they present their bodies, relationships, and capacities as valuable resources for others to exploit. "Women's value as wealth . . . does not denigrate their subjectivity," Strathern argues; rather, marriage and other binding agreements commit persons to following the will of others and to being treated as valuable acquisitions. Such personal exchanges are ongoing, multiple, and have some strategic value for both sides. "It would be an error," Strathern concludes, "to see certain people as always the objects of others' transactions, and equally an error to assume their natural, 'free' form is as subjects or agents."[98] Griselda's marriage instantiates the interplay of subjection and agency in Strathern's analysis. Griselda is both the object of Walter's exploitation and the agent of her own submission to it. I might attempt to write off one of these positions by arguing that Griselda wields the radically free will of Christian theology such that her choice is all her own, or on the contrary that her poverty and womanhood so constrain her that asking for her consent is just Walter's cynical screen for his tyranny. I propose instead that Griselda's situation represents, in heightened form, the complexity of women's positioning in the patriarchal, largely arranged, but also bilateral and consent-driven marriages of the late Middle Ages.[99]

Because Chaucer has revised Griselda's oath to make it clearly marital, it is worth considering her ongoing conduct in terms of marriage and the peculiar kind of subordination that characterizes women's position in marriage. A salient ritual parallel with the Ardres meeting is that words alone are insufficient to the task of transforming Griselda's status. Performance studies illuminate this situation by arguing that "performatives," words that accomplish fundamental changes in status, are inevitably citational. An entirely fresh and personal "I do" is an impossibility; instead, the oath of marriage takes uncertain meaning from acceding to a long and obscure history of prior instances.[100] Given the contingency of oaths, it is not surprising that they typically need ritual support. Not that rituals are any less afflicted by uncertainty; like the performatives they enclose, they base their authority on the shaky ground of iteration. At the same time, rituals seek to stabilize iteration by constructing elaborate bulwarks of words, gestures, and material endorsements.

Griselda's reclothing by Walter is just such a material endorsement. In the first place, it is an appropriate sign for their virilocal union—so appropriate that dressing the bride was a traditional responsibility of husbands in fourteenth-century Italy.[101] Providing brides with clothing incorporated them visually into their husbands' households and expressed their subordination to their husbands' kin and lineage.[102] As I noted above in relation to the ceremony at Ardres, one premise of ritual is that mimesis, along with formality and expense and celebration, can accomplish a transformation. A "newe markysesse" emerges from Griselda's reclothing together with her vows, Walter's declaration that "this is my wyf," his ring, the procession to his palace, and the day's celebrations (CT 4.369, 394). Stripping and reclothing Griselda identifies her newness with Walter's agency and status, as he commands that the ladies accompanying him remove her old clothes and dress her in new ones he has had made for the occasion: "for that no thyng of hir olde geere / She sholde brynge into his hous, . . . this mayde bright of hewe / Fro foot to heed they clothed han al newe" (CT 4.372–73, 377–78).

Even as Griselda's reclothing accomplishes her absorption into Walter's household and her subordination to him in marriage, it leaves visible a residual self that remains unincorporated into the "newe markysesse." The verbal signal of this residue is "unnethe" [hardly]. When she is reclothed, "unnethe the peple hir knew for hire fairnesse," and when she is living in Walter's palace, "unnethe trowed they . . . that to Janicle . . . she doghter were" (CT 4.384, 403–5). She is heavily revised ("translated," CT 4.385) into a new appearance, status, and behavior, yet a connection persists between the married Griselda and something prior.[103] In Annette Weiner's terms, this something would be Griselda's inalienable connection by blood to Janicula; in Marilyn Strathern's terms, it would be Griselda's constrained, subordinated will persisting alongside her self-objectification in marriage. Intriguingly, all versions of the Griselda story from Boccaccio's onward make Griselda's blood and her will interchangeable terms in Walter's testing of her. In order to satisfy his doubts that she has not really given up her own agency, Walter persistently invokes Janicula's blood marking both her and her children.[104] Janicula's residual blood is a plausible disguise for Walter's suspicion of her residual will, because both blood and will are beyond the parameters of "translation" into wifehood.

Walter's tests demand Griselda's continual surrender of blood and will through the years of their marriage. Her maternity and descendants must not count for her; the will she brings into marriage must be absorbed into his. Griselda responds to his concern in declaring her children to be not hers but only Walter's, and her will to be entirely at his service. Both of Walter's demands perversely expand the subordination of women's lineage and will in marriage, yet both gain some false purchase on plausibility from that conventional subordination.

The proof Walter needs and Griselda provides is a performance that recalls, in exaggerated form, the self-definition conveyed in badges and other personal signs. What is hidden in Griselda must find visible expression, and that exterior expression is what counts. Her heart stands in relation to her behavior as the motto "I will have none other" stands in relation to its bestowal in a badge: commitments and feelings hidden from view gain their merit and usefulness when they attain concrete expression in personal interactions. Walter's immediate motive is "to preeve hir wyfhod," to make her demonstrate her wifeliness, and in response Griselda demonstrates a perfect contiguity between her heart and her behavior.[105] This contiguity is an important revision from Petrarch's version, which often posits inner feelings that differ from Griselda's outward show. A single trace of these passages remains in the Clerk's narration, "I deeme that hire herte was ful wo" (*CT* 4.753), hedged by the conjectural "I deeme" and soon denied by Griselda herself: "I wol gladly yelden hire my place" (*CT* 4.843). She does not have a second secret identity unavailable to Walter but only one seamless self that exists in performance.

This totally performed self is most evident as Griselda departs from marriage. Here again Chaucer presses the tale toward confronting women's position in marriage at some cost to Petrarch's allegorizing tendency. The alterations pivot on Walter's stipulation concerning Griselda's dowry: "And thilke dowere that ye broghten me, / Taak it agayn; I graunte it of my grace" (*CT* 4.807–8). Petrarch's Griselda asserts that her dowry was "fides et nuditas" [nakedness and devotion].[106] This doublet makes nakedness the visible sign of virtue. Paired with "fides," Griselda's undressing recalls the many female saints who renounce their rich clothing, and wider icono-graphic and moral associations of clothing with self-glorification, and un-dress with humble piety.[107] In contrast, Chaucer's Griselda experiences a curiously double or failed memory at this point that considerably expands the scene. Her first recollection is that her only dowry was her old clothes:

> But ther as ye me profre swich dowaire
> As I first broghte, it is wel in my mynde
> It were my wrecched clothes, nothyng faire,
> The whiche to me were hard now for to fynde.
> O goode God! How gentil and how kynde
> Ye semed by youre speche and youre visage
> The day that maked was oure mariage!
>
> But sooth is seyd—algate I fynde it trewe,
> For in effect it preeved is on me—
> Love is noght oold as whan that it is newe. (*CT* 4.848–57)

Griselda's first version of her dowry is problematically material rather than allegorical: her old clothes are no longer at hand, so what will she wear home? Her poignant nostalgia for Walter's lost kindness clarifies that she is vulnerable to his manipulation at this point: his request that she depart with only her dowry risks shaming her by making her return home naked. Here the associations of undress with abjection, punishment, and public reproach dominate those with piety and virtue.[108] These added lines make Griselda's subsequent interpretation of her dowry seem a resourceful resis-tance to Walter's attempt to shame her: "To yow broght I noght elles, out of drede, / But feith, and nakednesse, *and maydenhede*" (*CT* 4.865–66). Asserting that her maidenhead was part of her dowry prepares for negoti-ating a smock in exchange. Indeed, the logic of the exchange draws on Griselda's earlier evocation of her marriage as a history of loss and muta-bility: "Love is noght oold as whan that it is newe." The smock she nego-tiates can recall her maidenhead's thin tangibility, but also its irrecoverable loss and the intact purity lost with it. "Lat me not lyk a worm go by the weye," she pleads in another Chaucerian addition, acknowledging again that nakedness would shame her now, however immune to shame she was as a virgin bride.[109]

Chaucer's substitution of "maydenhede" for Petrarch's "virginitas" does not, of course, fully substitute the physicality of marriage for Petrarch's spiritual concerns. Chaucer elsewhere uses the word "virginitee" frequently

(Virginia "floured in virginitee," and the Prioress's young martyr was "sowded to virginitee," *CT* 6.44, 7.579), but the term "maydenhede" fits Griselda's situation better because it encompasses the concrete, embodied coin of the hymen as well as the spiritual worth assigned to virginity. This double sense of maiden*head* and maiden*hood* anticipates both the material trade of hymen for smock and Griselda's insistence that it is morally incumbent on Walter not to refuse: "ye koude nat doon so dishonest a thing" (*CT* 4.876).[110] Reinforcing her virtue, she notes that Walter "semed" kind at their marriage: his performance, in contrast to hers, has been duplicitous. For her part, she demonstrates her relations to Walter down to the last detail of what she wears. Her clothing is not a screen but a contribution to her visibility; the smock she wears to leave marriage expresses her modesty but also acknowledges her lost virginity and Walter's ability to transform her marital and social status.

Griselda, however, works her own transformation when her persistence in devotion finally converts Walter from doubt to confidence in her transparency. Whatever the Clerk's audience, or Chaucer's, might make of Walter's exculpation of his conduct "til I thy purpos knewe and al thy wille," the fictional onlookers are unanimous concerning his relation to Griselda (*CT* 4.1078). Their celebration and their redressing Griselda "in a clooth of gold that brighte shoon" remake and even enhance her marriage, "For moore solempne in every mannes syght / This feste was, and gretter of costage, / Than was the revel of hire mariage" (*CT* 4.1117, 1125–27). These revelers endorse Walter's conduct and find it compatible with marriage—something to celebrate with remarriage rather than, for example, tyrannicide.

The Clerk's conflicting interventions make assessment more difficult for his audience and Chaucer's. The tale's envoy further resists simply concluding that the tale refers not to marriage but only allegorically to patience in adversity, or that it does approve women's marital subordination but not men's exploitation of it, or (most attractive in my view) that it depicts an exacerbated marital subordination in order to interrogate the subordination inherent in contemporary marriage practices. The envoy's inversions, its festive celebration of archwives and its recollection of the Wife of Bath's telling dissidence, extend and emphasize the interrogative, ironic mode of the tale as a whole. Instead of attempting to locate the tale's final position on marriage, I want to urge the significance of Griselda's purely enacted identity. She is so exaggerated in this regard as to be virtually inconceivable. Most readers indeed cannot do without imagining a private Griselda, however difficult to locate. David Wallace, in

his fascinating study of the tale's political implications, finally finds interiority in Griselda's fainting spell: "Once her ordeal is terminated Griselde
drops to the ground. Her public face falls with her and some time elapses
before she 'caught agayn hire contenaunce.' It seems, after all, that Griselde
contains a world of private feeling, an individuality that Walter . . . cannot
comprehend or take possession of."[111] Finding private feeling in a faint, in
the very absence of consciousness, illustrates the challenge Griselda poses
to any desire for interiority. In my view, Griselda's peculiar accomplishment is to have no interiority at odds with her performance. Where she is
not behaving, she herself is not. Certainly she has emotions and expresses
them, for example in speaking tenderly to her daughter and weeping at
their reunion, but her devotion cannot imply a hidden thought such as
"since I love my daughter, should I attempt to protect her from death?"

Griselda's total overtness is hardly naturalistic. It is a function of her
exemplarity rather than an imitation of life. At the same time, particularly
in Chaucer's version, Griselda's accessibility refers to contemporary marriage practices—for example, to the self-objectification Strathern describes
in unequal personal exchanges. More generally, Griselda's overtness refers
to a socially recognized way of being that is radically enacted rather than
private and contemplative. Her exemplarity and her historicity intersect
at just this point. She is a function of fable and exemplum, but also of
a secular culture that values the visible, palpable creation of identity in
rhetorical and material performance.

A final aspect of the Ardres ceremony and Griselda's wedding that makes
an important point about secular ritual is their deployment of worldly
rather than divine sanction for making their alliances. One explanation for
the peculiar prominence of clothing in both ceremonies is the near absence
of the institutional church. When Walter expels Griselda from marriage,
he has papal bulls counterfeited to license a second marriage, but the negotiation between Walter and Griselda in fact turns on papal ignorance.
Griselda's public undressing, her procession back to her father's house, and
his redressing her in "hire olde coote" are the substantial gestures that
accomplish her divorce (CT 4.913). The absence of the church is just as
notable at Griselda's wedding, when she and Walter "swere oure alliance"
without benefit of clergy and Griselda's reclothing does the ceremonial
work one might expect a church wedding to accomplish (CT 4.357). This
expectation is misplaced. Specifically, it is a product of the church's long
campaign to bring lay marriages under its control. In the late fourteenth
century, marriage was no longer a fully secular matter, but neither did it

require a church ceremony or even an after-the-fact blessing from a cleric. The legal systems of England, France, and Italy recognized marriages that involved only mutual vows exchanged in domestic settings, and at least statistically speaking, these secular marriages were still the norm. For example, in Ely between 1374 and 1382, 70 percent of the marriages in a register of legal cases were accomplished in secular settings.[112] Richard Helmholz concludes that a much larger range of legal cases "show the tenacity of the belief that people could regulate their own matrimonial affairs, without the assistance or interference of the Church."[113] At the same time, the church had defined marriage as a sacrament and was developing rituals that strove not just to bless the union but to produce it.[114] The fourteenth-century versions of the Griselda story reflect the still-marginal place of clerical sanction in marriage: of Petrarch's several translators, only Philippe de Mézières solemnizes Walter and Griselda's union with clerical intervention.[115] Richard II and Isabel did have a church wedding, but it was a small, ancillary affair in comparison to the ceremony at Ardres that preceded it.

The church's intrusion into marriage during these centuries recalls Franz Kafka's leopards in his mythologizing account of how rituals change: "Leopards break into the temple and drink the sacrificial chalices dry; this occurs repeatedly, again and again: finally it can be reckoned on before-hand and becomes a part of the ceremony." Jonathan Z. Smith cites this text alongside Plutarch's on the aggregative tendency of ritual: "At Athens, Lysimache, the priestess of Athene Polias, when asked for a drink by the mule drivers who had transported the sacred vessels, replied, 'No, for I fear it will get into the ritual.'"[116] I admit to a certain perversion in claiming that the church intervenes in marriage during the Middle Ages just as the leopard does and the mule driver might. Kafka and Plutarch are describing the tendency of rituals to absorb random accidents into their tradition, and the church's intervention into marriage was far from accidental. Moreover, the leopard and the muleteer are alien to the sacrosanct whereas the church would claim to be the very source of sanctification. My analogy between church and leopard is meant to stress that marriage was a coherent and self-sufficient event before the church's intervention. The Griselda story's ring-giving, oath-swearing, and redressing the bride have a deep history stretching back into antiquity. This durable secular ritual, based in traditions of lay practice rather than the sanction of priests, manifests a poly-semous, multiply authorized culture with diverse sources of validation for its social transformations.

2

Maytime in Late Medieval Courts

IN THE MAYTIMES OF FOURTEENTH- and fifteenth-century England and France, courtiers dressed up in plants, celebrated women for being daisies, and allied themselves with the parties of Leaf and Flower. This elite adaptation of a seasonal festival provides an especially well-documented interface between physical and verbal performance in a secular ritual. Wardrobe accounts and court poetry offer a rich archive on the practice of Maying. The first half of this chapter surveys the archive as a whole to discover ways in which courtly Maying shaped participants' sexuality and reiterated their privileged social position. The second half of the chapter turns to the problematic status of the persona in Maying. Like the poetic persona that indeterminately is and is not identifiable with the poet, a ritual participant typically is and is not engaged and defined by the ceremony. The ambiguous relation between performing persona and historical self generates creative participation in much Maying poetry, but in Chaucer's *Legend of Good Women*, it produces a radical critique of the ritual and its underpinning prescriptions for love and womanhood.

Lyrics about Maying are not obviously *part* of Maying; an anthropologist might align Maying poetry with the comments of informants who explain ritual symbols after the fact.[1] But Maying poetry presents itself also as a function of the occasion—an eyewitness account, an obligation to May, even an act of allegiance to flower or to leaf. I will consider the poetry of Maying to be both a source of information about Maying and an aspect of Maying itself. Rituals are inherently poetic in that they work through figuration: the symbolic representation, the metaphoric association, and the mimetic tactic are their most fundamental devices. The ineffability of figurations contributes to their ritual efficacy, but there is also a rhetorical component in ritual, a place for assertion and glossing, which again allies it to poetry. This degree of consonance makes poetry a peculiarly apt vehicle for expressing as well as explaining ritual. The two functions overlap in Maying poetry.

Technical information about wearing plants can be more enigmatic than illuminating. Does Froissart's notation that a garland is woven "sans esclice," without a flexible wooden frame to support it, signal the garland's extraordinary craftsmanship or its simple artlessness?[2] The claim that women not only dress in flowers but become them would be equally mysterious were it not heavily glossed in poetry.[3] Maying costumes draw meaning from fashion, livery, and ritual in varying proportions. For example, Deschamps writes that "En May voit on chascun de vert vestir; / On fait dossier es cours des arbrisseaux; / Fueilles porte qui veult estre nouviaux" [In May we see everyone dress in green; they have branches carried back to court; and whoever wants to be "nouviaux" wears leaves].[4] "Nouviaux" is wonderfully suspended between "in fashion" and "in season," linking social prestige to festive dress.[5] When the leaves Deschamps praises are taken as the dress of one Maying party, in contradistinction with the party of the flower, leaves and flowers recall shared liveries, simultaneously imagining Love as a temporal lord and making a space within Maying for real lords to perform maintenance in the distribution of festive liveries.

"Livery" has so many meanings in late medieval courts that Maying liveries are complex phenomena. For example, liveries of maintenance and favor might seem to suppress identity and mark the wearer simply as someone else's creature, but they were also widely understood to encourage lawlessness because the wearers sustained one another in misbehavior as well as sustaining their lord.[6] The very proliferation of badges, buttons, sleeves, and fuller liveries of maintenance in later fourteenth- and fifteenth-century England indicates that contemporaries understood the practice less as a disenfranchising surrender of autonomy than as a license to pursue personal agendas. In contrast, liveries of chivalric orders, such as the Order of the Star and Order of the Garter, invite a more regulated self promotion: these orders do not simply submerge knights in a fellowship of peers but press them to excel their fellows. In the idealizing program of these orders, which I discuss in Chapter 4, the pressure to outperform one's fellows is said to enhance the general good as well as personal renown.

Maying liveries draw on both kinds of affiliation, that of households or retinues held together by patronage on the one hand, and that of orders or voluntary associations of peers on the other. The chivalric orders, exclusive in their membership and grounded on defense and attack, resonate most with the parties of leaf and flower. Charles d'Orléans writes of a company in which "fut ordonné qu'on choisiroit . . . la fueille . . . ou la fleur pour toute l'annee" [it was decreed that each should choose the leaf or the flower for the coming year] and in response "prins la fueille pour livree" [I took the leaf as livery].[7] Choosing instead the flower, Deschamps writes, "son ordre prain et humblement reçoy, / Qui plus digne est d'esmeraude ou topace" [I take and humbly receive its order, which is more worthy than emerald or topaz], comparing its merit to the emblems of other orders.[8] The parties of flower and leaf are charged with defending their emblem through the year until the following May. This analogy between Maying parties and orders of peers informs historical distributions of green clothing recorded in wardrobe accounts for the first of May around the century's turn. Charles VI commissioned 26 houppelandes for high-ranking participants in a 1387 Maying at the Château de Beauté so that his companions would be dressed like himself ["pour estre vestus semblable à lui le premier jour de may"].[9] In 1400, Charles VI ordered no fewer than 352 green houppelandes for many ranks of his entourage, and here the distribution resembles more closely a household livery, that is, a regularly scheduled provision of clothing to groups within the household for their use in that season.[10] The commission of 1400, so much larger than that of 1387, refers not to dressing like the king but to wearing his livery: "pour eulx vestir de la livrée que ycellui seigneur a faicte le premier jour de may" [to dress them in the livery that this lord has made on the first of May].[11] Participants might imagine their livery to be that of May or the God of love himself, but to record that May's servants are indebted to Charles VI, this livery is marked from beyond Maying with the king's own emblematic *planta genista* [broom]. The twenty-six houppelandes of 1387 were embroidered with a branch of broom that took root behind the right shoulder and descended the left arm; the houppelandes of 1400 bore intertwined branches of broom and "may," probably honeysuckle.[12] This intertwining is particularly communicative, interlacing symbols of the May festivity and the sponsoring lord on the green ground of an extraordinary livery, not one of the scheduled liveries of maintenance, that expresses therefore the largesse that is particularly celebrated, I will argue, in elite Maying.

In sum, the liveried aspect of Maying costumes conveys a double message of allegiance and self-promotion and extends lordship into the terrain of ritual. The liveried self is poised between incorporation and distinctiveness, and the interaction of these two forces can be empowering. Livery's doubleness works for unique as well as for distributed garments. Pierre de Navarre in 1384 and Charles VI's brother Louis, in 1389 commissioned May houppelandes just for themselves, making evident that the ritual allegiance signaled by their green and leafy outfits does not obviate their distinctive self-adornment.[13]

Complementing the resonances between livery and May dress is the ritual significance of dressing in green, leaves, or flowers. As a physical gesture rather than a verbal statement, dress may seem a peripheral aspect of Maying. But gesture is crucial to ritual, as my next pages will seek to demonstrate. For Pierre Bourdieu, mimesis is what makes a ritual work; for Jack Goody, belief is less at issue in ritual than simple participation: going through the motions is exactly what's required.[14] This location of meaning on the surface of things, in the performance itself, explains in part why dress is so important in Maying.

Maying as Ritual

The best single illustration of how Maying proceeded in late medieval courts is Eustache Deschamps's "Lay de franchise," based on a 1385 celebration of May hosted by King Charles VI at the chateau of Beauté-sur-Marne.[15] Deschamps's persona endorses "la coustume . . . d'aler le may cueillir" [the custom of going to gather the may: "Lf" 12–13] as he rises at dawn to revere the season: "Sacrifier voulz mon cuer et offrir / Avec le corps et tout le vert vestir / Au gentil mois qui les doulz cuers avance / A leurs dames . . ." [I want to sacrifice and offer my heart with my body all dressed in green to the gentle month that advances all sweet hearts to their ladies: "Lf" 19–21]. His special care is to honor the daisy, the metonym of his beloved. In a beautiful enclosed park, he watches noble young people who are cutting flowers and little branches to make belts and chaplets such that "de verdure furent touz revestis" [they were altogether reclothed in greenery: "Lf" 123]. They speak and sing of love while others joust under the king's direction. The "flower" of the persona's devotions addresses the company to prove from literature and history that "sanz amour ne puet estre prouesse" [without love there can be no prowess: "Lf" 211]. Then the company processes back to the chateau of Beauté-sur-Marne for a feast, while the persona continues on his way to find Robin and Marion in a remote spot dining on water and cake, singing of love and recommending their simple life over the life of courts.

In only 300 lines, the "Lay de franchise" assembles virtually all the tendencies of court poetry on Maying in the later fourteenth and fifteenth centuries. The processional behavior of leaving court for nature and cutting branches and flowers to wear and to bring back to court is presented as a custom honoring May and celebrating love. This processional shape to Maying, out to nature and back to home, is a fundamental gesture of

Maying generally, whether popular or elite, as is dressing in green and greenery. Deschamps's Maying is restricted to courtiers, not only in that all the participants are "tresnoble . . . gent de parage" [very noble people of high birth: "Lf" 94–95], but also in the enclosed garden setting, the allegorical and rhetorical echoes from the *Roman de la Rose*, the jousting and feasting, and the contrasted pastoral bliss of Robin and Marion, whose love flourishes outside all these formalities and luxuries. The special reverence for the daisy does not appear in records of popular Maying; like the parties of Flower and Leaf, the identification of women with daisies appears to have been an elite contribution to spring celebrations. And finally, although Deschamps's account of Maying asserts the court's shared status and ideals, his poetic persona is detached, reflective, even at odds with some aspects of the celebration. This chapter will trace each of these characteristic aspects of elite Maying.

The best-known illumination of a Maying party (Figure 1), from the *Très Riches Heures du Duc de Berry* (c. 1415), elaborates the poetic record in emphasizing the processional aspect of the rite together with dressing in greenery. The seasonal aspect is evident in the image's calendrical representation of May and the sky's fusion with the zodiac of May above the forest. The trumpeting servants in their household livery and the subtle tracery of leafy garlands over luxurious clothing emphasize the high status of this Maying party, while the riders' turning heads indicate that they are a harmonious, communicating group. A less-known calendrical image (Figure 2) from the *Heures de Turin* (c. 1420) also represents the seasonal, processional, and exclusive dimensions of courtly Maying and adds the gesture of cutting greenery with a sword, an implement hardly suited to the task but suitably elite in compensation. Women ride postillion in heterosexual pairs, making the ritual's sexual component more explicit than in the earlier image of mixed but independently mounted men and women.[16]

As a thoroughly secular event, Maying could illustrate the relatively recent shift in anthropology from understanding ritual as a deeply traditional and magical practice, to a more historicized recognition that people make and alter ceremonies of all kinds in relation to their situations, constructing a repeatable performance that may call on the metaphoric powers of language and gesture rather than on supernatural powers. The goal of a secular ritual could be to reproduce and celebrate the group's identity, as in a flag-raising ceremony, or to accomplish a transformation, as in a marriage ceremony. To achieve their effects, rituals often solicit the participation of the entire community and ask a surrender of each person's will to the duty of performance, to an appropriate frame of mind, and to a

Figure 1. *Très Riches Heures de Jean, duc de Berry*. Chantilly, Musée Condé, MS 65, fol. 5, verso. Copyright Réunion des Musées Nationaux/Art Resource, NY.

Figure 2. *Heures de Turin*, fol. 5. By permission of G. Molfese e Figli, Torino.

social or sacred power that is beyond the control of the group. However unavailable it may be to the full understanding or control of participants, a ritual may be commented upon, elaborated, forgotten; its execution is a performance as well as a rite and as such may be a space for difference as well as for reproduction.[17] The tension between participants' absorption and their resistance is inherent to ritual and is one target of its operations.[18]

Maying poetry evokes ritual most transparently in claiming that the longstanding custom must be honored by all. Like Deschamps, Charles d'Orléans urges, "Alons au bois le may cueillir, / Pour la coustume maintenir" [let's go to the woods to gather the may in order to maintain the custom].[19] The obligation not only to participate but to feel appropriate emotions figures in many Maying poems: Christine de Pizan urges true lovers, "Soiez joyeux et liez sans retenir . . . Amours le veult et la saison le doit" [be joyful and happy without reservation . . . Love wishes it and the season demands it]; the king in Deschamps's "Lay de franchise" declares, "Au may sacrifions / Car nul de nous ne doit avoir sommeil; / Corps et penser et le cuer lui offrons" [we sacrifice to May, for none of us should be sluggish; we offer it our body and thought and heart: "Lf" 176–78].[20] Chaucer's description of Emelye's Maying repeatedly stresses obligation: "May wole have no slogardie anyght"; the season commands "every gentil herte . . . 'Arys, and do thyn observaunce.'"[21] The customary dress for Maying is green cloth or leaves and flowers: Emelye's "subtil gerland" is part of her "observaunce"; the lady in Jean Froissart's *Paradis d'Amour* makes a chaplet "de flourettes biel et doucet / Tel que l'adonne la saisons" [of little flowers sweet and lovely such as the season provides]; and Christine de Pizan declares that it is right to wear "chapiaulx jolis" [pretty garlands] and "Vestir de vert pour joie parfunir" [to dress in green in order to perform joy].[22]

What is this ritual accomplishing? Seasonal festivals tend to effect changes in the agrarian year, initiating the work of sowing for example. When Bishop Grosseteste condemns "games which they call the bringing-in of summer and autumn," he focuses on the rituals' transformative claim.[23] Bourdieu's account of ritual suggests that wearing green clothing and garlands could be read as a physical mimesis of spring's return. Bourdieu argues that ritual efficacy derives from emphatic reiteration, not from consciously worked out meaningfulness, and that reiteration is more importantly gestural and bodily than intellectual and verbal: "Rite is indeed in some cases no more than a practical *mimesis* of the natural process which needs to be facilitated."[24] Malory's knights who accompany Guinevere's Maying dressed in green clothing and "bedaysshed wyth erbis, mossis and floures in the freysshyste maner" might be accomplishing a return of spring in the most concrete terms.[25]

But the mimetic effect seems trivial in having, in this particular social context, no concrete need to fulfill: courtly Maying is sustained neither by a social conviction that spring will not return unless a rite is performed, nor by an agrarian impulse to influence the success of crops. The merely celebratory appearance of elite Maying could betray that it is not truly a ritual, but I believe its apparent triviality works to sustain its claim to eliteness. To be disconcerned with the productive implications of spring, and (as we will see below) to recast Maying as a celebration of sexual re-straint rather than of fecundity, is to ignore with some energy the pressing concerns of the agrarian sector. If wearing green clothing and plants does recall a mimetic desire to influence nature, it at the same time reorients that externally directed desire into an inner-directed self-revision that is (the reorientation itself would argue) a peculiar privilege of gentility.

Popular Maying, to the extent it can be recovered from records that are largely hostile to it, seems to have been a festival of release from con-straints, especially sexual ones: in diverse records, May festivities include wives taking revenge on husbands and going out without their permis-sion, young people spending the night in the woods together such that "scaresely the third parte of them returned home again undefiled," hang-ing garlands on trees to invoke spirits, and celebrating the outlaw freedom of Robin Hood bands.[26] Such behaviors construct an analogy between the release from winter's deprivations and release from cultural restraints on sexual, religious, and civic behavior.

Before the fourteenth century, Maying poetry incorporates some of this sense of licence and informality, but in its richest poetic elabora-tions toward the end of the century and into the next, courtly Maying contradicts much of its heritage.[27] It requires of lovers the sublimation that marks fine loving off from common: restraint and reverence are everywhere. Ladies may provide their lovers with chaplets, Christine declares, "Mais toutevoye / N'octroyez rien dont blasmer on vous doye" [but nonetheless, do not permit anything for which you could be blamed].[28] Guillaume de Machaut's "Dit de la Marguerite" concludes "Or me doint Diex grante pooir et vie / Pour li servir sans penser vilenie / . . . Pour ce que c'est de m'onneur le droit port" [Now God give me the life and power to serve her without a vulgar thought . . . for she is the true haven of my honor].[29] In Deschamps's "Lay amoureux" the central speaker is Honneur, who wears a flower chaplet and commands Youth to pursue love "Car amer et poursuire amende" [because loving and courting improve one]: love is fundamental to human society because it is the source of good manners, prowess, largesse, loyal marriage, and indeed salvation itself.[30] John Gower defies the claim that courtly Maying inculcates social and moral propriety when he calls May processions no more than "pleie."[31] Court poetry does so represent the Maying of shepherds and shepherdesses, who make garlands and sing of love and praise their simple life in unconstrained pastoral bliss, but this poetry is a foil to that of elite Maying.[32] The contrast between the carefree joy of the *pastourelle* and the didactic thrust of courtly Maying claims a status difference between the shepherd and the courtier. The price of admission to the groomed gardens of courtly Maying is the refined discernment that distinguishes elite from common status.

Courtly Maying does not simply assert elite status but works actively to conform its participants to a demanding standard of conduct. To accomplish this work, Maying must discover ways to make its demands appealing. Victor Turner's early work and more recent scholarship on ritual metaphor center on the complementarity within an effective ritual symbol between the normative values of the group and the individual desires of participants. A ritual symbol condenses these conflicting interests of the group and the participants into an apparently harmonious whole. Still, it may be possible to discern within the symbol, according to Turner, an "ideological pole," where the moral and social order expresses itself, and a "sensory pole," where feeling and desire gain representation. "The ritual symbol, we may perhaps say, effects an interchange of qualities between its poles of meaning. Norms and values, on the one hand, become saturated with emotion, while the gross and basic emotions become ennobled through contact with social values."[33] Turner's early and still influential analysis of the ritual process makes sense of the dual pressures in Maying poetry—the importance of constraint on the one hand and the lovers' desire on the other. These two poles, the regulatory and the passionate, unite in the concept of "fine" or "courtly" loving. Below I will argue that Maying works this fusion through two symbolic actions: going out into nature and back to court, and wearing and impersonating plants. In these actions Maying subsumes sexual desire into the social order. As Turner concludes, "ritual . . . is a mechanism that periodically converts the obligatory into the desirable. . . . The irksomeness of moral constraint is transformed into 'love of virtue.'"[34]

My discussion of sexual constraint and social hierarchizing in Maying modifies the Turnerian model in two respects. First, courtly Maying does configure sexual restraint as a reconciliation of private desire to the public good, but resurgent desire also lays claim to restraint and incorporates it into the private pleasure of fetishism. This contradictory movement suggests that Maying is not so system-maintaining as rituals are traditionally thought to be. Although Maying, like other rituals, claims to be a long-standing custom that simply requires observance, that claim disguises ritual's contingency on its own historical moment and its own participants' shaping interventions. John Kelly and Martha Kaplan conclude that rituals are "not reproductions from cultural templates or 'expressions' of structure, but instead are acts of power in the fashioning of structures."[35] The historicity of courtly Maying is particularly evident in its complex reshaping of a spring ritual around sexual constraint rather than sexual licence. Second, Turner's emphasis on the unifying function of ritual can only be illuminating in the case of Maying if this ritual's excluding function is also clear. Unifying and excluding reinforce one another in Maying, pressing the courtier toward a standard that defines itself in opposition to the common. As anthropologists have moved toward studying large-scale societies, the role of ritual in defining hierarchies has become more evident.[36] Elite Maying uses plants symbolically to enact the social and economic superiority of its participants. Bourdieu's concept of symbolic capital introduces ritual to its historical circumstances and helps explain how Maying sustains hierarchy. The apparent disregard for material needs and economic values in this elite ritual actually mobilizes symbolic capital, I will argue, to enhance participants' social standing.

Maying and the Amorous Law

"J'ay ouy parler en France," Deschamps begins one of his flower-and-leaf lyrics, "de deux ordres en l'amoureuse loy" [I've heard talk in France of two orders in the amorous law]: the apparently paradoxical "amorous law" aptly designates the ritual process by which controlling desire is made attractive.[37] The first and most universal gesture of Maying is going out from a domestic space into nature, and then returning at the end of the "observaunce." In popular Maying this movement acts out a distancing from social constraints, especially on sexuality, as noted above. In the poetry of courtly Maying, the natural space echoes rather than escapes the domestic space, grounding a construction of sexuality that refuses to distinguish between natural passions and cultural sentiments. Restraint, it appears, is universal—as native to birds as to humans.

One way to interpret the motion out from court and back again would be that it assumes and then crosses a nature/culture boundary. The dichotomy between nature and culture was so powerful in the work of Claude Lévi-Strauss that it governed many others (raw and cooked, naked and clothed), but Marilyn Strathern has warned that it is not a master dichotomy for all cultures. We tend, she argues, to find an organizing, conceptual difference between nature and culture wherever the data sustain a difference between interior and exterior, cultivated and wild, and so on, but we may instead be reading "feedback from our own input."[38] I believe that in Maying poetry, the movement out from court and back asserts the equivalence of the two spaces rather than their opposition, in order to ground its argument that the constraint of sexuality is a natural value to which participants should all subscribe.

The Floure and the Leafe and Chaucer's *Legend of Good Women* can briefly illustrate the contiguity of domestic and natural space. In the former, the narrator rises very early and takes a path overgrown with plants, apparently a solitary route away from cultured society, but she comes to an "herber" that is "benched" with turf like "welwet" [velvet], surrounded by a hedge cut "plain as a bord, of an [one] height"; "And shapen was this herber, roofe and all, / As a pretty parlor."[39] This arbor confounds the distinction between indoor and outdoor space. Does it do so by imposing culture on nature, by forcing grass and hedges into architectural shapes? The action that unfolds as the narrator watches from the arbor suggests otherwise: in that action, the nightingale and goldfinch represent allegiances, respectively, to the flower and to the leaf. A party of women and men celebrate their allegiance to the leaf in songs and jousts; then a party loyal to the flower is beset with troubles allegorically representing its members' superficiality, until they are all rescued by the party of the leaf, who feed them "plesaunt salades" and treat their sunburn with herbal ointments.[40] The distinctions important to this Maying scene, between virtuous restraint and amoral self-indulgence, are figured in the natural symbols of leaf and flower, nightingale and goldfinch. Nature is divided just as the human spirit is divided between higher and lower impulses.[41] This representation of Maying suggests that the arbor's turf benches and wall-like hedges are further representations of meritorious self-control, the orientation toward virtuous love that the nightingale celebrates and the leaf symbolizes. The arbor, like the garden of love in courtly poetry generally, reconstitutes much of the domestic sphere. It is removed certainly from daily duties and court intrigues, but coextensive with court life in articulating a relation between love and duty.

The Legend of Good Women similarly commingles the human and the natural. When the god of love makes his appearance, "a larke song above: / 'I se,' quod she, 'the myghty god of love. / Lo! yond he cometh! I se his wynges sprede'" (LGW G 141–43). This god of love, equally a god of humans and of birds (he even arrives on the wing), does not polarize nature and culture but rather fuses them in a comprehensive space where desire and restraint are likewise taken to be inseparable. Although his dominion over other creatures appears universal, among humankind the god of love distinguishes and particularly rules an elite. Following a familiar topos, the Legend mirrors the practices of courtship in the behavior of birds:

> [They] songen, "Blessed be Seynt Valentyn,
> For on his day I chees yow to be myn,
> Withouten repentyng, myn herte swete!"
> And therwithalle hire bekes gonnen meete,
> Yeldyng honour and humble obeysaunces
> To love, and diden hire other observaunces
> That longeth onto love and to nature. (LGW F 145–51)[42]

The birds' thanks to St. Valentine, solemn pledges, and humble observances validate courtly practices by instantiating them in nature. In so doing, the birds' observances revise the opposition between natural passions and cultural constraints that informs Turner's ritual process. Whereas that process brings "physiological experiences and desires" under the control of a "moral and social order," the poetry of Maying asserts that the most restrained self is most in consonance with nature. If Bourdieu's conception of mimesis can be extended from actions designed to affect the world to ones designed to affect the self, going out from court into nature and back might amount to a mimesis of the need to define the two spaces as one—a metaphorical performance of conforming the self "onto love and to nature."

A related symbolic gesture in Maying is cutting, carrying, weaving, and wearing plants. In part, working plants into ritual dress symbolizes the contiguity of natural and domestic spheres traced above. Courtiers add garlands, belts, and other decorations to their clothing as if enacting Derrida's insight about the supplement: donned in the course of Maying, a garland might seem a dispensable extra in the courtier's costume, but its very addition suggests that the costume is only complete once it is there, and that something was lacking before.[43] This sense of completion in dress reinforces the inclusiveness of moving from court to nature and back. But the leaf or flower supplement "completes" a participant's dress from outside the realm of dress (leaves are not cloth, a garland is not a hat or a crown), and this difference from seamless plenitude has two implications. One is that the supplement converts ordinary dress into ritual dress. The register or code of dress shifts from its everyday social meanings to signal "putting on a mood," conceding to the state of mind the festival requires.[44] Garlands of flowers and leaves are suited to joyful occasions, according to many classical and medieval sources; and Maying poets generally specify that green garments are appropriate to this festival.[45] But consonance in dress is even more significant than color, such that descriptions of Maying do not distinguish among the dress of individual participants but only among groups.[46] Donning a garland expresses submission to the ritual's pressure toward conformity and the rule of the general good: as Deschamps sums it up, "par l'amoureuse estincelle / se puet ly mondes reformer" [the world can be reformed by the spark of love].[47] At the same time, Derrida insists, because the supplement is an external addition, it betrays a failure to achieve true plenitude; it is "the mark of an emptiness."[48] The supplement's merely appended, detachable character and its location just where a lack can be felt associate it with the fetish. And indeed, one of the most seductive ways Maying uses plants is in a sublimation of sexuality that is fetishistic—that is finally less about restraint than about the diffusion of sexuality beyond mere satisfaction into a range of eroticized experiences of frustration.

Perhaps the most striking vestimentary image of the "amorous law" is the god of love's costume in the *Roman de la Rose*, made all of flowers but flowers worked into elaborate patterns:

> For nought clad in silk was he,
> But all in floures and in flourettes . . .
> And with losenges and scochouns,
> With briddes, lybardes, and lyouns,
> And other beestis wrought ful well.
> His garnement was everydell
> Portreied and wrought with floures,
> By dyvers medlyng of coloures.[49]

Weaving flowers into elaborate designs heightens the appeal of this costume, just as the god of love's many regulations for lovers should be
understood to intensify rather than dilute their experience of desire. Although later medieval poetry revises some of the more scandalous aspects
of the *Roman de la Rose*, that later poetry draws on the *Rose* tradition for a
perception of sweeping importance to the history of sexuality: that imped-
iments to desire enrich the experience of desire, rather than suppressing or
evading it. Concerning scopic pleasure, the god of love instructs the lover:

> The more thou seest in sothfastnesse,
> The more thou coveytest of that swetnesse;
> The more thin herte brenneth in fir,
> The more thin herte is in desir.[50]

Pain and pleasure are inextricable in the lover's experience, not because satisfaction is elusive but because desire encompasses its own reversals. The
oxymoron is the lover's figure, and lyric provides a discursive space for this
enlarged experience of desire. Where Maying poetry interrelates pain and
pleasure, it undercuts the ritual claim that love "puet ly mondes reformer"
[can reform the world]. A privatized ritual emerges beneath the one that
seeks social integration, a self-oriented rite that indulges rather than con-
trols desire. Fetishizing flowers is the primary gesture of this second ritual
process within Maying.

Flower Fetishes

Of the several metaphoric uses to which flowers are put in Maying poetry,
fetishization shapes desire most enticingly. I am broadening the sense of
fetishization, as do many revisionist readers of Freud, from his vivid story
of compensation for the discovery that mother has no phallus to a more
general sense that desire can organize with surprising energy around a
metonymy rather than a person.[51] But metonymy is still too associative
a figure for the fetish: when the handkerchief, the glove, or the daisy not
only substitutes for the absent lover but comes to be preferred, to be itself
the object of devotion, an "aesthetics of disavowal" creatively denies
absence by inventing a substitute presence.[52] In the relatively narrow definition developed by analyst Robert Stoller, this metonymic history must
be fully suppressed for the fetish to function erotically: the fetish "stands
for—condenses in itself—meanings that are, wholly or in crucial parts of the

text, unconscious." For Stoller, Maying poetry would provide a fictional representation of that unconscious "text" rather than instantiate genuine fetishization, but he would perhaps appreciate the recognition in this poetry that fetishization requires a narrative. In his memorable formulation, "a fetish is a story masquerading as an object."[53]

"Marguerite" poetry, equating women with daisies, does not always fetishize; usually it sustains a metaphoric relation between woman and daisy, albeit at times an obscure one:

> Toutes les fois que de ma main la cueil,
> Et je la puis regarder à mon veil
> Et li porter à ma bouche, à mon oeil,
>   Et à loisir
> Baisier, touchier, oudeurer et sentir
> Et sa biauté qui ne fait qu'embelir
> Et sa douceur doucement conjoir,
>   Riens plus ne veil.[54]

[Every time I gather it (or her) in my hand and can look at it at will and at my leisure kiss, touch, smell and feel both its beauty which only grows more beautiful and its sweetness sweetly conjoined, I want nothing else.]

Were it not for the metaphoric premise that all assertions concerning the marguerite are assertions concerning Marguerite, these lines culminating in "riens plus ne veil" would represent fetishistic substitution to the full. The erotic frisson instead arises from the claim to an expanded sensitivity, a doubled source of sensation that compensates for the intensified sublimation of the merely metaphoric looking, kissing, and touching. But some poets take the substitution of daisy for woman beyond metaphor. Froissart's fictions of how the daisy got its erotic charge illustrate the modern conception that the fetish compensates for and conceals a pivotal experience of lack. The courted lady in Le Paradis d'amour, instead of kissing the loving persona, makes him a daisy chaplet that each of them kisses before she crowns him with it.[55] The kisses' displacement onto the chaplet inverts the more widespread associations of garlands with sexual license, but the encounter is nonetheless satisfying: at this point the lover wakes from his dream quivering at the touch of Pleasure.[56] This fetishized resurgence of erotic energy within the courtly celebration of constraint recovers a certain consonance with popular Maying after all.

Froissart's "Dittié de la flour de la margherite" provides a double mythology for the daisy's fetishizing potential: daisies arose from the tears

of loss shed by Hero on the tomb of Cepheus; there Mercury picked them
to make a garland that won the love of Ceres—but only by messenger, and
apparently with only the effect that Mercury wears a chaplet ever after.[57]
May his fate be the same, the persona concludes; each time he sees daisies

> J'en cueillerai une ou deus en riant;
> Et si dirai, son grant bien recordant:
> "Veci la flour qui me tient tout joiant,
> Et qui me fait en souffissance grant
> Tous biens sentir."[58]

[I will pick one or two happily and say, remembering its (or her) great value, "Here
is the flower that keeps me all joyful and that makes me experience all good to the
fullest."]

Froissart's invented mythologies of loss and separation suffuse this no
longer metaphorical daisy so that, effectively severed from every absent
lover, it becomes the only source of "souffissance." A memory lingers of
his lady's "grant bien," distanced by the pronoun's equivocal reference to
the daisy as well as herself, but the lover's relationship in the lyric present
is with the flower alone.

The fetish has also a postmedieval history in ritual: the pidgin term
fetisso, for small objects of trade with peoples undergoing colonization,
soon came to signify small objects figuring in those peoples' rituals, but
figuring in superstitious ways alien to European Christianity: the intransi-
gent materiality that seemed to characterize the ritual fetish set the strange
religions apart. William Pietz argues that the fetish "originated in the
cross-cultural spaces" of early colonization, but he also traces its medieval
antecedents in suppressed magical practices that used small objects, carried
or worn about the body, to guarantee health or achieve other concrete
ends.[59] In courtly Maying, traces of the magical and the sexual fetish coin-
cide. Maying, together with many festivals originating outside the church,
make an alien space within Christendom well before the colonial era.
Leaves and flowers focus a ritual process that seeks to integrate desire into
a social and moral order without recourse to Christian sacraments. At the
same time, a counterprocess resists integration by severing the marguerite
from Marguerite, redefining it as a small but powerful extension of the
lover's body that elaborates his own eroticism. This fetishized daisy, a
material embodiment of the "amorous law" that absorbs frustration into
the experience of desire, escapes submission to the moralizing "amorous
law" that demands restraint for the greater good.

Ritual Exclusion

The two fundamental gestures of elite Maying, going out from court to gather plants and weaving, wearing, even becoming plants, invoke sexual restraint in part to assert the superiority of courtly to common loving, as I have argued above. Maying enacts social superiority still more evidently around the issues of production and consumption. For elite Maying, spring is not a season of concern for crops or for beginning agricultural labor; nature is itself directly and extravagently productive of leaves and flowers that are gathered and woven into garlands by courtiers themselves. The peasant's work and the artisan's craft need not intervene in this relation to the natural world. Three aspects of this relation, traced below, are its resistance to the place of labor in maintaining privilege, its claim to an enlarged privilege that can disregard material exchange values, and its mobilization of symbolic capital to enhance material privilege.

The parties of the Flower and the Leaf, an elite accretion to Maying, illustrate the elision of labor particularly clearly. In much medieval poetry, leaves and flowers together represent the whole scene of springtime. "The rose rayleth hire rode, / The leves on the lyhte wode / Waxen al with wille"; in a Maying lyric "Je gart le bos" [I guard the woods] from all but true lovers; "gart la raime / Et la flour du bois" [I guard the branch and the flower of the woods].[60] But in the later fourteenth century, these complementary leaves and flowers become the livery of contending parties within elite Maying.[61] The very triviality of their difference suits the parties to the leisure of the privileged: what could be less consequential than deciding whether to be loyal to a flower or to a leaf? Of course the two gain symbolic meaning in *The Floure and the Leafe*, where they stand for careless and constrained behavior, but their assigned meaning has little to do with physical properties inherent in flowers or leaves. In four lyrics Deschamps treats the choice as if it were consequential—"Qui est a choiz de deux choses avoir, / Eslire doit et choisir la meillour" [Whoever is choosing between two things must elect and choose the better one]—but the distinctions he makes are more elegant than weighty.[62] At one point Deschamps argues in favor of the flower "Qu'elle a beauté, bonté, fresche couleur, / Et rent a tous tresprecieux odour, / Et fait bon fruit que mains sont desirans" [that it has beauty, goodness, fresh color, and gives everyone a most precious scent, and makes good fruit that many desire], but he objects in another lyric that fruit "petit vault pour le corps maintenir" [is worth little for sustaining the body] whereas leaves shelter game of all kinds, "cerfs, bisches et chevriaux, / Sanglers et dains, connins et laperiaux" [harts, hinds, and roebucks, boars and deer, rabbits and bunnies].[63] Deschamps's shifting allegiance signals that one goal of the debate is clever argument on whichever side, but also significant is the direct relation he establishes between the elegant Maying parties and natural sustenance: the flower "makes good fruit" and the leaf fosters all sorts of game in a reenchantment of nature that no longer requires labor for sustenance.[64] In *The Floure and the Leafe*, similarly, the party of the Leaf restore the party of the Flower with herbal ointments and pleasant salads, needing no resort to prepared foods or medicines. There is a willful disregard for labor in these sce-narios—willful in that they are so overtly mere fantasies of a relation to nature. Leaf and Flower are icons of a mystified, deeconomized relation between participants and their own privilege.

Like choosing between leaf and flower, weaving and wearing garlands prizes the unproduced and uncrafted over the fabricated. But the garland is tied more fully to the true economics of Maying than the parties of flower and leaf, because it is only part of a costume that retains luxury as one of its merits. The dress of Maying taken as a whole does not so much reject a relation to the labor of inferiors as acknowledge and defy that rela-tion's importance. Donning garlands has been seen as an escape from courtliness, an escape expressing a pastoral impulse that plays at simplic-ity.[65] I believe the garland operates on the contrary, in this subset of May-ing poetry, to put down the challenge of pastoralism. Participants in elite Maying do not shed their clothing or "dress down," gestures that would indeed suggest a rejection of social position. Valuing garlands takes place within the system that also values fine dress. A group of ladies in *The Floure and the Leafe* wear white velvet garments trimmed with emeralds, and chaplets of woodbine, laurel, or agnus castus.[66] The chaplets, apparently as esteemed as velvet and jewels, recall the Black Prince's commutations of rents in exchange for "a red rose yearly at Midsummer."[67] The privilege of wealth expresses itself in the exercise of largesse, of disregarding exchange value altogether. The chaplet of a shepherdess may be innocent of eco-nomic meaning, but to wear a chaplet above velvet is a gesture of power: one deliberately puts off the headdress and values the materially valueless in its place. Thus largesse contributes to social standing; in the "Lay de franchise," the first didactic claim that "sanz amour ne puet estre prouesse" [without love there can be no prowess: "Lf" 211] quickly widens to the exemplary triad "Emprise, Amour, Largesce" [boldness, love, largesse: "Lf" 221]. From a position of economic strength, choosing a chaplet over a crown, a rose over a rent, expands one's standing rather than depleting it, because it implies a sufficiency so great that it need make no distinctions of value.

But when we note that valuing flowers enhances rather than diminishes the standing of courtiers, it becomes clear that the term "largesse" disguises the gesture's investment in social hierarchy. Bourdieu's conception of symbolic capital is illuminating here in that it rejects a distinction between material exchanges and negotiations involving other measures of value: we should "extend economic calculation to *all* the goods, material and symbolic, without distinction, that present themselves as *rare* and worthy of being sought after in a particular social formation."[68] Honor, smiles, even gossip are among the instances of symbolic capital Bourdieu suggests, and this kind of value does inhere in flowers for much Maying poetry: woodbine represents constancy, to draw again on *The Floure and the Leafe*, laurel represents hardiness, and agnus castus virginity.[69] Leaves and flowers stand for the elements of self-discipline by which participants in Maying lay claim to elite status. Valuing flowers, elite Maying appears to disregard material value, but more accurately expands value from the material to the symbolic realm.[70]

The most extended illustration of how flowers come to represent symbolic capital is "marguerite" poetry, which declares that women are themselves flowers insofar as they embody the virtues Maying enforces. The adored woman is a "tresdoulce fleur toute blanche et vermeille" [very sweet flower all white and red], her every attribute expressed in botanical sign language: "Ce qu'elle s'oeuvre et s'encline au soleil, / C'est à dire qu'en li n'a point d'orgueil" [that she opens and leans toward the sun, is to say that in her there is no pride]; the daisy's white stands for her purity and red for her timidity; "La grayne d'or est sens, qui vous conseille / De bien garder vostre honneur" [the gold seed is good sense, which counsels you to guard your honor well].[71] Through such metaphoric connections, plants of no economic value come to represent the symbolic capital of virtues: "also many vertues hadde shee / As smale florouns in hire corowne bee" (*LGW* F 528–29).

The metaphoric chain from plant to woman to virtue not only expresses the symbolic value of good conduct but also figures a ritual transformation, urging women to shape their identity through chastity and restraint. James Fernandez argues that metaphors are fundamental to ritual because they produce "movement in our understanding. . . . We learn something by the metaphoric choice of a domain to which the subject does not legitimately belong and within which he does not legitimately act." Arguing that rituals typically turn on metaphoric transformations for their participants, Fernandez asks, "What is more abstract and inchoate and in need of predication than a pronoun? Personal experience and social life cry out that we predicate some identity upon the I, the you, the he, the she, the they, the it."[72] What is it to be a daisy? Alceste in the *Legend of Good Women* has several intersecting relations to the daisy: she is dressed to appear like one, she is metaphorically equivalent to one, and she now *is* one by metamorphosis at the same time that she is also a queen. The narrator recognizes at first only the way her dress imitates a daisy, then hears from the god of love that she is "the quene Alceste, / That turned was into a dayesye," and then asserts the metaphoric relation himself: "And is this good Alceste, / The dayesie, and myn owene hertes reste?" (*LGW* F 510–11, 518–19) Already the narrator has called the daisy "of alle floures flour" and the ladies accompanying Alceste have kneeled to it singing "Heel and honour / To trouthe of womanhede, and to this flour / That bereth our alder pris in figurynge [that conveys figuratively the merit of all of us]" (*LGW* F 296–98).[73] "Alceste / The dayesie" is a sort of bootstraps operation, whereby Alceste's historical faithfulness to her husband inhered in the daisy through her metamorphosis, but now inheres in it independently of her, so that the daisy can represent the virtue of many women—can "[bere] our alder pris in figurynge." The metaphor that woman is a flower, then, accomplishes an elevation in her moral standing that sustains the wider claim of courtly Maying that heterosexual love is a refining experience. Women are flowers insofar as they constrain their sexuality—which reintroduces the relation between flowers and symbolic capital. Feminine chastity, honor, constancy all designate the sexual control which is most valued in "women on the market."[74]

Persona in Maying

The final sections of this chapter turn from the cultural work of courtly Maying to an inherent complication in getting the work done. Within ritual there is a negotiation to be effected, even a conflict to be overcome, between the participant and the event. Preceding sections of this chapter have drawn in part on Turner's thesis that rituals negotiate a conflict between the desires of bodies and the best interest of communities. A preliminary, underlying conflict exists between a participant's absorption in and resistance to the event itself: typically, people experience both grateful acquiescence to a ritual, such as a trial following a crime, and at the same time an uncomfortable sense of detachment and doubt. In Maying poetry, this double response to ritual tends to find expression in a persona, both because the persona is a ritual participant, in diegetic terms, and because the persona, in rhetorical terms, is itself a divided entity.

In rhetorical terms, "persona" refers not just to poetic voice but to voice sufficiently specified and fictionalized that readers and listeners must consider the degree of its overlap with the historical poet. This overlap may be greater or lesser but is always problematic. Persona registers the inaccessibility of the poet's historical self and at the same time constructs an accessible simulacrum that claims a connection to the historical poet. The indeterminacy of this connection is the source of the device's power: persona's protean masking asserts an authenticating connection to the historical poet but reaches fantastically beyond the constraints on self-presentation in the historical world. Medieval high culture knew the concept of persona and the term from classical poetry and theater, a heritage bridging written and performed self-presentation. Persona, of course, is a multifaceted concern for literary scholars, encompassing issues as diverse as tone, voice, narration, and characterization.[75] For investigating just the relation between poetic and ritual self-presentation, the salient aspect of poetic persona is its doubly historical and fictive quality, a doubleness which slides between extremes of total opposition (in the obtuseness of Chaucer's persona, for example) and productive fusion (in Deschamps's "Lay de franchise," discussed below).

The ritual self is similarly double: ritual invites participants to put on a mood and join a performance that escapes everyday conditions, thus rejecting a full connection with everyday life. Participants are both falsified and recognized; they are misrepresented in order to be invoked. Jack Goody characterizes rituals as "masks of the 'true' self," such that participants cannot be fully recognized, cannot be taken into account in all their particulars and complexities. But this only partial recognition prepares, at least potentially, for self-transformation, for profound engagement in the ritual.[76] I suspect that both the ritual persona and the poetic persona take their meaning and energy from the inseparable, indeed symbiotic, misrepresentation and invocation of the "true" self. Goody puts "true" in scare quotes, recognizing the already performed rather than natural status of the self that has come into ritual space. That prior self, with its complex allegiances and its comparatively long history, dons the awkwardly small and thin mask prescribed by the ritual as a strategy for getting through the performance, and perhaps profiting from it. Like the poetic persona, the ritual persona enacts the self as a temporally layered entity. This self-aware re-presentation characterizing both the ritual and the lyric persona is a salient feature of Maying poetry.

This chapter began by illustrating the characteristics of elite Maying with Eustache Deschamps's "Lay de franchise." Although his account of Maying asserts the court's shared status and ideals, Deschamps's persona is detached from the occasion insofar as he withdraws to observe it and re-flects again upon it after hearing Robin's words. Is the persona then himself divided, embodying an only partial commitment to the celebrated occasion? To most readers today, the relation between ritual absorption and resistance may appear simply oppositional; moreover, resistance appears consonant with modernity, individuality, and progressiveness while absorption appears "medieval" in the popular negative senses of universalizing, repressive, and retrograde. Certainly the two can pull against one another, but in some Maying poetry the tension between them is symbiotic and productive rather than oppositional. Deschamps's persona in the "Lay de franchise" is both participating in the Maying of the court and observing it, and his dual position is what allows him to contribute his crucial insight to the court at the close of the lay.

At the outset, the "Lay de franchise" locates custom in the memory of a generalized "one":

> Pour ce que grant chose est d'acoustumance
> Quant on la prant et poursuit des s'enffance
> Dure chose est qu'om se puist retenir
> De la laissier. ("Lf" 1–4)

[Because habit is a powerful force when one has and follows it from one's child-hood, it would be difficult for one to determine to leave it.]

This universal "one" soon unfolds into persona and "gens," other people: "Du moys de may me vint la souvenance / Dont maintes gens ont la coustume en France / En ce doulz temps d'aler le may cueillir" [I recalled the month of May, about which many people have the custom in France to go gather the may in this sweet season: "Lf" 11–13]. This contiguity of persona and others informs the lay's dramatic structure as the persona leaves his "hostel" to participate in Maying. He does so by observing others, yet the lay's pervasive claim is that the persona is a full participant. The frame of mind in which he sets out, "sacrifier voulz mon cuer" [I want to sacrifice my heart: "Lf" 19] is echoed in the king's assertion "Au may sacrifions" [we sacrifice to May: "Lf" 176]. Until he comes on the May-ing party, the persona's thoughts and actions sustain the "coustume du jour" [custom of the day: "Lf" 16] in his dressing in green, walking out, and contemplating "la tresdouce flour / Qui en bonté, en douçour, en honour / Et en tous biens, est la flour souveraine" [the very sweet flower, which in goodness, sweetness, honor, and all virtues is the sovereign flower: "Lf" 30–32]. This flower figures both the virtues of restrained sexuality that Maying inculcates and a particular woman who later embodies and articulates them: the flower glides ambiguously between generality and specificity to represent the desire of every and each participant. The persona's devotion to this flower's circulating centrality links him to the Maying he watches, particularly at the culminating moment of the festival, when "la flour" speaks authoritatively about the power of love throughout history.

The persona's observing does not remove him from the celebration but rather dramatizes a relation between his absorption in the festival and a certain detachment. The persona is not simply another Maying courtier, but any other participants might perform their distinctiveness as well, for example in lyric outbursts of their own. Indeed, the other participants' singing and reciting of "amoureus dis" makes a *mise en abime* with the poet's own lay finally offered to "celle flour" at the close ("Lf" 127, 308).[77] Deschamps poises his persona between experiencing the ritual as a devotional act and celebrating the equivalent experience of all.

The close of the "Lay de franchise," however, produces some stress around the persona's difference. The lay's final episode contrasts courtly Maying to Robin and Marion's simple meal and Robin's critique of court life:

> "Marion, deshonneste
> Sont grans mangiers et cilz qui les apreste . . . .
> J'ay franc vouloir et bonne souffisance,
> Ne je ne vuiel autre estat maintenir." ("Lf" 274–75, 298–99)

[Marion, great feasts are unworthy as are those who arrange them . . . . I have free will and good sustenance, nor do I want any other estate.]

Such feasting is unhealthy and even dangerous, what with the intrigues of courts. The persona's response is profound: his body shudders as he "panse et repance" [thinks and rethinks: "Lf" 303], and then accepts Robin's view that "trop est cours perilleuse balance" [the court is all too precarious: "Lf" 307]. Gaston Raynaud and Marian Lossing read this ending as Deschamps's categorical rejection of court life.[78] This reading neglects the curiously integrative gesture of the closing lines, which attribute the persona's enlightenment to "la flour":

Et Dieux vueille celle flour remerir
Et le doulz may qui m'ont fait avertir
Par Marion et Robin seure dance.
Or lui suppli que sa douce semblance
Reçoive en gré ce lay au departir. ("Lf" 308–12)[79]

[And may God reward that flower and the sweet May for advising me through
Robin and Marion of the right path. Now I beg her that her sweet countenance
receive with good will this lay at our parting.]

Marion and Robin are the mere agents of an enlightenment that is sub-
sumed, according to the persona, within the celebration of that flower who
was most embodied and articulate at the heart of the court festival. At the
moment of critique, the claim to a productive relation between incorporation and resistance becomes strongest. The reproach to courtly excess and
venality, which appears at first to be entirely at odds with the elite Maying
that preceded it, is instead a final contribution to the morally elevating
process of elite Maying. That contribution arises from an irreducible doubleness inherent in the ritual and poetic persona's masked performance of
a self both engaged in and transcending the particular occasion.

When this productive reciprocality between commitment and detachment
breaks down, chagrin and loss characterize the experience of Maying. In a
ballade written during Charles d'Orléans's captivity in England, his persona participates in Maying "en compaignie" by taking the livery of the
leaf. That night he reflects that his choice was appropriate:

Car, puis que par Mort perdu ay
La fleur, de tous biens enrichie,
Qui estoit ma Dame, m'amie . . .
Mon cueur d'autre flour n'a pas cure.

For syn thorugh deth y lost have (welaway!)
She which was sorse and flowre of all bewte
Which was my love, my swet hert and lade . . .
Of othir flowre, god wott, y take no quere.[80]

His reflection gives a private meaning to wearing the livery of the leaf
that is more profound than his companions' choices of leaf or flower. He
will serve the leaf loyally, he concludes, but he knows from his experience that "Il n'est fueille ne fleur qui dure / Que pour un temps" ["Ther
nys leef nor flowre that doth endewre / But a sesoun"].[81] His assertion
can be read in two ways. Most evident is that the ritual's celebration of leaf
and flower divorces this persona from the ritual, since his beloved's death

is so meaningful and so painful as to render both leaf and flower equally trivial in comparison. Choosing the livery of the leaf did make sense, but a negative sense arising from his loss of the only "flower" he could care about. This first implication of "Il n'est fueille ne fleur qui dure" contrasts the persona's private grief to the joy Maying requires. But this contrast is itself a second source of grief. If we take "fueille" to refer to the leaf or the party of the leaf, and "fleur" to refer his lady, the line becomes a zeugma, a figure that yokes radically different subjects to a single predicate: leaf and lady last only for a time. The zeugma expresses not only the triviality of Maying when measured against the persona's bereavement, but also the insubstantiality of the ritual's claim for the world-shaping importance of heterosexual courtship. Love is as soon lost as spring. The persona is twice bereaved, having lost both his lady and his belief in the ritual's importance.

Charles d'Orléans uses clothing in a range of poetic scenarios to present his persona, and to link his persona suggestively to his historical circumstances. In this process the persona unfolds into dramatic encounters among "mon cueur, penser et moy, nous trois" [my heart, thought, and I, we three], or similarly differentiated but organic relationships.[82] "Moy" in these scenes is not the persona in toto but its voicing, self-representing aspect. Yet the heart also voices itself, through dress: "Je suy cellui au cueur vestu de noir" ["Thus am y he whos hart in blak is gownnid"] visualizes and clothes the heart, giving silent pain a corporeal expression.[83] In other lyrics the heart wears the gray of hope, the blue of faithfulness, but most often black.[84] That Charles habitually wore black from the time of his father's murder through his years of captivity in England echoes the heart's dress in historical practice, reinforcing his lyrics' claim that affective states can be concretely and performatively expressed.[85] As Charles restages biographical material on the dehistoricized allegorical terrain of lyric, he corroborates his historical suffering even as he converts biography into compellingly allusive, generalized terms.

One such generalized scene of sorrow is the failure of Maying. In a striking image for the loss of any productive relation between ritual's recognition and falsification of the "true" self, Charles's heart wears green, but not the green of May:

> Le premier jour du mois de may,
> De tanné et de vert perdu,
> Las! j'ay trouvé mon cuer vestu,
> Dieu scet en quel piteux array!

Tantost demandé je lui ay
Dont estoit cest habit venu,
Le premier jour du mois de may.

Il m'a respondu: "Bien le sçay,
Mais par moy ne sera cogneu;
Desplaisance m'en a pourveu,
Sa livrée je porteray,
Le premier jour du mois de may."[86]

[The first day of the month of May, I found my heart dressed, alas, in brown and darkest green, God knows in what pitiful array. I asked my heart where this costume had come from, the first day of the month of May. He answered me, "I know well where, but it will not be known by me; Displeasure gave it to me; I will wear his livery the first day of the month of May."]

The company of Maying courtiers gives way here to a fully internal scene that compounds grief with the knowledge that grief should be banished by the festival. The livery "de tanné et de vert perdu" suggests an autumnal loss of green even as it recalls the green dress of Maying.[87] The "vert perdu" of the heart's dress refers as well to the house colors of Orleans, which were altered, first in response to the assassination of Louis d'Orléans in 1407 and again after the Battle of Agincourt, from *vert gai* to *vert brun* to *vert perdu* [bright or happy green to brown green to lost green] to reflect the ever worsening fortunes of the house.[88] This darkest green, named so evocatively lost green, marks the heart's distance from Maying: it is more accurately the livery of displeasure than of celebration. This displeasure remains unarticulated—"par moy ne sera cogneu"—detached from historical events and fixed without referent in the small, spare landscape of figuration. Thus "desplaisance" marks not just the heart's unparalleled livery but the loss of ritual engagement and of the masked relation between poet and persona.

Since the time of the Romantics we tend to identify the lyric with the solitude of a subjectivity enclosed in its own reflections. Medieval lyrics are better identified with voice and with a mobile selfhood located in communication as well as reflection. Performing in relation to the occasion of Maying as well as through his persona, Deschamps contributes to ritual as well as gaining from it. For Charles d'Orléans, losing the benefits of ritual is equivalent to losing contact with his poetic identity. Both poets understand ritual to demand engagement *and* misrepresentation, rather as the poetic persona claims *and* denies that it represents the poet. In ritual and in lyric, this doubleness expresses an identity always in process, a performative selfhood importantly located in mimesis.

Chaucer's Persona and Alceste's Dress

Always departing from his predecessors but always peculiarly sensitive to their meanings, Chaucer provides my last instance of Maying as a scene of self-presentation. A sixteenth-century portrait of Chaucer (Figure 3) commemorates his Maying persona in the *Legend of Good Women*. Above the poet's physical image are a daisy on the right, and the coat of arms traditionally ascribed to him on the left.[89] A death date of 1402, not quite correct, nonetheless contributes to the portrait's rhetoric of preservation and record. Preservation also dictates this portrait's reuse of the early Hoccleve portrait or one of its copies.[90] But the early image gets enlargement here. The poet stands on a floating cloudlike turf whose fragile artifice helps associate his human figure with two attendant figurations, the arms and the daisy. The daisy might express an extratextual tradition that Chaucer himself revered the daisy, but such a tradition would surely have its basis in the *Legend of Good Women*, where Chaucer's persona writes "in service of the flour / Whom that I serve as I have wit or myght" (*LGW* F 82–83). Thus the portrait oddly conjoins a representation of historical status, the coat of arms, with one of poetic self-presentation, the daisy. It is a visual translation of the poetic persona's doubleness, its enigmatic overlapping of connection to and difference from the historical poet.

The portrait positions the daisy as a complement to the coat of arms in order to assign the daisy a similarly emblematic, self-representing status. The two signs are intriguingly linked by their red and white color. The daisy is much faded in the portrait, but still recognizably a *bellis perennis* "white and rede, / Swiche as men callen daysyes in our toun" (*LGW* F 42–43). The arms are the same colors, *argent and gules, a bend counterchanged*. Given the natural inevitability of the daisy's red and white, the coat of arms seems to take its colors from the daisy in an intensely visual expression of "service of the flour." Priority, of course, is usually the reverse in coats of arms and emblems: the former are in principle inherited and fixed, the latter open to purely personal determination. The portrait appears to narrate an inverted process, in which the poet expressed his devotion to the daisy by adopting red and white arms. This romantic (and probably spurious) history for Chaucer's arms expresses again the permeable border between person and persona: a poetic and ritual self, produced and defined within Maying, seems to be bleeding back into the historical Chaucer, feeding his self-representation in arms as well as in poetry.

Chaucer's handling of the daisy is actually less self-enhancing than this portrait imagines. Chaucer revisits the fetishistic role that French poetry

Figure 3. Portrait of Geoffrey Chaucer. London, British Library, Add. MS 5141, fol. 1. By permission of the British Library.

developed for daisies, but he makes the failure of fetishization a first aspect of his persona's haplessness. The F text of the Prologue to the *Legend of Good Women*, which responds more fully to Maying traditions than the G text, sensitively represents the ambiguity of the referent of "la marguerite" in French by vacillating between "it" and "she" as pronouns for the daisy: Chaucer's persona is eager "to doon it alle reverence / As she that is of alle floures flour . . . / And I love it, and ever ylike newe" (*LGW* F 52–53, 56).[91] The persona then shifts from third to second person to address the flower: "ye ben verrayly / The maistresse of my wit, and nothing I. . . . / Be ye my gide and lady sovereyne!" (*LGW* F 87–88, 94) Metaphoric equivalence between daisy and woman prepares for fetishistic substitution as it becomes clear that this "lady sovereyne" is Alceste. But loving the daisy does not link Chaucer's persona to the unattainable woman through the powerful "souffisance" of fetishization that Chaucer would have known from his French sources. Instead, when Alceste is finally introduced to him, he distinguishes his gratitude to the woman from his affection for the flower:

> Wel hath she quyt me myn affeccioun
> That I have to hire flour, the dayesye.
> No wonder ys thogh Jove hire stellyfye,
> As telleth Agaton, for hire goodnesse. . . .
> In remembraunce of hire and in honour
> Cibella maade the daysye and the flour
> Ycrowned al with whit, as men may see;
> And Mars yaf to hire corowne reed, pardee,
> In stede of rubyes, sette among the white. (*LGW* F 524–27, 530–34)

This fascinating revision of the initial relation between Alceste and the daisy moves in two new directions, stellification and metamorphosis, that avoid fetishization. The daisy is either her earthly commemoration, if she is stellified, or her eternal self, if she is metamorphosed—either not Alceste or totally Alceste—but in either case not a fetishistic substitution that a lover could enjoy in sublimated devotion. The persona's worship of the daisy does recall the triumph of pleasure over constraint in French poetry, but here it becomes the pitiful resort of an outsider who cannot truly participate in Maying.

Chaucer evokes and then denies fetishistic pleasure to mark his persona's impotence, as do his disempowered stance before the god of love and his ineffectual defense of his writing. His depleted relation to the daisy betrays a certain detachment from Maying. Although he acts and writes "in service of the flour," the persona does not claim affiliation to the party of Flower or of Leaf (*LGW* F 82, 188–96; cf. G 69–80). Compounding his detachment is a curious resemblance between the daisy and the books he ostensibly leaves behind in May. The daisy opens at dawn, the persona pores over it all day in silence, and it closes when the light fails; its "white leves lyte" replace the leaves of his books without resituating him in relation to his community (*LGW* F 219).[92] Isolated from the parties that characterize elite Maying and situated more as an admiring reader than a participant, the persona next misses out on fetishization. Despite his reverence for Maying, there is little in it for him besides submissive admiration; there is neither the sense of community that gives ritual much of its appeal nor the erotic charge that fetishism can preserve within restraint. The persona's failure to fetishize the daisy, his alienation from the god of love, and his inability to turn fully from books to Maying prepare for an equally alienated reassessment of Maying itself.

Alceste's costume is a revealing way into Chaucer's optic on Maying. Although claiming that Alceste is a daisy is consonant with marguerite poetry's metaphorics, Alceste's daisy outfit is a bizarre literalization of the claim that woman is flower. Garlands, green cloth, and leaves dress both men and women in Maying, but a gold hairnet topping a crown of carved white petals, turning Alceste into an outsized daisy, has no parallel in lyrics or wardrobe accounts of costumes and liveries for May Day:

> And she was clad in real habit grene.
> A fret of gold she hadde next her heer,
> And upon that a whit corowne she beer
> With flourouns [petals] smale, and I shal nat lye;
> For al the world, ryght as a dayesye
> Ycorouned ys with white leves lyte,
> So were the flowrouns of hire coroune white.
> For of o perle fyn, oriental,
> Hire white coroune was ymaked al;
> For which the white coroune above the grene
> Made hire lyk a daysie for to sene,
> Considered eke hir fret of gold above. (*LGW* F 214–25)[93]

The clarity and detail with which Chaucer lays out this costume's imitation of a daisy contrasts with his short account of the god of love's more conventional silk embroidered with branches and leaves.[94] Alceste's unparalleled costume rejects the only partial equation of metaphor, whereby some qualities of the daisy overlap with some feminine qualities, to express both total metamorphosis and the simultaneity of its two poles in the timeless space of Love's garden. Metamorphosis is Chaucer's well-known addition to the classical story that Alceste was willing to die in place of her husband Admetus, and that Hercules rescued her from the underworld and returned her to Admetus out of admiration for her self-sacrifice. Hercules's reward, her return "out of helle agayn to blys" of married love, is doubled in Jove's stellification of Alceste and trebled in her metamorphosis into a flower designed by Cibella and Mars (*LGW* F 510–34, G 498–522). Showered in godly recognitions, Alceste's suffering for love provides the template for the "Seintes Legende of Cupide." The relation between Prologue and legends has seemed tenuous to many critics, and I do not deny that generic and thematic distinctions mark off the former from the latter. However, Alceste's metamorphosis, so concretely manifested in her costume, establishes a closer relation between Prologue and legends than other aspects of the Prologue might suggest.

Chaucer draws on the *Ovide moralisé* as well as Ovid's *Metamorphoses* to claim an important relation between divine justice and metamorphosis. In both sources, the heavens darken the mulberry in response to Thisbe's request that it take "noire coulour / En testimoine de dolur" [black color that testifies to sorrow], and in both sources Bacchus stellifies Ariadne's crown as part of his consolation when Theseus abandons her.[95] In general, however, Ovid's heavens are less oriented toward providing justice and solace than is the Christian order of the *Ovide moralisé*. Ovid's Bacchus consoles Ariadne because he loves her; in the *Ovide moralisé*, the stellification of her crown is a divine reward for faithfulness as well as a love gift. Philomela's transformation has no divine motive in Ovid's account, but in the *Ovide moralisé* as well as in Chrétien de Troyes's interpolated poem on Philomela, her persecuted virtue explains her transformation into the sweet-voiced nightingale rather than the less attractive birds Procne and Tereus become.[96] Chaucer used both sources, but his invented myth of Alceste's transformation draws particularly on the *Ovide moralisé*'s tendency to understand metamorphosis as a recognition of merit and a compensation for suffering. In Alceste's case these two motives are equally appropriate to her willingness to die for love. Here is a first link between Alceste and the saints of Cupid: virtuous suffering unites them. But within this paradigm there is a notable difference around metamorphosis: Alceste's transformation into a daisy makes more obvious and pointed that Chaucer deletes metamorphosis from the stories of Ariadne, Thisbe, and Philomela.

A first explanation for the disappearance of metamorphosis from the legends is that the Prologue stipulates it. Alceste specifies that the legends must be not only of good women but of "false men that hem bytraien," stressing the injustice and suffering in their stories rather than divine recognition and reward (*LGW* F 486). This emphasis aligns the legends with Ovid's *Heroides*, another important source for Chaucer, and with tragedy in its medieval sense of untranscendent worldly fortunes turning always to the worse. In contrast, Alceste's metamorphosis after her virtu-ous suffering might refer to Christian eternal life after martyrdom, as the title "Seintes Legende" and the Latin incipits and explicits naming women "martyr" suggest. In V. A. Kolve's reading, Alceste's desire to save her hus-band and her eternal reward establish "a pattern not of courtly loving but of the love that is charity," in sharp contrast with the legends' earth-bound miseries: "such suffering is without purpose, and without redemp-tive potential: tragedy in a pagan world."[97] In my view, the Prologue does not endorse Alceste so unequivocally. Her deference to the god of love's capricious authority, and more generally the god's imperfect understand-ing, argue that the Prologue's Christian imagery is ironic inflation for a scene that shares little with Christian eschatology.

The legends that follow the Prologue expand its creeping discomfort with Alceste as a model of love. Maying appears more attractive than it later proves, most evidently in the god of love's hostility to Chaucer's per-sona. His misreading and his imperious demand that the persona voice sentiments to his specifications call into question his choice of Alceste's virtuous suffering as the epitome of feminine loving. Does her subordina-tion of her own life to her husband's represent the best loving women do, and the kind of loving men should desire? Her own account of the god of love's capriciousness suggests otherwise: "Lat be thyn arguynge," she silences the narrator, "For Love ne wol nat countrepleted be / In ryght ne wrong; and lerne that at me!" (*LGW* F 475–77) Her overt acceptance of Cupid's authority in right or wrong suggests that dying in her husband's place was equally vacant of justice, equally a zealous subordination to authority rather than to right. James Simpson has argued in detail that Alceste is primarily "a signifier of Cupid," and that Cupid desires stories of feminine suffering so strongly because he is himself the instigator of suffer-ing, as his role in Dido's love for Aeneas most clearly betrays.[98] Love's court is an imperfect place despite its apparent glories. Its ruler is less than insightful, less than just, merely worldly and calculating in his con-cern for his stature and image. Here lies a second bond between Prologue and legends: the injustices Alceste accepts from the god of love adumbrate the lives of his other saints. In the light of the miseries to come, the clunky literalness of Alceste's daisy outfit as well as her deference to a tyranni-cal Cupid fall short of transcendence and figure a material, earthbound metamorphosis.

Alceste is not only Cupid's signifier but the point where Maying fails. Chaucer's persona, I have argued above, cannot win pleasure or merit from his devotion to her flower. Maying then yields place to something more like a trial, but an irregular trial without benefit of legal protections for the accused. David Wallace argues that Alceste's intercessory plea is "one of the most brilliant set-pieces of political rhetoric ever written," largely succeeding at rescuing Chaucer's voice while deferring to its oppressor's power.[99] At the same time, since Chaucer's voice is rescued for readers but apparently not for the dyspeptic Cupid, the god's negative judgment reemphasizes his capriciousness. As the persona fails to win the rewards of Maying and as the imperfect judicial ritual supersedes Maying, the luscious cocktail of sublimation, integration, and exclusivity Chaucer found in French sources becomes a disturbingly bitter cup.

Robert W. Frank sees no relation between the Prologue's Maying and what follows: "this delicate, sugary creation is allowed to go to waste, like an elegant wedding cake left melting in the hot sun."[100] I would emphasize that Alceste is not just a sugary creation of Maying but the first suicide for love and the voice that sentences the persona to commemorate her similars. Her story and her voice are much harsher and darker than the average wedding cake. Perhaps only in retrospect, as the legends reflect back on the Prologue, Alceste's outfit looks like an imposture rather than a true measure of immortal merit. Her stemlike dress and petal headdress, more outlandish than impressive, fabricate a claim to perfection that fails to deliver, just as Maying fails for this persona. Here the ironies and omissions that characterize the legends also find adumbration: Alceste and the women who follow her are not unequivocally admirable, and the persona's suppressed gestures toward their inadequacies sustain his artistic freedom despite the sentence to artistic suicide.

Chaucer's peculiar invocation of Maying finally to undermine Maying corresponds to his persona's further alienations from the parties of flower and leaf, from courtiers and lovers, from fetishistic satisfaction. A more mitigated alienation is characteristic of Maying poetry generally, as Deschamps and Charles d'Orléans have illustrated. The ritual persona, divided between resistance and absorption, is importantly performative. Taking part in Maying by wearing its livery, processing, weaving garlands, and singing lyrics implies a substantial connection between mimesis and self-definition. This mimesis is not simply acquiescence but a negotiation between, in Deschamps's case, engaging in elite Maying and endorsing Robin's critique, or in Charles's case, wearing the livery of the leaf and reinterpreting it.

This chapter began by arguing that while courtly Maying sometimes appears to be an escape from social regulation into "le doulc may qui fait coers esjoïr" [the sweet May that makes hearts rejoice], it celebrates inscription more substantially than release.[101] One compensation for its participants is that it simultaneously celebrates their social superiority by creating a symbolic economy of leaves and flowers that frees them from dependence on labor, values their largesse, and expands their capital beyond the merely economic. A more subversive compensation, traced in the second and third parts of this chapter, counters the ritual's incorporation of sexuality into a socially responsible "amorous law." Fetishizing flowers subsumes constraint within desire, shifting the "amorous law" from a merely regulatory to a richly erotic experience. As ritual dress, as fetish, and as livery, the green and leaves and flowers of Maying concretize its inscriptions and indulgences on the social stage of gesture and voice.

3

Joan of Arc and Women's Cross-Dress

JOAN OF ARC WAS THE DAUGHTER OF PEASANTS, but she spent the last two years of her life living, dressing, and leading troops as if she were a knight and a courtier. Her championing of the dauphin, crowned Charles VII through her efforts, together with her performance for the court of inquisition after her capture, provide a fascinating instance of self-presentation located at the nexus of clothing and actions that make clothing speak. Her verbal self-descriptions and her way of dressing shift under pressure, but that pressure more significantly reveals her firmest points of commitment.

Today, cross-dressing (wearing men's clothes without seeking to pass for male) and transvestism (any degree of adopting masculine identity, from cross-dressing to changing one's name and apparently one's sex) are on a continuum from routine to rare, with cross-dress now endorsed by Valentino and the armed services alike. In contrast, late medieval cross-dress and transvestism could both seem as radical as the modern decision to alter one's birth sex by passing or by undergoing hormone treatments or surgery—as radical in their rarity, perceived extremity, and the profundity of their implications for sexuality, though distinct in other ways. One crucial distinction is that medieval women's transvestism tended to avoid genital sex rather than to modify it: the familiar example is the transvestite saints, who escaped marriage by disguising themselves as monks and hermits. I believe this characteristic abstinence has misled modern scholars to conclude that medieval women's cross-dress had no implications for sexuality. Vern Bullough argues that whereas medieval sources attribute male cross-dressing to lust for women or effeminacy, women who conceal their sex are motivated by desire for the social advantages of men—protection from sexual assault, mobility, access to arms, and so on.[1] Caroline Bynum makes a similar point in generalizing from the case of Joan of Arc: "cross-dressing was for women primarily a practical device. . . . Perhaps exactly *because* cross-dressing was a radical yet practical social step for women, it was not finally their most powerful symbol of self."[2] I will argue instead that the deliberate evasion of genital sex is itself an expression of sexuality—of the complex of desires, birth sex, apparent sex, and gendered behaviors that make up the sexual aspect of any person. My position is that for Joan, cross-dressing *was* a "powerful symbol of self," and that she was mobilizing and shaping her sexuality through both her chastity and her clothing. To be sure, women could gain social authority by cross-dressing, but the act was understood to entail a wider claim to masculinity than to authority alone. In brief, Joan was engaged in a much more consequential behavior than today's cross-dress: the transgressive, sexual implications of cross-dressing in her time place it closer to our sense of transvestism, although that term's imbrication in modern sexology sets it apart from her practice.

Joan of Arc is by far the best-documented cross-dresser of the Middle Ages. She wore men's clothes almost continuously from her first attempts to reach the dauphin until her execution twenty-eight months later. When she set out from home, she was in women's dress; at Vaucouleurs she borrowed men's dress until some townspeople presented her with a set of men's clothes in which she completed her journey to Charles (a contemporary witness details a black doublet, a short black tunic, and a black cap on her now shorn black hair).[3] Joan may have continued to wear a dress on some occasions for the first few months of her mission: she gave a red garment, probably the red dress in which she had left home, to her godfather five months later; the 1429 treatise *De quadam puella* relates that Joan is as capable as an experienced war leader when on horseback "vestibus et armis virilibus induta" [clothed in male attire and armor]; "ubi autem de equo descendit, solitum habitum reassumens, fit simplicissima, negotiorum saecularium quasi innocens agnus imperita" [but when she descends from her horse, and assumes her usual clothes, she becomes completely naive, as inexperienced in the ways of the world as an innocent lamb].[4] This equation of femininity with ignorance and innocence might seem to restrict Joan's authority to the battlefield, but the mediating role the treatise assigns to clothing implies that masculine capability is as easy to acquire as masculine garments. If Joan's cross-dressing was indeed only occasional during the early months of 1429, this passage suggests what was to be gained by giving up female attire altogether.

Joan claims a new class status as well as masculine authority: she soon abandoned the sobriety of her black Vaucouleurs clothing and began to dress as a knight and courtier.[5] The *Chronique des cordeliers* mentions, in addition to her armor, "très noble habis de draps d'or et de soie bien fourrés" [very noble clothes of cloth-of-gold and silk well trimmed with fur]. Other records note a hat of blue silk or velvet with gold embroidery and a brim divided into four parts, a robe of scarlet Brussels cloth and a dark green tunic ordered for her by Charles d'Orléans, decorations of embroidered nettle leaves to represent the house of Orleans, and a slashed tunic of cloth-of-gold.[6] These records tally with the trial's charge that she dressed in "sumptuosis et pomposis vestibus de pannis preciosis et aureis ac eciam foderaturis" [sumptuous and magnificent clothes of precious fabrics and gold and also of furs], in clothes "curtis, brevibus, et dissolutis" [short, small, and dissolute: Pc 1: 207]. Joan is caught between two semiotics: the tailoring and luxury that express high status in secular circles are susceptible to moral objections from the clergy. But Joan refused to give up cross-dressing during the months of her imprisonment and trial. The twelve articles on which Joan was judged at the end of the trial describe her dress as "brevem tunicam, gipponem, caligas ligatas cum multis aguilletis . . . capillos tonsos in rotundum supra summitatem aurium" [a short tunic, doublet, and hose attached by many pointed laces; hair cut round above the ears].[7]

Joan's clothing was for her judges the visible expression of an aberrant sexuality. For them, cross-dress itself is polluting. Although her physical virginity was never in doubt, Jean d'Estivet, one of the major figures in her trial, is said to have called her "putana" and "paillarda" [whore, wanton].[8] The terms refer not to her sexual behavior but to her corrupted sexuality. Other adversaries call her "femme monstrueuse," "femme desordonnée et diffamée, estant en habit d'homme et de gouvernement dissolut" [monstrous woman, disorderly and notorious woman who dresses in men's clothes, whose conduct is dissolute].[9] For them also, her clothing testifies to a deformed sexuality.

Joan's supporters argue that she is enhanced rather than abased by acquiring masculinity: for Christine de Pizan she is "chose oultre nature" [something beyond nature], best described by alternating masculine inflections with feminine, but full of extraordinary virtue rather than vice.[10] However, even her supporters are uncomfortable with her cross-dressing. They tend to acknowledge only her armor, noting that it is necessary to defeating the English. A rare exception is Martin le Franc's later fifteenth-century *Champion des Dames*, which describes Joan's masculine civilian clothing (pourpoint, short robe, felt cap) and extends the instrumental argument from armor to street dress: "Armes propres habis requierent . . . / Aultres pour estre en ville affierent" [combat requires appropriate clothes; others are appropriate for being in town].[11] Yet the illuminators of his poem retain feminine dress for her, or feminized armor, resisting the full transgressiveness of her self-presentation (Figure 4). The only image of Joan from her own lifetime, in the margin of Clément de Fauquembergue's record of her victory at Orleans, comes from inside Paris and thus from an adversarial position, but it too avoids representing her cross-dress (Figure 5).[12] To be sure, women's dress is one way to identify Joan in a visual medium, but these images are sufficiently embedded in text that she would be easily identifiable even cross-dressed. Probably the rarity of cross-dress and the sanctions around it put up barriers to its representation that were insurmountable for her allies and adversaries alike.

In an earlier essay I wondered if the abstinence that accompanies Joan's cross-dress prepared for or restrained homoerotic desire, but it seems more likely to me now that abstinence is already itself the meaning of her sexuality.[13] Today we understand sexuality to be so fully based in genital behavior that virginity is almost irrelevant to declaring a position along the spectrum of object choices. People might know someone to be virginal, but virginity alone would define her sexuality less adequately than naming what her object choice would be if she were to make one! In Joan's

Figure 4. Martin le Franc, *Le Champion des Dames*. Grenoble, Bibliothèque municipale, MS 875 (352), fol. 330, verso. Copyright Giraudon/Art Resource, NY.

Figure 5. *Journal* of Clément de Fauquembergue, May 10, 1429. Paris, Archives nationales, MS XIA 1481, fol. 12. Document conservé au Centre historique des Archives nationales à Paris.

time however there is quite a rich understanding of celibacy and virginity as life choices that define and modify one's identity as a whole, shaping one's birth sex, social position, and self-presentation in complex but recognizable ways.

Chaste cross-dress manifests Joan's spirituality and shapes her sexuality in a performance of difference that should count as one of her most significant acts. Joan does not imitate the ascetic, sex-neutral dress of the transvestite saints, and she does not invoke Judith or Deborah or the Amazons to defend her actions.[14] "Illicterata et ignorans Scripturas" [unlettered and ignorant of Scripture: *Pc* 1: 328], Joan develops a self-definition that finds its closest resonances in popular piety and secular narratives.[15] Three contexts for investigating her practice are the minutes of her trial for heresy, the interrelation of cross-dress and virginity in her self-presentation, and the more generalized popular conviction that women who cross-dress can find themselves in substantial ways no longer women.

Inquisitorial Procedure and Self-Definition

Legal trials and proceedings across cultures are highly ritualized: they have special times and venues, and rules of decorum and evidence; they end by transforming the accused's status; they are binding on the whole community; and they appeal to divine law or weighty precedent for their authority. Two further characteristics of ritual make the medieval Christian inquisition particularly intriguing. First, rituals demand a performance. Whatever their means and ends, they ask and even coerce a more or less prescribed, regulated participation. Second, rituals sweeten their demand with a promise of gratification: health, absolution, adulthood, uniting the community, rewarding virtue. In Christian confession, for example, divine grace visits the submissive confessant. The ambiguous interpenetration of repression and reward sets the typical ritual apart from medieval inquisition. This ritual sides decisively with repression—or more accurately, it splits off repression, which is directed toward suspect individuals, from gratification, which is delivered instead to the purified Christian community. Inquisition labors under a peculiar handicap in this regard, but its structural awkwardness produces remarkable performances under interrogation. If the inquisition had better integrated demands with rewards, it might not have inspired the complex, richly resistant performances of aberration that accused heretics produced and the inquisition's bureaucracy recorded.

The peculiarities of inquisition contrast it to the sacrament of penance.

Both centered on a confession; both sought recognition of sin and heart-felt repentance; both were institutional procedures that generated manuals guiding and perpetuating their ideology and structure; both accrued a metaphorics of medicinal intervention and rescue.[16] The trial's opening exhorts Joan to "unburden her conscience" in a "confession of the full truth" and the statement written for her abjuration begins "je confesse que j'ay tres griefment pechié" [I confess that I have most greivously sinned].[17] The court declares on several occasions its charitable concern for Joan and its desire for "salutem vestram tam anime quam corporis" [your salvation in both soul and body].[18] Inquisition however is not sacramental but judi-cial, and its primary charge is not the salvation of the heretic but the health of the church. These distinctions have important consequences for the targets of penance and inquisition respectively. The sacrament of penance assumes that contrition has preceded confession, and that contrition is a desire to return from deviation to conformity with a certain general stan-dard.[19] In the orderly sequence of sin, conviction, contrition, and con-fession, the confessant's willing submission invites a relatively formulaic, prescribed exchange that identifies any obedient soul with all obedient souls. For the laity of the late Middle Ages, therefore, penance invited self-examination to be sure, but it was primarily sacramental, "un rite de puri-fication saisonnier, printanier."[20]

Inquisition is a ritual of purification for the community rather than for the individual. Infected by the "heresis pestiferum virus" [pestilential virus of heresy], inquisition's target must be cut from the body of the Christian community "tanquam membrum putridum" [like a rotten limb] so that it will not infect the community as a whole (Pc 1: 411–12). Inqui-sition replaces penance's solicitous concern for process ("how are you doing?") with a more probing demand for an account ("who do you think you are?"). Inquisition assumes a will to resist as well as an aberrant way of life. In so defining the accused, it undertakes an adversarial interroga-tion that seeks to neutralize the threat to the Christian community by whatever means necessary. The heretic is pressed to reform, but if she will not do so, the purification of the community can be accomplished through the sentence that excommunicates her, expels her from the faith, and aban-dons her to secular justice.

The two choices presented to a prisoner such as Joan who had beliefs and behaviors the court found heretical are far more radical than the ordinary Christian's gestures of contrition for sin. The heretic must accept either death or a dislocation of the self that, in positive terms, could be called a conversion.[21] Bringing the heretic to one of these choices can require long months of pressure that, again, might be seen as an effort to save one soul but are primarily concerned with saving the entire community from pollution. On the procedural level, inquisition replaces the putatively voluntary relation of confessor and confessant with exceptional coercions such as imprisonment, fettering, and torture. Inquisition elicits a physical performance of endurance (or collapse) as well as a creative rhetorical performance. If confession is a scene of self-examination, inquisition is one of self-production, or self-annihilation.

Although my emphasis is on differences between penance and inquisition, I agree with Talal Asad that both rituals assume a hidden, interior truth of the self that is painful to reveal.[22] The inquisition's accused are instructed "quod dicent plenam et veram veritatem" [to tell the whole and accurate truth] and to swear "non celabo veritatem" [I will not hide the truth].[23] The accused enjoys the radically free will of scholastic thought, with the capacity to choose sin or to repent and ask for grace. But the desire to speak truly that prepares for sacramental grace in confession is not assumed in the structure of inquisition. Here, a supplemental model of the truth of the self applies: the freedom of the will is so fundamental to the human soul that extreme pain "can move the taciturn will to speak, but not to lie."[24] Edward Peters demonstrates the connections between the theological doctrine of free will and the practical conclusion that torture, rightly executed, is not coercive but "conditional." That is, the will cannot be moved by force alone; "no torture can violate an individual's free will."[25] Peters and John Langbein trace the vociferous objections to torture during the Enlightenment that culminated in its general suppression until the twentieth century, and I would only add the startlingly apposite argument of John Locke (1689) on the "unreasonable, because unintelligible, Question, viz. Whether Man's Will be free, or no." The concept of a will free to choose in the absence of liberty is absurd, Locke argues, because the will cannot be free in and of itself. Freedom is one kind of power individuals may enjoy, and will is another kind of power; the former is not an attribute of the latter. Locke's pivotal illustration is torture: "A man on the Rack, is not at liberty to lay by the Idea of pain."[26] In Joan's time, a different anthropology pertained, under which pain judiciously applied could urge a free will to speak truly.

Joan's interrogation illustrates in several aspects "the torment and suffering of the body in order to elicit truth."[27] Long imprisonment was the inquisition's favored "interrogation technique," in James Given's phrase, and fetters appear in an Elizabethan list of instruments of torture.[28] Joan was fettered both during the day and at night by her legs to her bed. When her judges ask her what she thinks her voices meant by telling her "ne te chaille de ton martyre," which could mean "do not be concerned about your martyrdom" or "do not be concerned about your suffering," she says the word "martyr" must refer to the pain and adversity she is suffering in prison ["la paine et adversité qu'elle seuffre en la prison": *Pc* 1:148]. In the twelfth week of her interrogation, she was shown instruments of torture and admonished that they would be used if she were not truthful.[29]

The combined assumptions of inquisition that belief and behavior are accessible to verbalization and that coercion produces truthful accounts constitute the social reality in which Joan testifies. Whether or not we concur that these assumptions are accurate, they generate a remarkable performance in which Joan is deeply invested. For some readers, the coercions surrounding Joan's testimony render it a "hermeneutic nightmare" from which Joan's prior and current convictions are irrecoverable.[30] I believe, in contrast, that Joan's trial certifies her statements are an authentic effort to explain herself. The certification is that she burns. It is clear from her testimony that she does not want to die (indeed, that she greatly fears death, which was a problem raised by the Devil's Advocate at her canonization).[31] It is also clear that she is aware she will die if she does not find a way to accept the court's will. But she refuses to choose acceptable explanations for herself, with the exception of a three-day abjuration which she attempted, she says, in order to save her life rather than because her beliefs had changed. Her performative commitment to her self-description is extraordinary. She does shape her explanations and shift her ground, as I will discuss below, but she holds herself to a standard of accuracy she would rather die than abandon.

Most scholarship on Joan's testimony concerns her visions, religious faith, and political mission. Her judges were deeply concerned with her dress as well, and did not disengage it from her spiritual and political positions. Their concern reflects the total physical and rhetorical performance that inquisition demands of the accused and its global investigation of behavior as well as belief. The inquisitorial process assumes that behavior and belief inform one another—that behavior derives from belief but also perpetuates it. Thus Joan's judges press her from the start both to simply change clothes and to recognize that she should: the one tactic has no precedence over the other. Joan's beliefs and her clothes weigh alike in the court's assessment; together they constitute the identity the court will judge.

Joan was captured in May 1430 by Burgundian forces, sold to the English in November, and tried for heresy in Rouen during the following February,

March, and April by the bishop of Beauvais, Pierre Cauchon, and the papal
deputy inquisitor, Jean le Maistre, and well over a hundred assistants. Her
trial was deeply affected by the political moment, as were most inquisitorial trials of the Middle Ages and after. Joan was convicted of heresy in
May 1431, abjured during a public exhortation in the cemetery of St.
Ouen, but relapsed a few days later, reassuming the men's clothes she had agreed
to stop wearing and reporting that she heard her voices reproaching her
for having abjured them. The next day, the episcopal court declared her a
relapsed heretic, and she was burned by the secular authorities on the following day, May 30.[32] This was not, however, her only trial; when Charles
VII at last took control of Rouen eighteen years later, he initiated an investigation into the findings of her "procès de condamnation" which culminated in a "procès en nullité" that declared her conviction for heresy
to have been invalid.[33] Evidence collected at this second trial verifies the
records from the first: despite its obvious bias toward a martyred supporter
of Charles VII, the "procès en nullité" received much testimony sustaining
the accuracy of the record of Joan's words in the "procès de condamnation."[34] The original trial's procedures and conclusions, rather than the evidence taken from Joan, were the basis for nullification. Two manuscripts
descended from the French minutes of this trial survive.[35] Although Joan's
voice is in several ways constrained in the French minutes—by the questions her many inquisitors choose to ask, by certain omissions from the
minutes that were noted during the nullification trial, and by the notaries'
collating tendency to group responses to several questions together—it
appears that, in Joan's opinion as well as that of the notaries and other
witnesses, the French record of her statements is accurate.[36]

     Joan's first explanation for her dress is that it is merely instrumental
and without moral significance. In her testimony she refuses to charge
anyone with advising her to change clothes, stating instead that "il falloit
necessairement qu'elle changeast son habit" [it was necessary that she
change her clothes: Pc 1: 51]. Several of her early statements dismiss her
dress as a minor issue: "de veste parum est, et est de minori" [dress is a
small thing, among the littlest]; she cannot recall if Charles, or his wife, or
the ecclesiastical body that interrogated her for several days in Poitiers,
asked her anything about her dress.[37] These dismissive statements imply
that her cross-dress is motivated only by functional convenience. Indeed,
when offered women's clothes she responds that if she were allowed to
leave prison in them, she would wear them gladly: under those circumstances women's clothes, like men's in other circumstances, would serve
her purpose of resisting the English.[38] In a telling formulation she links

men's clothes directly to armed opposition: she "ne feroit pour rien le serement qu'elle ne se armast et meist en abit d'omme" [would never for anything swear not to arm herself and wear men's clothes: Pc 1: 168–69]. Associating transvestism with military goals and the exigencies of travel characterizes her contemporaries' justifications as well. Typically they mention her clothing only in relation to her arming for battle: in Percival de Cagny's chronicle, "elle print et se mist en habit d'homme et requist au roy qu'il luy fist faire armures pour soy armer" [she put on men's clothes and asked the king to have armor made with which to arm herself]; the *Chronique de la Pucelle* has her explain at Poitiers, "il fault, pour ce que je me doibs armer et servir le gentil Daulphin en armes, que je prenne les habillemens propices et nécessaires à ce" [because I must arm myself and serve the gentle Dauphin in arms, I must take the clothing that is suited and necessary for the purpose].[39]

In fact, however, there is much about Joan's dress that escapes instrumental explanations, both before and during her imprisonment. Joan cross-dresses at all times, not just for battle but in court, in prison, even to receive Communion. Her persistent cross-dressing requires an explanation that goes beyond mere instrumentality. How can it further her opposition to the English to refuse to wear a dress in church? This framing of the issue is concrete, not merely hypothetical, as the judges deny Joan's many requests for access to the sacraments until she has agreed to give up male attire.

Here Joan's self-justification takes a turn that is intriguingly different from that of her contemporary allies. She supplements the argument from instrumentality with the assertion that her cross-dressing pleases God, and later that she took it by God's command: "il plaist a Dieu que je le porte"; "je le fais par le commandement de nostre Sire et en son service" [it pleases God that I wear it; I do it on the command of our Lord and in his service: Pc 1: 67, 153]. She links her civilian attire to her military purpose in the assertion that "l'abit et les armes qu'elle a portés, c'est par le congié de Dieu; et tant de l'abit d'omme que des armes" [the clothing and the arms she has worn have been by the permission of God, and just as much the men's clothing as the arms: Pc 1: 227]. God's will becomes her standard explanation for why she will not leave off her male dress, even in order to hear Mass and take Communion at Easter. In the week before Palm Sunday she asserts that "quant a l'abit de femme, elle ne le prandra pas encore, tant qu'il plaira a nostre Sire" [as for women's clothes, she will not take them yet, until it pleases our Lord: Pc 1: 167]. In the week before Easter she replies concerning her clothes "qu'elle ayme plus chier mourir que revoquer ce qu'elle a fait du commandement de nostre Sire" [that she preferred to die rather than to abjure what she had done at the command of our Lord: *Pc* 1: 210].⁴⁰ Her insistence that she cannot leave off men's clothing in order to gain access to the sacraments is especially striking given her urgent pleas for access.

Joan's insistence on God's command that she cross-dress even in prison contrasts with the explanations generated during the nullification trial around threats to her chastity. The conditions of Joan's imprisonment were harsh. Rather than being held in an ecclesiastical prison with women attendants as was normal in heresy cases, Joan was guarded by English soldiers. A witness at the nullification trial stated that one of her guards had threatened to rape her and that the Earl of Warwick had replaced two guards and admonished the others; a number of witnesses explained her resumption of male clothing after her abjuration with accounts that her guards had removed her women's clothes from her room during the night, or had harassed her, or that an English lord had attempted to rape her.⁴¹ Other supporters linked her cross-dressing throughout her mission with her commitment to chastity.⁴²

The chastity motive suggested in nullification testimony arises at a convenient distance from the real conditions of Joan's imprisonment. Joan's male attire may have had some symbolic meaning for her guards, but it is important not to exaggerate the degree to which it could have protected her from rape. She continued to be identifiably female, she was fettered at all times, and she apparently slept undressed both in the field and in prison.⁴³ Only after her abjuration and relapse, when she rejected the women's dress provided for her at her abjuration, did Joan herself associate her clothing with the conditions of her imprisonment. Here Joan incorporates her defense of cross-dressing into her longstanding argument with the court that she should be in an ecclesiastical rather than a secular prison. Joan testifies that she resumed male attire because she is among men and because she was not allowed to hear Mass as promised and was not taken out of her fetters, but that if she were allowed to hear Mass and were transferred to a better prison, she would obey the Church Militant (*Pc* 1: 396–97). Her protest encompasses an oblique objection to being guarded by men, but that element of her protest is exceptional. During many weeks of interrogation, Joan, in contrast to her supporters before and after the trial, does not use sexual threat to explain her clothes. Admonished as late as May 2 that she is wearing men's clothes "sans neccessité, et en especial qu'elle est en prison" [without cause, and especially since she is in prison: *Pc* 1: 344], she answers, "quant je auray fait ce pourquoy je suis

envoyee de par Dieu, je prendray habit de femme" [when I have done what
I was sent to do by God, I will take women's clothes: *Pc* 1: 344]: even
when her interrogators refer to her imprisonment, she refers to God's will.

Claiming God's command to wear men's clothes exerts significant
counterpressure to the extraordinary pressure Joan receives from the court
concerning her masculine clothing.[44] Unlike her judges, I am not concerned to verify whether God told her to cross-dress, but rather to trace
how her self-description evolves during her mission and what it seeks to
accomplish. Joan's claim to divine sanction resists the court's authority in
favor of a higher one and counters the charge that cross-dress is immoral.
Claiming God's command dates back at least to Joan's first interrogation
by an ecclesiastical court, in Poitiers, two years before her trial for heresy.
Little record of the Poitiers interrogation survives, but the memoirs of
Pope Pius II report this defense of her cross-dress: "virginem sese ait;
virgini utrumque habitum convenire; sibi a Deo mandatum esse vestibus
ut virilibus uteretur, cui et arma tractanda essent virilia" [she said she was
a virgin, and it was suitable for a virgin to have both styles of dress; that
she had permission from God to wear masculine clothing, for whom also
masculine arms would have to be used].[45] If this report is accurate, the
continuity between Joan's earlier and later testimony is striking: God's
command is evoked in both interrogations in the context of establishing
the moral valence of cross-dressing, and divine sanction receives a corrob-
orating argument from instrumentality ("masculine arms . . . would have
to be used"). The fascinating claim that virginity licenses cross-dress is not
so overt in Joan's testimony at Rouen, but I will discuss below its muted
place in her self-defense.

Joan's judges at Rouen work to discredit the claim to divine sanction
by making Joan choose repeatedly between access to the sacraments and
cross-dressing. Indeed, Joan first anticipates condemnation when she refuses to wear a dress made up to her specifications. Asked on March 15
what sort of dress she might be willing to wear in order to hear Mass, Joan
provides detailed instructions:

Faictes moy faire une robe longue jusques a terre, sans queue, et me la baillez a aler
a la messe; et puis au retour, je reprandray l'abit que j'ay. . . . Baillez moy abit
comme une fille de bourgoys, c'est assavoir houppelande longue, et je le prendray,
et mesmes le chaperon de femme, pour aler ouyr messe. Et aussi le plus instamment
qu'elle peust, requiert que on luy lesse cest habit qu'elle porte, et que on la laisse
oyr messe sans le changier. (*Pc* 1: 157-58)

[Have made for me a long dress down to the ground, without a train, and give it
to me to go to Mass, and then on returning I will take again the clothes I have

now. . . . Give me clothing such as a daughter of a townsman would wear, that is a long houppelande, and I will take it and a woman's hood to go to hear Mass. And at the same time she asks as urgently as she can that they leave her in these clothes she is wearing, and that they let her hear Mass without changing them.]

Joan envisions a dress worn only to Mass, but her judges are more ambiguous about their deal with her, urging her to take women's clothing "du tout" and "simplement et absoluement" [completely, once and for all: *Pc* 1: 157] rather than just for this occasion. Joan refuses the dress on March 17:

Interroguee qu'elle dit a cel habit de femme que on luy offre affin qu'elle puisse aller ouyr messe: Respond: Quant a l'abit de femme, elle ne le prandra pas encore, tant qu'il plaira a nostre Sire; et se ainsi est qu'il la faille mener jusques en jugement, qu'il la faille desvestir en jugement, elle requiert aux seigneurs de l'Eglise qu'il luy donnent la grace de avoir une chemise de femme et un queuvrechief en sa teste. . . . Il luy suffist qu'elle soit longue. (*Pc* 1: 167–68)[46]

[Asked what she has to say about this woman's dress that they are offering to her so that she can go to hear Mass, she answers: As for the woman's dress, she will not take it yet, until it pleases our Lord; and if it comes to pass that she must be led to judgment, and if she must be undressed for judgment, she asks the lords of the church to give her the grace of a woman's shift and a kerchief for her head. . . . It (the shift) will be sufficient if it is long.]

One axis of Joan's resistance seems to be modesty: the houppelande is a particularly voluminous style, and the long shift she requests for judgment contrasts with the briefer undergarments ("shirts") that repentant men wore in public displays of guilt or for execution.[47] By stripping her for judgment, the court would make her expose her legs immodestly in her short man's shirt. In this case only, she would prefer the longer feminine equivalent. Joan also specifies a social niche in choosing a houppelande, a court fashion at the end of the fourteenth century that moved down to the bourgeoisie in the first decades of the fifteenth.[48] But these specifications are not sufficient when the moment for accepting the dress arrives. When neither physical modesty nor social dignity keeps Joan from accepting the dress, it appears that the change from masculine to feminine dress is the crucial one for her, the one that proves impossible to make. Under such pressure from the court, the strength of her preference for men's clothes indicates that cross-dressing holds a powerful place in her self-performance. The ritual's coercion has produced not acquiescence but clarity about her difference.

I began by proposing that inquisition is a peculiarly divided ritual in that it coerces suspected heretics in order to gratify the Christian community, but it partly overcomes this division by rewarding the coerced for submission to the court. To be sure, these rewards are no more than the lifting of deprivations, moving back toward zero from a position of severe lack. Having deprived Joan of access to the sacraments, the court can offer to reward her with access in return for wearing a dress. Viewed positively, this is simply a strategy for behavior change; viewed less generously, it apes the transformative power of the sacraments in a fully material register: "no grace without contrition" becomes "no admission without a dress." But inquisition's preoccupation with the material register does make ritual sense, in that rituals generally do blur the boundary between behavior and belief: the gestures appropriate to participation are the fundamental requirement; those gestures are taken to express some indistinct degree of belief.

And this encounter does have implications for belief as well as behavior. At the trial's end, Joan stands accused of "contempt for God's sacraments," on the evidence that "she preferred to keep her men's clothes rather than to attend Mass and take communion" (*Pc* 1: 148). The strategy is to make Joan's male dress look impious rather than superpious. The strategy was not lost on Joan. After this confrontation, she begins to avoid attributing her male clothing to God's will, using formulas for evasion such as "donnez moy dilacion" [grant me a delay] and "vous en estes assés respondu" [you have been sufficiently answered about this], and enigmatic responses such as "elle sçait bien qui luy a fait prandre l'abit, mais ne sçait point comme elle le doit reveler" [she well knows who made her take (men's) clothes, but she does not know at all how she should reveal it: *Pc* 1: 208]. Near the very end, she provides this example of how she prays: "tres doulz Dieu . . . je sçay bien, quant a l'abit, le commandement comme je l'ay prins; mais je ne sçay point par quelle maniere je le doy laisser. Pour ce, plaise vous a moy l'anseigner" [very sweet God, I well know concerning my dress by what command I took it, but I do not know at all in what way I should give it up. So may it please you to teach me that: *Pc* 1: 252]. Her now unattributed authority for cross-dress and her plea that God help her to abandon it show a painfully shifting and divided belief in contrast to her earlier clarity on this subject. Her prayer for help in giving up masculine dress seems to concur with the court that her own will to cross-dress is the impediment. Her will also intrudes, though asserted only hypothetically, when she testifies on Palm Sunday that if it were in her power to change to women's clothes, she would do so; and contradictorily, that if it were up to her, she would not change her clothes in order to receive Communion (*Pc* 1: 183).

Joan's elusive will resists the court by overlapping with but not quite disappearing behind God's will. Many women mystics of the later Middle Ages attribute their behavior to God's will, evading (with limited success) institutional attempts to regulate their behavior by presenting themselves as merely the channel for divine messages and interventions. That "merely" has the character of litotes, however, in claiming direct contact with God in place of the more mediated spirituality available to most Christians through the institutional church. The visionary risks appearing to be not the selfless vessel of the Lord but an ambitious self-promoter.[49] Joan's judges regard her claim to hear God's commands in this light, attending closely to aspects of her conduct such as her masculine clothing that might betray worldly aspirations. But Joan does not endorse their version of an exclusive relation between divine command and self-promotion. Her proverb "Aide toy, Dieu te aidera" [Help yourself and God will help you: Pc 1: 156] expresses her refusal to dichotomize divine and human agency—indeed, her tendency is to foreground the role of her own initiative in acting on God's will. In the struggle over whether to give up cross-dressing in exchange for access to the sacraments, Joan takes initiative by omitting to ask her voices if she may do so in the days before Easter, asking for delays in responding to questions about her dress, and insisting to her judges that cross-dressing should not be an impediment to taking Communion. Joan does not simply accede to what she understands as God's will, but shapes and supplements it through her strategic resistances to the court.[50]

Finally she asserts her own will as her motive: three days after abjuring and agreeing to wear a dress, she takes men's clothes again and says she took them "de sa voulenté, sans nulle contraincte, et qu'elle ayme mieulx l'abit d'omme que de femme" [of her own will, without anyone's constraint, and that she liked men's dress better than women's: Pc 1: 396]. Pressed for more of a justification, she adds "qu'il luy estoit plus licite de le reprendre et avoir habit d'omme, estant entre les hommes, que de avoir habit de femme" [that it was more appropriate for her to retake and have men's clothes, since she was among men, than to have woman's dress: Pc 1: 396]. At this point she is resigned to execution, saying "qu'elle ayme mieux faire sa penitance a une fois, c'est assavoir a mourir, que endurer plus longuement paine en chartre" [that she preferred to do her penance at once, that is by dying, than to endure any longer the pain of imprisonment: Pc 1: 399]. She has reached physical but not rhetorical collapse. Because she has claimed God's will is contiguous with her own, attributing her cross-dress to her own will is not at odds with attributing it to God's command. Another version of her characteristic proverb appears in testimony of Jean d'Alençon as "Operate, et Deus operabitur" [Act, and God will act].[51] In both versions, human agency can even anticipate God's will. On this final day, Joan's argument from instrumentality also resurfaces, shaped to the conditions of her imprisonment, in the claim that men's clothes are "licite" given that she has male guards. "Licite" carries a moral valence as well, licit in the sense of "proper" or "lawful," recalling Joan's claim that her cross-dress is not immoral.

To the end, Joan maintains that her male dress is useful, that it is not immoral, and that she prefers it to women's dress. Is that worth dying for? What is it that binds her clothing so tightly to her identity that she refuses so tenaciously to give it up? The answer lies in the connection her testimony has made between her dress and her virginity. This connection appears most overtly in the Poitiers testimony that it was suitable for a virgin to dress in men's clothes, suggesting that the purity of virginity exempts cross-dress from any taint of licentiousness. In her Rouen testimony, Joan connects virginity and cross-dress as two commitments to God's will: she pledged her virginity to God "tant qu'il plairoit a Dieu" [for as long as it pleased God: Pc 1: 123], and she will continue to cross-dress "tant qu'il plaira a nostre Sire" [for as long as it pleases our Lord: Pc 1: 167]. Virginity and cross-dress may later have a terminus, but only with God's permission; both express physically her devotion to God and to her mission.[52] Virginity has strong religious meaning for Joan; she indeed states that it is the single condition necessary for her salvation.[53] Aligning virginity with masculine dress validates the latter more subtly than invoking God's direct command, but this alignment has considerable cultural precedent and is finally Joan's surest ground of self-definition.

Virginity and Cross-Dress

By associating her dress to her virginity, Joan claims for them both the highest moral status, and assigns them a central importance in her identity. Here I will argue that Joan conceives both physical practices to be spiritually meaningful, but not in the sense that they move her closer to God. Rather, they express her mission in its substance; they are not ascetic practices but instead materialize her spirituality.

Above I have argued that Joan and her judges shared the inquisition's ritual premise that behavior has a substantial relation to belief. The consequentiality of cross-dress before and during this trial has to do as well with widespread popular perceptions about the relation of body to soul. In clerical writing and teaching as well as Joan's milieu of lay piety, body and soul were a duality to be sure, but also an interrelated system, a "psychosomatic unity" in Caroline Bynum's phrase.[54] Bynum traces late-medieval clerical and lay preoccupations with the resurrection of the body, visionary experience, transubstantiation, relics, and martyrdom to this general cultural sense that body and soul interrelate to express the self. One way to understand the unity of body and soul, but not I believe the most revelatory way to understand it for Joan's case, is that the late medieval body was (to quote Bynum again) "a means of access to the divine": the relic offers contact with the saint's spiritual power, the mortification of the flesh pushes the spirit upward in visionary or contemplative illumination, and the martyrs' endurance under torture brings them closer to God by imitating Christ's crucifixion.[55] In its role as a means of spiritual access, the body is clearly inferior to the spirit and the relation between the two has an ascending energy. But the energy of this relation flows in both directions, and for Joan's case it is particularly important to note the late-medieval corporeality of the soul—the ways in which spiritual power can express itself physically. Saints receive stigmata, visionary women experience physical ecstasy, holy bodies remain uncorrupted after death, the unconfessed are unable to swallow the eucharistic elements but particularly devout women can subsist for years on a diet of nothing but the eucharist.[56] In such cases, the "psychosomatic unity" provides, not access to the divine through the body, but instead something like divinity accessed and materialized in the body.

The examples just cited for this second category of the "psychosomatic unity," that is for the corporality of the soul, tend not to feel very congenial in the twenty-first century. The cultural validity of a downward flow of spirit into body is difficult to recover given the teleology of modernism, according to which the medieval world still believed the spiritual to be immanent, but later eras more correctly distinguished between the material here-and-now and the spiritual beyond. This modern version of Christian history can only make sense of medieval immanence as effectively tending toward transcendence—toward "access to the divine"—despite its awkward initial baggage of physicality. To the extent that the reverse was also true, that spirituality could be made physical, medieval belief looks superstitious and misguided.

For example, the body and soul figured in René Descartes's *Meditations* are a hierarchized and polarized dichotomy. Descartes begins from an apprehension of himself as made up of a "soul" that ponders and that guides his body—"a face, hands, arms and the whole mechanical structure of limbs which can be seen in a corpse"—but he concludes that his apprehension of this body might be delusional and has finally no relevance to his being: "Thought; this alone is inseparable from me. I am, I exist—that is certain. But for how long? For as long as I am thinking."[57] The mechanical or corpselike body figures a radical devaluation of the physical that grounds the free-thinking "view from nowhere" characteristic of Enlightenment and later modern thought.

This irrelevant body and its dichotomous relation to consciousness are resisted from several quarters in postmodern thought. Practice theorists argue that consciousness develops through daily repetition of bodily gestures; in Foucault's reversal of the connection, the consciousness generated by physical disciplines then turns back to constrain practice: "the soul is the prison of the body."[58] Butler similarly emphasizes the pressure on consciousness to reproduce norms in citational performances of gender.[59] Emerging variously from revisions of structuralist, psychoanalytic, and dramatic theory, these attempts to escape the Cartesian revolution share the tenet that body and consciousness are in close and reciprocal relation. Indeed, recent theory often gives more weight to physical practices than to consciousness in shaping and manifesting a self.

The postmodern challenge to the Cartesian individual's disembodied autonomy can help us read more sensitively the medieval relation between body and soul. Not that pre-Cartesian thinking was post-Cartesian—for example, nothing in the postmodern models I have cited accounts for an eternal soul or a resurrected body and, conversely, there is little sense in medieval thinking that the body could be *more* consequential than the spirit. But noting the premodern and postmodern consensus on the interrelation of body and consciousness, as well as the reciprocality of their expressions, may help familiarize Joan's self-presentation as "la Pucelle de Dieu," a cross-dressed virgin charged by God with saving France from English domination. In the course of her trial, Joan comes to argue that her virginity and her dress together manifest her consecrated mission. In isolation, Joan's virginity could signify an abnegation furthering spirituality—a rejection of the worldly in favor of the otherworldly, as in the assertions of nuns and virgin martyrs that their spouse is Christ. As a complement to secular cross-dress, Joan's virginity works instead to embody spirituality, signifying not rejection of the world but the entry of the spiritual into the world.

Joan grounds her authority on two widespread convictions, that virginity confers merit in the social realm and that divine sanction can have physical expression. Virginity has powerful secular and religious merit in women, protecting their value in the economy of heterosexuality until such time as they marry, and enacting their rejection of the sexual economy in favor of a spiritual life within religious practice. These two roles of virginity are to some degree at odds, the former presuming a genital sexuality to be engaged at marriage and the latter evading marriage definitively. In calling herself "Jeanne la Pucelle" instead of "Jeanne la Vierge," Joan aligns herself with the secular pattern of virginity, in which the stages of a woman's maidenhood, wifehood, and widowhood succeed one another.[60] In conjunction with her secular cross-dress, Joan's maidenhood works less to signal abnegation and rejection of the world than to claim status within its hierarchies. Kirsten Hastrup has argued that Joan would not have been able to lead men if she had not had the status of "Pucelle," unpolluted by sex and uncontained as yet by marriage.[61] One source of this worldly status was the belief that physical purity could draw special favor from God. Men who campaigned with Joan noted this effect concerning her person and her standard, which she testified was designed by her heavenly voices.[62] At the end of an indecisive day of fighting before Orleans, Joan "cepit suum vexillum in manibus suis, posuitque se supra bordum fossati, et instanti, ipsa sibi existente, Anglici fremuerunt et effecti sunt pavidi" [seized her standard in her hands and placed it on the edge of the trench, and as soon as she appeared there, the English trembled and took fear].[63] Joan's close companion Dunois cites this episode among several that indicated divine sanction for her acts.

An example from the legends of transvestite saints illustrates how cross-dressed virginity can incorporate holiness for all to see. I will come to this example, from the story of Eugenia, after a word on the relation between Joan and the "transvestite saints" as a group. Joan's contemporary defenders and modern scholars alike have cited these saints as a model for her self-presentation.[64] Valerie Hotchkiss has located 34 such saints, who are said to have lived from early Christianity through the fifteenth century.[65] In the majority of these saints' *vitae*, male dress is a fleeting strategy for escaping parents and husbands, but a few saints persist in transvestism for years. Christina of Markyate and Natalia, wife of St. Adrian, disguise themselves only briefly so as to accomplish narrow purposes, in contrast to Marina, whose father takes her with him to live in a monastery as Brother Marinus; Theodora, who atones for adultery by living as a monk; and Eugenia, who joins a monastery on realizing that Christianity holds a higher truth than "les arguments de Aristote, les ydees de Platon, et les enseignemens de Socrate" [Aristotle's arguments, Plato's ideas, and Socrates' teachings].[66] The latter examples come from the most widely circulated source for stories of transvestite saints in Joan's milieu, Jean de Vignay's translation of Jacobus de Voragine's *Legenda aurea*. Jean de Vignay's preface addresses "gens qui ne sont pas lectrés . . . tous ceulx et celles qui ce livre liront et ourront lire" [uneducated people . . . all men and women who will read this book or hear it read].[67] If Joan knew the stories of these saints, for example of St. Margaret evading marriage by cropping her hair and living for many years as "Brother Pelagius," they may have influenced her own refusal to marry and her pledge of chastity. However, Joan's practice contrasts with the saints' in important respects. The transvestite saints adopt ascetic dress that minimizes sexual difference and rejects the sex-marked position of the feminine. These women illustrate the profoundly hierarchical relation of the sexes in Christianity: their greatness lies in transcending their femininity and achieving a superior "masculine" asceticism. Joan in contrast does not conceal her sex in a male identity or repudiate her sex through asceticism; she continues to be known as Joan in her black doublet, her cloth-of-gold tunic, and her embroidered hat. Nor does Joan's testimony suggest that she regards her sex as a hindrance to her spirituality. And she does not retreat from the world but rather enters it more fully by cross-dressing.

Despite these differences, Joan's self-presentation parallels that of the transvestite saints in the important role they accord to dress within their self-definition. Often the saints' use of men's clothes begins as an instrumental gesture but later surpasses pure instrumentality to become a sign of virtue and an identifying feature. Like Joan, the transvestite saints link chastity to cross-dress in a process of self-transformation that both distinguishes the saint from her past and ties her to it. That is, the transvestite saints do not persist unrecognized in their new identities: if only at death, but often before death, their female sex resurfaces to impress the community with their remarkable triumph over feminine weakness or their innocence of some charge of paternity or rape. These stories differ in events from the course of Joan's life, but they recover diachronically the double identity that Joan maintains synchronically. When transvestism is no longer a disguise but an expression of spiritual transformation, it approaches a materialization of spirituality that defends the saints from censure, and could potentially defend Joan. In other words, although the saints' transvestism and chastity are importantly ascetic practices that give them access to the divine, a reverse current also flows from the divine into their physical practice, infusing their practice with special power to affect their communities.

The story of Eugenia is paradigmatic in this respect. She is the daughter of the provost of Alexandria, but leaves her family in male disguise in order to live in a monastery. Accused of attempting to rape a pagan woman, Eugenia (now Brother Eugenius) is taken for judgment before her own father. Because her accusers impugn the morals of Christians in general, Eugenia/Eugenius declares,

"je monstreray la verité et non pas par vantance, mais pour la gloire de Dieu." Et lors print sa cocte et la desrompit par dessoubz et par dessus jusques a la sainture et dist qu'elle estoit femme, si comme il apparut. Et dist au prevost: "Tu es mon pere et Claudiene est ma mere."[68]

["I will reveal the truth, not in order to boast but for the glory of God." And then she took hold of her tunic and tore it open from the bottom and from the top to the belt and said that she was a woman, just as it appeared. And she said to the provost: "You are my father and Claudienne is my mother."]

Figure 6. Saint Eugenia. Abbey of Mary Magdalene, Vézelay, nave capital 59. Photo by James Austin.

This physical revelation is the core of Eugenia's identity, the act that defines her in iconography and the manifestation of Christianity's power that converts her family. Two earlier medieval examples, a nave capital from Vézelay and an altar frontal from Catalogna, identify Eugenia through this dramatic gesture (Figures 6 and 7). Why is tearing apart her tunic the gesture that converts her family? Eugenia's female sex proves she could not be guilty of the charge of sexual aggression, but this is a relatively banal

Figure 7. Master of Soriguerola, Saint Eugenia. Paris, Musée des Arts Décoratifs. Photo: Union centrale des arts décoratifs.

revelation that only clears up a mistake.[69] More significant than her innocence of this specific accusation is the change Eugenia has worked on herself: her femininity is cleansed of its pernicious inferiority by being passed
through a male impersonation. Not only is Brother Eugenius innocent of
lust, Eugenia has escaped the limitations of her birth sex in the person of
this virtuous monk. We can assume that Brother Eugenius's ascetic life
brought her/him closer to God, but the legend is unconcerned with this
aspect of spirituality. The diegesis traces the reverse process, the manifestation of spirituality on the physical plane. The "verité" Eugenia reveals is
both her hidden female body and her right to her male name and garb. The
wonder of her spiritual transformation produces the wonder of her dual
self-presentation, and it is that physical expression of the spiritual that
amazes and converts her family.

Joan grounds her identity in the ideology of materialized spirituality,
but her judges find only materiality there. The faculty of the University of
Paris concurs at the end of the trial that, because her claim to divine sanction for her way of dressing is false, she is idolatrous in that she is preoccupied with her physical person to the exclusion of spirituality: "habenda
est suspecta de ydolatria et exsecracione sui ac vestium suarum demonibus,
ritum gentilium imitando" [she is to be held suspect of idolatry and of
consecrating herself and her clothes to devils, in imitation of the heathen
rite].[70] Like Eugenia, Joan claims a right to both her female origins and
an identity transformed by masculine attributes; like Eugenia's, Joan's true
identity resides not just in her female sex but in the interrelation of her
body and her masculine way of life. The Christian precedents for cross-
dressed virginity, together with the Christian conviction that spiritual
power can have physical manifestations, indicate that cross-dress was self-
defining for Joan. In more modern contexts that isolate body from soul,
Joan's masculine clothing might seem secondary, simply a reflection of
spiritual meaning. But her tenacity in cross-dress under the terrific pressure
of interrogation makes clear that her clothing amounts to a profoundly
consequential expression of her identity. It manifests her mission and God's
sanction. She cannot give up her cross-dress or her virginity without ceas-
ing to be "la Pucelle de Dieu."

Chose Oultre Nature

Simon Gaunt notes in his study of transvestite saints that "sexuality is central to the construction of sanctity in the Middle Ages."[71] Vows of chastity,

mystical marriage with God, martyrdom in sexually suggestive contexts, and cross-dress do not simply remove holy men and women from sexuality but continue to define them through reference to sexual identities they have reshaped and redirected. Gaunt's important perception can also be read the other way around, to say that sanctity is central to the construction of sexuality in this period. The preceding section concentrated on the spiritual implications of Joan's virginity and dress. Her spiritual practices, like those of Eugenia and other literary models, also have significant sexual implications.

Early in her trial, Joan was asked "se elle eust bien voullu estre homme" [if she really would have liked to be a man] when she set out on her mission. Joan responds with an evasive formula, "dit que autresfoys y avoit respondu" [she said she had answered this elsewhere], though no answer can be found in the record.[72] Since Joan's evasions tend to appear where a question does not allow for a response accurate to her convictions, it is possible that Joan did not believe that either "yes" or "no" would properly represent her position.[73] Our culture's current distinction between sex and gender, the former biological and bodily and the latter social and interpretive, even when we nuance that distinction by noting the indissociability of the one term from the other, is still sharper and more rationalizing than medieval conceptions of sexuality. For Joan's time it is not so clear that biological sex rather than social norms provide the importantly binary base for sexual identifications. All the categories appear less than firm, despite the rigor with which social institutions demanded conformity to accepted standards of behavior. Rigorous conformity in daily behavior is the ballast of a sexual system so mobile that dressing and living like a man can result in becoming one.

Joan Cadden and Miri Rubin have discussed medical and learned models in which either sex is latent at various points in human development, even in adulthood.[74] At the opposite pole from physiological theory lies the familiar theological premise that, as St. Jerome puts it, "as long as a woman is for birth and children, she is different from man as body is from soul. But when she wishes to serve Christ more than the world, then she will cease to be a woman, and will be called man."[75] Jerome neatly formulates both the dichotomous difference of the sexes and the fluidity of sexuality along the axis of virtue. The abbot to whom Eugenia appealed for admission to his monastery invokes a familiar pun to connect her male disguise and her conversion: "recte vir diceris, quia, cum sis femina, viriliter agis" [rightly do you call yourself a man ("vir diceris"), because you act virtuously / act like a man ("viriliter agis"), although you are a woman].[76]

Although this may seem a purely metaphoric invocation of manhood, it has bodily expression in several female saints who grow facial hair to avoid marriage and in St. Perpetua's vision of acquiring a male body as she is being carried into the arena for martyrdom.[77] A medieval listener might hear in these plots not only the teaching of women's inherent inferiority but also that women can adopt more of *vir* than *virtus* alone in their holy masculinity. A striking mistranslation of the *Legenda aurea*'s rather convoluted Latin illustrates this sexual elasticity: when the transvestite St. Margaret reveals that she did penance for the false accusation that as Brother Pelagius she had "fathered" an illegitimate son, the French translator has her say, "Je suis homme, je n'ay pas menti pour decepvoir, car j'ay monstré que j'ay eu vertuz d'omme" [I am a man; I have not lied in order to deceive you, for I have shown that I have the virtue of a man].[78] The mistranslation, which Caxton adopts as well in the English *Golden Legend*, illustrates how easily the saints' masculine *virtus* could glide for vernacular writers and readers toward a more global claim on masculinity.[79]

Joan does nothing so startling as claiming to be a man, but she does draw creatively on bellicosity in her conduct and testimony concerning warfare. Bynum argues that religious women who cross-dress continue to see themselves "in female images . . . not as warriors for Christ but as brides, as pregnant virgins, as housewives, as mothers of God."[80] Joan in contrast sees herself most accurately as a warrior, never drawing on imagery of pregnancy, motherhood, or nurturing, but she is a warrior with a difference: asked which she loved better, her standard or her sword, she replies that she loved the standard forty times better, and that she carried the standard herself in battle "pro evitando ne interficeret aliquem; et dicit quod nunquam interfecit hominem" [in order to avoid killing anyone; and she added that she had never killed anyone: *Pc* 1: 78]. She does approve her sword, "quia erat bonus ensis guerre et bonus ad dandum bonas alapas et bonos ictus, gallice *de bonnes buffes et de bons torchons*" [because it was a good sword for war and good for giving good slaps and good blows, in French "good whacks and good wallops": *Pc* 1: 78].[81] The French phrase testifies not only to Joan's colloquial vocabulary but again to her curious restraint about killing. Her sword seems less to threaten life than to punish and chastise in the manner of her weapon of choice, a heavy stick or *martin* by which she was known to swear ("par mon martin") and which she sometimes used on her own disobedient soldiers and their camp followers.[82] This diffidence about killing may also motivate Joan's discomfort with the term *chief de guerre*, which she used in a letter of warning to the king of England but repudiated during her interrogation, later explaining that "s'elle estoit chief de guerre, s'estoit pour batre les Angloys" [if she was a war leader, it was to fight the English].[83] Her letter indicates that she would rather the English simply left at her warning, though if they do not, "je les feray tous occire" [I will have them all killed: *Pc* 1: 221]: again she distances herself from the killing by however small a margin. She sees herself as a fighter, then, not a mother or a bride; but the modifications she brings to war leadership by carrying her own standard, refraining from killing, and preferring her stick and her standard to her sword constitute her refusal to succumb uncritically to the conventional model of the masculine warrior.

Among her contemporaries, only Christine de Pizan imagines positively a Joan who conflates masculinity and femininity in one persona. The *Ditié de Jehanne d'Arc* (1429) uses the masculine form "preux" for Joan while maintaining "preuses" to modify other heroic women. This grammatical crossgendering reinforces Christine's mixed imagery for Joan,

> le champion et celle
> Qui donne à France la mamelle
> De paix et doulce norriture,
> Et ruer jus la gent rebelle."[84]

[the champion, she who gives France the breast of peace and sweet nourishment, and who casts down the rebel host.]

The simultaneity of feminine and masculine attributes contrasts with *De quadam puella*'s version of pure sequentiality. To be sure, Christine finds nothing normal in this simultaneity. "Véez bien chose oultre nature!" [Here truly is something beyond nature!] concludes this stanza, and a similar passage rhymes the doubly gendered adjectives for Joan, "fort [m.] et dure [f.]" with "fors nature" [outside nature].[85] But Christine's "Pucelle de Dieu" is miraculous, supernatural rather than unnatural. She is elevated beyond sex by dedication to God yet also a credit to the feminine sex in general: "Hee! quel honneur au femenin / Sexe!"[86] Of all her contemporaries, Joan might have found Christine her most congenial advocate. The poet's urgently prophetic voice parallels Joan's, and the *Ditié*'s simultaneously masculine and virginal feminine "champion" recalls Joan's testimony on her conduct in war. Yet Christine's version of cross-gendering, in its poetic and miraculous harmony, floats at some remove above the conflicted and shifting self-presentation that Joan attempts under the pressure of interrogation.

The explanation Joan gives for cross-dressing after her relapse, that "elle ayme mieulx l'abit d'omme que de femme" [she likes men's clothes better than women's: *Pc* 1: 396] gains credit from earlier testimony revealing the ease with which she adapted to them from the beginning: when asked what reverence she showed to St. Michael at the Dauphin's court, she replied that she "se agenoulla et oulta son chaperon" [knelt and took off her cap: *Pc* 1: 118]. She inhabits the masculine gesture (uncovering the head to indicate reverence) as well as men's clothing. The faculty of the University of Paris invoke the figurative meaning of *habitus* to describe this expansion of masculinity from dress to practice: "relicto habitu muliebri, virorum habitum imitata est" [having given up women's way of dressing, she imitated the comportment of men: *Pc* 1: 363].[87] The literal and figurative reach of *habitus* in this accusation and the significance accorded to clothing and comportment as loci of identity anticipate Pierre Bourdieu's *habitus*, the accumulated gestures and structures of acculturated living that become so familiar as to seem the natural source and pattern for behavior in any new circumstance. It is tempting to think of Joan's *virorum habitum* in these terms, although it does not accurately match Bourdieu's *habitus*, so deeply ingrained as to be unconscious, "embodied history, internalized as second nature and so forgotten as history."[88] Joan's masculine way of life, consciously chosen but so meaningful that it exceeds explanation, is not "second nature" but "fors nature" [beyond nature] for Christine and other defenders who believe Joan to be supernaturally transformed. Nature is also the point of reference for her judges, who specify in the text of her abjuration that she sins "en portant habit dissolu, difforme et deshonneste contre la decence de nature" [in wearing dissolute, illshaped, and dishonest clothing against the decency of nature: *Pc* 1: 389]. Both Joan's *virorum habitus* and the nature she rejects appear more tenuous, conditional, and subject to interpenetration than in Bourdieu's paradigm. For Joan's defenders and opponents alike, nature, nurture, *habitus*, and divine intervention engage in ongoing negotiations that can substantially alter sexuality.

Extreme versions of these negotiations in secular literature indicate the importance of this cultural fantasy concerning sexuality. Several heroines of late epic and romance live in disguise as warriors. Yde of *Yde et Olive* and Blanchandine of *Tristan de Nanteuil* go so far as to marry, under somewhat forced circumstances, and avoid discovery by praying to God to change their sex to male.[89] The miraculous sex change endorses transvestism and its sexual component in particular. Yde and Blanchandine have engaged in a sort of bootstraps operation, finally achieving a full sex change by acting as if they had already achieved it.

Yde and Blanchandine contrast in the extent of their participation in masculinity before their sex change. Blanchandine is secretly married to Tristan while disguised, does not fight, and accedes to wooing, marriage, and God's will concerning her sex only because she believes Tristan has been killed.[90] Yde, who took up her disguise to escape her father's incestuous designs, proves herself in arms many times and so wins Olive's affection. Yde is not opposed to the marriage except in that she has "membre nul qua li puist abiter" [no member for having intercourse with her], and she wins Olive's complicity in concealing that lack after they have spent a fortnight kissing and cuddling.[91]

This affection, even physical affection, within the adopted male role is reminiscent of Ovid's Iphis, whose story reached late medieval French in the *Ovide moralisé* and in Christine de Pizan's *Mutacion de Fortune*. Iphis has performed in her male role since childhood, and despite her concealed sex she gladly accepts betrothal to Ianthe. Like Yde, Iphis believes her physical lack is the crucial impediment, even though she herself desires Ianthe as if physical lack were no impediment. In the *Ovide moralisé*,

> Se despere, et ne cuide mie
> Que joïr puisse de s'amie
> Et qu'à lui se puisse acoupler.
> Ce fet l'ardour croistre et doubler,
> Qui plus embrase la pucele.[92]

[She despairs, and thinks that she will never be able to enjoy her sweetheart and couple with her. That makes the ardor inflaming the maid grow and double.]

Iphis's conviction that women do not love women conflicts with her own love for Ianthe and implies that her love is an unforeseen consequence of her cross-dressed way of life. Again a divinity (Isis this time) resolves the dilemma by granting a sex change to make the marriage complete. Christine's retelling of the *Ovide moralisé* in her *Mutacion de Fortune* curiously foregrounds the role of transvestism just at the point of Iphis's sex change: "filz devint, par la soubtille / Deesse Vestis, qui deffit / Son corps de femme et filz le fit."[93] "Vestis," the name of a goddess substituted for Ovid's Isis, makes dress the sign under which the sex change takes place, since *vestis* is an inflection of the verb *dress*: the line could be understood, "she became a son, by the subtle goddess Dressed, who unmade her female body and made him a son."[94] *Vestis* could also be heard as a past participle in these lines: "she became a son, dressed by the subtle goddess, who unmade her female body and made him a son." This striking deployment of *dress* as a verb for bodily transformation again insists on the intimate relation between clothing and sexuality.

None of these texts can imply tolerance for historical instances of homoeroticism, yet within each narration the cross-dressed woman is a sympathetic figure.[95] The common, licit understanding these works share about female transvestism is that sharp distinctions cannot be made between hidden and manifest identities, between masculine clothing and masculine nature. I cite these works so briefly because my point is only that Joan's era had in circulation several such plots. The most widely circulated of these survives in *Lestoire de Merlin* and the *Roman de Silence*. It had popular origins as well as wide distribution, and it concentrates on the enigma of living as a man rather than the miracle of changing sex.[96] In this plot, which I illustrate from *Silence*, a young woman lives as a successful squire and knight until Merlin reveals her female sex and marries her to the king she has been serving. *Silence* is a complex, fascinating work on sexuality, which particularly deserves to be read alongside Alain de Lille's *Complaint of Nature* for its simultaneous insistence that there are strict sexual distinctions in nature and that humans persistently refuse to observe them. The narration claims a polarity between Silence's inner female nature and her outer male disguise, but also repeatedly confuses and denies this polarity.

During his years of passing, Silence is preoccupied not so much by the danger of discovery as by the persistent tension within himself between "nature" and "nurture," birth sex and apparent sex. (The narrator uses male pronouns to refer to Silence when he / she is passing as a boy and man, and I follow that lead because it is consonant with other ways in which the work troubles the relation between birth sex and sexual identity.) Nature and Nurture are fully personified in the narrative and in vigorous competition for Silence's identity. Often this polarized allegorization is said to correspond to Silence's hidden body versus his clothing: "Il est desos les dras mescine" [under his clothes he is a maiden]; "el a sos la vesteüre / Ki de tolt cho n'a mie cure" [what he has under his clothes has nothing to do with being male]; "Si est desos les dras meschine. / La vesteüre, ele est de malle" [and he is a girl beneath his clothes; only the clothing is masculine].[97] But the borderline between Silence's clothing and Silence is not really so clear. As for Eugenia and the secular heroines in disguise, dressing like a man shapes Silence's identity rather than simply concealing it. He acquires a comportment, manners, and skills that make him feel masculine: "Trop dure boche ai por baisier, / Et trop rois bras por acoler . . . Car vallés sui et nient mescine" [I have a mouth too hard for kisses, and arms too rough for embraces . . . for I'm a young man, not a girl].[98] Although Nature keeps insisting that only Silence's clothes are masculine, she spends three days at the end of the romance "a repolir / Par tolt le cors et a tolir / Tolt quanque ot sor le cors de malle" [refinishing Silence's entire body, removing every trace of anything that being a man had left there].[99] Nature gets the credit for Silence's resistance to sexual advances from a lascivious queen ("nel consent pas sa nature"; his nature did not consent to it), but genital sex is a last stand for Nature that emphasizes her failure to control other aspects of Silence's sexuality.[100] Indeed, Silence's body participates in passing by acquiring a fully masculine *habitus* that he refers to as his "nature" in a complaint to his father:

> "Vos savés bien de ma nature:
> Jo sui," fait il, "nel mescreés,
> Com li malvais dras encreés
> Ki samble bons, et ne l'est pas.
> Si est de moi! N'ai que les dras,
> Et le contenance et le halle
> Ki onques apartiegne a malle."[101]

["You know my nature very well. I am," he said, "believe me, like an inferior piece of cloth powdered with chalk, that looks good, but isn't. That's what I am! I have only the clothing and bearing and complexion that belong to a man."]

Silence's cross-dress began as an instrumental disguise but its daily practice has substantially reshaped him. By locating all the terms for his identity in a clothing metaphor (inferior cloth disguised by powdering chalk), Silence resists identifying with his birth sex alone and emphasizes the place of performance in constituting a self. The shift from female birth sex to "inferior" manhood is stressful, I would argue, because it is substantial rather than superficial.[102]

Joan may have heard such stories or may have absorbed the cultural fantasy they instantiate, that women could adopt male dress and comportment and find their sexuality deeply unsettled in consequence. The transgressive valence of sexual fluidity dominates the reactions of Joan's judges. Following the prohibitions in Deuteronomy and First Corinthians, they consider Joan's dress and short hair to be reprehensible violations of the feminine category—"contra honestatem sexus muliebris et in lege divina prohibita ac eciam Deo et hominibus abhominabilia et per ecclesiasticas sancciones sub pena anathematis interdicta" [against the uprightness of the female sex and prohibited by divine law, equally abominable to God and to men, and forbidden by ecclesiastical law under pain of anathema].[103] This unsettling effect of cross-dress is also implicit in the accusation quoted earlier that "relicto habitu muliebri, virorum habitum imitata est" [having given up women's way of dressing, she imitated the comportment of men: *Pc* 1: 363]: the recurrence of *habitus* in its literal and figurative senses argues that cross-dress and sexual deformation are inextricable. Joan's masculine *habitus* helps account for doubts about her sexuality when she presented herself to the dauphin: Jean Pasquerel testifies at the nullification trial that Joan was twice visited by women to determine "si esset vir vel mulier, et an esset corrupta vel virgo; et inventa fuit mulier, virgo tamen et puella" [if she were a man or a woman, and if she were deflowered or a virgin; and she was found to be a woman, but a girl and a virgin].[104] That women were chosen to make this determination suggests Joan's female sex was not in much doubt: male physicians would have been more appropriate investigators of sexual anomaly had it seemed likely that Joan was male. However, that the sex determination needed to be made at all indicates that Joan's cross-dressing and cross-behavior were perceived to complicate her sexuality.

Joan argued that her virginity licensed her revisions to sexuality, and I emphasize that her virginity should not be taken for disengagement from sexuality. Valerie Hotchkiss states that Joan had "no desire to masculinize herself," and Barbara Newman writes of "Silence's missing sexuality" when she resists the lascivious queen, as if the only site for sexual definition were between the sheets.[105] Marina Warner invokes the androgyne, an idealized nonsexual status, to describe Joan: "she was usurping a man's function but shaking off the trammels of his sex altogether to occupy a different, third order, neither male nor female, but unearthly, like the angels whose company she loved."[106] But gender theorists have argued compellingly that the concept of the androgyne, in its unconflicted wholeness, evades the issue of sexuality by idealizing it away.[107] Androgyny's prior sexuality, moreover, is conceived only in bipolar terms: only conventional masculinity and femininity come before androgyny, doing away with the possibility of any other sexuality. Androgyny evades sexuality while reasserting that it is binary; Joan's testimony, in contrast, draws on femininity and masculinity to present a *habitus* that matches neither. Joan's commitment to virginity frees her from genital sex, but her commitment itself, and her masculine dress and way of life, continue to shape her sexuality in the construction of "la Pucelle de Dieu." Not only her hostile judges but supportive works such as *De quadam puella* and Christine's *Ditié* understand her sexuality as a double construction that cannot be reduced to either femininity or masculinity. The fifth of twelve articles drawn up at the end of the trial charges that Joan cross-dressed and cut her hair like a man's, "nichil super corpus suum relinquendo quod sexum femineum approbet aut demonstret" [leaving nothing on her body that proves or reveals her female sex]; the Orleans manuscript stops at that while the full Latin record continues "preter ea que natura eidem femine contulit ad feminei sexus discrecionem" [except for what nature has provided her to distinguish the female sex].[108] The complete Latin accusation suggests that Joan's fault is the greater in that she has not crossed over entirely (like the transvestite saints perhaps) into a masculine position. Her body is the more visible and shameful for its imperfect containment in cross-dress. She occupies neither position in the gender binary, but contaminates both by combining them.

A contemporary chronicle published as *Le journal d'un bourgeois de Paris* reports Joan's last days as if they revolved around just her relation to clothing:

Lui fut monstré l'ordonnance et la place où le feu devoit estre fait pour l'ardoir bientost, se elle ne se revocquoit. Quant elle vit que c'estoit à certes, elle cria mercy et soy revocqua de bouche, et fut sa robe ostée et vestue en habit de femme, mais aussitost qu'elle se vit en tel estat, elle recommença son erreur comme devant, demandant son habit de homme. Et tantost elle fut de tous jugée a mourir, et fut liée à une estache qui estoit sur l'eschaffaut que estoit fait de plastre, et le feu sus lui, et là fut bientost estainte et sa robbe toute arse, et puis fut le feu tirée ariere, et fut veue de tout le peuple toute nue et tous les secrez qui pevent estre ou doyvent [estre] en femme, pour oster les doubtes du peuple. Et quant ilz orent assez et à leur gré veue toute morte liée à l'estache, le bourel remist le feu grant sur sa pouvre charongne qui tantost fut toute comburée, et os et char mise en cendre.

[They showed her the writ and the place where the fire would be built to burn her if she did not recant. When she realized that they meant what they said, she asked for mercy; she recanted with her lips and her clothes were changed, she was dressed like a woman. But no sooner did she see herself like that than she fell again into her former error and wanted to have her men's clothing back. She was at once unanimously condemned to death and was tied to a stake on the platform (which was made of plaster) and the fire lit under her. She was soon dead and her clothes all burned. Then the fire was raked back and her naked body shown to all the people and all the secrets that could or should belong to a woman, to take away any doubts from people's minds. When they had stared long enough at her dead body bound to the stake, the executioner got a big fire going again round her poor carcass, which was soon burned up, both flesh and bone reduced to ashes.][109]

This account is not entirely accurate to Joan's last days: the crucial elements of her abjuration and her relapse were whether she would disavow her voices and submit to the Church Militant. But clothing is an apt metonymy for all the issues of her trial, in that she identified herself so fully through it. Her body was not really the frontier of her self; she was projected into her clothing to a degree that confused those nature/nurture, body/clothing, female/male distinctions that Eugenia and Silence also confound. Burning off her clothing to leave only her body is a canny representation of the court's objection to her identity as a cross-dressed virgin. This account of the burning achieves (however belatedly) the court's goal of altering Joan's identity by removing her men's clothes. It is entirely appropriate to Joan's self-presentation that "doubts" can only be taken away from people's minds when she is a naked corpse, when she is no longer animating herself in and through her clothing.

Plate 1. Pierre Salmon, *Les Demandes faites par le roi Charles VI*. Paris, Bibliothèque nationale de France, MS français 23279, fol. 19. Cliché Bibliothèque nationale de France, Paris.

Plate 2. Claes Heinen, Gelre Herald: *Wapenboek*. Brussels, Bibliothèque royale de Belgique, MS 15652-56, fol. 56, verso. Copyright Brussels, Royal Library of Belgium.

Plate 3. Gervais du Bus and Chaillou de Pesstain, *Roman de Fauvel*. Paris, Bibliothèque nationale de France, MS français 146, fol. 34. Cliché Bibliothèque nationale de France, Paris

Plate 4. Jean Froissart, *Chroniques*. London, British Library, MS Harley 4380, fol. 1. By permission of the British Library.

4

Chivalric Display and Incognito

THIS CHAPTER LOOKS at some interrelated registers of self-representation
for knights: coats of arms, ancestor myths, disguise, and chivalric orders.
The informing conceptions about identity that unite these registers are
two: that ancestors define descendants because blood is not simply one's
own but is continuous through time; and, complementarily, that deeds consolidate identity because chivalric standing must be continually reasserted.
Chaucer's lyric "Gentilesse," sometimes anachronistically taken to assert
the irrelevance of birth and the sole supremacy of conduct in determining
merit, instead expresses the widespread conviction that status can be bequeathed, but virtuous conduct must complement it before true gentility
can be claimed. Geoffroi de Charny similarly argues that high status once
did, and should still, require superior conduct: "Ycelles genz ne ycelz
seigneurs n'estoient mie eslevez pour avoir les grans repos ne les grans
deduis ne les grans delices, mes pour avoir plus grans paines et travaulx
que nulz des autres" ["These personages and these lords were not raised up
to have great periods of rest nor great pleasures nor great delights, but to
endure more and to strive harder than any of the others"].[1]

An intriguing visual image for the double source of chivalric identity
in birth and performance comes from late medieval rolls of arms. Early
rolls represented shields only, and fifteenth-century rolls shift toward representing full figures of knights with their crests and shields. The most
celebrated of the medieval rolls is Gelre Herald's record of nearly 1700
shields, many accompanied by crested helmets, which he compiled from
about 1370 to 1395. The first leaf of his seventy-nine English coats of arms
(Plate 2) represents Edward III, his elder sons (without differences for
the sons' coats of arms), and eight vassals' coats of around 1382–90.[2] What
I find most evocative in these images is their half-animate, masklike, not-
quite-human dimension. The helmets recall heads, particularly as they
rotate from profile to full-face at the end of the second tier, but their
expressionless smoothness contrasts with the openmouthed, glaring animals' heads atop them. Wings, tails, and hackles raised, tongues and tusks

protruding, these crests are intensely animated. Their energy sets them apart from the helmets' blankness, yet as men wear them, the crested helmets become masks. What is the relation between the hidden man and the creature replacing his face? Crested helmet and shield together have the aspect of a costume, an adumbration of the armed knights that later armorials depict. On Gelre's pages, an implicit body informs the vertical arrangement of crest above helmet and helmet above shield, as well as the shields' forward tilt and the helmet's apparent mobility. Gelre's skill at poising these arms between inertness and animation manages to suggest both that arms are stable definitions of their bearers, and that they are dynamic features of living identities.

The first half of this chapter will provide context for just one of Gelre's representations, that of Thomas Beauchamp, fourth earl of Warwick (Plate 2, second tier, second from right). I survey the symbolic and social meanings of arms in the Hundred Years War, and then focus on one particularly well documented case, the claim of many families to descent from the Knight of the Swan. In this case, I will argue that the metonymic relation of descendants to ancestors feeds on the metonymies of totemism. The second half of this chapter turns away from ancestral relations to their complement in chivalric identity, individual achievement. The need to couple lineal with earned identity is particularly visible when knights deliberately conceal their arms under disguise, or supplement them with the regalia of orders of chivalry. Totemism imagines an ancient ancestry, and disguise imagines self-transformation in the moment, but the two operate analogously to lift the limits on self-definition. The singular knight and his hard-won reputation open up to new traits. In the specific practices of late medieval knights, totemism pulls chivalric identity back into family history, while disguise presses identity forward beyond achieved renown.

Ancestral Signs

How is a coat of arms a self-representation? It might seem that arms are only peripherally related to their bearers, and due really to their bearers' ancestry alone. Have they any more significant place in identity than a vestigial sobriquet such as "Chaucer," "Shoemaker," had in Geoffrey Chaucer's life? This familiarizing analogy does illustrate a first significance of arms: like inherited surnames, they link individuals to their forebears and recall what the social standing of those forebears was. Even in the comparatively mobile and forward-looking London circles Chaucer frequented, ancestry was far from inconsequential. Greater weight accrued to ancestry in some-what higher ranks than Chaucer's, in part because those ranks' superior legal and social standing were based in the premise that their superiority was a birthright. A coat of arms several generations old was a token of standing derived from ancestors who had carried those arms into com-bat. Around the time of the Norman Conquest, devices on banners and shields served to identify companies in battle, and soon after, they identi-fied single knights in tournaments as well as in battle. Coats of arms deploy a language of dress, whether because cloth banners were their earliest man-ifestation or because they were perceived as analogous to clothing: the heraldic tinctures "ermine" and "vair" [squirrel fur] and heraldic terms such as "fess" [tie] and "bend" [band] connect arms with furred, trimmed garments.[3] Soon coats of arms became more than battle dress. From about 1125 arms could be inherited, and began to connote pride of birth as well as chivalric performance. By 1300, a corollary sense developed that arms were proper to families, such that outsiders should not be able to adopt identical arms.[4] To emphasize the lineal claim, early arms often canted on a family name: crows (from French *corbeau*) for the Corbetts, hammers (from French *martel*) for the Martels, a hart for De Hertley.[5] These aspects of coats of arms express the importance of genealogy in late medieval justifications of power, and wider convictions as well that history should be understood as continuity rather than rupture.[6] An inherited coat of arms asserts not only a right to ancestral privileges but a selfhood founded in the living presence of forebears in the blood.

The military and lineal connotations of arms obscure (and are surely meant to obscure) the prominent place of innovation in their later medi-eval history. Arms were adopted with great frequency, rather than inher-ited, by the time of the Hundred Years War. Not only knights but undubbed gentles and esquires were choosing coats of arms, without any presumption that they would become knights or even landholders. One might compare such coats to self-naming, in contrast to surnames. It appears that Chaucer had red and white arms (see Figure 3, p. 66); their first surviving attestation is a seal used in 1409 by his son Thomas, inscribed "S[igillum] Gofrai Chavcier."[7] Why Chaucer chose red and white for his arms is obscure, but adopting arms is consonant with his title of esquire. Moreover, those who already held arms by inheritance might alter them in gestures of piety, commemoration, or imitation. Around 1395, Richard II impaled his arms with those of Edward the Confessor, a move the *Annales Ricardi Secundi* declared to be more proud than pious.[8] The dukes of Brittany adopted plain ermine arms, probably alluding to the name "Ermenie" often given to Brittany in romances. Regnier Pot and his fifteenth-century descendants substituted for their family's arms the arms attributed to an Arthurian knight, Palamides.[9] Crests provided similar opportunities for innovation. Earlier crests derived from the shield's devices, as do Edward III's leopard crest and Henry Percy's lion in Gelre's armorial (Plate 2; Percy is second from the right on the bottom tier).[10] As the use of crests became widespread after 1350, they more often diverged from the primary device. Some crests expressed family names and holdings: Roland de Trémereuc, lord of Plumoison, took his crest of a goose from the second syllable of his holding; Hervé le Coq, seneschal of Saintonge, supplemented his shield of two bars with a cock crest.[11] William Montague's griffin crest revives an older Montague coat, *azure, a griffin segreant or* (Plate 2, bottom tier, second from the left).[12] Thomas Beauchamp's swan crest reaches deeper into family history, to claim descent from the Knight of the Swan, who founded Godfrey of Bouillon's line (Plate 2, middle tier, second from the right).

A change in the function of arms encourages this tendency to invent, reinvent, and modify them. According to Maurice Keen, during the fourteenth and fifteenth centuries, arms became more widely diffused because they replaced knighthood as the criterion for "admission into the charmed circle of the chivalrous."[13] This expanded importance of arms as a token of chivalric standing gave arms a new source of prestige, but diluted their connection to actual military practice. More than practical communications in battle, arms came to signify a commitment to the ideals of chivalry. A strong connection did persist between arms and fighting, for example in the etymological fantasy that coats of arms are so called from the strength of men's arms that was required to win them: they have "the name of armes, because that the worshippe was getyn with the myght of manys armes."[14] The imaginary etymology linking French *armes* (from Latin: weapons) and English *arms* (from Anglo-Saxon: limbs) binds coats to prowess deep in history, even as their bond in present practice was weakening. Prowess continued to confer great prestige, as the second half of this chapter will indicate, but narrative and symbolic messages came to provide an alternate source of prestige. Revising arms and adding crests take advantage of the aura of meaningfulness that comes to surround arms: like the personal devices discussed in the first chapter, these revisions and inventions make personal assertions, suturing individuals to their arms even in the absence of chivalric exercise.

The colors, shapes, and devices on coats of arms seem to beg interpretation. In the later fourteenth and fifteenth centuries, interpretation became an important task of heralds.[15] Their treatises offer a profusion of meanings for arms, but it is the act of symbolization that preoccupies them, not the history or the authority of any particular meaning proposed. For one treatise, the color black signifies darkness, prison, and honor; for another, sorrow and humility; for another, black is meritorious because laws are set down in black ink.[16] The *Llyfr arfau* and its source, the *Tractatus de armis*, provide two explanations for swans in heraldry, neither with any relation to the Swan Knight's story: some heralds say a swan "signifies that the first to assume the arms was a good singer, for in Latin the two words are similar," but another says swans are appropriate for "handsome men of good countenance and long-necked, and for that reason they were granted these arms."[17] For the heralds, it is more important to indicate that arms have meanings than to agree on just what they mean. The international consistency that heralds establish for blazoning arms contrasts sharply with this indetermination around their symbolic import. Apparently, heralds recognized the potential of arms to signify, but were not concerned to regulate that aspect of arms.

Within particular families, however, determinate meanings do come to be claimed for arms, meanings that preserve ancestral deeds and myths. The family of Coucy said that their arms of gules and vair represented a red furred cloak that an ancestor on crusade "had cut in pieces and given to his companions for a device when they were surprised by the Turk without their surcoats of arms."[18] Stories of this sort multiply in the fourteenth and fifteenth centuries. Some claim enchanted ancestors, half human and half animal. Melusine of Lusignan grows a serpent tail in her Saturday bath; when her husband discovers this, she flies away a serpent forever. Michel Pastoureau argues that Jean de Luxembourg asserts his descent from Melusine by wearing a crest of a winged serpent in a washing tub. Pastoureau finds evidence that several similar ancestors were claimed through coats of arms.[19] Best documented is the use of a swan crest by the many insular and continental families putatively descended from the Knight of the Swan. Closing in narrowly on this claim to descent, I will argue that such animal and natural forebears have a totemic relation to descendants.

Totemic Swans

Medievalists often note that heraldic devices appear totemic, without pausing to define or substantiate their use of the term. The definition of totemism has a long history, so complex and contested that the term might

seem beyond redemption. On the contrary, both redefinitions and subtle
analyses of specific cases are flourishing in anthropological circles. Most
persistent in all formulations of totemism is its conception that certain
groups of humans have a connection to certain animals or other natural
entities. The connection is one of "mystical descent," which may have further implications such as special protection from the animal ancestor and
prohibitions on hunting or eating it. These implications vary, or they may
be absent; the core of totemic thought is the ancestral relation between
human and nonhuman.[20] The disputed aspect of totemism is just how to
understand this claim to descent. Claude Lévi-Strauss's *Totemism* disagreed
sharply with earlier anthropologists who were intrigued by the quality,
particularly the religious valence, of the relation between human and mystical ancestor. That relation, in Lévi-Strauss's view, was insignificant in comparison to the differentiating function of totemism within human society:
totemism asserts not so much "we are descended from a swan" as it asserts
"we are different from people who are not descended from a swan."
Totemism, in short, explains distinctions between human lineages by reference to the more evident distinctions between natural species.

Poststructuralist responses to Lévi-Strauss's highly influential argument tend to accept that totemism does differentiate among human lineages and clans, but to resist in various ways Lévi-Strauss's disregard for
the relation between humans and natural ancestors. Two strains in recent
writing on totemism concentrate on this relation and define it in terms of
metonymy. First, the ordinary ancestor-descendant relation, in medieval
Europe, is understood to be metonymic: ancestors are not reincarnated
in descendants, but they do have a significant association with them, both
biologically as cause and effect, and socially as holders down through time
of identical positions in the devolving lineage.[21] Where ordinary human
descent is already metonymic, such that ancestors are at a remove from
descendants but can confer prestige on them by association, the conceptual
ground is prepared for mystical ancestry. In the case of the Swan Knight,
the mystical ancestor fits neatly into an otherwise historical lineage, as the
grandfather of Godfrey of Bouillon. A second strain in recent responses
to Lévi-Strauss rejects his argument that totemic relationships between
humans and nature are simply irrational and have no relevance to the
true meaning of totemism. His nature-versus-culture model for all civiliza-
tions assumed that humans conceived their fundamental difference from
animals "sometime in the historic past when man for all time made his
passage from nature to culture"; intellection itself was founded in this
conceptual shift "from affinity with the animal to separation from it."[22]

The structuralists' nature-culture binary has not held up in current anthropology; with regard specifically to animals, for example, John Borneman
shows how richly horse breeds are understood through mythical histories,
genealogies of blood, and conduct codes, the very "strategies most often
used to constitute the kinship systems of human groups."[23] This "reverse
totemism," the projection of human characteristics into the animal world,
assumes a metonymic sensibility akin to that linking medieval Europeans
to their ancestors.[24] The descendants of a Yankee farmer might attribute
to him their pluck and industry, and similarly, the Morgan horse is seen as
plucky and industrious because of its historic association with the Yankee
farmer. There is surely a measure of irrationality in both perceptions, but
they are nonetheless worthy of investigation. Specifically, the Swan Knight's
story owes little to rational thought, yet its imaginative exploration of
contact between humans and animals gave rise to real badges, crests, and
seals, chosen to express the real authority of their users. The allure of this
imaginary contact was obviously substantial.

Swan Ancestry

The story of the Swan Knight is so evidently concerned with lineage, and
its concern with lineage so evidently mobilized in its audiences' practice,
that my first point about its totemic contribution is little more than an
observation: lineage is just as telling in most contexts whether it is literal
or fictive. To be sure, a swan ancestor could not validate a claim to land
in a court of law, but in many situations it is unproblematic whether an
ancestor is real, or only securely narrated as such. Real and narrated ancestors rub shoulders in the story of the Swan Knight: the families claiming descent from him were in fact descended from the line of Godfrey
of Bouillon, conqueror of Jerusalem on the First Crusade. Accreted to
Godfrey's ancestry at the beginning of the *Old French Crusade Cycle*, the
Swan Knight provided a marvelous origin for the great conqueror.[25] Some
ten generations later, in the fourteenth and fifteenth centuries, about two
hundred of Godfrey's descendants across Europe were using swans in their
badges and heraldry, and sponsoring new manuscripts and translations of
the Swan Knight texts.[26] Never mind that their genuine ancestor Godfrey
had won and ruled Jerusalem; the mythical ancestor was the one they
preferred for their self-representations. Their relation to the Swan Knight
was consolidated through a powerful narrative about lineage rather than
through lineage itself.

The Swan Knight's youth is all about lineage and legitimacy. In its most widely circulated medieval version, extant in nine French manuscripts and one in Middle English, a king's wife gives birth to seven children at once, each wearing a silver chain around its neck.[27] The king's mother substitutes seven puppies for the babies and sends the babies off to be killed. Instead they are abandoned in a forest and fostered by a hermit. The wife, accused of bestiality and promiscuity by the king's mother, is cast into prison. Some years later, the children are spotted in the woods, each wearing its precious chain, and the function of these chains becomes clear when the king's mother dispatches another minion to have them taken from the children. He is able to steal only six of them, the seventh child and the hermit being absent; when the chains are removed from the children's necks, they are transformed into swans. The king's mother has a silversmith melt down all the chains, as she believes, but in fact he uses only part of one chain to make one or two cups. Believing the children to be fixed forever in their swan bodies, the king's mother finally convinces her son that he should execute his wife. On the eve of her execution, an angel appears to the hermit and explains that the one remaining son is to rescue his mother. Despite his total ignorance of mothers, horses, and judicial combat, this son's innate nobility and God's help make it possible for him to defeat his grandmother's champion. With his mother freed and his grandmother's sundry injustices reversed, the young hero, who has been baptized Elias or Enyas, reveals the fate of the king's other six children. All the chains are recovered except for the one damaged to produce the silver cups, and all the children change back to human form except for the one swan without his chain, who arouses everyone's pity with his doleful cries and desperate self-wounding. The Middle English condensation ends with the baptism of the other children. In the vastly longer French cycle, an angel then tells Elias to join his swan brother and go wherever he leads him as the Knight of the Swan, "le Chevalier au Cygne." The swan pulls Elias in a boat to further adventures culminating in his marriage and the birth of Godfrey of Bouillon's mother.

Lineage is the plot's preoccupation from its opening, on the castle battlements, where the king looks down in envy on a woman carrying twin babies, and his unfortunate wife repeats the old libel that a woman with twins has known two men. Her seven children are conceived that night, as God wills, recalling other tales in which slandering a mother of twins produces a multiple birth. This version does not focus on correcting the wife's conduct; rather, her virtue is salient in its dichotomous relation to her mother-in-law's devilish evil. She "sette her affye [put her faith] in

Sathanas of helle" (*CA* 10, *B* 43). Instead of yielding to her son's progeny, the king's mother seeks to discredit the alien woman her son has married and kill their children; "Thenne hadde I þis londe hollye to myne wylle" [then I would have this land wholly in my control (*CA* 181); in the French manuscripts, her motive is her love of violence and treachery: "Onques riens tant n'amai con mordre et traïson" (*B* 2497)]. The old woman's accusation of promiscuity and bestiality condemns the king's exogamy, and his son's job is to restore his mother to credit, in order to restore her children to their place in the lineage. "Criste hath formeth þis chylde to fyȝte for his moder" (*CA* 200), the warning angel concludes; "c'iert .I. hom de grant pris et de grant signorie": he will be a man of great renown and great lordship (*B* 653). No mention of Jerusalem or crusade dilutes this message: the scene well illustrates Keen's comment on the Crusade and Grail cycles as a whole, that "secular aristocratic ideals, heroic and courtly, which had nothing to do with ecclesiastical ideology, remained basic to chivalry even in its most deliberate mood of religious commitment."[28] Similarly, when the angel appears to the Swan Knight soon after he has rescued his mother, the message concerns his honor (the prowess and marriage he will win) rather than a holy cause: "Tel cose t'avenra dont tu onour aras" [something will happen to you from which you will gain honor (*B* 2554)]. At court, the son begins by reproaching his father for being under the control of his grandmother; then he defeats his grandmother's champion, who reveals his depravity by striking at the cross on the son's shield. "'Kepe þy swerde fro my croyse,' quod chevelrye assygne," but his adversary scorns the cross (*CA* 328, *B* 1549–52). Again divine intervention sustains the lineal cause, as a serpent and a fire leap out from the shield to disable the opposition. Once his mother is freed, the son makes two related revelations to the king: "how he was his sone" ["vostre fius sui"], and that his siblings "ȝonder in a ryvere swimmen þey swannes" ["Vés encor mes freres et ma serour vallant / La jus en vo vivier u sunt cisne noant"; you can still see my brothers and my worthy sister down there in your fishpond where they are swimming swans: *CA* 347, 350; *B* 1786, 1816–17].

I will turn next to the ways these children and swans interrelate, but I want to emphasize that the plot's first totemic feature is its preoccupation with the Swan Knight's lineal right. It narrates into being a mysterious origin, both supernatural and divinely sanctioned, for Godfrey of Bouillon's line. To emphasize the importance of their mystery, the unlikely seven babies in their silver chains demand a long labor of legitimation from the narrator and the hero. The evil of the "olde qwene" (*CA* 227) and the might and right on Elias's side finally insert the swan children into their

lineage in both the narrative space of the poem and the imaginative space
of mystical ancestry. The success of the *Chevalier au Cygne* in both registers
is evident in the fifteenth-century *Rous Roll*, a record of ancestral deeds and
arms of the Beauchamp family. The *Rous Roll* declares that the Beauchamp
arms of six cross crosslets (Plate 2, middle tier, second from right) are
inherited from the cross on Elias's shield that defended him with fire: "the
angel gafe hym armys of Sylver a croscrosle of Gold." The roll's coats
of arms show the Swan Knight's single cross crosslet multiplying in his
descendants' arms.[29] But in fact, the Beauchamps had adopted cross crosslets well before marrying women of the Tony family, which claimed descent
from the Swan Knight.[30] Some 160 years after these marriages, mystical
descent from swans has become more compelling for the *Rous Roll* than the
actual history of the Beauchamps' cross crosslets. Indeed, one imaginary
lineage trumps another for John Rous: Guy of Warwick, a more proximate
legendary ancestor for the Beauchamp family, leaves no mark on these
Beauchamp arms. Rous authenticates his renarration of the swan legend
with the detail that the earls of Warwick own the cup made from one
swan's chain; "I have dronk of the same, I dar the better wryghten hyt."[31]
For this genealogist, the Swan Knight texts have produced an ancestor so
powerful as to erase others, both the first holder of the cross crosslets and
the legendary ancestor Guy, from meaningful relation to this Beauchamp
coat of arms.

In summary, one way that the Swan Knight achieves a totemic relation
to families is by occupying the same metonymic relation to descendants
that blood ancestors have. J. C. Crocker points out that totemic connections are of many kinds (metaphor, synecdoche, and mystical participation
in addition to metonymy may express the relationship between humans
and their ancestors), but he stresses metonymy's particular aptness for
expressing descent.[32] In a conceptual parallel that may well reinforce ancestral claims, devices and coats in general tend to be conceived as metonymies for their holders. A poetic lament of about 1449 begins "The Rote
is ded, the Swanne is goone, / The firy Cressett hath lost his lyght," with
interlinear glosses noting that the "Rote" is "Bedforde," the "Cressett" is
"Excetter," and the "Swanne" is "Gloucetter," Humphrey Plantagenet, duke
of Gloucester, fourth son of Henry IV.[33] Humphrey takes his swan from his
mother, Mary de Bohun, whose family descends from Godfrey of Bouillon's
grandparents Godfrey the Bearded and his wife Ida. For the Bohun family,
as for the other late-medieval families in this lineage, Godfrey the Bearded
and Ida have ceded their ancestral place to the Swan Knight and his fictional wife.

Swan Siblings

A second anthropological puzzle inherent in totemism is just what sort of relationship it establishes between humans and natural entities. Beyond the widespread claim to mystical descent, cultures formulate differently the meanings and implications of the relationship. Lévi-Strauss argued in *Totemism* that such differences were irrelevant; indeed they betray their irrelevance in their very variety, since his test of relevance was any structure's persistence across cultures. In place of particularities of the relation between humans and nature in different local cases, Lévi-Strauss valued the consistent capacity of totemism to structure and organize human groups. More recently, a counterbalancing attention to particular cases has inspired the richly detailed analyses of John Borneman, J. C. Crocker, and Stanley Tambiah.[34] Accepting that totemism's cross-cultural recurrences signal its imaginative power, these scholars look for its meanings both in its most recurring features and in the local particularities of its elaboration. Their comprehensiveness is well beyond the scope of this study. Crocker, for example, urges that any account of totemism "must rest on a complete ethnographic account of the logical connections between man and animal, culture and nature, perceived by the society."[35] I set aside phenomena such as the English king's ownership of swans, the descriptions of swans in bestiaries, and heralds' interpretations of swans, to concentrate narrowly on the Swan Knight's story and its mobilization in heraldry. This mobilization sought to invoke the Swan Knight's story, but claimed no relation to other thinking on swans.

What kind of relation with swans do Elias's descendants have? Since the children can be either humans or swans, according to whether they are wearing their chains or not, the *Chevalier au Cygne* does not produce a fully animal ancestor. Still, the animal connection is clearly what differentiates this ancestor from all the others in Godfrey's line—others that medieval families do not bother to represent in their heraldic practice. Indeed, the preoccupation with human-animal connections is intensified by making the swan children themselves both human and animal. The plot repeats this preoccupation again and again. At first, these echoes and repetitions seem to argue that animals are inferior to humans, and that humans should be completely distinct from animals. When the king's mother substitutes seven puppies for the stolen babies, the crime imputed to the babies' mother is heinous: "bothe howndes & men have hadde þe a wylle: / Thow shalt to prisoun fyrste & be brente aftur" [both hounds and men have had their way with you; first you will be imprisoned and then burned:

CA 79–80].³⁶ In the English condensation, young Elias is simply ignorant
about courts and combat, but in the French versions he has bestial qualities to emphasize his ignorance: he is as hairy as a bear, with long nails and
shaggy hair; "Houme fol et sauvaje mervelles resambloit" [he looked just
like a mad, wild man: *B* 889]. In his wildness he needs to ask the hermit
even about mothers: "qu'est mere? Et s'on le mangera? / Samble oisiel u
beste? Nel me celés vous ja" [what is a mother? Does one eat it? Does it
resemble a bird or a beast? Don't conceal this from me: *B* 747–48]. The
wild youth progresses from bestial to noble appearance as he is shaved and
dressed and instructed in chivalric conduct.³⁷ The last indication in Elias's
youth that animal status is inferior to human is the misery of the one
brother who cannot change back into human form: "He bote [bit] hym
self with his bylle, þat alle his breste bledde, / And alle his feyre federes
fomede upon blode, / And alle formerknes [darkens] þe watur þer þe
swanne swymmethe" (*CA* 360–62); "Par .III. fois est pasmés, puis brait a
grant alaine. / A son bec se demaine, toute la cars li saine" [three times he
fainted, then cried out loudly. He attacks himself with his beak, so that all
his flesh bled: *B* 1855–56]. Here again, a hierarchy between humans and
animals is in force.

But in other ways the *Chevalier au Cygne* allies humans to animals
and presents the alliance positively. The swan children's mother does not,
in fact, sin to conceive her strange children; she, and they, are virtuous
creatures worthy of repeated aid from God and the angels. French and
English versions suggest, if only in a single line, that God chose to make
the children thus (*CA* 170, *B* 494). Young Elias's conflation of mothers,
birds, and beasts ("what is a mother? . . . is it a bird or a beast?") has a profound resonance with his mother's birthing of babies that have changed
into swans. In this plot, it is actually not ignorant to suppose that a mother
could be a bird. The possibility of cross-species descent also informs the
king's mother's accusation that the mother has consorted with dogs, but
because that accusation has an evil origin and refers to the puppies substituted for the children, it actually cleanses the swan children's strangeness
of any negative taint. In other words, the king's mother's wickedness dis-
places the taint of abasement from the doubly formed children onto the
substituted puppies. A positive substitution answers that negative one
when God sends the abandoned babies a doe in place of a human nurse
(*CA* 113–17, *B* 368–76).

The children's shape-shifting provides the strongest connection between humans and animals. Fundamental to this connection is that the
children change shape without losing their human consciousness. In the

longer French versions, they recognize Elias as he feeds them bread and come to him when he calls them (*B* 554–78, 1840–46). The English version suggests their consciousness by adumbrating, at the moment of their first transformation, the sorrow of the one brother who will be fixed in his swan body: as their chains are cut off, they fly away "withe a rewfulle stevenne" [with a rueful cry: *CA* 149]. The English version also connects them more fully with the human than the avian by identifying their second transformation as a return to their "kynde," their natural group or true character: "Eche on chese to his, & turnen to her kynde / Bot on was alwaye a swanne for losse of his cheyne" [each one chose his own chain, and returned to their true nature, but one remained always a swan, for the loss of his chain: *CA* 357–58]. On the one hand, these details of the children's avian days make clear that they prefer human form. On the other hand, the powerful attraction they feel to their "kynde" emphasizes how extraordinary and mysterious is their capacity for shape-shifting. Far from being inferior to ordinary humans, the children provide a remarkable hero with a wondrous birth. Whether their source is the Christian God or the mother's fairy blood, the children's shifting bodies intimate that Elias is no ordinary mortal.[38]

This enhancement is less clear in Elias's own person, since he is never seen to alter his form, than in his ongoing relationship with his swan brother. The angel who instructs Elias to go on adventure with "le cisne, ton frere" [your brother, the swan: *B* 2556] inaugurates a relation in which the two rescue one another, pray together, and divide the work of guarding and exploring. The swan cannot speak, but he retains his human feeling and understanding. Elias is equally justified in addressing the swan "frere," brother, and in complaining that his brother has been taken from him: he accuses his grandmother, "ma mere a fait grand honte, mon frere tolu m'a" [you have greatly shamed my mother, and taken my brother from me: *B* 1909].[39] The divinely ordained arrangement for their adventures, that the swan brother guides Elias, pulling him in a boat by a silver chain, extends the connection between human and animal forms that was first worked by all seven children's silver chains (*B* 2555–59, 2619–22). The silver chain joining Elias to his swan brother focuses and interprets the children's earlier potential for vacillation: the swan brother enhances Elias's heroism through his loyalty and aid, through his perpetual embodiment of Elias's supernatural birth, and more enigmatically through his conjoined human and animal identity. The chain by which the swan pulls Elias concretizes the many links articulated in the sobriquet "Chevalier *au* Cygne." Elias is "with" the swan, "of" the swan, "from" the swan, thanks to the fortuitous

amplitude of the preposition *à*. The multiplicity of this relation, together
with its suggestive vagueness, make it compelling in the face of plausibility. Its "reverse totemism" associates humans and animals by projecting
human behavior, values, and relationships into animals. The resemblances
between human social organization on the one hand and natural species on
the other, which Lévi-Strauss held to be merely analogous sets of distinctions, prove also to be homologous relationships in reverse totemism: the
manlike swan and the children who fly away "with a rueful cry" imagine an
expansive connection to nature, as well as exploring the difference between
human and animal. Challenging Lévi-Strauss's dichotomy between nature
and culture, Tambiah concludes for his Thai village, but also for Lévi-
Strauss's discussion of dogs, horses, and birds in France, that both cultures
perceive "a similar complexity which expresses neither a sense of affinity
with animals alone nor a clear-cut distinction and separation from them,
but rather a coexistence of both attitudes in varying intensities which
create a perpetual tension."[40] Borneman's and Tambiah's emphasis on the
infusion of human characteristics into nature, but also the inscription of
human difference from nature, could take as its illustration the plot of
the Swan Knight's youth. Linking and distinguishing Elias and his swan
brother, the sobriquet "Chevalier *au* Cygne" draws power from the complexity of their cross-species relationship.

The multiple relation between knight and swan encoded in this sobriquet may explain why the Middle English poem substitutes the sobriquet
for Elias's baptismal name (Enyas in Middle English) when the other children are baptized:

> Thenne þey formed a fonte & cristene þe children;
> And callen Uryens þat on and Oryens another,
> Assakarye þe thrydde & gadyfere þe fowrthe;
> The fyfte hette rose, for she was a mayden;
> The sixte was fulwedde chevelere assygne. (*CA* 365–69)

[Then they formed a font, and christened the children; and called one Uriens and
another Oriens, Zachary the third and Gadifer the fourth; the fifth was called Rose,
for she was a maiden; the sixth was baptized Chevalier au Cygne.]

The Middle English redactor's intention is probably not to erase Enyas's
earlier baptism but to recall it, such that the final line quoted above should
be understood "the sixth, the Chevalier au Cygne, had already been baptized." In that case, his sobriquet overlays his baptismal name, rather than
replacing it completely. In either case, it is striking that the Middle English
poem should so prefer his sobriquet that it alone is used from the moment

he is knighted.[41] This preference accomplishes, in very condensed form, the alliance of knight and swan that the French manuscripts narrate at length.

Swan Crests

The totemic relation of swan to knight, both as mystical ancestor and in this second sense of totemism as an expansive relation to nature together with an endorsement of difference from it, seems particularly to inform the use of swan crests. In crests, more often than in supporters or devices on the shield itself, medieval families express their descent from Elias. Crests, emblematic objects surmounting the helmet, were comparative latecomers to heraldic dress. Crests were superfluous to identification in battle, given the other marks that knights already displayed; their primary use was in tournaments, as well as in representational media such as seals, effigies, and plaques.[42] Fragile painted constructions of leather, wood, cloth, feathers, and animal skin, crests have only rarely survived into the present. The Black Prince's leopard crest in his funeral achievements is the only extant exemplar from Britain. Considerably bigger than the helmet itself, at 74 centimeters to the helmet's 31, the Black Prince's crest is of "moulded leather and canvas, covered with gesso on linen and painted" (see Plate 2: Edward III's leopard crest is similar).[43] The leopard crest comes directly from the royal coat of arms, as do many earlier crests. At the height of their use, from about 1340 to 1460, crests often supplement rather than echo the shield's devices. But unlike badges, crests were not distributed to followers: they are unique to their wearers, or to their wearers' lineage.[44]

Explanations for what it meant to wear a crest range from transgressiveness to mere ornamentation.[45] Most crests have no surviving verbal explanations, but the use of swans by Godfrey of Bouillon's descendants is easier to gloss than the use of crests in general. In this case it is clear that the crest represents descent from the Knight of the Swan. What makes a helmet crest the appropriate locus for asserting this claim? The alchemy of masking is at least part of the answer. Masking is the production of a second face that stands in some relation to the first—but there are many possible relations, many theories of personality informing the practice, many contexts that shape it across times and cultures. Admixtures of sham and conviction, overt play and underlying seriousness, are broadly typical of ceremonial and ritual masking.[46] Disguise and masking were pervasive court practices during the Hundred Years War, and I discuss some further instances later in this chapter and in the next. In each case, the mechanism differs and needs consideration within its particular context. For crests, the context is twofold: tournaments in which a helmet is actually worn with its crest, and representational media such as rolls of arms, seals, and effigies. Tournaments make an especially ceremonial frame for masking and disguising; they provide heightened performances of chivalric supremacy, dramatizing (inaccurately but compellingly) the authority and courage that "those who fight" contribute to the social fabric. The central place of literary imitation in tournaments invites reading a swan crest in terms of the swan texts. Lest the crest appear simply transitory and fanciful in its tournament role, it is important to recall that it routinely appears on seals, tombs, and property marks, that is, on more stable and more obviously committed self-representations than tournament gear. Figure 8 represents Thomas Beauchamp, third earl of Warwick, on his seal of 1344. Here the shield's fess and cross crosslets together with the swan crest represent Thomas's authority. The crest's role in legal and commemorative self-representation as well as in tournaments indicates that its meaning is more than merely playful.

Excellent historical work has refuted the conviction of Johan Huizinga and his followers that late medieval tournaments were empty shows, frivolous pageants that did no real cultural work. Malcolm Vale and Maurice Keen recover substantial connections between tournaments and warfare; Michel Stanesco, Juliet Vale, and Louise Fradenberg emphasize the continuity between self-defining display in tournaments and in all other spheres of chivalric engagement.[47] Showiness is hardly dichotomous with substantiality in this culture of honor and renown. Particularly in the ritualized space of tournaments, we should expect the brightest flashes of display just where the culture's most important claims are being conveyed. At the same time, such displays are more likely to dazzle than to inform: Moore and Myerhoff note of secular ceremonies in general that they "epitomize the made-up quality of culture and almost invite notice as such. Yet their very form and purpose is to discourage untrammeled inquiry into such questions. Ceremonies convey most of their messages as postulates."[48] Despite their assertive rather than analytical mode, tournaments do stage heraldic and ancestral claims in readable ways. In the case of tournament crests, Michel Pastoureau argues for an element of masking, which he specifies as an interplay between concealing and revealing: a double process hides and defends the knight's face while also presenting a false face signifying aggression and dominance.[49] His argument for doubleness is sustained by the physically doubled presentation of helmet below, crest above. Rather than taking over the facial surface of the helmet, turning it into a mask in its own right, the crest sits atop a hidden face still represented in the smooth impassibility of steel. The cap of maintenance, the coronet, or the wreath from which the crest springs further insists that the helmet represents a head, not just a support for the crest. For swan crests however, Pastoureau's dichotomy between true and false faces, hiding and showing, seems less apt than his recognition that self-presentation through crests is importantly double. Supplementarity more accurately describes this doubleness than substitution: the crest enhances identity even as it intimates that identity was not complete without it. This doubleness is already inherent in the aristocratic principle that lineage counts. The bearer of arms "is who he is" both through his own performance and through his ancestry.

Figure 8. Seal of Sir Thomas Beauchamp, third earl of Warwick, 1344. London, British Library, seal no. 5662, obverse. By permission of the British Library.

Invoking ancestors is one of the oldest and most widespread functions of masking: classical Latin "persona" referred to ancestral masks as well as stage masks, and death masks molded in wax and plaster have been important to family and national ideology in Western Europe as recently as the nineteenth century.[50] These masks were never worn, but they were revered as continuations (not just likenesses) of the ancestor. In his account of four types of masking, Ronald Grimes notes that effigies and death masks were "regarded with awe and reverence" because they represented the worthiness and prestige of the deceased, and invoked their authority in the present. Where masks are worn with this intention of fixing and invoking the power of others, Grimes argues that concealment is not the essential process at work, but rather "concretion," a fusing of the masked impersonator and the represented person's power.[51] Whether all crests could so operate is an open question, because virtually nothing is known about the meanings most of them intend. But in the context of the swan legend, the swan crest on the Beauchamp helmet spells out the process of concretion: it supplements the living knight's steely face with an invocation of Elias's exceptional knighthood. Thomas Beauchamp's identity is not concealed in this kind of masking but rather is suffused with his mystical ancestor's identity. Moreover, the double arrangement of helmeted head plus animal crest expresses the contradictory relation of humans and animals in totemism: expansion and contact on the one hand, but distinction and separation on the other. A swan crest could work in practice just as the swan legend works rhetorically, to claim an enhancing connection to the animal world through this mystical ancestor, while also acknowledging the difference and loss that suffuses Elias's relation to his swan brother.

The concretion of ancestor and descendant is implicit not only in crests but in the coat of arms altogether. Shield, surcoat, and crest constitute the masking of a present self in ancestral authority, whether real or invented. The present self is not concealed but marked and enlarged in this kind of masking. Robert de Tony's arms, as they are described in the *Siege of Carlaverock*, illustrate the process:

Blanche cote et blanches alettes
Escu blanc et baniere blanche
Avoit o la vermeille manche
Robert de Tony ki bien signe
Ke il est du chevalier a cigne.[52]

Nicholas Harris Nicolas translated these lines "A white surcoat and white

alettes, a white shield and a white banner, were borne with a red maunch
by Robert de Tony, who well evinces that he is a Knight of the Swan."[53]
The poet makes whiteness, often repeated, stand for the Tony's swan ancestry; the red noted just once might recall the pitiful self-wounding of Elias's
swan brother, but that reference is less clear.[54] The final couplet stresses the
symbolic nature of this ancestry in the *rime riche* "signe/cygne": the coat
of arms itself signals ancestry, but the homonymic swan-sign extends the
symbolic energy from heraldry in general to this mystical ancestor in particular. A literal if awkward translation would be "Robert de Tony signals
well that he is of, or from, or by the Knight of, or from, or with the Swan."
The preposition *de* expressing Robert's relation to Elias has the same evocative indeterminacy as the preposition *à* expressing Elias's relation to swans.
The effect is again totemic: literally vague but symbolically secure, Robert's
relation to the swan partakes of both connection and detachment, in an enhancing process that has more to do with vivid assertion than historical fact.

   Thus coats of arms in their entirety, not crests alone, fuse the knight's
ancestry to his present self. The second half of his knighthood, according
to chivalric principles, resides in prowess and the renown accorded to it. A
quick indication of the crucial role of prowess is that Thomas Beauchamp's
seal (Figure 8) and the arms of his son Thomas Beauchamp (Plate 2) are
identical: in their maturity, father and son cannot be distinguished in
heraldic terms. Both occupy an inherited role and perpetuate its ancestral
authority. Turning now to the vitally prospective realm of chivalric deeds,
I concentrate on how their expression of identity expands and individuates
the retrospective identity visualized in coats of arms.

Chivalric Incognito

In romances from the twelfth century onward, and in tournaments from
the thirteenth onward, disguise is a frequent strategy for presenting the
chivalric self.[55] Occasionally these knights in disguise are seeking to conceal
themselves from scrutiny and judgment, but in most cases chivalric incognito, as a written motif in romance and chronicle and as a historical practice, amounts to a peculiar kind of self-dramatization that invites rather
than resists public scrutiny.[56] This function of incognito becomes clearer
when placed in relation to other means by which late medieval knights display their identity, in coats of arms, badges, and the insignia of orders of
chivalry. All these gestures, I will argue, construct an identity that calls persistently on the chivalric community's recognition in order to constitute

itself, but that retains as well a suppressed and threatening potential for alienation from that community.

My reading of chivalric dress and disguise reconsiders a familiar dispute about medieval and modern selfhood. Renaissance scholars have long characterized the Middle Ages as the time before individuality. Stephen Greenblatt's most influential claim is that only in the Renaissance did people begin to fashion individual identities self-consciously, to choose and value "a distinctive personality, a characteristic address to the world, a consistent mode of perceiving and behaving."[57] Jacob Burckhardt much earlier argued that in the Middle Ages "man was conscious of himself only as a member of a race, people, party, family, or corporation—only through some general category."[58] That "only," that dichotomy between identity conceived independently of others and in terms of others, has also conditioned medievalists' counterclaims that individuality is a medieval phenomenon as well as a modern one. Robert Hanning has argued that the driving tension of the romance genre is between the striving hero's private desires and his social commitments. The protagonist's sense of self precedes encounters with the world: "The great adventure of chivalric romance is the adventure of becoming what (and who) you think you can be, of transforming the *awareness* of an inner self into an *actuality* which impresses upon the external world the fact of a personal, self-chosen destiny, and therefore of an inner-determined identity."[59] Peter Haidu, in contrast, argues that the opposition between inner self and external world is an entirely modern conception: "Le Moyen Age nous lisant ne peut que s'émerveiller à la vue d'un système social produisant des sujets s'opposant, aux meilleurs moments de la vie, à la société et au système de valeurs encodées qui les fondent en tant que Sujets" [the Middle Ages would be amazed to see our social mechanism that produces people who oppose, in their most shining moments, the very society and value system that has constituted them as subjects]. Looking specifically to Chrétien de Troyes's *Yvain*, Haidu concludes that the choice offered there is between a fully social identity and no identity at all.[60]

For both sides of this debate, a division, indeed an irreconcilable opposition, distinguishes the individual from society: the medieval self is either determined by social forces, or confronts them in a dialectical struggle over that determination. This oppositional conception itself has a history, one moment of which is articulated with particular clarity in the work of John Locke. Locke and his contemporaries convinced the architects of the American Revolution that each and every "man" had a primary duty to question "received Opinions" on every matter of importance to his daily conduct; each man's reason was his means to liberation from "the secret motives, that influenced the Men of Name and Learning in the World, and the Leaders of Parties" to further their own interests.[61] Locke is the first theorist to propose that everyone, not just the philosopher, must take a dialectical stance to social precedent and authority, and that to resist and interrogate is the essence of liberty: "he is certainly the most subjected, the most enslaved, who is so in his Understanding."[62] Students of the novel will recall Ian Watt's argument that Locke's version of the autonomous individual in confrontation with the social world is crucial to the generic shift from romance to novel in the eighteenth century.[63] Although Locke's sharp distinction between self and world has been shaken by the post-modern insight that identity is brought into being by social forces, Locke's sense of the confrontational, even adversarial relation that persons should take toward those social forces has continued within postmodernism. The long predominance of this oppositional relation constricts our ability to imagine other moments in the complex history of subjectivity.

In considering chivalric identity, we might imagine Locke's premises stood on their heads, or, from the medieval perspective, righted from their postmedieval inversions. Precedent and social consensus become reliable measures of merit rather than dangerously misleading "Opinions," and the relation between the self and those measures becomes largely mutual and interpenetrating rather than oppositional. Independent selfhood is not the goal of social life but a threat to it, a state of alienation that is to be avoided rather than sought out. And the isolated self does not precede confrontation with the world—is not the starting point for building an identity—but is rather an effect, and a largely negative one, of the quest for renown.

My argument contrasts with the two important perspectives on chivalric selfhood. Louise Fradenberg argues brilliantly for a psychological tension between chivalry's production of identity in performance and a preceding Lacanian interiority; this oppositional tension presses the subject "to create a relation between an interiority and the exteriority of the image."[64] In contrast, on the issue of chivalry Lee Patterson argues for an undifferentiated, publicly defined identity: "It is essential to grasp, as our initial premise, that chivalry entailed a form of selfhood insistently, even exclusively, public. It stressed a collective or corporate self-definition and so ignored the merely personal or individual."[65] I agree with Patterson that chivalric performance is better imagined as the very origin of the chivalric subject, not the place where a prior, private self strives to incorporate performance; however, I will argue below that a "personal or individual" identity can be founded in renown in this court culture for which the individual is not the questioning opponent of social precedent. Accorded by the chivalric community, this individuality derives from, rather than precedes, public judgment.

I will first outline several cases that locate identity in the estimation of the community, and then go on to argue that chivalry sustains a peculiar kind of individuality based on one's capacity to win esteem. Finally, I will analyze the risk of misjudgment in this identity system. When the community charged with assigning merit misreads a performance, the knight's alienation from the misreading adumbrates Locke's oppositional relation of self and world, but this opposition marks the collapse rather than the starting point of chivalric self-definition.

Incognito and Renown

Early instances of chivalric performance informed by narrative are Edward I's Round Table celebrating the conquest of Wales (1284) and the Picardy tournament (1278) presided over by a Dame Courtoisie and a Queen Guinevere who welcomed to the lists a "Chevalier au Lyon," a suite of damsels he had rescued, and his lion.[66] The Knight of the Lion imitates Chrétien de Troyes's disguised hero Yvain, in disgrace and attempting to remake his reputation as the "Chevalier au lÿon . . . / qui met sa poinne a conseillier / celes qui d'aïe ont mestier" ["þe knight with þe lyown: / He helpes al in word and dede, / Þat unto him has any nede"].[67] The historical impersonation of Yvain's impersonation illustrates the double attraction that the motif of incognito holds for late medieval courts: the motif invites both the invention of similar disguises and the impersonation of literary figures. "Incognito" in its many fourteenth-century manifestations encompasses both concealed identity modeled after romance plots and fictive identity borrowed from them.

A striking instance of the latter, according to Juliet Vale's compelling interpretation of the records, is provided by Edward III: having participated in the 1334 Dunstable tournament as "Monsr. Lyonel" (a Round Table knight and cousin to Lancelot, chosen perhaps for the "lions" on the royal coat of arms), Edward expanded the impersonation of Lionel in so naming his third son in 1338. Vale further suggests that the green hangings ordered for Lionel of Antwerp's betrothal recall the green ground on which the "arms of Lionel" ["schuchon' de armis Lyonel"] were embroidered on hangings of 1334, and that those tournament arms were passed on to Lionel of Antwerp at his birth.[68] Edward continued to participate incognito in later tournaments, as a simple knight bachelor at Dunstable in 1342 and in the arms of his follower Thomas de Bradeston in 1348.[69] At least one English knight of the period, Sir Thomas Holand, used adopted arms reminiscent of those in romance: although he bore his family's coat of arms in his early twenties, his later armorial seals of 1354 and 1357 as well as the Antiquaries' Roll (c. 1360) record his use of a plain sable shield.[70] Holand may have used his plain arms only in tournaments, but in any case they seem to refer to the plain arms used by disguised knights in romances.

The kind of disguise at issue here is the most common of all in romance: protagonists adopt plain or fabricated arms in combat, often just for the space of a decisive tournament. The narrative pretexts for such disguises are various. Chrétien's Cligés and Hue de Rotelande's Ipomedon are new knights seeking to prove themselves as they enter adulthood; Partonope of Blois and Chrétien's Yvain have committed offenses against their lovers that they are striving to redress. In all these cases, chivalric incognito is a public act, one of definition and redefinition that speaks to onlookers. Incognito does conceal information, but does so only temporarily in order to focus attention on the judgment of present actions without regard for lineage, past achievements, or past failures.

Texts from the Hundred Years War illustrate that winning renown (los, ⸙ pris, name, renommee) requires submission to a semiosis of performance and display. The protagonist of the Middle English Ipomadon uses multiple disguises, yet his layered self-presentation, which the English redactor attributes to his perpetual sense that he is not yet worthy of his lady, culminates in major scenes of revelation linking his screen identities together. For example, after a three-day tournament designed to find a husband for his lady, Ipomadon intends to "wend my way / To gette me more worshipe, yff I may," but he sends his burgess host to court with the red, white, and black horses he used in the tournament and two more horses won from two rivals there.[71] Presenting each major figure in the narrative with one of these equine tokens, the burgess claims the renown for Ipomadon that Ipomadon is reluctant to claim for himself. At this point Ipomadon's three tournament disguises and two of his court personas come together, but his name and lineage remain concealed: his chief rival, Cabanus, tries to find out "where he was borne & what he hatte [what he was named]," but in the absence of that information he must still concede that "A worthleer knyght þen he is one / Under the cope of heyven is none."[72] Ipomadon's merit in arms is the more firmly established for its independence from his lineage, although his lineage, discovered much later, consolidates his meritorious performances. As each disguise is changed for another, reassumed, and ultimately lifted, Ipomadon strives not really to conceal himself but to articulate his construction of a self fully constituted in renown, in the perception and judgment of his society.

Incognito serves Partonope much as it does Ipomadon, concentrating the public eye on the moment of action in order to establish an identity independent of affiliations with the past. In contrast to Ipomadon, Partonope is afflicted with failure when he attends the three-day tournament that will determine Melior's husband: he has disobeyed Melior's magical interdiction, exposing their love to public shame, and must now appear in disguise because, he believes, Melior has rejected contact with him forever. His plain silver shield stands for his superior performance: in the *bon mot* of a participant praising one of his victories, "The white shelde þinketh not to dey / At þis tyme" [the white shield isn't planning to die just yet].[73]

Where a past fault is the motive for disguise, there is a refashioned identity concealed beneath the incognito, but the strategy of romances is typically to externalize both the fault and the penance. Yvain's recollection that he has forgotten to return to his wife coincides exactly with a public reproach for his oversight, transforming what could be an occasion for private guilt into a public scene of shame. The Middle English adaptation of Chrétien's work, *Ywain and Gawain*, does away more thoroughly than its source with Ywain's prior identity by insisting that his fault negates it altogether. His wife's messenger calls into question his knighthood and his lineage:

> It es ful mekyl ogains the right
> To cal so fals a man a knight. . . .
> Sertainly, so fals a fode
> Was never cumen of kynges blode,
> That so sone forgat his wyfe.[74]

No wonder this "unkind cumlyng" [unnatural little upstart] runs maddened from court and later declares "I am noght worthi to be sene. . . . I was a man, now am I nane."[75] Ywain, like Partonope, reconstructs his manhood in deeds of chivalry, disguised as the Knight of the Lion.

These literary instances clarify Edward III's adoption of a chivalric disguise when his city of Calais was in danger of being recaptured by the French. Edward's exploit is noted in several chronicles, but Froissart's most fully elaborates the interactions between English and French combatants.[76] When Edward learned that Geoffroi de Charny had offered money to the

captain of the garrison at Calais in return for access to the city, the king
(together with the Black Prince and certain reinforcements) came in
secrecy from England to Calais, instructed the garrison captain to appear
willing to admit the French, and fought against the French force "sans cog-
nissance de ses ennemis, desous le banière monsigneur Gautier de Mauni"
[without the knowledge of his enemies, under the banner of Sir Walter
Manny].[77] Froissart makes much of this incognito, pointing it out repeatedly in the course of his account; his late redaction adds the comment,
"Bien monstra la li gentils rois Edouwars que il avoit grant desir de con-
batre et amour as armes, qant il s'estoit mis en tel parti et tant humeliiés
que desous le pennon mesire Gautier de Manni, son chevalier" [there the
noble King Edward showed well that he had a great desire for combat and
love of arms, when he took part in such an action and so humbled himself
under the banner of his knight Sir Walter Manny].[78] Edward fights hand
to hand particularly with Eustache de Ribemont; again Froissart insists
"Mesires Ustasses ne savoit a qui il se conbatoit; mais li rois le sçavoit bien,
car il le recongnissoit par ses armes" [Sir Eustache did not know with
whom he was fighting, but the king knew him well, for he recognized him
by his arms].[79] Edward's disguise works, like those of romance, to concentrate attention on his fighting skill and courage independently from his
established status as sovereign and military leader. The initial effect is
paradoxical—the leader now a follower, the sovereign on a footing with
the soldier—but Edward integrates his disguise with his kingship by staging a scene of revelation and judgment to follow the scene of incognito,
inviting the captured knights to a dinner on the night of their defeat at
which he mingles with them, wearing not a crown but a chaplet of silver
and pearls. Edward reproaches Geoffroi de Charny and praises Eustache
de Ribemont.

Adonc prist li rois le chapelet qu'il portoit sus son chief, qui estoit bons et riches,
et le mist et assist sus le chief à monsigneur Ustasse, et li dist ensi: "Messire
Ustasse, je vous donne ce chapelet pour le mieulz combatant de toute la journée de
chiaus de dedens et de hors, et vous pri que vous le portés ceste anée pour l'amour
de mi. Je sçai bien que vous estes gais et amoureus, et que volentiers vous vos
trouvés entre dames et damoiselles. Si dittes partout là où vous venés que je le vous
ay donnet. Et parmi tant, vous estes mon prisonnier: je vous quitte vostre prison;
et vous poés partir de matin, se il vous plest."[80]

[Then the king took the chaplet that he was wearing on his head, which was fine
and rich, and put it on Sir Eustache's head, and said to him, "Sir Eustache, I give
you this chaplet for being the best combatant of the entire day of those within and

those without, and I beg you to wear it this year for love of me. I know well that you are gay and amorous, and that you willingly find yourself in the company of ladies and maidens. So say wherever you come that I gave this to you. And during this time, you are my prisoner; I excuse you from imprisonment, and you may leave in the morning if you please."]

Edward reconstitutes the military encounter as a festive occasion, an event very like a tournament, of which he is the judge in apportioning the honors. War and tournament reveal here their close allegiance, their shared preoccupation with honor (versus Charny's attempt to suborn) and with testing and measuring participants.[81] Edward adopts the role of sovereign observer of the day's events (as if despite his participation in the field he was nonetheless aware of all the action "dedens et de hors"), but he simultaneously enhances his exploits in the field by choosing his own adversary as the best combatant. Eustache, in wearing his prize, will publish as well the exploit of Edward and the victory of Edward's party.[82]

Froissart, and presumably Edward before him, draws on a semiosis of disguise that is common to the conventions of tournament and romance. Edward conceals his identity in combat as do Ipomadon and others, but as in those cases the incognito is ultimately lifted and renown credited to the now-known knight. In Froissart's account the crucial revelation to the French, noble adversaries, exemplifies the transnational pursuit of chivalric renown in romances; and the "dames et damoiselles" who are to be the audience for Eustache's narrative recall the feminine associations of romance: beyond as well as within the genre, women are said to have a special susceptibility to romance and tend to be invoked for an audience in fact more mixed. Edward's imitation of literary incognito provides a second level of disguise for the English king as a hero of romance, and his exploit's literary analogues prepare for its return to narrative in the accounts of Eustache and Froissart.

The pivotal function of chivalric incognito, then, is to establish or revise the perception of others concerning the disguised knight's merits. That is, incognito is not significantly self-concealing and self-protecting but the reverse: the disguised knight draws the curious and judgmental eye and stands clear of his past to be measured anew. The full semiosis of incognito requires that the knight complete his adventure by giving up the disguise and incorporating the renown he has won into his earlier identity. As *Ywain and Gawain* summarizes, "þe knyght with þe liown / Es turned now to Syr Ywayn / And has his lordship al ogayn."[83] This trajectory towards revelation is characteristic of romance adventures: the wandering knight, isolated from the court's view, fully achieves his adventures only when they are reported—whether by himself or by his captives and emissaries—back to the courtly audience.

Limitations of Renown

If chivalric disguise is a language of self-presentation rather than a means of self-concealment, then incognito is on a continuum of visible signs through which knights perform and manipulate their identity. Turning from disguise to other adopted marks of identity, my argument widens from the claim that the chivalric self is first of all in the gift of the community, to claim as well that this selfhood may ultimately find itself alienated from the community that established it.

For the public nature of chivalric identity does not do away with tensions analogous to the modern struggle between individual and society, or the postmodern pressure on subjectivity from its constitutive social matrix. A kind of individuality—distinct from modern individuality and postmodern subjectivity alike—comes into play at the point of opposition between chivalric brotherhood and that brotherhood's charge to each knight to distinguish himself. The chivalric community both asserts its seamless accord and demands differentiation. The Order of the Garter, for example, represents the equivalence of its members in their shared regalia and a nonhierarchical organization. Yet it also institutionalizes its members' difference from those knights not admitted to the order and further from each other, in that their original seating arrangement in the choir of St. George's chapel apparently reflected two tournament teams of twelve members each, one under the Black Prince and the other under Edward III.[84] Founding the order in part to declare the unity of interests among his most loyal supporters and in part to foster contests among them, Edward followed the design of tournamenting confraternities generally, and perhaps specifically that of the Order of the Band, whose statutes require each new member to run two courses against two members of the order at the first tournament held after his initiation.[85] The regalia worn by members of John II's Order of the Star unites them visibly in the colors vermillion, black, and white, which probably carried the significances contemporaneously ascribed to them in Geoffroi de Charny's *Livre de chevalerie* for the dress of squires about to receive knighthood: white for sinlessness, vermillion for the blood a knight is prepared to shed, black for mortality.[86] The order's robes and the colors of investiture urge a spirit of common purpose and shared identity. Yet each member was charged at the order's annual feast to recount his "aventures, aussy bien les honteuses que les glorieuses" [adventures, the shameful as well as the praiseworthy] for the purpose of designating "les trois princes, trois bannerez et trois bachelers, qui en l'année auront plus fait en armes de guerre" [the three princes, three bannerets, and three bachelors who during the year have accomplished the most in the arms of war].[87] Charny's *Livre* similarly posits both a universal "ordre de chevalerie" made up of all true knights and the principle "qui plus fait, miex vault" ["he who does best is most worthy"], which becomes the refrain of his opening pages.[88]

The orders of the Garter and the Star, established in mid-century by Edward III and Jean II, overtly imitated Arthur's Round Table, implying their founders' imitation of Arthur and their members' imitation of his knights. The Arthurian inspiration for the orders of chivalry licenses a turn to literature for some insight into the paradoxical relation between injunctions to chivalric fellowship and to individual distinction. *Sir Gawain and the Green Knight*, particularly because it ends with the founding of an order of chivalry, might be expected to comment on this double imperative. Throughout the poem Gawain is declared the paradigm of knighthood. His pentangle illustrates the virtues to which all knights might aspire. To Bertilak's courtiers he is "þat fyne fader of nurture" [that fine father of manners]; in Bertilak's assessment "As perle bi þe quite pese is of prys more, / So is Gawayn, in god fayth, bi oþer gay kny3tez" [as the pearl next to the white pea is of more worth, so is Gawain, in good faith, next to other fair knights].[89] Both metaphors assert relation as well as superiority; Gawain is comparable to other knights but also excels them on all the scales of commitment and achievement implicit in the pentangle's mathematics. In Charny's terms he surpasses the "preux" and the "souverainement preux" to count among "les plus souveraines."[90] When Arthur's courtiers adopt Gawain's green girdle on his return, they honor Gawain's superiority in the same gesture that strives to reintegrate him into the "ordre de chevalerie" in general and this new order in particular.

The court's response, however, is problematic. Gawain asserts that the green lace is the bend of his blame and the token of his transgression, but the courtiers laugh loudly and found a brotherhood whose members will each wear this "bende abelef hym aboute of a bry3t grene" [band slantwise about him of a bright green: 2517]. Are the courtiers *over*estimating Gawain's success, carelessly laughing and failing to recognize the spiritual fault he sees emblematized in the "token of untrawþe" [token of un-troth: 509]? Or are they rather *under*estimating Gawain's success, presumptuously adopting as their own this "pur token / Of þe chaunce of þe grene chapel" [fair token of the adventure of the green chapel: 2398–99] to which only Gawain's extraordinary adventure can give the right? Even if they are perceptively asserting their own inferiority in adopting the baldric, thereby declaring their aspiration to become as "imperfect" as Gawain, they are rejecting his own negative assessment of his actions. The interpretive impasse that Gawain—and each reader—faces in this scene foregrounds the problem of interpretation itself that is the weak link in a system of individual honor dependent on public recognition. Misrecognition is always possible. The court's perhaps insightful, perhaps ignorant judgment and Gawain's contrasting judgment of his performance raise questions about how accurately deeds can get translated into renown.

It is immediately tempting to attribute the gap between Gawain's and the court's assessments of his adventure to a fundamental alienation of the private self known only to itself from the ignorant outside world. Casting Gawain's predicament as a dichotomy of "inner" and "outer" identities is natural to the modern view of selfhood, but I believe that Gawain throughout the romance is identified with his public reputation alone, and that the sense of interiority arising at the work's end derives from the conflict over what measure of renown to accord his most recent exploits.

The tests of courage and courtesy Gawain undergoes in his adventure were, according to Bertilak, designed "to assay þe surquidré, ȝif hit soth were / Þat rennes of þe grete renoun of þe Rounde Table" [to test your pride in the great renown, if it be true, of the Round Table: 2457–58], echoing his declared motive at the poem's outset (258–64) and his taunt "Now is þe revel and þe renoun of þe Rounde Table / Overwalt wyth a worde of on wȝes speche" [now is the revel and the renown of the Round Table overwhelmed by a word of one man's speech: 313–14]. As the Round Table's representative, Gawain, even in his intimate conduct with Bertilak's wife, is subject to constant measurement against the standards of—and his own prior reputation for—courteous and chivalric behavior. "Þou art not Gawayn" is the persistent reproach of Gawain's male and female challengers as they demand that he live up to the ideals of his court (1293, 1481, 2270). His challengers speak as if "Gawain" were simply metonymic for an ideology of knighthood. His identity is articulated and judged by others; his task is to perform the chivalry and courtesy imputed to him as perfectly as possible.

The signs of identity Gawain bears further emphasize its public nature. The pentangle on Gawain's shield blazons his virtues in a visible calculus of fives and in a narrative register that appears to be beyond counterinterpretation. Many critics have noted the firmness and stability with which the pentangle's "endeles knot" (630) of interlocked virtues are "harder happed on þat haþel þen on any oþer" [fixed more firmly on that knight than on any other: 655], and the contrasting mobility with which the green girdle is draped, knotted, and interpreted.[91] Gawain's final way of wearing the girdle "Abelef as a bauderyk [slantwise as a baldric] bounden by his syde, / Loken under his lyfte arme" (2486–87) revises his heraldic sign. The pentangle has made a muted but unmistakable return in Gawain's second arming, when he completes his preparations for meeting the Green Knight by donning "his cote wyth þe conysaunce [surcoat with the badge] of þe clere werkes / Ennured upon velvet"—his badge or cognisance having been the pentangle at his first arming (2026–27).[92] In this period, armed knights typically bore their coats of arms on their surcoats as well as their shields.[93] When Gawain arms for the second time, the girdle maintains something of its character as a belt, wrapped twice around Gawain's waist, but after he comes to see in it the "syngne of my surfet" [sign of my transgression: 2433] he takes to wearing it crosswise. For a fourteenth-century audience, the "bende abelef" that Gawain ties across his "cote wyth þe conysaunce" would have recalled a heraldic bend, a deliberate revision Gawain has blazoned on his earlier "bytoknyng of trawþe" (2517, 2026, 626).[94]

That Gawain blazons a new identity reflective of his adventure breaks the pentangle's "endeles" stability and reasserts the performative nature of chivalric identity. But the difference between the meaning Gawain attributes to the girdle and the meanings urged by Bertilak and Arthur's courtiers marks the point where Gawain is, finally, estranged from his community. The text's focus on renown ends in a crisis of renown, as Gawain's sense of shame divides him from both his past position as the Round Table's best representative and the present "broþerhede" of knights in green baldrics (2516). Gawain's differing sense of self does not precede but rather derives from his participation in a chivalric economy of identity conceded in return for deeds. His trajectory from an identity fully constituted in renown toward an identity unavailable to public understanding exactly reverses the narrative, familiar from a thousand novels, of an independent youth at odds with tradition. From Locke's modern perspective, the kind of estrangement from social consensus that Gawain experiences on his return to court is the universal precondition of individuality; from a medieval chivalric perspective, however, Gawain's estrangement amounts to a failure in the system of renown that has generated his individuality.

Identity Beyond Renown

Marked and overwritten with the colors and symbols that convey his identity, Gawain makes himself available to the reading of others, and his own words of shame carry little weight with them. That Gawain's new token is a feminine garment invites Marjorie Garber's thesis on the transvestite: he/she is one who fails to fit, who embodies a problematic not just of gender but of other classifications—here of the imperfect coordination between exploits and renown.[95] The crisis of interpretation with which *Sir Gawain and the Green Knight* ends could contextualize the motto of the Order of the Garter, "honi soit qui mal y pense," which appears at the end of the unique manuscript of *Sir Gawain*.[96] The order's motto recalls a number of parallels between Gawain's experience and the account, perhaps spurious but widely attested, that the Order of the Garter began with Edward III retrieving a garter fallen during a dance at court from a woman's leg. When his courtiers' reactions suggested that his gesture was beneath a king's dignity, Edward is said to have responded with the order's motto, "shame unto him who thinks ill of it," turning unfavorable interpretations of the act back onto the interpreters and further forestalling criticism by founding an order in which the worthiest men of England and Europe would go about wearing the emblem of the incident.[97]

Historians are suspicious of this account of the order's inspiration, preferring to attribute it to Edward's claim to the French throne and specifically to the Crécy campaign.[98] Yet the earliest surviving accounts of the Garter's origins offer instead the story of the woman's garter. *Tirant lo Blanc*, whose author was in England from March 1438 to February 1439, has it that the dancing woman was of little standing and that the king wore her garter for several months before the protests of courtiers and displeasure of the queen led him to utter the (mangled) motto "puni soit qui mal y pense" and to found the Order of the Garter to consolidate the merit of his action.[99] In 1534 Polydore Vergil, a careful historian, endorsed the "popular tradition" that the Order of the Garter began with the king's retrieval of "a garter from the stocking of his queen or mistress"; Vergil comments, "English writers have been modestly superstitious, perhaps fearing to commit lèse-majesté if they made known such unworthy things; and they have preferred to remain silent about them, whereas matters should really be seen otherwise: something that rises from a petty or sordid origin increases all the more in dignity."[100] The Garter motto in the Gawain manuscript, which makes best sense in terms of the "popular tradition" about the Garter, may indeed be that tradition's earliest trace—earlier by a few decades than the English material published in *Tirant lo Blanc*.

Here I am arguing neither that the Garter foundation story is necessarily true, nor that the Gawain poet alludes to it, but rather that the Garter motto written at the end of the Gawain manuscript records a contemporary perception of similarities between the foundation stories of the two brotherhoods. According to these stories, both orders begin with interpretive crises in which Edward and Gawain understand the feminine token differently from their courts. Both men can be said to cross-dress, although not simply because they transfer a woman's garment to their own bodies. Edward's and Gawain's gestures recall the common practice among knights of wearing bits of feminine clothing as love tokens. Such tokens do not disturb the gender binary but on the contrary assert the knight's heteronormativity, signaling even in battle and tournament that he is actively engaged in courting a woman. In contrast, the garter and girdle narratives carry a potential for shame: Edward stoops to retrieve an intimate garment as his courtiers titter; Gawain breaks his troth as he accepts the lady's girdle. At the point where shame still inheres in the action and the garment, Edward and Gawain could be said to cross-dress, with all the loss of status that represents for men in the heterosexual paradigm.[101] As Gawain explains his plight to himself, "wyles of wymmen" have brought down mankind from the first (2415). The potential shame is suppressed as the feminine garment becomes a token of honor for a new chivalric brotherhood. It is this radical change from shame to honor that involves the adopted garments in the gender hierarchy and invites the notion of transvestism.

In that moment when they can be described as cross-dressing, Edward and Gawain dramatize the risk of submitting to public judgment and the gap where their interiority might be distinguished from their renown. But the glimmer of interiority seems chimerical as both narratives quickly bring it to public light. According to Polydore Vergil, Edward "showed those knights who had laughed at him how to judge his actions" by transforming a sexually charged situation into an affair of state that actively defends against illicit interpretation.[102] Stephen Jaeger cites Vergil's account of the Order of the Garter in a compelling series of instances in which courts fabricate a public, asexual discourse from the language of sexuality and intimate interactions.[103] In support of Jaeger's argument, I would point out that Edward's two most durable mottos, "honi soit qui mal y pense" and "it is as it is," embroidered again and again on his tournament costumes and hangings, his beds and tents, assert control over interpretation and deny that multiple interpretations might have merit.[104]

Similarly, Gawain's apparently private interactions with Bertilak's wife, as noted above, are immediately generalized by reference to courtly standards and turn out to be not a genuine seduction but a test of *treupe* that Gawain goes about confessing and signaling with the girdle. The court's reading of his adventure, and the Garter motto appended in the manuscript, deny the shameful potential in Gawain's interactions with Bertilak's wife. Yet this is not to say that the potential was never there at all. The feminine associations of the two garments are not completely erasable—they persist at least in the foundation stories of each order—and their persistence dramatizes the more visibly how powerful the court's ability to suppress and redefine can be. In the garter and girdle narratives the illicit holds an important role as that which is denied in order to establish that which constitutes noble identity: the illicit is the trace of a potential for private identity that the aristocracy actively rejects in favor of a public identity constituted in renown.

Gawain's green baldric, blazoned over his pentangle, represents a belated interiority that amounts to the difference between his sense of shame and his court's admiration. Edward's and Gawain's situations differ in that the king asserts sovereign control over his court's interpretation, whereas Gawain finds his self-assessment overridden by Arthur's and the court's approval of his performance. The private sense of self his adventure has produced in him is marginal, and perhaps transient as well, as he faces the court's conclusion that the green baldric is to represent "the renoun of the Rounde Table" (2519). This chapter began by insisting on the lineal aspect of chivalric dress, in crests and coats of arms that claim merit and power from ancestors. In striking contrast, chivalric disguise and the orders of chivalry locate further measures of honor and dishonor in the gift of the community. Far from negotiating a tension between private self-perception and a potentially contradictory public perception, chivalric dress and disguise seek to move from one public estimation to a higher one; far from valuing and sheltering an inner self from misestimation, the disguised knight generates a public dialectic concerning his two or several identities. But where there is conflict within the community's judgment, or between the adventuring knight's self-assessment and the assessment of his peers, such conflict betrays the precariousness of basing identity in public consensus.

5

Wild Doubles in Charivari and Interlude

THIS CHAPTER HAS TWO INTERTWINED GOALS: to trace how courts themselves generate inversions and disruptions of courtly decorum and to discover how these disruptions function within the identity of a participating courtier. My conviction, as in other chapters, is that framed ceremonial performances provide intensified situations for self-expression. These expressions can be recovered only through careful attention to the formalities framing them. Some formal contexts are relatively well known, such as tournament and marriage, but the less familiar charivari and interlude of this chapter need closer attention in their own right. They are particularly spatial, costumed events, more closely allied to theater than are the other events in my purview, yet they do not offer the anonymity and falsification we might associate with theater. Instead, the charivaris and interludes of this chapter invite courtiers to incorporate disruptive, oppositional, wild behaviors into their elite identities.

The great halls of aristocratic households were complexly figured spaces of display, hospitality, charity, and performance. The halls' daily and festive uses marked them first with their owners' authority and then with their milieu's responses. Decorated with paints, overlapping tapestries, and cupboards displaying valuable serving plate, the hall further enhanced its owners' image by seating household members and lesser guests along the hall's sides, with heads of household and greater guests at the hall's end, often on a dais. Feasting enacted largesse on a grand scale and filling the alms dish at each meal dramatized the wealthy's generosity to the poor. On ordinary days, food was the medium joining and stratifying lord, household, guests, and the wider community, but on days of celebration, food accompanied music, dance, and various enactments in the center of the hall that celebrated the marriage, the state visit, or the seasonal festival in progress. At such events, even food acquired a rhetoric, colored and shaped into a coat of arms, or sculpted from meat and bean pastes into a castle. These edible "entremets" or side-dishes gave their name to "des entremès vifz, mouvans et allans par terre" [living and moving entremets] in the hall's central space.[1] I take *Entremets* and its English equivalent *interlude* to be the most capacious terms for a range of performances—dances, illusions, disguisings, challenges, mock battles, pantomimes—that involved household members as both actors and spectators.[2]

Later developments in theater history have obscured the roles that courtiers took in these performances. Theater historians might have seized with more energy on the wardrobe accounts of costumes made up for Edward III's Christmas *ludi* at Guildford in 1347 and Otteford in 1348, if they had coincided with payments made to "king's players" or other emerging professional groups. The performers who wore the "viseres" of silver-headed angels and men with beards, the tunics painted with peacock's eyes, the "capita de wodewose" and "capita virginum" [heads of wild men and virgins] were most likely members of the household itself, unrewarded because the events were in large part amateur, and participation was understood to be as celebratory as onlooking.[3]

The household's inner hierarchy may have dictated that the lesser members more often performed for the greater, but even heads of household and their immediate families took part. The tanned wolf skins René of Anjou gave his son for a "mourisque du roy Adrastus" [disguising/ dance of King Adrastus] suggest an enactment of Adrastus's first encounter with his future son-in-law Polynices, who wears a lion's skin when he first appears at Adrastus' palace. The wolf skins may have been an available substitute for the lion's skin, and King René could have impersonated King Adrastus without needing a costume specific to the role.[4] James IV had robes made for masking, and Charles d'Orléans wrote a lyric for recitation in the course of a danced interlude:

> Venuz sommes en ceste mommerie,
> Belles, bonnes, plaisans et gracieuses,
> Prestz de dancer et faire chiere lie,
> Pour resveillier voz pensees joieuses.[5]

[We have come in this mumming, we who are lovely, virtuous, pleasing, and gracious, ready to dance and make happy cheer in order to awaken your joyous thoughts.]

Charles writes in the voice of a company of women, and he may have read the poem himself, as he regularly read his other poetry in court, to accompany the women's mumming.[6] At the court of Mahaut of Artois, a mock tournament of six masked ladies and six knights celebrated St. Bartholomew's night, with Mahaut's son Robert bursting out of a three-headed serpent.[7] Further traces in chronicles and wardrobe accounts make clear that high-ranking members of households took part in interludes.[8]

In these court festivities there was not so sharp a distinction between costumed participants and passive onlookers as would later characterize theatrical performance.[9] The interlude's space was not reserved for performance alone; interludes asked to be taken for real events by usurping a daily living space. Indeed, interludes often exploited their location in the hall by staging interactions that turned onlookers into performers. Masked visitors to Richard II's manor in Kennington on February 2, 1377, set before the young prince a gold ball, a gold cup, and a gold ring, each of which he won from them in a game of loaded dice they conveniently supplied.[10] According to Froissart's account of the 1393 dance of wild men, which I will discuss below, Charles VI survived only because the Duchess of Berry caught hold of him, pulling him away from his companions to ask him who he was. Froissart's account may not reflect just what happened on that occasion, but at the least it made sense to him that a spectator could have inserted herself thus into the interlude. Interludes do not construe their audience as passive spectators but as the dramatic context and occasion for the interlude, which might call on them to speak, dance, or perform in other ways appropriate to its fictions.

From the spectrum of performances that took place in halls, I will consider a narrow band that is especially intriguing in its riotous, undisciplined aspect. It has become a commonplace that "carnivalesque" celebration is not exclusive to oppressed groups, nor consistently liberating for them. Richard Schechner argues that the New Orleans Mardi Gras "privileges the already privileged," and Joseph Roach aligns it with other performances "whereby elite cultures produce themselves by contrast with the excluded."[11] Roberto DaMatta opposes New Orleans' carnival to Brazil's, which expresses social oppositions but more importantly strives for their reconciliation.[12] Emmanuel Le Roy Ladurie's study of carnival and tax insurgency in sixteenth-century Romans discovers complex social and financial considerations influencing who joined in violent protest and who stood aside.[13] These analyses share a nuanced reading of concrete instances that does not lose sight of the persistent features of carnival: high spirits but low pleasures, inversions and parody, transgressions, noise, rejection of institutional authorities and constraints.

The cases in this chapter contrast with most instances of the carnivalesque in speaking almost entirely inside court space, rather than commenting across social strata. The cavorting wild men of Charles VI's court performed for their peers in the course of celebrating a wedding. The

best-informed chronicler of this event frames it as a charivari, a noisy bois-
terous protest against an irregular marriage. Historians and anthropologists classify charivari as a form of "popular justice" rather than an elite
behavior. The first and fullest literary representation of a charivari, from
Chaillou de Pesstain's additions to the *Roman de Fauvel*, will ground my
counterargument that charivari is not exclusively popular, nor is it concerned with adjudication. I will close by discussing how *Sir Gawain and
the Green Knight*, composed around the time of the charivari in Charles
VI's court, uses similar tactics and the space of interlude to confront
Arthur's court with its deficiencies.

     An important concern of cultural studies has been how those without
much power have asserted themselves, and how their culture "mattered in
the play and negotiation of hegemonic practices."[14] One of the many ways
oppressed culture matters is how the more powerful relate to it—how those
in power stage their own contentions by drawing on rituals of inversion that
are not generally considered to be among their resources. An analogy from
Bourdieu's discussion of the traditional house is helpful in conceptualizing
the place of disruptive and mocking behavior in courts. In the context of a
town, Bourdieu notes, a house is defined as a feminine space by contrast
with masculine space outside the house, but within itself, considered as its
own symbolic universe, a house has both masculine and feminine spaces.
One symbolic scheme, the masculine/feminine distinction, is applied differently in two logical universes, but people negotiate the difference without
much strain.[15] The court makes similar distinctions concerning disruptive
and mocking performances, associating such unruliness both with an "outside" of wild nature and unsophisticated commoners and with an "inside"
of self-critique and self-transformation. Wild dress of several kinds (animal, hybrid, savage, green) has the potential for carrying courtiers in both
directions, outward and inward, as they perform for aristocratic audiences.

Charivari

Judicial records and ecclesiastical prohibitions detail the characteristic features of late medieval charivaris: they took remarriages or unsuitable marriages as their occasion, and they noisily and rudely insulted the newlyweds;
their participants were typically young men, disguised or cloaked by darkness, who could sometimes be appeased with money for drinking. In 1362
a bridegroom was threatened with a charivari because his fiancée "avoit
esté deux autres fois mariee et aussi pour ce qu'il ne l'avoit oncques esté"

[had been married two other times whereas he had never been married], folding the typical motive of widows' remarriages into the less common motive of unequal or inappropriate ones.[16] Charivari's disruption of irregular marriages questioned the church's authority over marriage, and ecclesiastical prohibitions vigorously condemn the horrid, obscene, insulting, wicked, insolent conduct and language that charivaris directed at the newlyweds.[17] These comparatively articulate insults were accompanied "pulsatione patellarum, pelvium et campanarum, eorum oris et manus sibilatione, instrumento aerugiariorum, sive fabricantium, et aliarum rerum sonorosarum" [with clanging plates, basins and bells, whistling and handclapping, and banging on brass objects and other sonorous things].[18] The later English term for charivari, "rough music," records the defining importance of unharmonious racket in this ritual. Masks and disguises turn up somewhat less often in the records than noise, but there is mention of cross-dressing, veiling, false faces, and wicked masks ["cum larvariis," "cum falsis visagiis," "sub turpi transfiguratione larvarum," "larvis in figura doemonum"].[19] Sometimes the charivari disperses if paid "un franc à boire"; sometimes its contained hostility breaks into serious violence that lands the participants in courts of law.[20] Perhaps the least stable feature of medieval charivari is its location: prohibitions place it at the church door, in the cemetery, or outside the newlyweds' house; judicial records indicate a procession to the house was often involved.[21]

For my fourteenth-century cases, this list of charivari's most normative features is sufficient; historians of the later charivari find its occasions diversifying, its participants including women, its unruliness varying from place to place.[22] Explanations of what might be going on in this ritual vary as well. Lévi-Strauss's deep-structure analysis is that eclipses, earthquakes, and irregular marriages require noisy resistance to "an anomaly in the unfolding of a syntagmic sequence."[23] In a response to Lévi-Strauss, E. P. Thompson urges that historical moments and contexts continually reshape charivari such that its description must emphasize innovation over system: it is "un révélateur extrêmement sensible des changements dans la définition des rôles sexuels ou matrimoniaux."[24] The dominant view of charivari, as Violet Alford puts it, is that "Rough Music is the beginning of popular justice." Natalie Davis's articles provide the most extended argument that charivaris accomplish "local folk justice" and maintain "family order."[25] Davis concludes that charivari's "license was not rebellious. It was very much in the service of the village community."[26] As Davis recognizes, however, the forms and the energy of charivari have more in common with carnival behavior than with moral and civic conservatism. Like carnival, charivari is noisy, indecent, disruptive, joking, and aggressive, particularly against women.[27] Moreover, the "folk justice" model faces the difficulty that charivari fails if its purpose is truly to regulate marriage: there is no historical indication that charivari worked as a deterrent to irregular marriages, and they survive the ritual of charivari intact.[28]

In my view, charivari is not a quest for justice. Sexuality is indeed pivotal in fourteenth-century charivari, and so is opposition to the church's sanction for remarriage: as carnival proleptically inverts Lent, so charivari retrospectively inverts a marriage ceremony. Neither lay festivity destroys or even reshapes its target, but both make it an opportunity for iconoclastic reveling. Rodney Needham, commenting on social anthropology's preoccupation with discerning order, urges also the importance of "those practically universal usages and beliefs by which people create disorder, i.e. turn their classifications upside down or disintegrate them entirely."[29] My sense of the medieval cases collected by Roger Vaultier, Claude Gauvard, and Altan Gokalp is that charivari figures itself as a transgression on a transgression: it takes what could be considered an irregular marriage as an excuse for breaking out in riotous behavior. The work of the charivari is to point out, indeed to play up, the irregularity of the marriage in question, not in order to chasten it but in order to provide the charivari's riotousness with the excuse of a prior, instigating riotousness.[30] Charivari, I believe, both mocks and claims a kinship with irregular marriage: it declares that the marriage too is indecent, does violence to the order of things, and takes advantage of the community just as the charivari takes advantage of the irregular marriage. Rather than resisting the (often slender) insult to propriety the offending marriage has registered, charivari expands on that insult.

I illustrate this argument with the *Roman de Fauvel* and the 1393 dance of wild men, but my review of the judicial and ecclesiastical texts is meant as a provocation to scholars to reconsider the ruling interpretation that charivari is "popular justice." My cases will question both terms of that interpretation: although charivari is widely characterized as a rural and village ritual, it not only appears in courts but appears as a practice of courtiers.[31]

Chaillou de Pesstain's Charivari

The fullest as well as the earliest depiction of a charivari in medieval literature occurs in one extraordinary manuscript of the *Roman de Fauvel*. An allegorical satire on the success that vices enjoy in the world, *Fauvel*

denounces the allegorical figure of these vices, a horse called Fauvel
(faus-vel, false veil), who is assiduously curried by all estates, reigns over
Fortune's realm, and marries her courtier Vaine Gloire.[32] This 1310–14
composition attributed to Gervais du Bus, a French royal clerk, survives in
fourteen manuscripts. One of these, Bibliothèque nationale de France, MS
français 146, features extensive textual interpolations and musical additions that were composed and collected by Chaillou de Pesstain. "Mesire
Chaillou de Pesstain," according to the title ascribed to him in the manuscript, was a knight or at least a secular rather than a cleric.[33] His revised
Roman de Fauvel, completed around 1318, adds 169 musical pieces and
expands the episode of Fauvel's marriage by about 2000 lines, adding a lavish wedding feast, a charivari with many rude songs, a tournament that
pits vices against virtues, and Fauvel's visit to a fountain of youth. In sum,
as Fortune declares in suspending the indecisive tournament, the end to
Fauvel's power is not yet in sight. Chaillou's "edition" is a multilayered
assemblage of inventions and borrowings studded with music and images.
Its elegant manuscript suggests an aristocratic milieu.[34] The manuscript
was prepared around 1318–22 as a royal presentation volume in the mode
of a mirror for princes, its allegory pointed against the last corrupt years
of Philip IV (d. 1314) and his sons.[35]

This court manuscript offers from the Middle Ages the only fictional
as well as the only visual representation of a charivari, generally thought to
be a popular form. Fauvel's charivari is instead a meaningful court event. It
does begin in the streets: as Fauvel jumps into bed with his new wife Vaine
Gloire, a superlative charivari ["onques tel chalivali": E 682] breaks out
"par les quarrefours / De la ville par mi les rues" [at city intersections in
the streets: E 684–85]. The racket, petty aggressions, and disguises accord
with accounts of historical charivaris. Clanging pots and kettles compete
with cowbells, drums, and other instruments of "paramusic" as the revelers
break windows and doors and throw salt into wells. Costumes and masks
hide them from accountability but also repeat the disorder of their music
and mayhem: some wear their garments inside out, some wear monks'
robes, not in reverence to monasticism but in desecrations analogous to
those who expose their behinds and toss dung in people's faces.

How is this misbehavior related to Fauvel's wedding night? Its per-
petrators go wherever they choose without fearing Fauvel's men, implying that they could have reason to fear them ["Cil qui le font par tout se
boutent, / Fauvel ne sa gent point ne doutent": E 689–90]. As the charivari ends, a reciprocal disregard marks Fauvel's relation to it: whoever else
might have been displeased, Fauvel was more interested in the pleasures

he was having with his wife (E 766–70). This adversarial relation between the charivari and Fauvel is not tinged with the least indication of moral opposition to Fauvel's marriage. Indeed, Chaillou inserts an atypical figure into the charivari, a roaring giant called Hellekin, whose associations with destruction and death deny that this charivari could be considered an appeal to justice or morality in the face of Fauvel's marriage.[36] The charivari has an adversarial relation to Fauvel, not in resisting or protesting to him, but in unmasking his pretensions to propriety and refinement. The masked revelers tear away the "faus vel" of court ceremony and official sanction by exaggerating and acting out the impropriety that underlies Fauvel's marriage. The royal marriage and the charivari mirror one another, in an equivalence unflattering to the sovereign but belligerently celebrated by the revelers.

This amoral expansion on impropriety characterizes medieval charivaris in general, as I have argued in the preceding section of this chapter. I want to argue as well that Chaillou de Pesstain's charivari exposes the sovereign to ridicule not so much from the "popular" position of the streets as from within the court's own discursive and architectural space.[37] Modern readers may have overlooked this aspect of the charivari because it is more evident in relation to the manuscript's illuminations and songs than in the narrative text alone. The full experience of BNF 146 is unfortunately fragmented in early editions, which parceled out text and lyrics and did not adequately reproduce music and illuminations.[38] To begin with the illuminations, the episode's first and fourth in particular locate the charivari in relation to the court. The second and third illuminations, smaller representations of Hellekin and his followers, do not relate their figures to onlookers or settings, but the first and fourth surround the reveling figures with an audience and architectural elements. Conventionally dressed, courtly men and women, in decorous poses that suggest disapprobation as well as attentive spectatorship, stand in stone enclosures to the sides of the charivari's tumultuous movement.[39] In the episode's first illumination (Plate 3), Fauvel approaches his wedding bed above two tiers of revelers; the fourth illumination (Figure 9) works as a continuation of the first with the same three-tiered plan but with the charivari and its audience occupying all three tiers.

Michael Camille has noted that the charivari illuminations in BNF 146 offer "the only occasion in French manuscript illumination when scatological antics, monstrous masks and ludic spectacle occur not in the margins but in the centre of the page," yet the shift is less complete than it appears.[40] Grotesque appearances and behaviors have moved from marginal to central position, but the manuscript's text and music indicate that marginal social positions have not made the move. The opening hyperbole that "onques tel chalivali / Ne fu fait des ribaus de fours" [never was such a charivari made by street ruffians: E 682–83] turns out to evoke low status for comparison, only to exclude it from this event: this charivari is surpassingly sophisticated as well as surpassingly rowdy. Visual cues to the court's selective usurpation include the rebec player in the first illumination, who fits the iconography of court entertainment rather than the paramusic of charivaris, and the special costumes themselves, which look

Figure 9. Gervais du Bus and Chaillou de Pesstain, *Roman de Fauvel*. Paris, Bibliothèque nationale de France, MS français 146, fol. 36, verso. Cliché Bibliothèque nationale de France, Paris.

more like purchased artisans' work than the improvised disguises in the
legal records.[41] BNF 146 reinvents charivari as an expression of rowdy violence of, by, and for courtiers. This is a peculiarly elite poaching, a theft
from the realm of the disenfranchised that allows those in power to be
divided against themselves both socially, in denigrating a king, and indi-
vidually, in complicating the decorum typically incumbent on their status.
A closer look at the illuminations and music will demonstrate that this
charivari purloins some low trappings, but speaks and acts in courtly space.

In some respects the arrangement of the two larger illuminations does
associate the charivari with an "outside" to the court. The first illumination
(but not the others) shows grass under the revelers' feet; low stone walls
as well as the illuminations' framing compartments separate the courtly
onlookers from the charivari itself. Other elements suggest a closer relation
to Fauvel's court. If we think of his bedroom as a "soler" located on an
upper floor, the first illumination (Plate 3) looks more like the unfolding
of a single building than its inside and outside. The rooftop pinnacles
that rise alongside the bedroom reinforce the sense that it is above other
rooms, with the low walls in front of the spectators then suggesting interior balconies or galleries rather than places from which to view the street.
I would not attempt to argue that the charivari is clearly taking place inside
Fauvel's palace, but the layout can be read that way partly because other
elements reinforce the connection between court and charivari. The spectators' attentiveness, their smaller size, and their marginal position sustain
the charivari's invasive energy. The revelers seem not exactly to dance nor
exactly to process but to move in lively confusion appropriate to usurping
the wedding's decorum and its courtly space.[42] The stance of the first reveler directly below Fauvel mirrors Fauvel's body position as he "saut eu lit"
[jumps into bed: E 681]. Connecting the wedding night most closely to the
charivari is Fauvel's masklike horse's head. The preceding illuminations
suggest that Fauvel's representation in the charivari is not just accidentally
similar to that of the revelers. At first in BNF 146, Fauvel appears entirely
as a horse, for example when the estates are grooming his various parts;
most often he resembles a centaur, sitting on a horsey bottom but gestur-
ing and speaking with human arms and head; occasionally he has a human
body but a horse's head.[43] In the first charivari illumination, Fauvel's head
anticipates many of the masks below in its bestiality, its grotesque in-
appropriateness to a human body, and its implication that baser impulses
are having their way. At the same time, Fauvel's horse's head contrasts
with that of the only reveler shown in profile below, the last figure in the
bottom tier, whose sideways pose reveals the mask's artifice and the human

head beneath it.[44] His mask is a passing disguise under his human control; Fauvel's profiled head reveals that his bestiality is no mere mask. The repetition of Fauvel's stance in the first reveler and his profile in the last artfully conveys that the revel below imitates the marriage above, and conveys as well that the revelers, masked but still human, are more worthy occupants of courtly space than Fauvel himself.

Supplementing the illuminations' insertion of the charivari into the court's space are twelve "sotes chançons" [foolish songs] assigned to the revelers, and one long motet assigned to the women accompanying Hellekin. With the addition of these songs, the representation of charivari in BNF 146 reaches its full complexity.[45] The first large, three-tiered illumination precedes the passage describing costumes (E 697 ff.), and nine of the "sotes chançons" follow the initial account of the charivariseurs' misbehaviors (after E 720). Two small images of Hellekin and his followers accompany the next forty lines of the text, followed in midcolumn by the motet of the women accompanying him. This motet ends two leaves later with the second three-tiered illumination of the charivari proper (Figure 9), which is framed with three more "sotes chançons." The episode closes with Chaillou's assertion that "Onc chalivali si parfaiz / Par desguiser, par diz, par faiz / Ne fu com cil en toutes choses" [there was never a charivari so perfect in every way, in its disguises, its words, and its deeds: E 761–63]. Indeed this charivari is exceptional in having so many "diz" as the musical numbers provide: typically noise replaces words in this ritual, as Chaillou's own depiction at first asserts (E 705–34). The charivari's music continues the double relation to courtliness that the illuminations also reflect. In their songs, the revelers address the elite culture of the court on its own terms and in its own media, as well as moving in opposition to it.

Most of the "sotes chançons" are fragments that offer some simple inversion of a propriety. Decorum is evoked only to be affronted by farting, insults, and cacophony.[46] Two are more complex *fatrasies* that mark a turning point in that genre's history, when parodic citations of courtly lyric join up with nonsense verse. *Fatrasies* were an elite entertainment that consisted in stuffing a conventional court lyric with comically inappropriate material; despite their frequent resort to scatology, *fatrasies* entertained the Valois court one Easter as well as on more ordinary occasions.[47] The revelers' first song is an especially pointed illustration of this parodic but sophisticated reworking of courtly lyric: the *fatrasie*'s decorous courtly version appears just a few leaves earlier in the manuscript, during Fauvel's attempt to win Fortune for his wife. (Fortune, after a long lecture on her close relation to Reason and God, affiances him instead to her associate

Vaine Gloire.) This motet of a suffering lover (c. 1280), which Ernest Hoepffner traced back to the *Dit d'amour* of Nevelon Amiot, suits the elevated social milieu and the apparently refined sentiments of Fauvel's courtship.[48] By reducing this motet to comic and blasphemous nonsense, the revelers insist again, this time in a musical register, that Fauvel's behavior is actually as venal as the charivari itself.

The revelers' first "sote chançon" is an elite manipulation of an already elite exemplar that claims a space in courts for rude foolishness. The motet that Hellekin's followers sing is a more conventional insiders' performance, "highly imaginative and thoroughly charming" in the judgment of musicologist Hans Tischler, "a little masterwork that even today retains its charm."[49] It voices arguments in a Maytime debate on whether it is wise to love. Voices of "la blanche princesse," "la duchesse," "la tres noble marquise" express conventional sentiments: true love is virtuous, but the most loyal often suffer; eventually love rewards loyalty, reason, and restraint, so loving is on balance a good thing.[50] What such a motet could be doing in the middle of a charivari is an ongoing puzzle for scholars.[51] I propose that the Maytime motet situates the charivari socially, just as the figure of Hellekin situates it morally. Braying, devilish Hellekin overwhelms any sense that the charivari is a force for justice; the perfectly sophisticated motet overcomes any sense that the charivari is popular. To be sure, it wears a popular look in its disruptive upending of decorum, its initial location in the streets, and the household instruments of its paramusic (cooking pot, pestle, meathook). But the thoroughly elite project that is BNF 146 borrows all these elements considered popular for an event that moves within court circles.

Ritual Costume in *Fauvel*

If *Fauvel*'s charivari is neither popular nor aimed at justice, if it is a court event that mimics the venality of Fauvel's marriage, how does its elite location affect its meaning? What is it aiming to accomplish? This charivari's atypical emphasis on costume betrays a certain strain in fitting courtiers into rowdy, oppositional positions. They need masks not only to protect themselves from retribution but to displace them from a social identity incompatible (it would seem) with disorderly violence. Medieval elites were in fact adept at rowdiness and lawlessness in general, but the symbolic identification of rowdiness with lower social strata is no weaker for that.[52] *Fauvel*'s charivari enhances elite misbehavior by attributing a raw popular energy to it, while also preserving markers of elite status such as the *fatrasie*, the motet, and the rebec. These doubly licensed charivariseurs, powerful in their popular license and their elite status as well, express in their costumes every symbolic process of the ritual: denigration, revelry, redefinition, and transformation.

Denigration is the most obvious trajectory in the charivari and its costumes. I emphasize charivari's predilection for the carnivalesque celebration of venality, but it is also designed to shame the supposedly venal couple. The illuminations in BNF 146 denigrate this marriage by multiplying Fauvel's suspect hybridity in the revelers' costumes. The text notes their "barboeres" [bearded masks: E 741], but the illuminations show animal masks as well, and masks with prominent teeth and noses, familiar iconographic signs for enemy races and villains (Plate 3, Figure 9).[53] "Trop estoient lès et sauvages" [they were very ugly and savage: E 740] summarizes their noisy violence but could describe as well the illuminations' bared behinds, exposed undergarments, furry legs, disreputable hats, shaved fools' heads, and desecrated monks' robes.[54] One reveler wears a woman's face with a wimple but with masculine leggings, adding sex to the incongruous mixtures that others accomplish by combining tunics with fur, or topping human clothes with a bestial head. These costumes represent denigration in process by mixing more with less dignified elements. One of the "sotes chançons," "Nous ferons des prelaz gorpiz et des larrons mestres" [we will make foxes of the prelates and masters of the thieves], similarly articulates denigration as a transformation from high to low, or a transgression from low into high.[55] All this abasing hybridity ridicules a king made of a horse as well that horse-king's venal marriage.

Revelry aligns this charivari's denigrations to carnival rather than to judicious protest. The revelers respond to Fauvel's indecency with exaggerated indecencies of their own, not with didactic satire. Their noisy excess, disruption, and bodily indulgence fit Bakhtin's classic definition of carnival.[56] These open, overflowing bodies "n'avoient pas les bouches closes / De bien crier et de fort braire" [didn't close their mouths to shouting well and braying loudly: E 764–65]. For Bakhtin, carnival could only be a popular protest against official culture, but this charivari fits the wider range of possibilities now granted to carnival. Parodic laughter, which was for Bakhtin popular laughter, drives the courtly *fatrasies* the revelers perform, and their verbal inversions find material expression in masking as animals, fools, women, and other inferiors. The revelers' hybrid presentation asserts disharmony and complexity within Fauvel's own milieu, but the pleasure of displacement exceeds all its plausible motives. If mocking Fauvel were the revelers' only goal, a Fauvel disguise would suffice, as for the many children who masked as Richard Nixon on the Halloween nearest his downfall.[57] The variety, playfulness, and transgressiveness of *Fauvel*'s costumes surpass instrumentality to pursue the wider pleasures Needham notes when "people . . . turn their classifications upside down or disintegrate them entirely."

Redefinition is, nonetheless, one trajectory in this revel, and it too is visible in the intensely metaphorical costumes. A ritual process strikes metaphoric connections in order to express and work through a problem. In court Maying and in its poetry, for example, women are said to be flowers in order to redefine the problem of sexual restraint as a source of pleasure. The flower gets metaphoric energy from its displacement to femininity, and ultimately it can become a sexual fetish (see Chapter 2). In *Fauvel*'s charivari, the problem is corrupted power. Fauvel embodies inferior desires usurping the human soul and upending the social order in which animals should serve humans. To quote J. C. Crocker on ritual masks, the revelers' masked displacements toward bestiality are a "physical emblematizing of verbal metaphor," the metaphor that corrupted power is bestial.[58] The revelers are not simply reveling; their counter-representation of Fauvel's marriage redefines it from the participants' point of view in contrast to the sanction of the celebration and of Fauvel's own authority.[59] In their surrender to baseness, the revelers represent what has happened to kingship in its alliance with vainglory. But their redefinition seems to drive only their wild revel, not a solacing social transformation.

Transformation of the marriage is not available to charivari, any more than carnival can transform Lent, but in *Fauvel*'s charivari the participants do transform themselves. In every culture, masking is associated with transformation, whether that involves leaving one spiritual plane for another, or one social status for another, or just playfully one persona for another. Medieval Christianity was especially hostile to masking because classical and pagan practices of masking to make contact with the gods were still uncomfortably proximate. Christianity's perfectly just universe should obviate any need for humans to influence or interrogate the divinity.[60] Over the centuries, the Christian church has approved masking only for a few crucial transformations (e.g., winding sheet, wedding veil). The persistent power of masking is evident, however, in the medieval church's continual prohibitions and its oft-repeated argument that masking is dangerous and sinful, an argument compactly expressed in the double meanings of *larva* [mask/demon] and *masca* [mask/evil spirit].[61] Compared to sacramental transformations, those of secular masking may be small and fleeting, but they take some substance from the deep-rooted cultural and religious belief that a physical transformation can invoke or manifest a metaphysical one. Masking remains dangerous because it opens the hidden self to substantial change.

That is, rather than just concealing identity (as a robber's bandana would), the masks and costumes of *Fauvel*'s charivari provide courtiers with a new identity from which they can talk back to the court. The revelers sing in courtly genres and situate themselves in courtly space, but for the time of performance, they set themselves against the court by displacing the social position grounded in their known faces and practiced self-depictions. A distinctive feature of this transformation is that it does not turn on unmasking, an important trajectory in chivalric disguise (Chapter 4) and in the court mummings to be discussed later in this chapter. Unmasking is a diachronic process that transfers masked behaviors back to the unmasked self: the Knight of the Lion's exploits belong to Ywain once it is clear who the Knight of the Lion was. In *Fauvel*, the work of masking is synchronic rather than sequential. The bestiality and vulgarity of the adopted disguise overcome the constraints inherent in courtly subservience to sovereignty, without quite erasing the privileged access to courtly forms in which the revelers register their mockery. Their masked identities are doubly hybrid, imitating Fauvel's allegorical doubleness (from upper to lower body) but also superimposing new features over their prior ones. The text recounts the revelers' appearance in terms of this latter doubling:

> Li uns ont ce devant darriere
> Vestuz et mis leur garnemenz;
> Li autre ont fait leur paremenz
> De groz saz et de froz a moinnes.
> L'en en congneüst un a poinnes,
> Tant estoient tains et deffais. (E 698–703)

[Some had put on and arranged their garments inside out; others had adorned themselves in big sacks and monks' robes. They could hardly recognize one another, they were so stained and abased.]

They can "hardly" recognize each other; they have changed but not completely. This layering revises the participants' identity, if only for the moment of performance. Harsher, ruder, louder than their quotidian selves, these costumed courtiers have a fine time wreaking havoc in their own home.

In summary, the displacements these costumes choose, downward trajectories toward inferior status, are appropriate to denigration, to revelry, and to redefining an irregular marriage; in addition, they constitute an elite poaching on social and natural terrain that lies outside courts. Drawn into this court performance, the costumes' inferior elements transform identity, if only for the moment, in substantial compensation for the ritual's inability to transform the irregular marriage itself.

January 1393: Court Charivari and Interlude

Mesire Chaillou's elite poaching adumbrates historical moments in later fourteenth-century courts. The Abbé de Choisy's *Histoire de Charles VI* cites a source now lost for a 1389 charivari at the remarriage of Queen Isabeau's lady-in-waiting Catherine. The queen's officers attacked the revelers and beat her husband, not recognizing him among the other troublemakers.[62] Eustache Deschamps devotes one of his verse letters to recounting an all-night harassment similar to charivari at the Château de Beauté. Several courtiers (among them "madamoiselle de Dreux, / Madame des Bordes aussi") banged on the couple's door, made various kinds of racket, sang bawdy songs, and got a little page to imitate a tournament herald by shouting "faictes vo devoir" [do your duty] to the beleaguered husband. Deschamps praises their efforts with the flagrant double entendre of "villenie," vulgar status and vulgar behavior rolled into one: "que nulle ne die / Ce ne soit gieux sanz villenie" [may none say these are not vulgar tricks].[63] Borrowing lowness for their playful assault on marriage links Deschamps's courtiers to Charles VI and five companions who dressed as wild men in January 1393 at a banquet celebrating Catherine de Fastavarin's third marriage. This Catherine is the same favored lady-in-waiting whose second marriage Isabeau arranged in 1389; for all three of her weddings the queen provided trousseaus and sponsored festivities.[64] The wild men's antics at Catherine's wedding feast find a place in chronicles, most notably Jean Froissart's *Chroniques* and the *Chronique du Religieux de Saint-Denys*, because four of the men died when a torch ignited their pitch-and-flax disguises; a fifth had the presence of mind to throw himself into a tub of water for rinsing dishes. Charles alone did not catch fire. On these details and the names of the participants the chronicles agree, although they differ on many other points.[65]

An illumination from Philippe de Commines's fifteenth-century copy of Froissart's *Chroniques* (Plate 4) can briefly introduce both the performance and its terrible end.[66] Musicians play in the gallery, costumed men jump about, seated and standing spectators look on almost as if the dance

had not yet gone wrong. The flames on the costumes curl out not so differently from the greenish flax representing wild hair, and the barking lap-
dog seems as likely to be threatening the disguised intruders into courtly
space as to be sounding an alarm at the fire. Disaster is of course obvious
not only in the flames but in the onlookers' helpless handwringing, the tub
of water where one man saves himself, and the fallen clubs that represented
the wild men's uncultured violence. But the image seems to preserve a
prior moment as well. The burning men's diverse, leaping poses resemble
those in the *Fauvel* illuminations of charivari, and the men's bared teeth
recall masks of the kind the *Fauvel* revelers wear. Close inspection reveals
that the wild men wear not the "barboeres" of *Fauvel* but brown half-
masks together with bushy false beards and hair to match the greenish
color of their tight costumes. Those teeth are their own, grimacing in pain,
but the grimaces themselves are uncannily appropriate to the wild disguises, as the dog's bared teeth emphasize. Through these details the illuminator conveys something of the performance that preceded the fire. One
man's attempt to tear off his costume even records that it was stitched in
place when he donned it, rather than buttoned, so as better to resemble
real skin.[67] In conjoining earlier and later moments, the illuminator may
mean their relation to be no more than sequential, or there may be a causal
implication like that between the wild man's lust and his death by fire in
the illustration to an Alexander romance (Figure 10). There the wild man

Figure 10. *Le Livre et la vraye hystoire du bon roy Alixandre*. London, British
Library, MS Royal 20 B.xx, fol. 64. By permission of the British Library.

appears twice, in mirror relation to himself, first reaching out for a naked woman that Alexander's men are offering to him as experimental bait, and then toppling into a fire as Alexander's men execute him for his failure to behave in a civilized manner.[68] In the Froissart illumination, the overlap of wild dancing and painful writhing may imply a similarly causal relation between the two moments.

The chronicles of Jean Froissart and Michel Pintoin (the Religieux de Saint Denis) are close to the event, and I credit all their details, even when they conflict, insofar as they represent what seemed plausible to Froissart and Pintoin in the kind of performance they are narrating. Neither says he was present at the event; Froissart wrote his account four to six years later and Pintoin wrote about ten years later.[69] For Pintoin, the event was a reprehensible charivari; for Froissart, it was a welcome interlude at the wedding feast.

Since my preoccupation is with the performance itself rather than its catastrophic end, I will review the chroniclers' interpretations of that end only briefly. Pintoin's chronicle is deeply committed to the supremacy of church over state, to a hierarchical social model that the king defends, and to the common good over private interests.[70] On all counts, Pintoin objects to Charles VI's performance: it mocks a sanctioned marriage, involves the king in base behavior, and breaks all the rules of social decorum ["jura omnia moresque honesti"]. In short, "humani generis adversarius ad interitum eorum preparaverat insidias" [the enemy of the human race must have laid this ambush to destroy them]. Nonetheless, with the help of a guardian angel and divine grace ["angelica cooperante custodia et divina gracia mediante"], the king was held apart from his companions at the crucial moment when a spectator accidentally inflamed the costumes.[71] Pintoin organizes the event's evil end around one participant, Hugh de Guisay, who had the perversity of treating his servants and peasants as beasts, making them get on all fours and bark, or riding and spurring them like horses. Nobles rejoiced at his agonizing death, and commons along the route taken by his coffin called out "Bark, dog!" in mockery of his old commands.[72] Pintoin does not articulate the connection, but an implicit analogy links the courtiers' mimicry of wild men to the bestial mimicry Hugh forced on his people, imputing the wrongful abasement in both cases to Hugh's wickedness. Charles gets angelic aid, but the base sexuality of the other dancers is suitably punished as the fire burns its way down their bodies "quod genitalia cum virgis virilibus frustratim cadencia sanguine madefacerent pavimentum" [so that their genitals and penises, falling into pieces, drenched the floor in blood].[73]

Froissart throws a warmer glow of pathos and misfortune around the event. It was an "esbatement," an amusement, designed by Hugh de Guisay as part of the wedding-night festivities. Yvain, bastard son of Gaston Fébus, attempted to guard against torches being brought near the flammable costumes, but Louis d'Orléans carelessly ignited one of them. Four others caught fire, but the king had moved toward the ladies, as his youth inspired him ["ainsi que jeunesse le portoit"]. The duchess of Berry had detained him, demanding his name, and when the fire broke out she covered him with her long gown ["elle le bouta dessoubs sa gonne et le couvry pour eschiever le feu"]. Yvain dies crying out "save the king!" and the unhappy adventure ["ceste pesme et doulente aventure"] ends with Louis's long apology. For Froissart, youth replaces Pintoin's evil inspirations and guardian angel as the agent of events. Youth pushed Louis to carelessness just as it pushed the king toward the ladies, and it inspired the "esbatement" in the first place: the king was behaving too youthfully ["trop jeunement se mainenoit"]; he should leave his youthful idleness ["jeunes huiseuses"] for behavior more suited to his station.[74] Peter Ainsworth argues compellingly that the episode culminates a large narrative pattern counterbalancing the promise and the folly implicit in youth, as well as a pattern of "tragic retribution" leading from Gaston Fébus's murder of his own heir to Yvain's selfless death.[75]

Froissart's injudicious "esbatement" suits his secular interpretation that youthful folly blasts the promise of youth; Pintoin's immoral charivari fits his theological argument that sinful corruption calls forth heavenly intervention on the king's behalf. On the details of the performance, the two accounts are in better agreement. The six young men wear tight-fitting cloth garments on which a coat of pitch affixes strands of teased-out flax, to imitate thick body hair. Froissart notes twice that the costumed men are so hairy from head to foot ["du chief jusques à la plante du piet"] that no one can recognize them; Pintoin adds masks to the hairy body costumes ["cum larvis facies abscondissent"].[76] The wild men enter the hall of the king's Hôtel de Saint-Paul, where the wedding celebration already involves masking and dancing ["on danssa et mena grant revel"; "omnes, breviloquio utens, cum mimis et instrumentis musicis usque ad noctis medium tripudiendo choreas continuaverunt"].[77] Pintoin says the wild men dance "choreas sarracenicas," probably a Latin equivalent for the court dance called *moresque*, but their version of the dance is infernal ["instinctu dyabolico agitati"].[78] They run here and there making gross gestures and imitating the horrible howls of wolves ["gestus deformiores huc illucque discurrendo ceperunt exercere, et tandem more lupino horrissonis vocibus ululantes"].[79] Pintoin means his dancers to match the behavior of charivariseurs, who he says attack a widow's remarriage by wearing disguises, acting immodestly, and insulting the couple in all sorts of ways.[80] Froissart's tamer "esbatement" centers on disguise and discovery; Charles leads the other five men, who are chained together and presumably move or dance in imitation of wild men.[81]

It is impossible to recover whether this event was intended as a charivari or an interlude consonant with other wedding festivities. At the least, Pintoin believed that charivari was in the repertoire of fourteenth-century courtiers.[82] A charivari on this occasion would have been peculiarly divisive, setting the king directly against the queen (sponsor of the marriage) and even against his own part in the wedding arrangements (he himself sponsored the fesitivities, according to both chroniclers). Misogyny is no stranger to courts, but mocking Catherine's remarriage would seem flatly irreconcilable with the other revels that followed the wedding. Given these counterindications, and this chapter's focus on charivari above, I will concentrate on Froissart's account, which introduces a new context for court wildness.

Froissart's version of the event is less a culturally recognized ritual (like charivari) than an improvised theatrical performance. Many contrasts between ritual and theater distinguish charivaris from interludes: the latter do not seek to transform a wrong condition, to invoke or even refer to transcendent forces, or to be stable repeatable events, collectively created in community tradition. Interludes, however, share more with ritual and ceremony than with play. They are designed to celebrate festivals, they assume a participatory audience rather than an audience of passive observers, and they contribute to the festival's goals—consolidating a host's dominant position, making a nationalist statement to foreign visitors, celebrating a religious holiday or a wedding.[83] Finally, interludes celebrate stratification: like entries, coronations, and tournaments, they are condensed, intensified enactments of elite superiority. The substantial social meaning inherent in interludes makes all the more puzzling what Charles VI and his companions could have meant by dressing as wild men, if their performance was indeed an interlude, as Froissart claims.

The only clue to the event's meaning on which every chronicle concurs is the disguise itself. Wild men and women have several important resonances for late medieval courts. First, their naked hairiness stands in defining opposition to dress. In travel and adventure narratives, wild men and women often reside beyond the fringes of Europe, but they can also be nearby inhabitants of the deep woods, as the Middle English term "wodewose" denotes.[84] In both cases, to be wild is to be beyond civilized constraint, a fundamental trait that suits wild men to carnivalesque disruptiveness.[85] Further, a teleology of wildness and civilization associates wildness with youth, and civilization with maturity. Lost children can grow up wild: Tristan de Nanteuil, Valentine's brother Orson, and Elias are wild men of the woods who later become accomplished knights.[86] Louise Fradenberg has anlayzed James VI's tournament disguise as a Wild Knight in these terms, as "the story of the king's own emergence from wildness"; his tournament "is a way of taking leave of the joys of a violent, rebellious, wild past."[87] Froissart seems especially attuned to the anteriority of wild men in his repeated claims that the king's youth motivated his participation.

A salient expression of wild men's uncivilized state is their uncontrolled sexuality. Hayden White argues that "desire incarnate . . . without even consciousness of sin" is a medieval contribution to the wild man's difference from civilized humans.[88] In the episode from Alexander's history (Figure 10), the wild man's unfettered sexuality is his pivotal strangeness, the one determining his death. Froissart's version of wild sexuality is less aggressive, in that Charles VI approaches the ladies of the court just to show himself off. His heterosexual display recalls the familiar medieval topos that women can tame the sexuality of wild men, transforming them from their purely erotic state into the obedient suitors of conventional courtliness.[89] Although this topos endorses domestication and self-control, it also imagines a prior time of engaging wild sexuality directly, a titillating encounter between the civilized woman and the still wild man. Charles dances that encounter for the ladies of the court, and then experiences a kind of domestication with the duchess of Berry, who first constrains him and demands his name, then protects him under her skirts from fire.[90] Well might Pintoin have preferred a guardian angel to this emasculating rescue! The Harley manuscript's illumination (Plate 4) captures the passive subjection Froissart exacts as the price of Charles's survival. As the other wild men meet their terrible fate, Charles's upturned face, outstretched hand, and one bare foot are just visible from within the duchess's sheltering embrace. In the text, the duchess extends her domestication by directing the king to go change his clothes and console the queen. Charles's submission to the duchess and the queen expiates or at least mitigates the transgressive sexuality the young men endorsed by dressing as wild men.

When wildness is nearby rather than exotic, humans can slide in and out of it. Lovers like Tristan may go wild with grief and take to the woods, and rulers like Nebuchadnezzar may go mad and live like beasts.[91] It is tempting to connect the wild men of January 1393 to Charles VI's attacks of madness. His first attack preceded the wedding celebration by a few months, in May 1392, and the second followed it in June 1393. His symptoms included fearful delusions, violence toward his followers, and destruction of his clothing.[92] Some historians conjecture that Charles "lost the remains of his feeble wits" when the wild men burned before his eyes, but no medieval chronicler connects the episode to Charles's failing health.[93] An appealing conjecture, no more than that, might be that dressing as a wild man seemed to Charles an effective way to redefine his one preceding episode of madness, now in the past. Transforming his real behavior into symbolic behavior, he could be acknowledging his madness but also asserting his control over it. There are better indications, however, that the wild men of 1393 were meant to represent not madmen but a strange people: they constitute a band (whereas madmen of the woods are solitary), they look alike, and they are purposeful and communicative, not unaware and confused. All in all, mystery and sexuality, rather than madness, govern their representation.

The strangeness of wild people has at the same time a certain familiarity that distinguishes them from Moors and monopods. Whether they are from Asia or the woods down the road, their difference is not that between cultures but between any culture and none. Wild men and women are stripped of all culture, and as such are mirror images of courtiers minus language, religion, chivalry, courtesy, and clothing. Their uncivilized status is in tension with the context of a court festival. Richard Bernheimer therefore calls Charles's disguise "outright treason to the knightly ideal"; Fradenberg's subtler analysis of wild disguises notes "court culture's intense preoccupation with the mannering of the body and its perhaps equally intense nostalgia for the bodily 'freedom' thus sacrificed."[94] Sacrifice and loss offer a significantly different optic on the dance of wild men than a carnivalesque release of suppressed energy. The difference is between wanting to recover something from without and wanting to release something from within. Although it might appear, particularly within the history of carnival justifications, that Charles and his companions are letting out their suppressed wildness, they might instead be attempting to restore a loss, to reverse a sacrifice, by impersonating what they were "before" they were courtiers. Given that Froissart's disguising is meant, not as a hostile disruption to a wedding but as a celebratory contribution, the wild dance may represent not an overpowering wildness that threatens the court but a fictive recovery of wildness that actually enhances courtly status. As for Maying, the model of the supplement seems right to me: the wild costume adds a dimension to the courtier's identity, but the act of adding it betrays that the courtier's identity has been incomplete until now.

For this model of the disguising to work, the dynamic between masking and unmasking would be essential, and Froissart pepares for that dynamic as the king moves toward the ladies "pour luy monstrer" [to show himself] although he "ne se vouloit nommer" [did not want to name himself].[95] The distinction between appearance and name creates a tension between them that the performance should engage. In Froissart's syntax, both Charles's costume and his name are reflexive properties of "himself" ["luy," "se"], but they are disunited in the space of performance. The duchess catches Charles's hand "par esbatement," through the same playful spirit that names the event itself, indicating that her insistence on his name is appropriate to the event's dynamic. Discovering the king, either naming or unmasking him, will catch up wildness within his already established courtliness.

These six dancers demonstrate the category-busting potential of play that Don Handelman notes in his study of Christmas mummers in Newfoundland. In that wild mumming, as in Froissart's, "the power of the idea of play is in its capacities for dissolution."[96] The dancers' intimidating strangeness and rude undress, together with their desire to be recognized in their strangeness and rudeness, are their means of reaching outward for sources of energy that are normally prohibited to them. Their interlude surpasses play through its affiliation to a court wedding, a ritual that substantially transforms sexual status. Performing wild sexuality both complements marriage's invitation to sex and counterbalances marriage's constraints on sex. By hitching their performance to a marriage, the wild dancers imply that ritual precedent for fusing wild and elite identities can be found in the sexual license and constraint that marriage so potently combines.

This short, wordless performance may seem to share little with the Christmas interlude in *Sir Gawain and the Green Knight*, but the Green Knight figures in a purely fantastic register what Froissart's courtiers desire. The Green Knight is superlatively wild and courtly by turns, and even simultaneously. The wonder of his wildness, together with Bertilak's subtler version of it, elaborate the late-medieval fascination with how wildness might supplement courtliness.

The Green Knight's Challenge: Can Wildness Be Courtly?

The Christmas festivities that open *Sir Gawain and the Green Knight* play on the interdependence of literary tradition and historical imitation. As in contemporary courts, music, dancing, gift exchanges, and feasting prepare for an interlude that engages courtiers in more substantial self-definition, while maintaining the festive mood. Arthur "at hert hade wonder" after the Green Knight's imponderable performance, but he attributes his wonder to theatrical craft: "Wel bycommes such craft upon Cristmasse," Arthur explains, "Laykyng of enterludez [playing of interludes], to laȝe and to syng, / Among þise kynde caroles [seemly dance-songs] of knyȝtez and ladyez."[97] Reducing the Green Knight's bloody beheading to just a festive interlude beats a retreat from Arthur's earlier desire for "sum aventurus þyng," such as a challenger demanding "sum siker knyȝt / To joyne wyth hym in justyng, in jopardé to lay, / Lede, lif for lyf" [some true knight to joust with him, in jeopardy to lay life for life: 93, 96–98]. Arthur's proposal that the interlude was not a magical wonder but a crafted pleasure claims that its terror is manageable if he can get its genre right: his is a first effort to deflect Morgan's desire "your wyttez to reve [take away], / For to haf greved Gaynour and gart [caused] hir to dyȝe." (2459–60) But in fact this interlude draws on both sources of power, the magical and the ludic; it resembles the wonders that interrupt the feasts of romance but it also recalls historical interludes' comparatively earthbound effects. The Green Knight is similarly suspended between portentious wonder and festive materiality, figuring in himself the attempt historical interludes make to mystify the noble life.

From the earliest twelfth-century romances, Arthur's Pentecost feast tends to attract alien, distressed, or threatening visitors who draw knights into adventures. The *Livre de Caradoc*, the *Alliterative Morte Arthure*, and Chaucer's *Squire's Tale* continue the visits; Malory's angry, pleading, and warning interrupters of feasts carry thirteenth-century examples into the fifteenth. Historical interludes strive to capture these interruptions' wonders. The gift of the flying brass horse in the *Squire's Tale* could be the model for several mechanical "entremets" at Philip of Burgundy's 1454 banquet, as described by Mathieu d'Escouchy: "Apprès, par le plus hault de la salle, parti d'un bout un dragon tout ardant, lequel vola la plus part de la longueur de la salle, en l'air, et passa tout oultre les gens, que nul ne sceut qu'il devint" [Then, from the highest part of the hall, a dragon all enflamed appeared from one corner and flew most of the length of the hall, in the air, and passed beyond everyone such that none knew what had

become of it].[98] Escouchy's account values the illusions' mystery rather
than attempting to provide explanations. His "nul ne sceut qu'il devint"
perpetuates enigma as do the two departures of the Green Knight: "To
quat kyth he becom [what land he went] knwe non þere" (460; cf.
2477–78). Aurelius's brother in the *Franklin's Tale* shows a similar appreciation for banquet illusions:

> For ofte at feestes have I wel herd seye
> That tregetours, withinne an halle large,
> Have made come in a water and a barge,
> And in the halle rowen up and doun. (F 1142–46)

Charles V of France presented roughly this illusion to Emperor Charles
IV at a banquet in January 1378. The *Chronique de Charles V* praises how
lightly the false boat moved, just as if it were floating on water, and how
vividly the ensuing action depicted Godfrey of Bouillon's conquest of
Jerusalem.[99] The chronicle's illumination (Figure 11) echoes the text's appreciation for illusion by floating the boat on what appear to be real waves,
though without color, breaking into the frame of the hall from somewhere
exterior to it. The mast of the boat fuses into the picture's frame, or more
accurately the frame fuses with the mast and enters the boat along with it,
doubly supporting Godfrey's banner at the mast's top. These visual signs
that the boat is an illusion signal as well that the mayhem to the right of
the banquet table is another stage effect.

Charles V's interlude may have had an element of challenge, according
to Laura Hibbard Loomis: Charles himself was considering a crusade in
these years, influenced by his friend and counselor Philippe de Mézières.
He may have been urging the idea to Charles IV by dramatizing Godfrey's
international effort (his banner is flanked in the illumination by those of
England, Flanders, and Jerusalem).[100] At Philip of Burgundy's more overtly
challenging banquet, the crusading vows of a hundred knights were sworn
on a live pheasant. So many knights wanted to record their oaths that some
had to be put off until the following day.[101] "The Vows of the Heron" (1338)
attributes the Hundred Years War to a French knight's banquet insult:
Robert of Artois carries a roasted heron into Edward III's hall, accompanied by minstrels and singers, and presents the heron to Edward with
the explanation that the most cowardly of birds is an appropriate dish
for a king so cowardly that he will not seize his own heritage in France. In
response, Edward III and many followers swear on the heron to devastate
France.[102] At a feast for the knighting of his heir in 1306, Edward I swore
on two swans ornamented with gold to avenge the death of Comyn, and

many other knights followed his example.[103] Perhaps most like the Green
Knight's challenge is Lodewij van Velthem's account of Edward I's marriage banquet in the *Spiegel historiael* (1316). A series of costumed visitors
from the age of Arthur interrupt the feasting, accuse Edward's courtiers of
cowardice, and press them to take revenge on the Welsh until the king and
knights agree to do so.[104] Van Velthem's accuracy is more suspect than that
of other chroniclers, but they concur that an appropriate kind of interlude
engages courtiers in responding to challenges, and binds them with oaths
that may have long consequences.

Figure 11. *Chronique de Charles V*. Paris, Bibliothèque nationale de France, MS
français 2813, fol. 473, verso. Cliché Bibliothèque nationale de France, Paris.

In an amusing *mise en abime* of these contemporary restagings, the Gawain poet imitates them in turn, while also restoring them to the magical register. The Green Knight's visit to Arthur's court draws on the literary premise that important challenges mark important feasts, the very premise for historical imitations of literary challenges. Victoria Weiss points out that the Green Knight's timely entrance between first and second courses and the intensely visual impact of his performance recall historical interludes; Carl Lindahl finds traces of mumming in the Green Knight's initial silence, and the recollection of a stage trick in noting just before the beheading that the Green Knight is "herre þen ani in þe hous by þe hed and more" [taller than anyone in the household by a head and more: 333].[105] If that line does refer to the stage trick for beheading giant adversaries (cutting off an artificial head worn atop the performer's own), I would say the reminiscence works not to deflate this scene's magic but to celebrate poetry's power to invent an imposing adversary that historical performance could only fake.

One further way in which historical interludes inform the Green Knight's performance is its emphasis on clothing. In the illumination from the *Chronique de Charles V* (Figure 11), costume is important to distinguishing diners from crusaders, and crusaders from Saracen defenders (who have stained brown faces and turbanlike cloths wrapped around their helmets). Among the crusaders, Godfrey of Bouillon's leadership is evident in the repetition of his arms on the leading crusader's surcoat and the boat's most prominent banner: his sign frames the event from left and right. The diners are also costumed in the regalia of their offices; the repetition of Charles V's fleur-de-lis robe in the wall hangings behind him not only picks him out as the host and the king but also provides a visual analogy between himself and the celebrated Godfrey, the only other figure whose arms repeat themselves in the scene. Godfrey's arms frame the table, and Charles's focus the table on himself. The artist's implication is that Godfrey's heroism accrues to his descendant Charles, who may further link himself to Godfrey by undertaking a new crusade. The meanings of costume are less evident in *Sir Gawain*, where in Larry Benson's phrase "everything is obvious but the solution."[106] Still, the Green Knight's costume should be readable, if his appearance is meant to recall an interlude, in which costume is an important aspect of performance.

The oft-noted tensions in the Green Knight's appearance—between monstrousness and manliness, threat and restraint, wildness and ornament, strangeness and familiarity—contribute to that effect Arthur experiences as wonder and critics as ambiguity or undecidability. The Green Knight's horse can speak to these unresolved tensions. The knight's horse is his complement in many ways: in color, in exceptional size and power, in the splash of red sparks he throws back at his departure like a memory of blood and holly berries. The horse's trappings are as embroidered, enameled, and bejeweled as the knight's clothing, but it is particularly the hair of each creature that is juxtaposed: "Wel gay watz þis gome gered in grene, / And þe here of his hed of his hors swete" [right handsome was this knight dressed in green, and the hair of his head was in suit with his horse's: 179–80]. *Swete* later describes the consonance of the courtiers' dress with Gawain's, when all adopt the green baldric "for sake of þat segge, in swete to were" [for the sake of that man, to wear it in suit: 2518]. It connotes a close alliance, a standing together. How might the horse's hair be "in swete" with the knight's? The much-noted ambiguity of the Green Knight's hair and his bush-like beard trimmed to resemble a "kyngez capados" seems to leave comparison with the horse for a sartorial simile, but immediately again the relation of the man's and the beast's hair is noted ("Þe mane of þat mayn hors much to hit lyke": 186–87). This relation can resolve a bit of the ambiguity in the knight's appearance, in that we have no trouble iden-tifying the horse's hair with his prior nature and its trimming with just this performance, for which it is "Wel cresped an cemmed [curled and combed], wyth knottes ful mony" (188). If the man's and the horse's hair are truly comparable, both should be imagined as uncivilized, natural features that have been contained and made elegant for their court appearance. Several more lines on the managing of mane and tail reinforce this history: the ani-mal's hair, twisted up with gold thread and then bound in green bands set with stones that are themselves tied with a thong in an intricate knot hung with golden bells, could hardly be more elaborately contained (189–95). In light of this passage's alignment of knight and horse, the knight's appear-ance too should be read as the containment of a prior wildness, a carapace of elegance strapped on all but his bristling brows and rolling red eyes.

    In the long aftermath John Spiers's "anthropological approach" to *Sir Gawain*, the critical currents have flowed hard against seeing any rela-tion between the Green Knight and wild men, green men, vegetation gods, anything woodsy.[107] Searching for avatars beyond the work's own cultural context is obviously mistaken. But wild men have extensive representation in court arts, in contrast to the other sources that have been suggested for the Green Knight: green devils, Celtic fairies, and "green men" attributed to folk rituals and perhaps represented in foliate heads.[108] Commonplaces about wild men do inform the Green Knight, although his wildness works very differently than in other court performances this chapter has examined.

Wild men and women appear frequently in medieval court interlude, tournament, royal entry, dance, charivari, manuscript illumination, and even sartorial ornament: a cape made for the dauphin around 1349 was embroidered with maidens emerging from a castle to joust with wild men; Edward III had a velvet robe embroidered with blue garters and "wode-woses."[109] *Wynnere and Wastoure* imagines "ane hathell . . . Wroghte als a wodwyse alle in wrethyn lokkes" [a nobleman dressed as a wild man all in tangled locks] as a kind of champion or guardian of the king's pavilion; the wild man wears a helmet trimmed with a gold leopard crest and the royal arms.[110] Preceding sections of this chapter have detailed further ways in which wild men are plausible referents for the Green Knight's size, boldness, violence, connections to nature, and general strangeness. His color as well, although I will argue below for its wider reference to nature, could refer to wild men: their hairy bodies are sometimes greenish (Plate 4), and they sometimes wear leaves and twists of vine. To be sure, in the Green Knight's performance, wildness is radically transformed. In Chaillou's charivari and Froissart's dance of 1393, wildness is a risky enterprise. Adopted just for brief performances, wildness has a clearly transgressive, riotous quality that supplements courtly decorum but retains as well a certain incompatibility with it.

In striking contrast, the Green Knight has stabilized wildness inside courtliness. His dress, demeanor, physique, and speech are impeccable, and because they are so perfectly accomplished, his "wild" size, greenness, and fierceness make him more intimidating than all the wolves and worms and "wodwos" Gawain battles on his journey (720–23). The Green Knight is not less worthy than other courtiers for his wildness; indeed, he claims to be much worthier: he is a man to these "berdlez chylder," he disputes their reputation as "burnes best . . . Stifest under stel-gere," and he enjoys the ability to survive his own beheading (259–60, 280). As befits an interlude, the locus for expressing this wild courtliness is the knight's visual appearance, his clothed body over which the poem hovers for so many lines. Beyond the performance itself, he still holds wildness inside knighthood: he came from somewhere, he leaves for somewhere, he reappears somewhere else. Here again, as in the beheading's allusion to stage trickery, the poet evokes a staged interlude partly for the effect of flying free of it, to achieve in poetry the perfect incorporation of wildness that is so paradoxical and transient for historical knights.

The Green Knight's powerful stasis of wildness in courtliness contrasts with the transgression and revelry that wild men represent in other court performances. A few critics have argued that the Green Knight's game, his

rudeness, and his beheading recall carnival's violent iconoclasm.[111] On the
contrary, his game rejects the freedom of carnival inversions and revelry. In
Handelman's analysis, game is a "domestication of the ideation of play. . . .
Within it, the flux of play is harnessed to orders of cosmos and world,
often as a metaphor for regularity."[112] The Green Knight's game, as the rest
of the poem makes clear, is just such a modeling of the already established
order, a test of chivalry's and courtesy's most fundamental demands. His
challenge, though rudely intoned, asks the court to match its high reputation for merit, not to overturn it. The courtiers do seem to make a ghoul-
ish mockery of the knight's severed head, kicking it about as Londoners are
said to have kicked about Archbishop Sudbury's head in the Rising of
1381.[113] But the Green Knight simply ignores the court's mockery, if it is
that, and turns his severed head right back to the business of Gawain's
pledge. In his vivid theatricality and his capacity to perform courtliness
while remaining imponderable to the court, the Green Knight is a "mer-
vayl among þo menne," not an iconoclast (466). Indeed, his contained
wildness turns out to offer a model from which Gawain and his fellows
might learn a superior courtliness.

This didactic aspect of wildness is less visible in current critical writing on *Sir Gawain* than the didacticism of its vernacular theology. Throughout the Gawain poet's works, as Elizabeth Kirk notes, "the chivalric ethos
and especially the image of aristocratic life in the household of a great
lord provide an illuminating metaphor for the ethical and religious life."[114]
Much of Gawain's experience weaves the language of sin and penance
together with the language of nurture and social duty: "He cared for his
cortaysye, lest crabayn he were, / And more for his meschef 3if he schulde
make synne, / And be traytor to þat tolke þat þat telde a3t" [he was concerned for his courtesy, lest he appear boorish, and more for his hurt if he
should fall into sin, and betray the trust of the lord of the house: 1773–
75]. The risk of "synne" is more compelling than the risk of boorishness,
but the two can be voiced together, and betraying a host's confidence is
just as serious as "synne" itself. It is a tribute to the poem's success at inte-
grating Christian and courtly values, at least on a figurative level, that their
incompatibilities rarely surface, but the mere presence of theological concerns in the poem has tended to press critical readings in orthodox directions. In important contrast, Nicholas Watson details the concessions that
theology makes to lay values in order to spiritualize courtliness throughout the Cotton Nero manuscript: "Focusing not on his sources' emphasis
on the inner life nor on their devotionalism but on their use of the *rhetoric*
of purity, their spiritualised aestheticism, this writer sought to undo the

theological system which consigned his lay readers to the status of *medi-ocriter boni*, and make them equal to contemplatives in the acceptability of their lives to God."[115] The Green Knight plunders that rhetoric of purity in absolving Gawain at their second encounter: "Þou art confessed so clene, beknowen of þy mysses, / And hatz þy penaunce apert of þe poynt of myn egge, / I halde þe polysed of þat plyȝt" [you have confessed so cleanly, acknowledging your faults, and have taken your penance plainly at the point of my blade, that I hold you cleansed of that offence: 2391–93]. Gawain's unflinching courage as the axe's third blow cuts him is the chivalric substitute for fifty Pater Nosters. To be sure, the Green Knight's rhetoric of penance is metaphorical, but it does dignify Gawain's lay chivalry with a sacramental analogy. The Gawain poet's tailoring of spirituality to fit a beheading game, remarkable in its own right, prepares for an even less spiritual, more earthbound commitment to what the Green Knight calls love of life.

When Gawain leaps back from the Green Knight's third blow and fiercely, fearlessly forbids him to strike again, "in hert hit hym lykez": the Green Knight approves it in his heart (2335). He explains that Gawain was disloyal to conceal the green girdle, but his love for his life mitigates the lack:

> Bot here yow lakked a lyttel, sir, and lewté yow wonted [did not show fidelity];
> Bot þat watz for no wylyde werke [fine crafting], ne wowyng [seduction] nauþer,
> Bot for ȝe lufed your lyf; þe lasse I yow blame. (2366–68)

Modern editors insert strong punctuation in the middle of line 2368, but that punctuation evades the complexity of this typical Middle English syntax shift. "For ȝe lufed your lyf" is both third in the series "þat watz for no wylyde werke, ne (for) wowyng nauþer" and a subordinate clause that explains "þe lasse I yow blame": "but I blame you the less because you loved your life." Heavy punctuation in the middle of line 2368 over-simplifies the relation between the first and second halves of the line; the syntactic division is as plausibly strong between lines 2367 and 2368, giving "for ȝe lufed your lyf" two possible relations to the rest of the period. The theologically coherent sense for line 2368 would be "your love of life was a less blameworthy motive for disloyalty than two other motives would have been," but placing the stronger syntactic division a half-line earlier, at the end of line 2367, invites the sense "but your disloyalty is less blameworthy because love of life was your motive." Theological orthodoxy suffers a blow

in this assertion that loving life is a positive value. Some readers will prefer to reject the syntactic ambiguity and hear only that love of life is not so
reprehensible as covetousness and lust. However, the reading that love of
life is actually meritorious gains plausibility from the Green Knight's and
Bertilak's performance throughout the work.

   Sir Gawain unfolds largely from Gawain's limited point of view and
concentrates on Gawain's shifting identity (Chapter 4). It hardly seems relevant, in comparison to Gawain, whether the Green Knight and Bertilak
have a coherent identity or not. For my purposes, however, it is important that their consciousness is single, and only their appearances double.
In the revelations at the end of the romance, the Green Knight makes no
distinction between the "I" of "I hyȝt þe a strok," referring to the Green
Knight's feinted blow, and "I sende hir to asay þe [test you]," referring
to Bertilak's instructions to his wife (2341, 2362). "My wyf," "my hous,"
"at home," "my meny" may suggest by accumulation that Bertilak is the
prior and more durable manifestation, but Helen Cooper points out that
we never hear "whether the Green Knight 'really' is Sir Bertilak under
enchantment, or whether he really is primarily the Green Knight (as the
guide suggests, with his account of the grisly inhabitant of the Green
Chapel) who is merely playing the host as a means of waylaying Gawain."[116]
Cooper's proposal that Bertilak is as likely to be in disguise as the Green
Knight points toward further connections between them. Indeed, Bertilak's
responses to Gawain are persistently disguised: he reacts as if truly "learning" that his guest is Gawain, he conceals that he already knows the connection between Gawain and the Green Chapel, and he pretends total
ignorance as he receives kisses from Gawain each day of their bargain
(908–9, 1068–69, 1392–94, 1644–47, 1938–39). His confidence in his deception seems strongest when he offers his hood on a stick as a mirthmaking
prize he will strive to defend (983–87). This compact revisitation of the
beheading game imitates the opening interlude, but now Bertilak has
become the disguise for the Green Knight. Additional links between the
two performances are the fused conclusion for the beheading and exchange
games, the energy and boldness of the two figures, and their profound
attachment to nature and the joy of life it represents in this work. Only the
last of this series would be controversial for most readers.

   More than the redeployment of wild men links the Green Knight to
nature. Scholars have found an extraordinary variety of significances for
the color green, at least when looking beyond the poem itself, in lapidaries,
encyclopedias, drama, ballads, blazon, and anecdote.[117] *Sir Gawain* and its
immediate court context give particular weight to the association of green

with nature. The Green Knight carries holly "Þat is grattest in grene when grevez [groves] ar bare" (207). His other shape, Bertilak, is devoted to aristocratic hunting, a secular ritual that assigns great value to encountering nature. The conventional color of hunting is green, like the color of Maying, the other ritual of late medieval courts that strikes a relation with nature. These substantial associations of green with the natural world, expressed not only in poetic metaphor but in court practice, make it certain that this knight's greenness has to do with nature. His "enker-grene" skin is, of course, supernatural as well, compactly identifying Morgan's magic with an untranscendent, earthbound process that the *Franklin's Tale* calls "magyk naureel" in contrast to spirit-conjuring.[118] But the evocation of nature holds its own enigma: what is nature in this work, and what is its place in the Green Knight's and Bertilak's performance? As I have argued concerning both Maying (Chapter 2) and animal ancestors (Chapter 4), nature seems to stand in defining opposition to culture, but in late medieval courts, the dichotomy is not absolute. Lévi-Strauss argued influentially that the nature/culture distinction (nature is not-us) is a universal, fundamental understanding that conditions all others. Recent anthropology, however, casts doubt on the distinction's organizing function. To be sure, in medieval terms, the book of Genesis puts Adam in charge of naming animals and gives him dominion over the earth, setting him apart from the rest of creation. Likewise, both hunting and Maying differentiate, in their costumes and practices, between civilized indoor and natural outdoor spaces. But the differentiation prepares for the rituals' dissolution of the boundary and for substantial interpenetration between the two realms.

As practiced by the medieval aristocracy, hunting was a richly elaborated ceremony. Its regulations and metaphoric meanings made it a socially expressive event, with particularly strong connections to heterosexual courtship.[119] Hunting acculturates nature through the forest laws that secure elite control, the codified rules of the chase, the specialized roles of "cacheres" and "trystors" and "vewters," and the systematic neatness of butchering called "wodcraftez" (1139, 1146, 1170, 1605). Where human and animal spheres truly interpenetrate in hunting, it becomes an experience about life and death for humans, not just about the life and death of animals. In offering this privileged contact with natural forces, hunting becomes a defining masculine exercise rather than a food-gathering chore. A rhetorical mark of human interaction with animals is the anthropomorphizing of the deer "doted for drede" [dazed with dread], the boar "breme . . . and braynwod" [brave and frenzied], the "wylé" fox named Reynard (1151, 1580, 1728). As animals rise metaphorically toward the

human, their deaths gain symbolic importance for the humans who kill
them. Hunting confers further control over life when animals are brought
back to civilized space, butchered or trophied as a head or a pelt, and represented there as having been alive outside. The deer become "venysoun"
and their tails become tallies; the boar's head calls forth the day's story
as the host "schewez hem þe scheldez, and schapes hem þe tale" [shows
them the cuts of meat and tells them the tale (1375, 1377, 1626)]. The story
and the meat consolidate the hunter's privileged interaction with life and
death, such that Gawain's feigned horror at the boar's (inert) head is neither
phony nor patronizing but a legitimate way to praise the hunter (1634).

The intercalation of hunting scenes and temptation scenes in *Sir
Gawain* can seem significant, even ominous, because of the portentious
relations that hunting establishes between humans and animals. To some
extent, as critics have noted with caution, Gawain is Bertilak's quarry. That
analogy predicts only death and dismemberment for him. The anthro-
pomorphism of the angry boar and the wily fox could run backward, this
reading suggests, to animalize Gawain into prey. The lure of the girdle
could prove to be a lethal snare. But the love of life that enables the Green
Knight to pardon him more clearly aligns Gawain with Bertilak's and the
Green Knight's engagement in nature, an engagement conferring heightened control over life as well as an identity expanded beyond the walls of
chamber and hall. Gawain's stratagem of using the girdle to defend himself against the Green Knight does recall Reynard's wiliness, but it also partakes of the hunter's aggressive, amoral confrontation with death, and the
Green Knight's ability to snatch life back from his own bloody beheading.
The Green Knight's wildness works in consonance with Bertilak's hunting
to urge the value of loving life. Magic rather than ritual pulls nature into
him, but he expresses as a "mervayle" what Bertilak expresses in his ener-
getic practice, the possibility of containing natural forces as powerful as life
and death within a cultured persona.

The poem's aesthetic register as well expresses love of life. The gor-
geously nostalgic depiction of the passing year Gawain lives as his last
("þus ȝirnez þe ȝere in ȝisterdayez mony" [thus the year passes away in
many yesterdays: 529]) is almost entirely about rain and sun, forests and
fields, birds and seeds. Even the harshest weather is intensely beautiful—
the hard icicles forming over Gawain as he sleeps, the red sun rising over
frost as the fox hunt begins: "Ferly fayre watz þe folde, for þe forst
clenged" [the world was wondrously fair, for the frost was clinging: 1694].
The products of courtly culture as well have strong visual and sensual
appeal in *Sir Gawain*: a mantle, a shield, a piece of embroidery can seem

just as splendid as the rising sun. Finding beauty so pervasively throughout natural and courtly spaces unites them in aesthetic equivalence, echoing their union in the Green Knight's person. The culminating image for
his strangeness expresses this comprehensive aesthetic: all the courtiers
wonder that a man and a horse could "growe grene as þe gres and grener
hit semed, / Þen grene aumayl on golde glowande bryȝter" [grow green
as the grass and seem even greener, than green enamel on gold glowing
brighter: 235–36].[120] The poem's double appreciation for nature and craft is
so pervasive as to constitute a stance in itself on the issue of loving life, and
a supporting context for Gawain's desire to preserve his own. His motive
for concealing the green girdle, "for ȝe lufed your lyf," acknowledges a
value the poem has endorsed in its aesthetic register and dramatized in the
dual performance of Bertilak and the Green Knight.

The Green Knight is not a wild man, but the social history of wild
men clarifies his function and his relation to Bertilak. He has every cultured accomplishment, but he is also fully in touch with the natural world.
His performance in Arthur's court is a mystified, perfected version of
what Froissart's wild men of 1393 were attempting in their performance.
Chaillou de Pesstain's charivari makes a similar claim that wildness can
be a useful practice, despite its transgressiveness. For Michel Pintoin, sin
and transgression are the whole story, expressing a far less subtle conflict
between secular and religious values than *Sir Gawain and the Green Knight*
explores. In all these representations, recovering wildness requires departing from perfect decorum, but often the departure finally, if fleetingly,
enlarges and empowers courtliness.

Conclusion

My chapters have treated formalized, ceremonial, and ritual situations that invite self-definition into visible and audible performance. The functional design of these situations has been one of my concerns: charivari, interlude, and inquisition have wider agendas that specify what kind of self-definition can happen within them. For example, inquisition's commitment to the health of the Christian community as a whole restricts the potential resolutions for the confrontation between Joan of Arc's lay piety and the ecclesiastical court. Quite differently, charivari takes advantage of an apparently irregular marriage to make a space for complicating courtly decorum with riotous resistance and critique. A unifying tendency in these events is that they assert the superiority of elite groups and define elite distinctiveness. This stratifying energy is particularly evident as Joan's judges demand her submission to the Church Militant, and as tournaments stage the magnificence of chivalry, but it is more subtly present in every ritual case I have examined.

Both elite difference and personal identity can be so authoritatively asserted in ritual because its framed, ceremonial structures credit performances with special seriousness. Rituals overtly claim that self-transformation can be accomplished by words and gestures. The ingrained gestures of everyday life (Bourdieu's *habitus* and Butler's citationality) are profoundly self-constituting as well. Courts require both ritual and daily occupation to define themselves—to turn from spaces into places, in de Certeau's terms. The two modes of occupation are on a continuum, as Griselda's marriage has illustrated: her performative wedding vow, which instantly transforms her marital and social status, commits her to years of performing its terms in terribly concrete situations. It is not evident exactly how rituals, already so various, are related to everyday practices, themselves so variously formalized. Many cases, however, such as the Griselda story's link between marriage oath and married life, the use of crests as ancestor masks but also as seals and property marks, and the overlapping of festive and theatrical impulses in interludes, demonstrate that ritual and quotidian behavior are in ongoing contact for medieval elites.

The concept of performance makes a connection between daily self-presentation and more elaborately designed ceremonies, festivals, and rituals. Performance encompasses the accouterments, gestures, and words through which people express their relation to a particular social moment. These expressions might be relatively intuitive or strategic, conventional or improvisational, but they are so grounded in shared meanings that they convey as much about the social order as they do about singular selves. The two registers are intimately related: a knight or a lady, by taking part in a tournament or a courtly Maying, is simultaneously demonstrating virtues said to be class-specific and attempting to enhance personal honor (for prowess in the one case, chaste sexuality in the other). Distinction from other groups looks perfectly compatible with distinction from other members of the group, but I have argued that singular and shared identity can be at odds: for example, basing chivalric identity in renown submits it to the risk of misjudgment by the chivalric community. Alienation and conflict can result from misjudgment, but only because the community's judgment was given such authority in the first place. These publicly displayed and assessed selves do not fit the more modern categories of the "individual," with its implication of neatly bounded, free-floating coherence, or "subjectivity," with its quite different implication of a complexly constrained psychology largely hidden from view. The medieval term "self" and the more recent term "identity" have seemed to me to translate the confidence that court ceremonies place in the substantiality of visible expression: what people manifest and articulate is what counts about them, not what is hidden and unexpressed. Performance is a reliable measure of who one actually is.

My account of court conceptions of selfhood does not attempt to define the full range of conceptions for all medieval milieux, nor to delineate the continuities and breaks between medieval and modern conceptions. I do mean to counter a persistent impression among postmedieval scholars that, insofar as medieval people did not highly value their interiority, they were quite simple creatures compared to us. The rhetorics of disguise and masking, of cross-dress and heraldry, illustrate the rich elaboration of personal significance around physical signs that is only possible when appearance, not hidden interiority, is taken to be meaningful. The motto "rien ne m'est plus" [nothing means more to me] does express an occulted singular desire, but values it by publicizing and circulating it, converting whatever is unique and private about it into negotiable social coin. In addition to resisting a teleology of increasingly complex selfhood as the centuries progress, my emphasis on secular identity is meant to counterbalance medievalists' attentiveness to Christian conceptions about the self in theological writing. The radically performed identity of secular rituals contrasts in some respects with Christian emphases on hidden desires and on examining the soul, although Joan's trial demonstrates that inquisition does assume that spirituality is embodied and enacted. All in all, my cases begin to suggest that the history of the self is a more intricate, nonlinear, even contradictory story than its scholarship has yet recognized.

Especially in the public forums of late medieval courts, material signs such as dress, emblems, coats of arms, and masks make crucial contributions to identity. Literary studies risk misinterpreting verbal assertions without the complement of material evidence. Bodily guises and disguises are not really inert things but substantial communications, less immediately readable than words but structured along lines similar to those structuring identity: any category important to defining a self in late medieval courts, such as rank, honor, or sex, can find direct expression in dress. But more than merely posting identity, material signs can shift it in new directions. Joan of Arc's cross-dress defines, together with her virginity, a concretized spirituality that is her primary evidence of God's sanction. Several times in these chapters I have returned to Derrida's account of the supplement to describe the relation of dress to identity. For example, a coat of arms adds ancestral connections to a knight's self-representation, enlarging and specifying his social position, but at the same time acknowledging that he is incomplete, not fully himself, unless the ancestors are taken into account. The coat of arms both confers ancestral merit on the descendant and subordinates him to those ancestors. Similar vacillations are inherent to personal signs of all kinds, enhancing their capacity to mobilize and modify identity.

Postmedieval conceptions of identity tend to assert that the true self is within, and that self-presentation is therefore more or less a false front. My chapters have offered many counterexamples that locate selfhood in external performance. Several currents in performance studies have resisted the dichotomy between inner genuineness and outer falseness, by historicizing the dichotomy itself, by analyzing situations in which behavior constitutes as well as expresses identity, and by suggesting that interiority is an effect generated within performance itself. The medieval elites of this study offer their own arguments against discounting performance or seeing it in dichotomous relation to interiority. Masking and disguise provide the most obvious, if counterintuitive, examples. *Fauvel*'s charivari, Ywain's disguise, and the wild man costume of Charles VI stage meaningful self-definitions. Certainly masking and disguise can function as falsifications. But in diverse instances I have discussed, they amount instead to identity claims accruing to the soon revealed self, or translucent layers that revise the still visible self.

One reason that modern scholars have not taken these self-definitions seriously is that ritual, like social performance more broadly, has been redefined as falsification from the Reformation onward. For religious and secular reformers alike, ritual's showiness is suspect and its emphasis on gesture over belief seems mistaken. The crests and coats of arms in which tournament combatants dress and the fantastic identities they adopt are ostentatious indeed, but I have argued they are ostentatious in the functional rather than the pejorative sense: they show forth identity with the serious purpose of accruing renown. Similarly, at Ardres in 1396, Richard II and Charles VI spent so much time and money on exchanging personal signs and holding hands because they believed this ritual demonstration appropriately expressed their commitment to changing the relationship between England and France. In many medieval instances, showiness and gesture are not void of commitment but instead mark the moments where commitment is deepest.

Given the sparse and fragmented evidence surviving from late medieval courts, it is fortunate that identity in these courts was not simply verbalized but was instead more broadly performed. Self-definition left marks not just on parchment but in cloth and steel, not just in poetry but in gestures and ceremonies. Had the elites of the Hundred Years War identified themselves with their hidden thoughts, they would have had no need for their brilliant array of talking garments, growling masks, flower fetishes, ancestral totems, and mimetic rituals. In the traces of their material performances, together with their words, they can still make themselves known today.

Notes

Introduction

1. Indeed, scholars have long imagined a shadowy medieval semiconsciousness that precedes modern identity's "birth" in the Renaissance and "evolution" to the present. Now that scholars are rejecting metaphors of maturation and the ideology of unchecked melioration that underwrites them, the metaphors of protean plurality, forgetting and loss, rhizomic resurfacings, detours and ruptures that characterize recent cultural histories promise less patronizing attitudes toward medieval self-consciousness. For reviews of scholarship and signs of change in its terms, see Lee Patterson, "On the Margin: Postmodernism, Ironic History, and Medieval Studies," *Speculum* 65 (1990): 87–108; Roy Porter, Introduction to *Rewriting the Self: Histories from the Renaissance to the Present*, ed. Roy Porter (London: Routledge, 1993), pp. 1–14; John D. Cox and David Scott Kastan, "Demanding History," and Margreta de Grazia, "World Pictures, Modern Periods, and the Early Stage," introduction to *A New History of Early English Drama*, ed. John D. Cox and David Scott Kastan (New York: Columbia University Press, 1997), pp. 1–5, 7–21; James Clifford, "On Ethnographic Self-Fashioning: Conrad and Malinowski," in *Reconstructing Individualism: Autonomy, Individuality, and the Self in Western Thought*, ed. Thomas C. Heller, Morton Sosna, and David E. Wellbery (Stanford, Calif.: Stanford University Press, 1986), pp. 140–62.

I am not investigating what may constitute consciousness per se, a question for disciplinary and interdisciplinary work in philosophy, neurobiology, evolutionary psychology, and cognitive science. Rather, I am investigating self-consciousness: how people conceive and articulate themselves in their language and behavior.

2. On the concept of a court and its application to the late fourteenth century, see Nigel Saul, *Richard II* (New Haven, Conn.: Yale University Press, 1997), pp. 327–65; Gervase Mathew, *The Court of Richard II* (London: Murray, 1968); Richard Firth Green, *Poets and Princepleasers: Literature and the English Court in the Late Middle Ages* (Toronto: University of Toronto Press, 1980); C. Stephen Jaeger, *The Origins of Courtliness: Civilizing Trends and the Formation of Courtly Ideals, 939–1210* (Philadelphia: University of Pennsylvania Press, 1985); Daniel Poirion, *Le Poète et le prince: L'Evolution du lyrisme courtois de Guillaume de Machaut à Charles d'Orléans* (Paris: Presses Universitaires de France, 1965).

3. Michel Foucault, "About the Beginning of the Hermeneutics of the Self: Two Lectures at Dartmouth," *Political Theory* 21 (1993): 221; Caroline Walker Bynum, "Did the Twelfth Century Discover the Individual?" *Journal of Ecclesiastical History* 31 (1980): 4; John F. Benton, "Consciousness of Self and Perceptions of

Individuality," in *Renaissance and Renewal in the Twelfth Century*, ed. Robert L. Benson and Giles Constable (Cambridge, Mass.: Harvard University Press, 1982), pp. 263–95; Brian Stock, "Reading, Writing, and the Self: Petrarch and His Forerunners," *New Literary History* 26 (1995): 725. Aaron Gurevich finds little self-consciousness outside St. Augustine's *Confessions*, in *The Origins of European Individualism*, trans. Katharine Judelson (Oxford: Blackwell, 1995).

4. For instance, Poirion, *Poète et le prince*; Michel Zink, *The Invention of Literary Subjectivity*, trans. David Sices (Baltimore: Johns Hopkins University Press, 1999); Anne Berthelot, *Figures et fonction de l'écrivain au XIIIe siècle* (Montréal: Institut d'Etudes Médiévales, 1991); Kevin Brownlee, *Poetic Identity in Guillaume de Machaut* (Madison: University of Wisconsin Press, 1984). Lee Patterson has most penetratingly explored the language of secular identity, e.g., *Chaucer and the Subject of History* (Madison: University of Wisconsin Press, 1991); "Making Identities in Fifteenth-Century England: Henry V and John Lydgate," in *New Historical Literary Study*, ed. Jeffrey N. Cox and Larry J. Reynolds (Princeton, N.J.: Princeton University Press, 1993), pp. 69–107.

5. Examples of current work are Andrew Parker and Eve Kosofsky Sedgwick, eds., *Performativity and Performance* (London: Routledge, 1995); Joseph Roach, *Cities of the Dead: Circum-Atlantic Performance* (New York: Columbia University Press, 1996); Elin Diamond, ed., *Performance and Cultural Politics* (London: Routledge, 1996); John J. MacAloon, ed., *Rite, Drama, Festival, Spectacle: Rehearsals Toward a Theory of Cultural Performance* (Philadelphia: Institute for the Study of Human Issues, 1984); important precursors are Victor Turner's and Richard Schechner's many works on theater, ritual, and performance.

6. Other subgroups such as mystics, contemplatives, and theologians value interiority more highly, and seem to experience interiority more complexly, than the lay elites I call courtiers; at the same time, the sacrament of penance, eremetic writing, and the *vitae* of mystics concur that interiority must be exteriorized, examined, and published in order to become meaningful.

7. Charles Taylor, *Sources of the Self: The Making of Modern Identity* (Cambridge, Mass.: Harvard University Press, 1989), pp. 14–24, 152–55.

8. Sarah Beckwith, *Signifying God: Social Relation and Symbolic Act in the York Corpus Christi Plays* (Chicago: University of Chicago Press, 2001), p. 154; C. Stephen Jaeger, *Ennobling Love: In Search of a Lost Sensibility* (Philadelphia: University of Pennsylvania Press, 1999).

9. Johan Huizinga, *The Autumn of the Middle Ages*, trans. Rodney J. Payton and Ulrich Mammitzsch (Chicago: University of Chicago Press, 1996), pp. 92, 103.

10. Pierre Bourdieu, "L'Illusion biographique," *Actes de la recherche en sciences sociales* 12, nos. 62–63 (June 1986): 69–72; Norbert Elias, *The Civilizing Process*, vol. 1, *The History of Manners*, trans. Edmund Jephcott (New York: Urizen, 1978); Erving Goffman, *The Presentation of Self in Everyday Life* (Garden City, N.Y.: Doubleday, 1959) and *Interaction Ritual: Essays in Face-to-Face Behavior* (Chicago: Aldine, 1967).

11. Michel de Certeau, *The Practice of Everyday Life*, trans. Steven Rendall (Berkeley: University of California Press, 1984); Marshall Sahlins, *Culture and Practical Reason* (Chicago: University of Chicago Press, 1976); Pierre Bourdieu, *Outline of a Theory of Practice*, trans. Richard Nice (Cambridge: Cambridge University Press, 1977); see also Marcel Mauss, *Sociology and Psychology: Essays*, trans.

Ben Brewster (London: Routledge, 1979), pp. 95–123 ("Body Techniques"). Only with a certain hindsight can these diverse works be gathered together under the heading "practice theory"; I adopt the term with that reservation, in order to recognize the breadth of intelligence that has contributed to thinking on the relation between body and self-consciousness.

12. On tactics for change see especially de Certeau, *Practice of Everyday Life* and Anthony Giddens, *Central Problems in Social Theory* (Berkeley: University of California Press, 1979), pp. 1–48, 198–225.

13. Jack Goody, "Against 'Ritual': Loosely Structured Thoughts on a Loosely Defined Topic," in *Secular Ritual*, ed. Sally F. Moore and Barbara G. Myerhoff (Amsterdam: Van Gorcum, 1977), pp. 25–35.

14. Richard Schechner, *Between Theater and Anthropology* (Philadelphia: University of Pennsylvania Press, 1985), pp. 35–116.

15. In addition to the citations above, particularly influential studies have been Michel Foucault, *Discipline and Punish: The Birth of the Prison*, trans. Alan Sheridan (New York: Pantheon, 1977); Judith Butler, *Gender Trouble: Feminism and the Subversion of Identity* (London: Routledge, 1990), and *Bodies That Matter: On the Discursive Limits of "Sex"* (London: Routledge, 1993); Marshall Sahlins, "The Sadness of Sweetness: The Native Anthropology of Western Cosmology," *Current Anthropology* 37 (1996): 395–415: "human needs and drives are indeterminate as regards their object because bodily satisfactions are specified in and through symbolic values—and variously so in different cultural-symbolic schemes" (p. 404).

16. Pierre Bourdieu, *Distinction: A Social Critique of the Judgement of Taste*, trans. Richard Nice (Cambridge, Mass.: Harvard University Press, 1984), p. 3.

17. A few important titles on these general issues are Herbert Blau, *Nothing in Itself: Complexions of Fashion* (Bloomington: Indiana University Press, 1999); Fred Davis, *Fashion, Culture, and Identity* (Chicago: University of Chicago Press, 1992); J. C. Flugel, *The Psychology of Clothes* (New York: International Universities Press, 1969); Anne Hollander, *Sex and Suits* (New York: Knopf, 1994); Valerie Steele, *Fetish: Fashion, Sex, and Power* (New York: Oxford University Press, 1996).

18. Arjun Appadurai, ed., *The Social Life of Things: Commodities in Cultural Perspective* (Cambridge: Cambridge University Press, 1986); *World Archaeology* 31, no. 2 (1999): Chris Gosden and Yvonne Marshall, eds., *The Cultural Biography of Objects*. An important collection on the political and economic vitality of cloth in many cultures is Annette B. Weiner and Jane Schneider, eds., *Cloth and Human Experience* (Washington, D.C.: Smithsonian Institution Press, 1989).

19. Christopher Allmand, *The Hundred Years War: England and France at War, c. 1300–c. 1450* (Cambridge: Cambridge University Press, 1988). A small sample of the work on English-French interactions during the period: Philippe Contamine, Charles Giry-Deloison, and Maurice H. Keen, eds., *Guerre et société en France, en Angleterre et en Bourgogne, XIVᵉ–XVᵉ siècle* (Villeneuve d'Ascq: Centre d'Histoire de la Région du Nord et de l'Europe du Nord-Ouest, 1991); *La "France anglaise" au Moyen Age: Actes du IIIᵉ congrès national des sociétés savantes (Poitiers, 1986)* (Paris: CTHS, 1988); Andrew Wathey, "The Marriage of Edward III and the Transmission of French Motets to England," *Journal of the American Musicological Society* 45 (1992): 1–29; Julia Boffey, "English Dream Poems and Their French Connections," in *Literary Aspects of Courtly Culture*, ed. Donald Maddox and Sara Sturm-Maddox

(Cambridge: D.S. Brewer, 1994), pp. 113–21; Mary-Jo Arn, ed., *Charles d'Orléans in England (1415–1440)* (Woodbridge, Suffolk: D.S. Brewer, 2000).

Chapter 1. Talking Garments

1. Léon de Laborde, *Les Ducs de Bourgogne: Etudes sur les lettres, les arts, et l'industrie pendant le XVe siècle*, part 2, *Preuves*, 3 vols. (Paris: Plon, 1849, 1851, 1852), vol. 3, no. 6241 (year: 1414).

2. Jean-Bernard de Vaivre, "Troisième note sur le sceau du comté de Charolais au temps de Jean Sans Peur," *Archivum heraldicum*, 3–4 (1982): 34–36; Laborde, *Ducs de Bourgogne*, part 2, vol. 3, no. 6229; Alice Planche, *Charles d'Orléans ou la recherche d'un langage* (Paris: Champion, 1975), pp. 683–87; Juliet Vale, *Edward III and Chivalry: Chivalric Society and Its Context, 1270–1350* (Woodbridge, Suffolk: Boydell, 1982), p. 65.

3. De Vaivre, "Troisième note," p. 34; Joan Evans, *Dress in Mediaeval France* (Oxford: Clarendon Press, 1952), pp. 40–42, 54–55. At a moment of reconciliation in 1406, John wore Louis's device for a tournament: Laborde, *Ducs de Bourgogne*, part 2, vol. 1, pp. 21–22.

4. See, e.g., Michel Pastoureau, *Figures et couleurs: Etudes sur la symbolique et la sensibilité médiévales* (Paris: Léopard d'Or, 1986); Jean Froissart, *"Dits" et "débats"*, ed. Anthime Fourrier (Geneva: Droz, 1979), pp. 57–59. A fine demonstration that color symbolism has social and economic sources is Jane Schneider, "Peacocks and Penguins: The Political Economy of European Cloth and Colors," *American Ethnologist* 5 (1978): 413–47.

5. Elizabeth Salter, "The Timeliness of *Wynnere and Wastoure*," *Medium Aevum* 47 (1978): 40–65; Malcolm Norris, *Monumental Brasses: The Memorials*, 2 vols. (London: Phillips and Page, 1977), 1: 9–10; 2: fig. 15; *Monumental Brasses: The Craft* (London: Faber and Faber, 1978), figs. 120–21 (n.b. Robert or William de Setvans); for more examples see Michel Pastoureau, *Traité d'héraldique*, 3rd ed. (Paris: Picard, 1997), pp. 250–53; Winifred Hall, *Canting and Allusive Arms of England and Wales* (Canterbury: Achievements, 1966). On heraldic dress for women, see note 72 below, and Chapter 4, note 13.

6. See, e.g., G. R. Owst, *Literature and Pulpit in Medieval England* (Oxford: Blackwell, 1961); Odile Blanc, "Vêtement féminin, vêtement masculin à la fin du Moyen Age: Le Point de vue des moralistes," in Pastoureau, ed., *Le Vêtement*, pp. 243–51; Diane Owen Hughes, "Regulating Women's Fashion," in *A History of Women in the West*, vol. 2, *Silences of the Middle Ages*, ed. Christiane Klapisch-Zuber (Cambridge, Mass.: Belknap Press, 1992), pp. 136–58. On erotic and social meanings of dress, see E. Jane Burns, *Courtly Love Undressed: Reading Through Clothes in Medieval French Culture* (Philadelphia: University of Pennsylvania Press, 2002).

7. Claire Sponsler, *Drama and Resistance: Bodies, Goods, and Theatricality in Late Medieval England* (Minneapolis: University of Minnesota Press, 1997), pp. 1–23; Alan Hunt, *Governance of the Consuming Passions: A History of Sumptuary Law* (New York: St. Martin's Press, 1996), pp. 110–13, 132–36.

8. H. M. Zijlstra-Zweens, *Of His Array Telle I No Lenger Tale: Aspects of Costume, Arms and Armour in Western Europe, 1200–1400* (Amsterdam: Rodolpi, 1988),

p. 6; Kay Staniland, "The Great Wardrobe Accounts as a Source for Historians of Fourteenth-Century Clothing and Textiles," *Textile History* 20 (1989): 275–81 (cost of labor well under 10 percent for court clothing: p. 280).

9. See, e.g., Saul, *Richard II*, pp. 200–201, 263–64, 369; Paul Strohm, *Hochon's Arrow: The Social Imagination of Fourteenth-Century Texts* (Princeton, N.J.: Princeton University Press, 1992), pp. 57–74, 179–85; Françoise Piponnier, *Costume et vie sociale: La Cour d'Anjou, XIVᵉ–XVᵉ siècle* (Paris: Mouton, 1970), pp. 243–59.

10. Kay Staniland, "Court Style, Painters, and the Great Wardrobe," in *England in the Fourteenth Century: Proceedings of the 1985 Harlaxton Symposium*, ed. W. M. Ormrod (Woodbridge, Suffolk: Boydell, 1986), pp. 236–46.

11. Kay Staniland, "Medieval Courtly Splendour," *Costume* 14 (1980): 7–23; the wardrobe account of this outfit is published in W. Paley Baildon, "A Wardrobe Account of 16–17 Richard II, 1393–4," *Archaeologia* 62 (1911): 497–514 (quotation at p. 511); C. M. Woolgar corrects the attribution of the account: *Household Accounts from Medieval England*, ed. C. M. Woolgar, 2 vols. (Oxford: Oxford University Press, 1992–93), 1: 37–38. Staniland follows Baildon on the probable meaning of "hancelyn": "Medieval Courtly Splendour," p. 14.

12. Staniland, "Great Wardrobe Accounts," p. 280; *Chaucer Life-Records*, ed. Martin M. Crow and Clair C. Olson (Oxford: Oxford University Press, 1966), pp. 148–62, 402–8, 535–37.

13. Mary Douglas and Baron Isherwood discuss this problem in *The World of Goods* (New York: Basic Books, 1979); see also Alfred Gell, "Newcomers to the World of Goods: Consumption Among the Muria Gonds," in *The Social Life of Things: Commodities in Cultural Perspective*, ed. Arjun Appadurai (Cambridge: Cambridge University Press, 1986), pp. 110–38.

14. Louis Claude Douët-d'Arcq, *Comptes de l'argenterie des rois de France au XIVᵉ siècle* (Paris: Renouard, 1851), pp. xlii–xliii (a six-piece robe, with further examples); during a sixteen-month period the English royal accounts show 20,677 miniver skins used in garments mainly for Edward III: Staniland, "Courtly Splendour," pp. 10–11; Staniland defines miniver and pured miniver, p. 10.

15. Jean Baudrillard, *For a Critique of the Political Economy of the Sign*, trans. Charles Levin (St. Louis: Telos, 1981), pp. 80–82, 130–42 (quotation at p. 80); Sahlins, *Culture and Practical Reason*, pp. 166, 169, 196.

16. Recently Werner Sombart's thesis that the demand for luxuries is the original motor of capitalism has regained some attention in studies concerning the social meanings of objects. His thesis could draw credibility from evidence that well before the Middle Ages prestige uses of new materials such as iron, copper, and gold preceded by several centuries their use in practical, technological applications: Werner Sombart, *Luxury and Capitalism*, trans. W. R. Dittmar, int. Philip Siegelman (Ann Arbor: University of Michigan Press, 1967); Arjun Appadurai, "Introduction: Commodities and the Politics of Value," in *Social Life of Things*, pp. 36–39; Colin Renfrew, "Varna and the Emergence of Wealth in Prehistoric Europe," in *Social Life of Things*, pp. 141–68; Hunt, *Governance of the Consuming Passions*, pp. 89–95.

17. Elisabeth Crowfoot, Frances Pritchard, and Kay Staniland, *Medieval Finds from Excavations in London, 4. Textiles and Clothing c. 1150–c. 1450* (London: HMSO, 1992), pp. 150–98; Margaret Scott, *A Visual History of Costume: The Fourteenth and*

Fifteenth Centuries (London: Batsford, 1986), pp. 16–18. The best general intro-
ductions to clothing of this period are Evans, *Dress in Mediaeval France*; Victor
Gay, *Glossaire archéologique du moyen âge et de la renaissance*, 2 vols.
(1887; reprint,
Paris: Picard, 1928); Stella Mary Newton, *Fashion in the Age of the Black Prince*
(Woodbridge, Suffolk: Boydell, 1980); and Piponnier, *Costume et vie sociale*.

18. Jennifer Harris, "'Estroit vestu et menu cosu': Evidence for the Construction of Twelfth-Century Dress," in *Medieval Art: Recent Perspectives: A Memorial
Tribute to C. R. Dodwell*, ed. Gale R. Owen-Crocker and Timothy Graham (Manchester: Manchester University Press, 1998), p. 90. Harris argues that the practices
leading to "fashion" are appearing in the twelfth century, but she concedes that
twelfth-century cutting relies on "essentially geometric shapes" and that tailoring
is elementary in comparison to "cutting-to-fit" (pp. 90, 99). Similarly, Christina
Frieder Waugh notes the twelfth-century dependence on lacing to achieve a good
fit, and describes garment construction as "quite simple, almost disappointingly
so"; "very simple, hardly any different from the cut of earlier medieval clothing":
"'Well-Cut Through the Body': Fitted Clothing in Twelfth-Century Europe," *Dress*
26 (1999): 3–16 (quotations at pp. 3, 4).

19. Newton, *Fashion*, pp. 1–13; 108–9 (quotation at p. 3); Françoise Piponnier,
"Une Révolution dans le costume masculin au XIVᵉ siècle," in *Pastoureau*, ed.,
Le Vêtement, pp. 225–42; Anne Hollander, *Sex and Suits* (New York: Knopf, 1995),
pp. 14–49.

20. Geoffrey Chaucer, *Canterbury Tales*, frag. 10, ll. 412–31, in *The Riverside
Chaucer*, 3rd ed., ed. Larry Benson (Boston: Houghton Mifflin, 1987); for further
comments on court dress including defenses of it see Patricia J. Eberle, "The Poli-
tics of Courtly Style at the Court of Richard II," in *The Spirit of the Court: Selected
Proceedings of the Fourth Congress of the International Courtly Literature Society
(Toronto 1983)* (Cambridge: D.S. Brewer, 1985), pp. 168–78.

21. *The Brut, or the Chronicles of England*, ed. Friedrich W. D. Brie, EETS o.s.
131, 136 (London: Oxford University Press, 1906, 1908), 2: 296–97; for the translation I have drawn on Newton, *Fashion*, p. 9; *The Brut* uses the *Chronica Johannis
de Reading et anonymi Cantuariensis, 1346–1367*, ed. James Tait (Manchester: Manchester University Press, 1914), pp. 88–89.

22. Peter Stallybrass and Ann Rosalind Jones are two hundred years late with
their claim that "the connection between fashion and change emerged in the
Renaissance," when the term "fashion" began to describe not only creating and
making in general, but also rapidly changing styles of dress: *Renaissance Clothing
and the Materials of Memory* (Cambridge: Cambridge University Press, 2000), p. 5.
For fifteenth-century uses of the term in that sense, see Hans Kurath et al., eds.,
Middle English Dictionary (Ann Arbor: University of Michigan Press, 1952–), under
"fascioun." Fourteenth-century chroniclers know the concept without yet using the
term. More important is Stallybrass's and Jones's demonstration that Renaissance
dress is not superfluous to identity but constitutes and commemorates it, linking
the operations of dress in the Renaissance to its operations in the late Middle Ages.

23. For example, J. C. Flugel, *The Psychology of Clothes* (New York: International Universities Press, 1969), pp. 137–54; Jean Baudrillard, *Simulations*, trans.
Paul Foss, Paul Patton, and Philip Beitchman (New York: Semiotext(e), 1983), pp.
83–84; Appadurai, "Introduction," *Social Life of Things*, pp. 24–26.

24. Hunt, *Governance*, p. 112.

25. On the relation between personal devices and heraldry, see Pastoureau, *Figures et couleurs*, pp. 125–37; on the dates when badges were widely used, see Colette Beaune, "Costume et pouvoir en France à la fin du Moyen Age: Les Devises royales vers 1400," *Revue des sciences humaines* n.s. 55, no. 183 (July–September 1981): 125–46. Edward seems to have taken the ostrich feather from his mother Philippa's set of personal signs: Nicholas Harris Nicolas, "Observations on the Origin and History of the Badge and Mottoes of Edward Prince of Wales," *Archaeologia* 31 (1846): 350–84.

26. Huizinga's peculiar misfortune was to concentrate his attention on secular social practices that he could only, within the progressivism of the early twentieth century, judge again and again to be "primitive," "childlike," "superficial," and "almost paganly naïve": Johan Huizinga, *The Autumn of the Middle Ages*, trans. Rodney J. Payton and Ulrich Mammitzsch (Chicago: University of Chicago Press, 1996), chap. 11, "Forms of Thought in Practice," pp. 251, 256, 261, 268, 270, 281, 283, et passim. The weakness of medieval thinking, in Huizinga's view, was that it took from scholasticism the principle that every concrete instance exemplifies an ideal form. The "hollow and superficial character" of medieval minds was "directly spawned by general formalism"; badges specifically, like proverbs, strove to associate specific behaviors to generalized ideals and truths, making specious, casuistic connections that flattened and distorted reality (p. 281). It is well established by now that all aspects of medieval thought do not conform to the precepts of scholasticism. Learned philosophy and court dress are unlikely to be governed by the same principles of intelligibility.

27. Pierre Salmon, *Les Demandes faites par le roi Charles VI, touchant son état et le gouvernement de sa personne, avec les réponses de Pierre Salmon, son secrétaire et familier*, ed. G.-A. Crapelet (Paris: Crapelet, 1833). The work has, despite this edition's title, a first part, "Les Demandes" and a second part, "Les Lamentacions et les épistres de Pierre Salmon," in which Salmon relates his travels on Charles's behalf, notably to Richard II's court following his marriage to Isabel. For information on manuscripts, see the edition, pp. xvii–xxii; for information on the illuminations, see Sandra L. Hindman, *Christine de Pisan's "Epistre Othea": Painting and Politics at the Court of Charles VI* (Toronto: Pontifical Institute, 1986), pp. 115, 124, 127, 176; Millard Meiss, *French Painting in the Time of Jean de Berry: The Boucicaut Master* (London: Phaidon, 1968), pp. 124–25.

28. For John the Fearless using hops as a device, see Laborde, *Ducs de Bourgogne*, part 2, vol. 1, nos. 154, 198, 201, 239; the crossbow bolt held by another courtier may identify him as the king's master of crossbowmen, John of Hangest: R. C. Famiglietti, *Royal Intrigue: Crisis at the Court of Charles VI, 1392–1420* (New York: AMS, 1986), p. xvi.

29. Houppelande: a single outer garment common to both sexes, popular from the last decades of the fourteenth century, belted, with long sleeves and a collar, full-length for women and either full-length or shorter for men (Douët-d'Arcq, *Comptes de l'argenterie*, pp. 383–84; Newton, *Fashion*, pp. 57–58, 127–28). Charles's star-shaped neck ornament does not reflect any of the devices associated with him in Hindman's exhaustive account: *Christine de Pisan's "Epistre Othea"*, pp. 45, 108, 119, 123, 146–54, 176–78.

30. Beaune, "Costume et pouvoir," pp. 136–37. This winged white hart and the motto "jamais" appear on the left rear tapestry of London, British Library, MS Harley 4380, fol.1 (Plate 4).

31. Beaune, "Costume et pouvoir," p. 138.

32. Jean-Bernard de Vaivre, "A propos des devises de Charles VI," *Bulletin monumental* 141 (1983): 92–95; Louis Claude Douët-d'Arcq, *Nouveau recueil de comptes de l'argenterie des rois de France* (Paris: Renouard, 1874), pp. 143, 160–61, 172, 194, 198–99; Evans, *Dress in Mediaeval France*, p. 40; a brocaded velvet woven with broom cods and the motto "esperance" survives as a chasuble: Lisa Monnas, "Fit for a King: Figured Silks Shown in the Wilton Diptych," in *The Regal Image of Richard II and the Wilton Diptych*, ed. Dillian Gordon, Lisa Monnas, and Caroline Elam (London: Miller, 1997), 165–77.

33. De Vaivre, "Devises de Charles VI," p. 95; Derek Pearsall, ed., *The Floure and the Leafe and The Assembly of Ladies* (1962; reprint Manchester: Manchester University Press, 1980), p. 27.

34. See, respectively, Salmon, *Demandes*, p. xix; Famiglietti, *Royal Intrigue*, p. xv; Evans, *Dress*, p. x, pl. 26; Pastoureau, *Figures et couleurs*, p. 133.

35. A. C. Fox-Davies, *A Complete Guide to Heraldry*, rev. J. P. Brooke-Little (London: Nelson, 1969), p. 146. A similar gold tiger rampant ("un grant tigre rampant d'or") was embroidered on the left sleeve of red houppelandes made for Charles and Louis d'Orléans in 1394: Paris, Archives Nationales, MS KK 24, fol. 94v. For the tiger in Charles's manuscripts, see de Vaivre, "Devises de Charles VI," pp. 94–95. A rampant animal similar to that in the Salmon manuscript appears again on Charles's sleeve in Paris, Bibliothèque nationale de France, MS français 836, fol. 1 (frontispiece to Christine de Pizan's *Poésies*).

36. On Charles's madness, see Chapter 5. I hazard the association between the adoption of black and the onset of illness in 1393 because mental illness was largely treated with "hagiotherapy," to borrow Brachet's term: prayers, blessings, devotions, and pilgrimage are repeatedly prescribed (Auguste Brachet, *Pathologie mentale des rois de France* [Paris: Hachette, 1903], p. lxxvii). Black, according to Schneider's wide-ranging study, connotes "austerity and opposition to indulgence"; its associations with mourning, clerical, and monastic dress converge around "pious self-restraint" and the "ascetic ideals of the good Christian," precisely the orientations Charles's hagiotherapy endorsed ("Peacocks and Penguins," pp. 415, 421, 426).

37. Paris, Archives Nationales, MS KK 24, fol. 94v: on the two houppelandes embroidered with a gold tiger rampant, the inscription embroidered on the tiger's collar is called the king's motto: "j'aime la plus belle de la divise du roy."

38. Jean Froissart, *Oeuvres de Froissart*, ed. Kervyn de Lettenhove, 25 vols. (Brussels: Victor Devaux, 1867–77), 5: 417–18. Froissart reports (5: 425) that Jean de Clermont died in the next day's battle, but not in combat with John Chandos. For my study, Froissart is a valuable resource for the very reason many historians have avoided him: he shapes his narration of events so as to exemplify chivalric principles and aspirations. Whether or not Jean and Chandos spoke as Froissart reports, their encounter conveys Froissart's contemporary understanding of how knights used their personal signs. On Froissart's wider use of blue, see Peter Ainsworth, "Heralds, Heraldry and the Colour Blue in the Chronicles of Jean Froissart," in *The Medieval Chronicle: Proceedings of the 1st International Conference on the Medieval*

Chronicle, Driebergen/Utrecht, 13–16 July 1996, ed. Erik Kooper (Amsterdam: Rodopi, 1999), pp. 40–55. Another apposite text, written a bit late for inclusion in this study, is *The Assembly of Ladies*, in *The Floure and the Leafe and The Assembly of Ladies*, ed. Pearsall.

39. Nicholas Harris Nicolas, *The Scrope and Grosvenor Controversy*, 2 vols. (London: Samuel Bentley, 1832).

40. Various religious, political, and familial keys have been proposed for the unnamed object of devotion (Christ, salvation, a baby, a deceased husband, a crusade, etc.) but surely the devices draw power from concealing their object from view. Marie's device even means its own contrary, that is, either "nothing means more to me" or "nothing is left for me." See Beaune, "Costume et pouvoir," p. 125; Poirion, *Le Poète et le prince*, pp. 65–66; R. C. Famiglietti, *Tales of the Marriage Bed from Medieval France (1300–1500)* (Providence, R.I.: Picardy Press, 1992), pp. 74–75; Laborde, *Ducs de Bourgogne*, part 2, vol. 3, nos. 6732, 6954.

41. Enguerrand de Monstrelet, *La chronique d'Enguerran de Monstrelet*, ed. Louis Douët-d'Arcq, 6 vols. (Paris: Renouard, 1857–62), 2: 58; de Vaivre, "Troisième note," pp. 34–35.

42. Famiglietti, *Royal Intrigue*, p. xv; de Vaivre, "Troisième note," p. 34.

43. D'Arcy Jonathan Dacre Boulton, *Knights of the Crown: The Monarchical Orders of Knighthood in Later Medieval Europe, 1325–1520* (New York: St. Martin's Press, 1987), pp. 428–30; on livery collars see C. E. J. Smith, "The Livery Collar," *The Coat of Arms*, n.s. 3, no. 151 (Autumn 1990): 238–53.

44. *Procès de condamnation et de rehabilitation de Jeanne d'Arc*, ed. Jules Quicherat, 5 vols. (Paris: Renouard, 1841–49), 5: 112–13, 259. For further examples of gifts and distributions of personal signs, see Piponnier, *Costume et vie sociale*, pp. 231–59.

45. Jonathan J. G. Alexander, "The Portrait of Richard II in Westminster Abbey," in *The Regal Image of Richard II*, ed. Gordon, Monnas, and Elam, p. 205.

46. Pastoureau, *Figures et couleurs*, pp. 125–37; Huizinga's *Autumn of the Middle Ages* remains an influential source for this developmental model of selfhood over the centuries. Among other flaws, Huizinga's analysis ignores the negotiability of badges.

47. On the intersections between badges, coats of arms, and supporters see H. Stanford London, *Royal Beasts* (East Knoyle, Wilts: Heraldry Society, 1956); Pastoureau, *Figures et couleurs*, pp. 125–37. For visual representations of badges and livery collars contemporary with the Salmon manuscript, see Anne D. Hedeman, *The Royal Image: Illustrations of the "Grandes Chroniques de France," 1274–1422* (Berkeley: University of California Press, 1991), pp. 153–77.

48. Some important extensions to the alliance were negotiated at the Ardres ceremony, although not all were later carried out. For details, see Saul, *Richard II*, pp. 225–32, 353–54.

49. "L'Entrevue d'Ardres," ed. Paul Meyer, *Annuaire-Bulletin de la société de l'histoire de France* 18 (1881): 209–15. The MS, Oxford, Oriel College 46, dates from around 1400; it copies this record into a compendium of pieces on English government: see Henry O. Coxe, *Catalogus codicum MSS. qui in collegeiis aulisque Oxoniensibus*, vol. 1 (Oxford: Typographeo Academico, 1852), under Oriel College, p. 17. Other accounts of the Ardres meeting are: *Annales Ricardi Secundi*, in

188 Notes to Pages 22–24

Chronica monasterii S. Albani, ed. Henry Thomas Riley, Rolls Series, no. 28, vol. 3 (London: Longmans, 1866), pp. 188–94; Froissart, *Oeuvres*, ed. Kervyn, 15: 302–6. Although Michel Pintoin pays little attention to dress, he does recognize ceremonial uses of the landscape, gesture, and gift exchange: *Chronique du Religieux de Saint-Denys*, ed. and trans. M. L. Bellaguet (1842), intro. Bernard Guenée, 6 vols. in 3 (n.p.: Comité des Travaux Historiques et Scientifiques, 1994), 2: 450–73.

50. "Entrevue d'Ardres," pp. 212–15. A full-page illumination of this meeting in Salmon's *Demandes*, Paris, Bibliothèque nationale de France, MS fr. 23279, fol. 54, emphasizes the processional aspect of the meeting: Richard and his retinue ride in pairs out of London as Charles and his retinue ride out of Paris toward Ardres. Isabel's carriage follows most of the French retinue.

51. Douglas and Isherwood, *World of Goods*, p. 64; also Jonathan Z. Smith, "The Domestication of Sacrifice," in *Violent Origins: Walter Burkert, René Girard, and Jonathan Z. Smith on Ritual Killing and Cultural Formation*, ed. Robert G. Hamerton-Kelly et al. (Stanford, Calif.: Stanford University Press, 1987), pp. 191–205, on "the scholarly fantasy that ritual is an affair of the *tremendum* rather than a quite ordinary mode of human social labor" (p. 198). The dichotomy between sacred and profane is foundational for Emile Durkheim, *The Elementary Forms of the Religious Life*, trans. Joseph Ward Swain (London: Allen and Unwin, 1915); and Arnold van Gennep, *The Rites of Passage*, trans. Monika B. Vizedom and Gabrielle L. Caffee (Chicago: University of Chicago Press, 1960).

52. Sally F. Moore and Barbara G. Myerhoff, eds., *Secular Ritual* (Assen: Van Gorcum, 1977); Peter Arnade, *Realms of Ritual: Burgundian Ceremony and Civic Life in Late Medieval Ghent* (Ithaca, N.Y.: Cornell University Press, 1996).

53. Stanley J. Tambiah, *Culture, Thought and Social Action: An Anthropological Perspective* (Cambridge, Mass.: Harvard University Press, 1985), p. 153 (his emphasis); compare Douglas and Isherwood, *World of Goods*, p. 65: "the more costly the ritual trappings, the stronger we can assume the intention to fix the meanings to be."

54. Saul, *Richard II*, p. 231; for comparable expenses on the French side, see Léon Mirot, "Un Trousseau royal à la fin du XIVᵉ siècle," *Mémoires de la Société de l'histoire de Paris et de l'Ile-de-France*, 29 (1902): 151–58; Douët-d'Arcq, *Choix de pièces inédites relatives au règne de Charles VI*, 2 vols. (Paris: Renouard, 1863–64), 1: 130–34.

55. "Entrevue d'Ardres," pp. 220–24.

56. Jonathan Z. Smith, *Imagining Religion: From Babylon to Jonestown* (Chicago: University of Chicago Press, 1982), p. 63 (his emphasis). A curious overlap between ritual mimesis and personal devices enfolds the latter into the former: both, following Smith's analysis, express hopes and commitments that are projected into an ideal future. "What is crooked will be made straight"; "I will have none other": the predictive, aspiring, tenor of many personal devices suits them well to ritual use, in that ritual too asserts an ideal future in the face of difficulty.

57. "Entrevue d'Ardres," pp. 212–13. In relation to the tiger Charles wears in the Salmon manuscript, it may be noted that Charles also gave Richard an alms dish of gold ornamented with four tigresses: "Entrevue d'Ardres," pp. 214–15; *The Antient Kalendars and Inventories of the Treasury of His Majesty's Exchequer*, ed. Francis Palgrave, 3 vols. (London, PRO, 1836), 3: 370.

58. Mirot, "Trousseau royal," p. 154; on this record see John H. Harvey, "The Wilton Diptych—A Re-examination," *Archaeologia* 98 (1961): 9.

59. Douët-d'Arcq, *Choix de pièces inédites*, 1: 130; "Entrevue d'Ardres," p. 219. Charles's gift of the broom collar to Richard and Richard's adoption of it argue against Hindman's conjecture that the motto *jamais* with the *planta genista* signifies *never Plantagenet*, an anti-English message that would be inappropriate to this peace-making context (*Christine de Pisan's "Epistre Othea"*, p. 177).

60. *Annales Ricardi Secundi*, p. 190; Richard wears a "cervum de liberata propria" (p. 189); on the third day of the ceremony, Charles's badge of a hart is again said to be the "cervus de Regis Angliae liberata" (p. 193).

61. Marian Campbell, "'White Harts and Coronets': The Jewellery and Plate of Richard II," in *Regal Image of Richard II*, ed. Gordon, Monnas, and Elam, pp. 100–102; Harvey, "Wilton Diptych," pp. 7–8.

62. Beaune, "Costume et pouvoir," p. 143; Richard's wardrobe and exchequer records for the ceremony do not survive. Monnas, "Fit for a King," p. 170, cites a 1386 record of blue velvet robes for Richard and Anne embroidered with couched white harts and "diverse sayings" [div's' dictamin'].

63. Boulton, *Knights of the Crown*, p. 428; Douët-d'Arcq, *Nouveau recueil*, pp. 143, 160–61, 192–201; London, *Royal Beasts*, pp. 4, 65; Campbell, "'White Harts and Coronets,'" pp. 98–99.

64. Harvey, "Wilton Diptych," p. 9 et passim.

65. M. V. Clarke, *Fourteenth Century Studies*, ed. L. S. Sutherland and M. McKisack (Oxford: Clarendon Press, 1937), p. 272.

66. Annette B. Weiner, *Inalienable Possessions: The Paradox of Keeping-While-Giving* (Berkeley: University of California Press, 1992).

67. Weiner, *Inalienable Possessions*, p. 150; according to Froissart, the duke of Gloucester understands gifting to express Charles's withheld power: his comment on receiving extraordinary gifts at an earlier stage of these negotiations is "ens ou royaulme de France est toute richesse et toute puissance" [in the kingdom of France resides all wealth and power]: *Oeuvres*, ed. Kervyn, 15: 297.

68. Harvey, "Wilton Diptych," p. 11.

69. "Entrevue d'Ardres," p. 217. Anne's livery collar appears in exchequer records: *Antient Kalendars*, ed. Palgrave, 3: 341 ("i. coler de la livere la Roigne que Deux assioll ove un ostrich"), 3: 357 ("un coler du livere de la Royne Anne de braunches de rose maryn"). John Gough Nichols argues that the entries refer to a livery collar using both rosemary and ostrich motifs: "Observations on the Heraldic Devices Discovered on the Effigies of Richard the Second and his Queen in Westminster Abbey," *Archaeologia* 29 (1842): 51. Soon after the wedding, the duke of Aumarle gave Isabel a collar of broom cods, rosemary, and an ostrich in a similar fusing of her French device with Anne's devices: Douët-d'Arcq, *Choix de pièces inédites*, 2: 275. Broom is embroidered on two "corsets" and a "chambre" in Isabel's trousseau: Mirot, "Trousseau royal," pp. 143, 146.

70. "Entrevue d'Ardres," pp. 217–18; Charles also wears the hart badge again and, in place of his broom collar, "la sygne du soleil en son arme" [the sign of the sun on his arm], a sign he used intermittently from 1381: de Vaivre, "Devises de Charles VI," p. 95. Like the broom and the hart, the sun overlaps in Richard's and Charles's use: Monnas, "Fit for a King," pp. 167–68.

71. Catherine Bell, *Ritual Theory, Ritual Practice* (Oxford: Oxford University Press, 1992), p. 98; Pierre Bourdieu, *Outline of a Theory of Practice*, trans. Richard Nice (Cambridge: Cambridge University Press, 1977), p. 120 (text altered slightly to correct syntax). Bourdieu concludes that ritual gestures are not at all metaphoric but totally prediscursive; my position is that ritual gestures can be metaphoric, though gesture and referent are even less clearly related than vehicle and tenor in linguistic metaphors.

72. "Entrevue d'Ardres," p. 218. The French record of Isabel's trousseau describes this costume as embroidered with pearls of fleurs de lis and with the quartered arms of France and England ("ouvrées de broderie de perles de fleurs de liz et escartelées des armes de France et d'Engleterre"): Mirot, "Trousseau royal," p. 143. Richard may be referring to his alliance with France by switching from red garments to blue for third day of the ceremony: "Entrevue d'Ardres," p. 217.

73. "Entrevue d'Ardres," p. 219. Richard's first wife, Anne, was similarly called a gift to the English in a contemporary verse, but the *Westminster Chronicle* objects that since Richard gave a large dower for her but she brought no dowry, "it seemed that she represented a purchase rather than a gift": *The Westminster Chronicle, 1381–1394*, ed. and trans. L. C. Hector and Barbara F. Harvey (Oxford: Clarendon Press, 1982), pp. 24–25.

74. Claude Lévi-Strauss, *The Elementary Structures of Kinship*, trans. James Harle Bell, John Richard von Sturmer, and Rodney Needham (Boston: Beacon Press, 1969); Weiner, *Inalienable Possessions*, discusses backgrounds to Lévi-Strauss in the work of Marcel Mauss and Bronislaw Malinowski. Within feminist literary studies, the most influential versions of the exchange-of-women model have been Gayle Rubin, "The Traffic in Women: Notes on the 'Political Economy' of Sex," in *Toward an Anthropology of Women*, ed. Rayna R. Reiter (New York: Monthly Review Press, 1975), pp. 157–210; and Luce Irigaray, "Women on the Market," in *This Sex Which Is Not One*, trans. Catherine Porter with Carolyn Burke (Ithaca, N.Y.: Cornell University Press, 1985), pp. 170–91.

75. Jack Goody, *The Development of the Family and Marriage in Europe* (Cambridge: Cambridge University Press, 1983), esp. pp. 232–39. Goody responds extensively to the work of Georges Duby and Diane Owen Hughes, who weigh more heavily the patrilineal features of European kinship.

76. Goody, *Development of the Family*; the term "patrimonium" is used by Stanley Chojnacki, "The Power of Love: Wives and Husbands in Late Medieval Venice," in *Women and Power in the Middle Ages*, ed. Mary Erler and Maryanne Kowaleski (Athens: University of Georgia Press, 1988), p. 130.

77. Goody, *Development of the Family*, pp. 19–21; several local studies of dowry and dower practices reach similar conclusions, e.g., Martha Howell, *The Marriage Exchange: Property, Social Place, and Gender in Cities of the Low Countries, 1300–1550* (Berkeley: University of California Press, 1998); Andrée Courtemanche, *La Richesse des femmes: Patrimoines et gestion à Manosque au XIVe siècle*, Cahiers d'Etudes Médiévales 11 (Montreal: Bellarmin, 1993); Chojnacki, "Dowries and Kinsmen in Early Renaissance Venice," *Journal of Interdisciplinary History* 5 (1975): 571–600.

78. Weiner, *Inalienable Possessions*, pp. 66–97 (quotation at p. 73). For a history of the shifting term "inalienable" in discussions of gifting, see Jane Fair Bestor,

"Marriage Transactions in Renaissance Italy and Mauss's *Essay on the Gift*," *Past and Present* 164 (August 1999): 6–46.

79. "Entrevue d'Ardres," p. 219: "luy comanda d'estre foyal et plesante a son filtz d'Engletere."

80. See the letters and petitions demanding her return to France following Richard's death in Douët-d'Arcq, *Choix de pièces inédites*, 1: 185–87, 193–97.

81. Grant McCracken, "Clothing as Language: An Object Lesson in the Study of the Expressive Properties of Material Culture," in *Material Anthropology: Contemporary Approaches to Material Culture*, ed. Barrie Reynolds and Margaret A. Stott (Lanham, Md.: University Press of America, 1987), p. 107.

82. Influential discussions of marriage in relation to the tale are Christiane Klapisch-Zuber, "The Griselda Complex: Dowry and Marriage Gifts in the Quattrocento," in *Women, Family, and Ritual in Renaissance Italy*, trans. Lydia Cochrane (Chicago: University of Chicago Press, 1985), pp. 213–46; and Carolyn Dinshaw, *Chaucer's Sexual Poetics* (Madison: University of Wisconsin Press, 1989), pp. 132–55. Both note the importance of clothing in the tale's representations of marriage and divorce.

83. Philippe de Mézières, *Letter to King Richard II*, ed. and trans. G. W. Coopland (New York: Barnes and Noble, 1976), pp. 42, 115 ("Or pleust a Dieu, tres debonnaire prince, que, pour nourrissement de paix de la crestiente et consolacion de vostre royale personne, il vous vousist ottroier et mander une tele espouse et compaingne comme il fist au marquis de Saluce, apelee Griseldis," p. 115).

84. Ibid.; Philippe de Mézières, *Le Livre de la vertu du sacrement de mariage*, ed. Joan B. Williamson (Washington, D.C.: Catholic University of America Press, 1993).

85. J. Burke Severs, *The Literary Relationships of Chaucer's "Clerkes Tale"* (New Haven, Conn.: Yale University Press, 1942); see also Elie Golenistcheff-Koutouzoff, *L'Histoire de Griseldis en France au XIVᵉ et au XVᵉ siècle* (Paris: Droz, 1933); and Amy W. Goodwin, "The Griselda Story in France," in *Sources and Analogues of Chaucer's "Canterbury Tales"*, ed. Robert Correale and Mary Hamel (Cambridge: Boydell and Brewer, forthcoming).

86. The most recent edition is *L'Estoire de Griseldis en rimes et par personnages (1395)*, ed. Mario Roques (Geneva: Droz, 1957); the introduction summarizes debate on whether Philippe de Mézières was its author.

87. Severs, *Literary Relationships*, p. 288; trans. Robert Dudley French, *A Chaucer Handbook*, 2nd ed. (New York: Appleton-Century-Crofts, 1947), pp. 291–311 (quotation at p. 311). Charlotte Cook Morse demonstrates that, despite Petrarch's demurral, his early copyists and readers did take his text to be about marriage: "What to Call Petrarch's Griselda," in *The Uses of Manuscripts in Literary Studies: Essays in Memory of Judson Boyce Allen*, ed. Charlotte Cook Morse, Penelope Reed Doob, and Marjorie Curry Woods (Kalamazoo, Mich.: Medieval Institute Publications, 1992), pp. 263–303.

88. Severs, *Literary Relationships*, p. 288. *Le Menagier de Paris*, *Le Livre du chevalier de la Tour Landry*, and Christine de Pizan's *Livre de la cité des dames* address the tale to female audiences.

89. Philippe, *Livre de la vertu*, pp. 153, 155–56.

90. Severs reproduces these two versions on facing pages in *Sources and Analogues of Chaucer's Canterbury Tales*, ed. W. F. Bryan and Germaine Dempster (1941; reprint Atlantic Highlands, N.J.: Humanities Press, 1958), pp. 288–331.

91. Severs, *Literary Relationships*, p. 255.

92. For example, in French the women who reclothe Griselda at her wedding dislike handling her old clothes; these same old clothes no longer fit her properly when she returns home; and the sergeant who takes her daughter is not just "suspecta" [threatening], as in Petrarch, but "de laide figure" [ugly of face] and "rude et lourde" [rough and forceful] in his gestures: Severs, *Literary Relationships*, pp. 265, 271, 281; see also pp. 136–73. Compare Chaucer's *Clerk's Tale, Canterbury Tales* 4.375–76, 913–17. Subsequent references to Chaucer's text appear in my text and notes with the abbreviation *CT*. For a fresh approach to the complexities of reading clothing in the *General Prologue* to the *Canterbury Tales*, see Laura F. Hodges, *Chaucer and Costume: The Secular Pilgrims in the General Prologue* (Cambridge: D.S. Brewer, 2000).

93. Examples are *CT* 4.456–62, 581, 621–23, 696–97, 719–21, 902–3, 932–38.

94. Severs, *Literary Relationships*, pp. 4–6.

95. French, trans., *Chaucer Handbook*, p. 297; Latin text and French text: Severs, *Literary Relationships*, pp. 264–65.

96. Walter also fuses marriage and the oath of obedience in "I wol axe if it hire will be / To be my wif and reule hire after me": *CT* 4.326–27. On the contrasting Latin and French handling of the scene, see Severs, *Literary Relationships*, p. 240.

97. *CT* 4.507–9, 646–47, 654–56. Elizabeth Fowler, "Civil Death and the Maiden: Agency and the Conditions of Contract in *Piers Plowman*," *Speculum* 70 (1995): 760–92, argues that women's consent in marriage is so constrained by their subordination as to be "impoverished" and perhaps altogether vitiated (p. 785); compare below Strathern's argument for a more substantially engaged agency in self-subordination.

98. Marilyn Strathern, *The Gender of the Gift: Problems with Women and Problems with Society in Melanesia* (Berkeley: University of California Press, 1988), p. 331. Annette Weiner considered her argument against the exchange-of-women thesis to be at odds with Strathern's, because Strathern remains committed to exchange itself, to the idea that gifting is about transferring value, such that her discussion of marriage exchange cannot escape configuring women as possessions to be conferred (Weiner, *Inalienable Possessions*, pp. 14–15). For Weiner, the defining feature of wifehood is that it simultaneously confers and withholds access to the myriad relations of blood and power that a woman bears; this simultaneity of conferring and withholding characterizes gifts of objects as well. I believe Strathern and Weiner are more in alliance on the implications of traditional marriage than Weiner conceded: both scholars emphasize the complexity of women's position, which requires them to surrender much of their value and activity to a husband's control; both argue that marriage does not obviate women's status in other relationships that interpenetrate the marital relationship.

99. On consent, see James A. Brundage, *Law, Sex, and Christian Society in Medieval Europe* (Chicago: University of Chicago Press, 1987), esp. pp. 236–38, 436–37; Christopher N. L. Brooke, *The Medieval Idea of Marriage* (Oxford: Oxford University Press, 1989), pp. 128–43; Jacqueline Murray, "Individualism and Consensual

Marriage: Some Evidence from Medieval England," in *Women, Marriage, and Family in Medieval Christendom: Essays in Memory of Michael M. Sheehan, C.S.B.*, ed. Constance M. Rousseau and Joel T. Rosenthal (Kalamazoo, Mich.: Medieval Institute Publications, 1998), pp. 121–51; and Shannon McSheffrey, "'I will never have none ayenst my faders will': Consent and the Making of Marriage in the Late Medieval Diocese of London," in *Women, Marriage, and Family*, pp. 153–74. A valuable treatment of marriage in relation to lineage, identity, and women is Sarah Kay, *The "Chansons de geste" in the Age of Romance: Political Fictions* (Oxford: Clarendon Press, 1995).

100. J. L. Austin, *How to Do Things with Words* (Cambridge, Mass.: Harvard University Press, 1962); Andrew Parker and Eve Kosofsky Sedgwick, eds., *Performativity and Performance* (New York: Routledge, 1995). Jacques Derrida began the analysis of Austin's performatives along these lines: *Margins of Philosophy*, trans. Alan Bass (Chicago: University of Chicago Press, 1982), pp. 321–27.

101. The clothes these new husbands provided, and that brides carried and wore as they processed to their new homes, were typically worth from a third to two thirds as much as the dowry: Bestor, "Marriage Transactions." Klapisch-Zuber first pointed out that "the references to contemporary weddings are undeniable" in the Italian versions of the tale: "Griselda Complex," p. 230.

102. Hughes, "Regulating Women's Fashion." Clothing and other ornaments figure among English and French husbands' marriage gifts as well, though not so predictably as in Italy. Charles VI had Isabeau of Bavaria dressed for their wedding in a silk robe embroidered with gold, but they later provided their daughter Isabel's wedding dress for her marriage to Richard II: *Chronique du Religieux* 1: 358–59; Mirot, "Trousseau royal," p. 130. Aristocratic marriages of the period required an especially luxurious robe for the bride, but not necessarily one presented by the husband. The groom's family prepared a robe of white silk and gold brocade for Jeanne of Luxembourg's marriage to Philip of Burgundy's son, but John II of France provided his own daughter's dress of sanguine velvet with pearls when she married Charles the Bad (Famiglietti, *Tales*, pp. 65–66; Newton, *Fashion*, p. 31). White was not a standard color for wedding dresses until the eighteenth century: Phillis Cunnington and Catherine Lucas, *Costume for Births, Marriages and Deaths* (New York: Barnes and Noble, 1972), pp. 60–63.

103. Griselda's "translation" has been a touchstone for scholars' discussions of Chaucer's manipulation of his sources: Dinshaw, *Chaucer's Sexual Poetics*, pp. 132–55; David Wallace, *Chaucerian Polity: Absolutist Lineages and Associational Forms in England and Italy* (Stanford, Calif: Stanford University Press, 1997), pp. 285–87.

104. *CT* 4.481–83, 624–37, 792–95; Walter's people find low birth a plausible motive for rejecting Griselda, *CT* 4.724–25, 792–95, 904–10, 990–91.

105. Walter's motive: *CT* 4.452, 454, 495–97, 620–21, 699 (quoted), 707, 786–87, 1044, 1056, 1075, 1078.

106. Severs, *Literary Relationships*, p. 280; French, *Chaucer Handbook*, p. 306.

107. Petrarch's Griselda further evokes the moral valence of clothing in saying that Walter's finery has "enriched me to the point of envy": Severs, *Literary Relationships*, 280; French, *Chaucer Handbook*, p. 306. See also Cristelle L. Baskins, "Griselda, or the Renaissance Bride Stripped Bare by Her Bachelor in Tuscan *Cassone* Painting," *Stanford Italian Review* 10 (1991): 153–75.

108. My third chapter treats moral valences of dress and undress more fully.

109. *CT* 4.880. In Petrarch's version, maidenhead is not part of Griselda's dowry and the smock appears as an afterthought, a revision of the idea that nakedness expresses Griselda's virtue. The smock's belated appearance might argue that Petrarch feels the pull of social as well as spiritual implications in the tale. Kathleen Davis argued for political resonances in the exchange of smock for hymen, in "Limit of the Nation: The Hymen and Griselda's Smock," paper given at the Modern Language Association, Toronto, December 1997.

110. Larry Scanlon resists contradictions between moral and marital interpretations in his argument that Griselda's conduct consecrates marriage by treating Walter's demands as if they were sacred, thus defining marriage itself as "an arena of spiritual struggle": "What's the Pope Got to Do With It? Forgery, Didacticism and Desire in the Clerk's Tale," *New Medieval Literatures* 6 (2002).

111. Wallace, *Chaucerian Polity*, p. 288 (quoting *CT* 4.1110).

112. Michael M. Sheehan, *Marriage, Family, and Law in Medieval Europe: Collected Studies*, ed. James K. Farge (Toronto: University of Toronto Press, 1996), pp. 38–76.

113. R. H. Helmholz, *Marriage Litigation in Medieval England* (Cambridge: Cambridge University Press, 1974), p. 31: "Historians have sometimes thought that with the definitive formulation of the canon law in the later twelfth and thirteenth centuries, lay habits, or at least lay beliefs, fell quickly into line. But it is not so." See also Brundage, *Law, Sex, and Christian Society*, pp. 494–503.

114. Brundage, *Law, Sex, and Christian Society*, pp. 236, 254, 431–32.

115. Golenistcheff-Koutouzoff, *L'Histoire de Griseldis*, pp. 115–26, surveys the fourteenth-century versions of the tale in France. The dramatic version of Philippe's translation preserves his addition of a bishop; Philippe may be its author: *Estoire de Griseldis*, pp. vii–ix.

116. J. Smith, *Imagining Religion*, p. 53.

Chapter 2. Maytime

1. Pierre Bourdieu warns that "the informant's discourse owes its best-hidden properties to the fact that it is the product of a semitheoretical disposition, inevitably induced by any learned questioning": *Outline of a Theory of Practice*, trans. Richard Nice (Cambridge: Cambridge University Press, 1977), p. 18. Bourdieu's claim that mimetic behavior rather than intellection is fundamental to ritual leads him to divide interpretive commentary from ritual more sharply than do many anthropologists.

2. Jean Froissart, *Le Paradis d'amour, L'Orloge amoureus*, ed. Peter F. Dembowski (Geneva: Droz, 1986), *Paradis*, l. 1621.

3. Verbal ascriptions of meaning are a vital part of what Roland Barthes has dubbed the "fashion system." Barthes argues that the descriptions of clothing in fashion magazines provide not just an account of how the clothing looks but vital information on its significances. His analysis demonstrates (against his very thesis) that clothing is less a language in itself than a code needing linguistic interpretation:

see Jonathan Culler, *Structuralist Poetics: Structuralism, Linguistics, and the Study of Literature* (Ithaca, N.Y.: Cornell University Press, 1975), pp. 32–40, and Marshall Sahlins, *Culture and Practical Reason* (Chicago: University of Chicago Press, 1976), pp. 179–204, both on Roland Barthes, *The Fashion System*, trans. Matthew Ward and Richard Howard (Berkeley: University of California Press, 1983). Also useful for medievalists is Odile Blanc, "Historiographie du vêtement: Un Bilan," in *Le Vêtement: histoire, archéologie et symbolique vestimentaires au Moyen Age*, ed. Michel Pastoureau (Paris : Léopard d'Or, 1989), pp. 7–33.

4. *Oeuvres complètes de Eustache Deschamps*, ed. Le Marquis de Queux de Saint-Hilaire, SATF 9, 11 vols. (Paris: Firmin Didot, 1878–1903), 4: 262–64 (no. 767), ll. 35–37.

5. The editor's gloss reads "à la mode," but "nouviaux" evokes as well the new season and the renewal of the earth. Cf. the intersection of renewal and adornment in a May lyric of Christine de Pizan: "Tout se revest; il n'y a arbre nu" [everything reclothes itself; no tree is naked], so all should wear "Chapiaulx jolis, violetes et roses" [pretty chaplets, violets and roses]: *Oeuvres poétiques de Christine de Pisan*, ed. Maurice Roy, SATF 22, 3 vols. (Paris: Firmin Didot, 1886–96), 1: 235–36 (no. 25), ll. 14 and refrain.

6. Evidence stressing the license livery offers is analyzed by Paul Strohm, *Hochon's Arrow: The Social Imagination of Fourteenth-Century Texts* (Princeton, N.J.: Princeton University Press, 1992), pp. 57–74, 179–85; see also Françoise Piponnier, *Costume et vie sociale: La Cour d'Anjou, XIVe–XVe siècle* (Paris: Mouton, 1970), pp. 243–59; Frédérique Lachaud, "Liveries of Robes in England, c. 1200–c. 1330," *English Historical Review* 111 (1996): 279–98.

7. Charles d'Orléans, *Poésies*, ed. Pierre Champion, CFMA 34, 56, 2 vols. (Paris: Champion, 1923, 1927), 1: 85–87 (ballade 61), ll. 6–10.

8. Deschamps, *Oeuvres complètes*, 4: 259–61 (no. 765), ll. 35–36. David Wallace, *Chaucerian Polity: Absolutist Lineages and Associational Forms in England and Italy* (Stanford, Calif.: Stanford University Press, 1997), p. 353, hears the language of indentures of retaining in Chaucer's passage on the two Maying parties, "I nam withholden yit with never nother": *The Riverside Chaucer*, ed. Larry Benson, 3rd ed. (Boston: Houghton, 1987), Prologue to the *Legend of Good Women*, version F, l. 192. Subsequent references to the Prologue appear in parentheses in the text with the designation *LGW* (versions F or G).

9. Louis Claude Douët-d'Arcq, *Nouveau recueil de comptes de l'argenterie des rois de France* (Paris: Renouard, 1874), p. 294. On the same houppelandes see also pp. 116, 129–31, 196–97, 290. A similar provision for 61 houppelandes for 1 May 1399 is published in Léon de Laborde, *Glossaire français du Moyen Age à l'usage de l'archéologue et de l'amateur des arts* (1872; reprint Paris: Laget, 1994), p. 368.

10. Household liveries were not always marked with colors or emblems distinguishing the house, and were sometimes not even given in clothing but in sums of money that stood for clothing, but most typically these regular seasonal distributions were garments that represented the household in some visible way.

11. Louis Claude Douët-d'Arcq, *Choix de pièces inédites relatives au règne de Charles VI*, 2 vols. (Paris: Renouard, 1863, 1864), 1: 163–167 (quotation at p. 163); see also Douët-d'Arcq, *Nouveau recueil*, pp. xliv–xlvii. Philip the Bold's household

records indicate his participation in the king's Maying parties in 1385, 1390, and 1400: *Itinéraires de Philippe le Hardi et de Jean sans Peur, ducs de Bourgogne (1363–1419)*, ed. Ernest Petit (Paris: Imprimerie Nationale, 1888), pp. 177, 222, 297.
    12. Douët-d'Arcq, *Nouveau recueil*, p. xlvi: "ouvrées de broderie sur la manche senestre de deux branches de may et de genestes entortillez ensemble"; see also pp. 196–97. "May" in English refers to hawthorne and "le mai" in French to woodbine or honeysuckle or other greenery, according to Derek Pearsall, *The Floure and the Leafe and The Assembly of Ladies* (1962; reprint Manchester: Manchester University Press, 1980), p. 27. On broom taken over from the Valois by the Plantagenets, see John H. Harvey, "The Wilton Diptych: A Re-examination," *Archaeologia* 98 (1961): 8–9.
    13. Léon de Laborde, *Les Ducs de Bourgogne: Etudes sur les lettres, les arts et l'industrie pendant le XVe siècle*, part 2, vol. 3, *Preuves* (Paris: Plon, 1852), no. 5449; see also no. 5487 for six houppelandes ordered by Louis for May 1, 1390.
    14. Jack Goody, "Against 'Ritual': Loosely Structured Thoughts on a Loosely Defined Topic," in *Secular Ritual*, ed. Sally F. Moore and Barbara G. Myerhoff (Amsterdam: Van Gorcum, 1977), p. 33; Bourdieu, *Outline of a Theory of Practice*, p. 116; see also Bourdieu, *The Logic of Practice*, trans. Richard Nice (Cambridge: Polity Press, 1990), pp. 200–270.
    15. Deschamps, "Lay de franchise," *Oeuvres complètes*, 2: 203–14 (no. 307); John L. Lowes, "The Prologue to the *Legend of Good Women* as Related to the French *Marguerite* Poems and the *Filostrato*," *PMLA* 19 (1904): 603–7. Line references for the "Lay de franchise" appear in the text in parentheses with the designation "Lf."
    16. For basic information on the MSS and their artists, see *The "Très Riches Heures" of Jean, Duke of Berry, Musée Condé, Chantilly*, intro. Raymond Cazelles, Jean Longnon, and Millard Meiss (New York: Brazillier, 1969); *Heures de Turin: Quarante-cinq feuillets à peintures provenant des "Très Belles Heures" de Jean de France, Duc de Berry*, intro. Albert Chatelet and Paul Durrieu (Turin: Erasmo, 1967).
    17. On ritual and performance see Sarah Beckwith, "Ritual, Theater, and Social Space in the York Corpus Christi Cycle," in *Bodies and Disciplines: Intersections of Literature and History in Fifteenth-Century England*, ed. David Wallace and Barbara A. Hanawalt (Minneapolis: University of Minnesota Press, 1996), pp. 63–86; Rosalind C. Morris, "All Made Up: Performance Theory and the New Anthropology of Sex and Gender," *Annual Review of Anthropology* 24 (1995): 574–79; Joseph Roach, "Kinship, Intelligence, and Memory as Improvisation: Culture and Performance in New Orleans," in *Performance and Cultural Politics*, ed. Elin Diamond (London: Routledge, 1996), pp. 217–36; Richard Schechner, *Between Theater and Anthropology* (Philadelphia: University of Pennsylvania Press, 1985); Victor Turner, *From Ritual to Theatre: The Human Seriousness of Play* (New York: PAJ Publications, 1982).
    18. On secular rituals see John D. Kelly and Martha Kaplan, "History, Structure, and Ritual," *Annual Review of Anthropology* 19 (1990): 119–50; John J. MacAloon, "Olympic Games and the Theory of Spectacle in Modern Societies," in *Rite, Drama, Festival, Spectacle: Rehearsals Toward a Theory of Cultural Performance*, ed. John J. MacAloon (Philadelphia: Institute for the Study of Human Issues, 1984), pp. 241–80. Useful medieval studies include Peter Arnade, *Realms of Ritual:*

Burgundian Ceremony and Civic Life in Late Medieval Ghent (Ithaca, N.Y.: Cornell University Press, 1996); Gordon Kipling, *Enter the King: Theatre, Liturgy, and Ritual in the Medieval Civic Triumph* (Oxford: Clarendon Press, 1998); and Stewart Gordon, ed., *Robes and Honor: The Medieval World of Investiture* (New York: Palgrave, 2001).

19. Charles d'Orléans, *Poésies*, 1: 70–71 (ballade 48), ll. 4–5.

20. Christine de Pizan, *Oeuvres poétiques*, 1: 217 (no. 9); see also 1: 235–36 (no. 25), 1: 239–40 (no. 28).

21. Chaucer, *Riverside Chaucer*, *Canterbury Tales*, 1.1042–45; on the Mayings in this tale see Lorraine Kochanske Stock, "The Two Mayings in Chaucer's *Knight's Tale*: Convention and Invention," *Journal of English and Germanic Philology* 85 (1986): 206–21.

22. Froissart, *Paradis d'amour*, ll. 1612–13; Christine de Pizan, *Oeuvres poétiques*, 1: 217 (no. 9, l. 21); 1: 235–36 (no. 25, l. 8).

23. Ronald Hutton, *The Rise and Fall of Merry England: The Ritual Year, 1400–1700* (Oxford: Oxford University Press, 1994), p. 56.

24. Bourdieu, *Outline of a Theory of Practice*, p. 116; see also pp. 97–109 on the agrarian calendar.

25. *The Works of Sir Thomas Malory*, 3rd ed., ed. Eugène Vinaver, rev. P. J. C. Field, 3 vols. (Oxford: Clarendon Press, 1990), 3: 1122.

26. Natalie Zemon Davis, *Society and Culture in Early Modern France* (Stanford, Calif.: Stanford University Press, 1965), p. 141; *Floure and the Leafe*, p. 27; *La Minute française des interrogatoires de Jeanne la Pucelle*, ed. Paul Doncoeur (Melun: Argences, 1952), pp. 107, 201; Hutton, *Rise and Fall*, pp. 28, 31–33; T. F. Thiselton-Dyer, *British Popular Customs* (London: G. Bell, 1876), pp. 216–17, 224, 235.

27. On the poetic heritage see Joseph Bédier, "Les Fêtes de mai et les commencemens de la poésie lyrique au Moyen Age," *Revue des deux mondes* 4th ser. 135 (1896): 146–72.

28. Christine de Pizan, *Oeuvres poétiques*, 1: 239–40 (no. 28), ll. 23–24.

29. Guillaume de Machaut, *Oeuvres*, ed. Prosper Tarbé (1849; reprint Geneva: Slatkine, 1977), p. 128.

30. Deschamps, *Oeuvres complètes*, 2: 193–203 (quotation at l. 190); see also 2: 210–211.

31. John Gower, *Confessio Amantis*, in *The Complete Works of John Gower*, ed. G. C. Macaulay, vols. 2–3 (Oxford: Clarendon Press, 1901), 1: 2021–37, 6: 1832–53.

32. Examples are *Oeuvres de Froissart: Poésies*, ed. Auguste Scheler, 3 vols. (Brussels : Devaux, 1870–72), 2: 343–46, 348–50 (pastourelles 17, 19); Christine de Pizan, *Oeuvres poétiques*, 2: 242–44 (two bergeriettes).

33. Victor W. Turner, *The Forest of Symbols: Aspects of Ndembu Ritual* (Ithaca, N.Y.: Cornell University Press, 1967), pp. 28, 30; see also Turner, *The Ritual Process: Structure and Anti-Structure* (Chicago: Aldine, 1969); J. David Sapir and J. Christopher Crocker, eds., *The Social Use of Metaphor: Essays on the Anthropology of Rhetoric* (Philadelphia: University of Pennsylvania Press, 1977).

34. Turner, *Forest of Symbols*, p. 30.

35. Kelly and Kaplan, "History, Structure, and Ritual," p. 140.

36. For example, Stanley J. Tambiah, *Culture, Thought, and Social Action: An Anthropological Perspective* (Cambridge, Mass.: Harvard University Press, 1985), esp.

pp. 123–66; Stuart Hall and Tony Jefferson, eds., *Resistance Through Rituals: Youth Subcultures in Post-War Britain* (London: Hutchinson, 1976).

37. Deschamps, *Oeuvres complètes*, 4: 259–61 (no. 765), ll. 1–2.

38. Marilyn Strathern, "No Nature, No Culture: The Hagen Case," in *Nature, Culture and Gender*, ed. Carol P. MacCormack and Marilyn Strathern (Cambridge: Cambridge University Press, 1980), p. 179. Margaret Lock discusses anthropologists' "perceived opposition between nature and culture, now recognized as a product of Western metaphysics" in "Cultivating the Body: Anthropology and Epistemologies of Bodily Practice and Knowledge," *Annual Review of Anthropology* 22 (1993): 135.

39. *Floure and the Leafe*, ll. 49–70. On courtly gardens see Derek Pearsall and Elizabeth Salter, *Landscapes and Seasons of the Medieval World* (Toronto: University of Toronto Press, 1973), pp. 76–118; on architectural uses of plants in medieval gardens, see Sylvia Landsberg, *The Medieval Garden* (London: British Museum, 1996), pp. 49–54.

40. *Floure and the Leafe*, l. 412.

41. In John Clanvowe's "The Cuckoo and the Nightingale," the two birds similarly articulate the distinction between carefree, pleasure-seeking love and a love from which "cometh al goodnesse, / Al honour, and [eke] al gentilnesse": in *Chaucerian and Other Pieces*, ed. Walter W. Skeat (Oxford: Clarendon, 1897), pp. 347–58 (quotation at ll. 151–52). I have not considered "The Court of Love" (in *Chaucerian and Other Pieces*, pp. 409–47), because its sensibility is more clerical than courtly.

42. Deschamps's "Lay de franchise" extends the connection between nature and court to the closing feast, for which the hall is "tendu de vert, de riches draps paré" [hung with green, decorated with rich cloths: "Lf" 249] and has "un ciel entier sur la table" [a whole cloth sky suspended over the table: "Lf" 253].

43. Jacques Derrida, *Of Grammatology*, trans. Gayatri Chakravorty Spivak (Baltimore: Johns Hopkins University Press, 1974), pp. 144–45.

44. Mary Ellen Roach and Joanne Bubolz Eicher, "The Language of Personal Adornment," in *The Fabrics of Culture: The Anthropology of Clothing and Adornment*, ed. Justine M. Cordwell and Ronald A. Schwartz (The Hague: Mouton, 1979), p. 18.

45. Jack Goody, *The Culture of Flowers* (Cambridge: Cambridge University Press, 1993), pp. 66–79, 157–65; George L. Marsh, "Sources and Analogues of 'The Flower and the Leaf,'" *Modern Philology* 4 (1906–7): 121–67, 281–327.

46. In *Floure and the Leafe*, for example, all the followers of the Leaf wear white clothing of more or less luxurious fabric and trim. The effect is of a house color or livery differently executed to indicate different ranks.

47. Deschamps, *Oeuvres complètes*, 2: 193–203 (quotation at ll. 319–20).

48. Derrida, *Of Grammatology*, p. 145.

49. *The Romaunt of the Rose*, in *Riverside Chaucer*, ll. 890–98. The original reads "il n'avoit pas robe de soie, / Ainz avoit robe de floreites, / Fete par fines amoreites. / A losenges, a escuciaus, / A oiselez, a lionciaus / Et a betes et a liparz / Fu sa robe de toutes parz / Portrete, et ovree de flors / Par diverseté de colors": Guillaume de Lorris and Jean de Meun, *Le Roman de la Rose*, ed. Félix Lecoy, 3

vols., CMFA 92, 95, 98 (Paris: Champion, 1973, 1975, 1978), vol. 1, ll. 876–84. See also Pierre-Yves Badel, *Le Roman de la Rose au XIVe siècle: Etude de la réception de l'oeuvre* (Geneva : Droz, 1980).

50. *Romaunt of the Rose*, ll. 2465–68. The original reads "Qui ce qu'il aime plus regarde / Plus alume son cuer et larde; / Cil larz alume et fet flamer / Le feu qui fet les genz amer": Guillaume, *Roman de la Rose*, vol. 1, ll. 2333–36.

51. Useful revisions and consolidations of work by Freud, Marx, and others on the fetish include Emily Apter, *Feminizing the Fetish: Psychoanalysis and Narrative Obsession in Turn-of-the-Century France* (Ithaca, N.Y.: Cornell University Press, 1991); Laura Mulvey, "Some Thoughts on Theories of Fetishism in the Context of Contemporary Culture," *october* 65 (Summer 1993): 3–20; William Pietz, "The Problem of the Fetish, I," *Res* 9 (Spring 1985): 5–17; Pietz, "The Problem of the Fetish, II," *Res* 13 (Spring 1987): 23–45.

52. Mulvey, "Theories of Fetishism," p. 9.

53. Robert J. Stoller, *Observing the Erotic Imagination* (New Haven, Conn.: Yale University Press, 1985), p. 155.

54. Machaut, *Oeuvres*, p. 124 ("Dit de la Marguerite"). On "Marguerite" poetry see Lowes, "Prologue to the *Legend of Good Women*"; James I. Wimsatt, *The Marguerite Poetry of Guillaume de Machaut*, University of North Carolina Studies in the Romance Languages and Literatures, 87 (Chapel Hill: University of North Carolina Press, 1970).

55. Froissart, *Paradis d'amour*, ll. 1675–1723.

56. Ibid., ll. 1683–85.

57. "Tant l'ama que tous soirs et tous mains, / Quels temps qu'il fust, kalendes ou toussains, / Un chapelet en portoit" [he so loved it (or her) that every evening and morning, whatever the weather or time of year, he wore a chaplet of them]: Froissart, *Poésies*, ed. Scheler, 2: 209–15, ll. 133–35. On the names and the invented mythology see M. Bech, "Quellen und Plan der 'Legende of Good Women' und ihr Verhältniss zur 'Confessio Amantis,'" *Anglia* 5 (1882): 363–64. On the place of daisies and their relation to poetic persona in Froissart, see Claire Nouvet, "The 'Marguerite': A Distinctive Signature," in *Chaucer's French Contemporaries: The Poetry/Poetics of Self and Tradition*, ed. R. Barton Palmer (New York: AMS, 1999), pp. 251–76.

58. Froissart, *Poésies*, ed. Scheler, 2: 209–15, ll. 180–84.

59. Pietz, "Problem of the Fetish, I," p. 5; "Problem of the Fetish, II," pp. 31–36.

60. *The Harley Lyrics*, ed. G. L. Brook (Manchester: Manchester University Press, 1956), p. 44 (no. 11, ll. 13–15); Joseph Bédier, "Les Plus anciennes danses françaises," *Revue des deux mondes* 5th ser. 31 (1906): 408–9.

61. The names of various adherents survive; on the historical context and references of flower-and-leaf poetry, see G. L. Kittredge, "Chaucer and Some of His Friends," *Modern Philology* 1 (1903): 1–18; Marsh, "Sources and Analogues of 'The Flower and the Leaf,'" pp. 124–43.

62. Deschamps, *Oeuvres complètes*, 4: 257–58 (no. 764), ll. 1–2. Carl Lindahl, *Earnest Games: Folkloric Patterns in the Canterbury Tales* (Bloomington: Indiana University Press, 1987), pp. 46–61, suggests a competitive aspect to the writing of

May poetry like that of the London Pui, which accorded prizes to poems at each of its meetings.

63. Deschamps, *Oeuvres complètes*, 4: 259–60 (no. 764), ll. 14–16; 4: 262–64 (no. 767), ll. 46–48.

64. "The discovery of labor presupposes the constitution of the common ground of production, i.e., the disenchantment of a natural world henceforth reduced to its economic dimension alone" (Bourdieu, *Outline of a Theory of Practice*, p. 176).

65. For example, Pearsall and Salter, *Landscapes and Seasons*, p. 28; Goody, *Culture of Flowers*, pp. 164–65.

66. *Floure and the Leafe*, ll. 141–61.

67. *Register of Edward the Black Prince*, ed. M. C. B. Dawes, 4 vols. (London : HMSO, 1930–33), 4: 114, 192–93.

68. Bourdieu, *Outline of a Theory of Practice*, p. 178 (his emphasis).

69. *Floure and the Leafe*, ll. 473–90 and notes.

70. Bourdieu continues, "symbolic capital, a transformed and thereby *disguised* form of physical 'economic' capital, produces its proper effect inasmuch, and only inasmuch, as it conceals the fact that it originates in 'material' forms of capital which are also, in the last analysis, the source of its effects" (*Outline of a Theory of Practice*, p. 183; his emphasis). This claim is harder to work out in examples: how might a smile or honor be understood as originating in material capital? Perhaps by the same circularity we can easily see in largesse: material wealth is what makes it possible to appear unconcerned with wealth, and that disconcern contributes symbolic capital to the dispenser of largesse, precisely because largesse disregards material calculation. Any behavioral standard such as a code of honor or hospitality is facilitated by economic privilege, a "luxury" few can afford, but one that draws its effect from appearing to arise from values other than economic ones.

71. Machaut, *Oeuvres*, p. 124 ("Dit de la Marguerite"); Deschamps, *Oeuvres complètes*, 3: 379–80 (no. 539), ll. 1, 5–6; compare 4: 261 (no. 766), l. 1, which addresses a man as "Tresdouce flour, Elyon de Nillac." On the workings of metaphor in this poetry, see Peter W. Travis, "Chaucer's Heliotropes and the Poetics of Metaphor," *Speculum* 72 (1997): 399–427.

72. James W. Fernandez, "The Performance of Ritual Metaphors," in *The Social Use of Metaphor*, pp. 103, 106.

73. On the "flos florum" topos from antiquity into the Middle Ages, see Peter Dronke, *Medieval Latin and the Rise of European Love-Lyric*, 2nd ed., 2 vols. (Oxford: Clarendon, 1968), 1: 181–92.

74. See Chapter 1, note 74.

75. See Gerald A. Bond, *The Loving Subject: Desire, Eloquence, and Power in Romanesque France* (Philadelphia: University of Pennsylvania Press, 1995), pp. 1–18; Paul Zumthor, *La Lettre et la voix: De la "littérature" médiévale* (Paris: Seuil, 1987); David Lawton, *Chaucer's Narrators* (Cambridge: D.S. Brewer, 1985); Joyce Coleman, *Public Reading and the Reading Public in Late Medieval England and France* (Cambridge: Cambridge University Press, 1996).

76. Goody, "Against 'Ritual,'" p. 32.

77. Deschamps, "Lf" 127, 308. Making poems for Maying is a convention of the festival: cf. *LGW* F 422–23.

78. Deschamps, *Oeuvres complètes*, ed. Raynaud, 11: 45–46; Marian Lossing, "The Prologue to the Legend of Good Women and the *Lai de Franchise*," *Studies in Philology* 39 (1942): 15–35.

79. Lowes, "Prologue to the *Legend of Good Women*," p. 607, believes the "flour" is Marguerite de Bourgogne and "au departir" refers to her departure from Beauté soon after her wedding. A historical referent for "la flour" would not preclude the poet's metaphoric refigurings, and "au departir" within the poem's diegesis must first of all refer to the end of this festival.

80. Charles d'Orléans, *Poésies*, 1: 85–87 (ballade 61), ll. 2, 14–16, 19; *Fortunes Stabilnes: Charles of Orleans's English Book of Love. A Critical Edition*, ed. Mary-Jo Arn (Binghamton, N.Y.: Medieval and Renaissance Texts and Studies, 1994), pp. 215–17 (ballade 64), ll. 2239–41, 2244.

81. Charles d'Orléans, *Poésies*, 1: 85–87 (ballade 61), ll. 34–35; *Fortunes Stabilnes*, pp. 215–17 (ballade 64), ll. 2259–60.

82. Charles d'Orléans, *Poésies*, 1: 154–55 (ballade 98), l. 9; for extended discussions see Alice Planche, *Charles d'Orléans ou la recherche d'un langage* (Paris: Champion, 1975), pp. 626–73; Claudio Galderisi, "Personnifications, réifications et métaphores créatives dans le système rhétorique de Charles d'Orléans," *Romania* 114 (1996): 385–412.

83. Charles d'Orléans, *Poésies*, 1: 36–37 (ballade 18), l. 25; *Fortunes Stabilnes*, pp. 163–64 (ballade 18), l. 758. I have altered the spelling "hurt" to "hart" to clarify the translation. See also Planche, *Charles d'Orléans*, pp. 33–34, 675–80; Daniel Poirion, *Le Poète et le Prince: L'Evolution du lyrisme courtois de Guillaume de Machaut à Charles d'Orléans* (Paris: Presses Universitaires de France, 1965), pp. 64, 569–80.

84. For example, Charles d'Orléans, *Poésies*, 1: 261–64 (complainte 2), l. 49; 1: 56–57 (ballade 37), l. 21; *Fortunes Stabilnes*, l. 4807 (no French equivalent).

85. Pierre Champion, *Vie de Charles d'Orléans* (Paris: Champion, 1911), pp. 57, 104, 117, 191.

86. Charles d'Orléans, *Poésies*, 2: 312 (rondeau 39). The place of this rondeau in Charles's manuscript suggests a date not long after his return to France. Deschamps also wrote several lyrics about failed Mayings; for example, *Oeuvres complètes*, vol. 3, nos. 415, 420, 481.

87. On "tawny" and black see Cecily Clark, "Charles d'Orléans: Some English Perspectives," *Medium Aevum* 40 (1971): 259.

88. *Procès de condamnation et de réhabilitation de Jeanne d'Arc*, ed. Jules Quicherat, 5 vols. (Paris: Renouard, 1841–49), 5: 112–13. The robe and cape presented by the house of Orleans to Joan of Arc was crimson and "vert perdu": Laborde, *Ducs de Bourgogne*, pt. 2, vol. 3, no. 6441.

89. On the coat of arms, see Chapter 4, note 7; on the portrait, see Robert F. Yeager, "British Library Additional MS 5141: An Unnoticed Chaucer *Vita*," *Journal of Medieval and Renaissance Studies* 14 (1984): 261–81. Yeager identifies the flower in the portrait as the English double daisy, *bellis perennis*.

90. This early portrait in Hoccleve's *Regiment of Princes* shows only head and bust (London, British Library, MS Harley 4866, fol. 91).

91. On the earlier date of F and the tendency of editors to obscure it, see Ralph Hanna III, *Pursuing History: Middle English Manuscripts and Their Texts* (Stanford, Calif.: Stanford University Press, 1996), pp. 184–85. In an interpretive register, Wallace notes the "bookish pastness and finality of G" in contrast to F, "which had evoked so brilliantly a sense of current occasion": *Chaucerian Polity*, p. 6; see pp. 337–78. Reading that sense too literally, William A. Quinn argues that F is "a script to be applauded," written perhaps for a May festival but in any case for a performance, whereas G is recast for a less participatory manuscript public: *Chaucer's Rehersyngs: The Performability of the "Legend of Good Women"* (Washington, D.C.: Catholic University Press, 1994), pp. 4–11 (quotation at p. 4).

92. Lisa Kiser notes the relations between Alceste and a muse and proposes that "of alle floures flour" recalls the flowers of rhetoric: *Telling Classical Tales: Chaucer and the "Legend of Good Women"* (Ithaca, N.Y.: Cornell University Press, 1983), p. 43.

93. On *flourouns* and *leves* as terms for petals, see Lowes, "Prologue to the *Legend of Good Women*," pp. 631–33, 677, and the notes in *Riverside Chaucer*.

94. The G text reinforces the comparative conventionality of Cupid's dress by substituting a garland for the sun he wears as a crown in the F text (F 227–28, 230–31, G 160–61). Wimsatt discusses Chaucer's use of "marguerite" poetry for Alceste's costume, noting its literalization of what is metaphorical in that poetry: *Marguerite Poetry*, pp. 36, 63–64.

95. *Ovide moralisé*, ed. C. de Boer et al., vol. 2 (Amsterdam: Müller, 1920), bk. 4, ll. 1021–22; vol. 3 (Amsterdam: Noord-Hollandsche Uitgeversmaatschappij, 1931), bk. 8, ll. 1131–1394; Ovid, *Metamorphoses*, ed. Frank J. Miller, 2nd ed., rev. G. P. Goold, 2 vols. (Cambridge, Mass.: Harvard University Press, 1921), bk. 4, ll. 164–66; bk. 8, ll. 176–81.

96. Ovid, *Metamorphoses*, bk. 6, ll. 661–74; *Ovide moralisé*, vol. 2, bk. 6, ll. 3661–718 (but cf. bk. 6, ll. 3849–52, where all three are said to have been changed to birds by the gods in vengeance for their sins).

97. V. A. Kolve, "From Cleopatra to Alceste: An Iconographic Study of *The Legend of Good Women*," in *Signs and Symbols in Chaucer's Poetry*, ed. John P. Hermann and John J. Burke, Jr. (University: University of Alabama Press, 1981), pp. 174, 152.

98. James Simpson, "Ethics and Interpretation: Reading Wills in Chaucer's *Legend of Good Women*," *Studies in the Age of Chaucer* 20 (1998): 91. Alceste's problematic glorification could raise the question of whether women who wrote Maying poetry, that is, Christine de Pizan and probably the author of *Floure and the Leafe*, took a distinctive stance toward Maying concerning its differentiations between masculinity and femininity. The question could be essentializing, but it has merit insofar as women do write from a different social positioning than men.

99. Wallace, *Chaucerian Polity*, p. 366. Simpson, "Ethics and Interpretation," associates the constrained situation of the legends' women with the constraints placed on the persona in the prologue, but in his view Alceste's rhetorical and social positioning is closer to Cupid than to the legends' women.

100. Robert W. Frank, Jr., *Chaucer and "The Legend of Good Women"* (Cambridge, Mass.: Harvard University Press, 1972), p. 26.

101. Froissart, *Poésies*, ed. Scheler, 2: 194–208 ("Le joli mois de may"), l. 170.

Chapter 3. Joan of Arc

1. Vern L. Bullough, "Transvestism in the Middle Ages," in *Sexual Practices and the Medieval Church*, ed. Vern L. Bullough and James A. Brundage (Buffalo, N.Y.: Prometheus, 1982), 43–54; Bullough is still reaching this conclusion in "Cross Dressing and Gender Role Change in the Middle Ages," in *Handbook of Medieval Sexuality*, ed. Vern L. Bullough and James A. Brundage (New York: Garland, 1996), p. 232.

2. Caroline Walker Bynum, *Holy Feast and Holy Fast: The Religious Significance of Food to Medieval Women* (Berkeley: University of California Press, 1987), 291 (her emphasis). Jonathan Goldberg makes a case for not ruling sexuality out of discussions of cross-dressing in *Sodometries: Renaissance Texts, Modern Sexualities* (Stanford, Calif.: Stanford University Press, 1992), 105–16.

3. In the account of the Greffier de la Rochelle, "elle avoit pourpoint noir, chausses estachées, robbe courte de gros gris noir, cheveux ronds et noirs, et un chappeau noir sur la teste": Jules Quicherat, "Relation inédite sur Jeanne d'Arc," *Revue historique* 4 (1877): 336. Jean de Nouillompont testifies that Joan cross-dressed slightly earlier in clothes of a member of his household: *Procès en nullité de la condamnation de Jeanne d'Arc*, ed. Pierre Duparc, 5 vols. (Paris: Klincksieck, 1977–88), 1: 290; see also 1: 296, 299, 306 (hereafter cited as *Procès en nullité*).

4. *De quadam puella*, in *Procès de condamnation et de réhabilitation de Jeanne d'Arc, dite la Pucelle*, ed. Jules Quicherat, 5 vols. (Paris: Renouard, 1841–49), 3: 412 (hereafter cited as *Procès de condamnation et de réhabilitation*). This treatise is sometimes attributed to Henri de Gorcum, sometimes to Jean Gerson: see Georges Peyronnet, "Gerson, Charles VII et Jeanne d'Arc: La Propagande au service de la guerre," *Revue d'histoire ecclésiastique* 84 (1989): 334–70. Anne Llewellyn Barstow translates *De quadam puella* into English in *Joan of Arc: Heretic, Mystic, Shaman* (Lewiston, N.Y.: Edwin Mellen, 1986), 133–41. Jean Morel testifies that in mid-July 1429 he received from Joan "unam vestem rubeam quam habebat ipsa indutam" [a red garment she had worn]; several witnesses recalled that when Joan arrived in Vaucouleurs "erat induta veste mulieris rubea" [she was wearing a red woman's garment]: *Procès en nullité*, 1: 255, 299.

5. On the sobriety attributed to black, see Jane Schneider, "Peacocks and Penguins: The Political Economy of European Cloth and Colors," *American Ethnologist* 5 (1978): 413–47. Black also connotes high standing; it was a new fashion among the aristocracy at the end of the fourteenth century, and through the fifteenth "les princes et les nobles d'Occident manifestent pour elle un goût marqué": Françoise Piponnier and Perrine Mane, *Se vêtir au Moyen Age* (Paris: Adam Biro, 1995), pp. 89–92 (quotation at p. 90). Joan testifies that a moribund baby she prayed over at Lagny "estoit noir comme sa coste" [was as black as her tunic], *Procès de condamnation de Jeanne d'Arc*, ed. Pierre Tisset with the assistance of Yvonne Lanhers, 3 vols. (Paris: Klincksieck, 1960–71), 1: 103 (hereafter cited in notes and in text as *Pc*).

6. Adrien Harmand, *Jeanne d'Arc: ses costumes, son armure* (Paris: Leroux, 1929), esp. pp. 261–71, 320, 361–63; *Procès de condamnation et de réhabilitation*, 5: 112–13.

7. *Pc* 1: 377; on *aguilletis* (points or aiguiettes) see Geoff Egan, Frances

Pritchard et al., *Dress Accessories c 1150–c 1450, Medieval Finds from Excavations in London 3* (London: HMSO, 1991), pp. 281–90.

8. *Procès en nullité*, 1: 349, 351. Jean Toutmouillé recalls Joan saying she was virginal at her death: 1: 40–41. Her adversaries' common nickname for her, "La Putaine," refers to her name for herself, "La Pucelle," but reverses her claim to purity.

9. *Procès de condamnation et de réhabilitation*, 4: 382, 406. The pleasure Joan took in her clothing was an issue in her canonization trial as well: see Henry Ansgar Kelly, "Joan of Arc's Last Trial: The Attack of the Devil's Advocates," in *Fresh Verdicts on Joan of Arc*, ed. Bonnie Wheeler and Charles T. Wood (New York: Garland, 1996), pp. 205–36.

10. Christine de Pizan, *Ditié de Jehanne d'Arc*, ed. Angus J. Kennedy and Kenneth Varty, Medium Aevum Monographs n.s. 9 (Oxford: Society for the Study of Mediaeval Languages and Literature, 1977), 1: 192; see the third section of this chapter, "Chose oultre nature."

11. Martin le Franc, *Le Champion des dames*, ed. Robert Deschaux, 5 vols., CFMA 127–31 (Paris: Champion, 1999), 4: ll. 16985, 16987. On the manuscripts and illuminations, see vol. 1, pp. x–xx.

12. Clément de Fauquembergue, *Journal de Clément de Fauquembergue*, ed. Alexandre Tuetey, 3 vols. (Paris: Renouard, 1903–15), 2: 306–7. For a range of images, see Regine Pernoud, *Joan of Arc by Herself and Her Witnesses*, trans. Edward Hyams (New York: Stein and Day, 1966); and [Albert] Le Nordez, *Jeanne d'Arc racontée par l'image* (Paris: Hachette, 1898).

13. Susan Crane, "Clothing and Gender Definition: Joan of Arc," *Journal of Medieval and Early Modern Studies* 26, no. 2 (Spring 1996): 297–320. Still a valuable starting place on this issue is John Bugge, *Virginitas: An Essay in the History of a Medieval Ideal* (The Hague: Nijhoff, 1975); Judith M. Bennett discusses how scholarship is currently handling the continuities and gaps between medieval records and recent theories of sexuality: "'Lesbian-like' and the Social History of Medieval Lesbianisms," *Journal of the History of Sexuality* 9 (2000): 1–24. Bennett would categorize Joan's cross-dress as "lesbian-like," a behavior that is hypothetically consonant with same-sex desire but, more importantly, is a practice that disturbs normative self-presentations. The reactions of Joan's contemporaries amply testify to this latter effect.

14. For her defenders, Joan is reminiscent of Camilla and the Amazons, the transvestite saints of the early church, and the biblical Deborah and Esther. Stephen G. Nichols observes of such comparisons that "each . . . provides Joan with a different identity and genealogy": "Prophetic Discourse: St. Augustine to Christine de Pizan," in *The Bible in the Middle Ages: Its Influence on Literature and Art*, ed. Bernard S. Levy (Binghamton, N.Y.: Medieval and Renaissance Texts and Studies, 1992), p. 67. For a comprehensive discussion of literary responses in Joan's lifetime, see Philippe Contamine, "Naissance d'une historiographie. Le Souvenir de Jeanne d'Arc, en France et hors de France, depuis le 'procès de son innocence' (1455–1456) jusqu'au début du XVIᵉ siècle," *Francia* 15 (1987): 233–56; Deborah Fraioli, "The Literary Image of Joan of Arc: Prior Influences," *Speculum* 56 (1981): 811–30; and Fraoli, "Why Joan of Arc Never Became an Amazon," in *Fresh Verdicts on Joan of Arc*, pp. 189–204.

15. Etienne Delaruelle, *La Piété populaire au Moyen Age* (Turin: Erasmo, 1975), pp. 355–74 ("La Spiritualité de Jeanne d'Arc").

16. See the essays by Nicole Bériou, Pierre-Marie Gy, and Jacques Chiffoleau in *L'Aveu: Antiquité et Moyen-Age* (Rome: Ecole Française de Rome, 1986).

17. *Pc* 1: 37 ; 1: 389: "requisivimus ut, pro acceleracione presentis negocii et exoneracione proprie consciencie, plenam veritatem super hiis diceret de quibus in materia fidei interrogaretur, non querendo subterfugia vel cautelas ab ipsius veritatis confessione divertentes."

18. *Pc*, e.g., 1: 380–81, 383, 410–11.

19. Lester K. Little comments on these features of confession : "Les Techniques de la confession et la confession comme technique," in *Faire croire: Modalités de la diffusion et de la réception des messages religieux du XIIᵉ au XVᵉ siècle*, ed. G. Barone, J. Berlioz, J. Chiffoleau, and A. Vauchez (Rome: Ecole française de Rome, 1981), pp. 87–99; Thomas N. Tentler surveys confessional writing: *Sin and Confession on the Eve of the Reformation* (Princeton, N.J.: Princeton University Press, 1977). Confessors had a limited role in defending orthodoxy, but medieval writers on this subject argued that confessions were privileged communications that confessors should not pass on to inquisitors: Little, "Techniques," p. 96; James B. Given, *Inquisition and Medieval Society: Power, Discipline, and Resistance in Languedoc* (Ithaca, N.Y.: Cornell University Press, 1997), pp. 199, 204–5. On inquisitors' manuals see A. Dondaine, "Le Manuel de l'inquisiteur," *Archivum fratrum predicatorum* 17 (1947): 85–194; on confessors' manuals see John T. McNeill and Helena M. Gamer, *Medieval Handbooks of Penance* (New York: Columbia University Press, 1938).

20. Jacques Chiffoleau, "Sur la pratique et la conjoncture de l'aveu judicaire en France du XIIᵉ au XVᵉ siècle," in *Aveu*, p. 352. To be sure, confession was not always voluntary, but the resulting evasions rendered it yet more formulaic as opposed to substantially self-descriptive: Jean Delumeau, *Sin and Fear: The Emergence of a Western Guilt Culture, 13th–18th Centuries*, trans. Eric Nicholson (New York: St. Martin's Press, 1990), pp. 463–79.

21. Annie Cazenave, "Aveu et contrition. Manuels de confesseurs et interrogatoires d'inquisition en Languedoc et en Catalogne (XIIIᵉ–XIVᵉ siècles)," *Actes du 99ᵉ Congrès national des Sociétés savantes, Besançon, 1974, Philologie et histoire* (Paris: Bibliothèque Nationale, 1977), 1: 333–52.

22. Talal Asad, *Genealogies of Religion: Discipline and Reasons of Power in Christianity and Islam* (Baltimore: Johns Hopkins University Press, 1993), pp. 83–124.

23. Cazenave, "Aveu et contrition," p. 339, quoting from manuals for inquisitors.

24. Edward Peters, "Destruction of the Flesh—Salvation of the Spirit: The Paradoxes of Torture in Medieval Christian Society," in *The Devil, Heresy and Witchcraft in the Middle Ages: Essays in Honor of Jeffrey B. Russell*, ed. Alberto Ferreiro (Leiden: Brill, 1998), p. 139.

25. Peters, "Destruction of the Flesh," pp. 138–39; as Peters summarizes his argument, "every ideology presupposes a particular anthropology" (p. 146). Excellent overviews are Edward Peters, *Torture* (Oxford: Blackwell, 1985) and John H. Langbein, *Torture and the Law of Proof: Europe and England in the Ancien Régime* (Chicago: University of Chicago Press, 1976). Peters and Langbein trace medieval

arguments against torture as well as those justifying it. Jody Enders relates theories of torture to medieval literature in *The Medieval Theater of Cruelty: Rhetoric, Memory, Violence* (Ithaca, N.Y.: Cornell University Press, 1999).

26. John Locke, *An Essay Concerning Human Understanding*, ed. Peter H. Nidditch (Oxford: Clarendon Press, 1975), pp. 239–40.

27. Peters, *Torture*, p. 1; several further early and late medieval definitions are cited here.

28. Given, *Inquisition*, pp. 52–65 (quotation at p. 53); Edward Peters, *Inquisition* (New York: Macmillan, 1988), p. 141.

29. *Pc* 1: 348–50; Pierre Cusquel testifies three times at the nullification trial that he saw an iron cage designed to hold Joan in a standing position, but that he never saw her in it: *Procès en nullité*, 1: 187–88, 1: 219, 1: 452.

30. Steven Weiskopf, "Readers of the Lost Arc: Secrecy, Specularity, and Speculation in the Trial of Joan of Arc," in *Fresh Verdicts on Joan of Arc*, p. 115; the essay in this volume by Karen Sullivan makes a similar point. In my view, even Joan's warnings that she cannot reveal certain things (*Pc* 1: 38–39, 45–46, 69) are better understood as part of her verbal self-construction than as evidence for the falsity of the trial record.

31. Henry Ansgar Kelly, "Joan of Arc's Last Trial," pp. 205–36.

32. The best edition of the records of this trial is *Pc* (see note 5 for citation). Still useful for both trials, with supplementary material, is *Procès de condamnation et de réhabilitation* (see note 4 for citation).

33. The best edition of records from this trial is *Procès en nullité* (see note 3 for citation); some extracts are available in English in Régine Pernoud, *The Retrial of Joan of Arc*, trans. J. M. Cohen (New York: Harcourt, Brace, 1955).

34. On the scope and accuracy of the first trial's records see also *Pc* 3: 17–41. On irregularities in the trial's procedures, see Henry Ansgar Kelly, "The Right to Remain Silent: Before and After Joan of Arc," *Speculum* 68 (1993): 992–1026; and Peters, *Inquisition*, pp. 69, 73.

35. *Pc* edits the two manuscripts deriving from the French minutes—Urfé (Bibliothèque nationale de France, MS lat. 8838) and Orleans (Bibliothèque Municipale d'Orléans, MS 518)—alongside the capacious Latin record established by Thomas de Courcelles, who assisted at Joan's trial, and the notary Guillaume Manchon. This latter collects letters, charges, records of interrogation and deliberation, votes, and sentences for the entire proceeding, drawn up a few years after Joan's death. Another complete and heavily annotated edition of the two French manuscripts is *La Minute française des interrogatoires de Jeanne la Pucelle*, ed. Paul Doncoeur (Melun: Argences, 1952). An English translation of the Orleans manuscript is *The Trial of Joan of Arc, Being the Verbatim Report of the Proceedings from the Orleans Manuscript*, trans. W. S. Scott (Westport, Conn.: Associated Booksellers, 1956). Latin acts were also produced during and just after the trial: a *procès-verbal* based on the French minutes and an *Instrumentum sententiae* summarizing the trial, Joan's abjuration, and her sentencing. Later copies of the *Instrumentum* survive: *Documents et recherches relatifs à Jeanne la Pucelle*, ed. Paul Doncoeur and Yvonne Lanhers, vol. 2, *Instrument public des sentences* ... (Paris: Argences, 1954). For evidence during the nullification trial about the generation and accuracy of the French minutes, see *Procès en nullité*, 1: 67–68, 181–83, 207, 214–18, 222–23, 243, 245–46, 414–28, 436.

36. Testimony from the nullification trial traces in fascinating detail how records from the first trial were generated. To summarize briefly, two official notaries and occasionally some other recorders kept running notes in French during the interrogations. The notaries compared their texts each day after dinner and drew up the minutes of the trial, still in French. One of the notaries, Guillaume Manchon, submitted his minutes to the authorities in charge of the nullification trial. Remarkable as it is to have a French record of Joan's interrogation, it is yet more remarkable that Joan considered herself its coproducer. The surviving copies of the minutes record, and testimony at the nullification trial recalls, numerous occasions on which Joan demanded that her responses be corrected in the record, admonished the notaries to be more careful, asked for a copy of the work to be sent to Paris if she was to be interrogated again there, and refused to answer questions she felt she had already answered. Instead she replies "luisés bien vostre livre et vous le trouverés" [read your book carefully and you will find it], or "vous estes respondus de ce que vous en aurez de moi" [you already have as much of an answer as you will get from me]: *Pc*, e.g., 1: 147, 154, 160, 169, 205, 208, 337; *Procès en nullité*, 1: 360. The French minutes were read aloud to Joan at the end of the weeks of interrogation for her corrections: *Pc* 1: 181–82. After the minutes' completion, according to the Orleans manuscript, when a herald at the cemetery of St. Ouen cried out that she was a heretic, Joan retorted "qu'il n'estoit pas vray, ainsy qu'il est escript ailleurs" [that it was not true, as was written down elsewhere]: *Minute française*, p. 273.

37. *Pc* 1: 75, 93–94. Where there are gaps in the French minutes, I quote from the Latin record of Thomas de Courcelles.

38. *Pc* 1: 168: "se on luy donnoit congié en abit de femme, elle se mectroit tantoust en abit d'omme et feroit ce qui luy est commandé par nostre Seigneur" [if they let her go in a woman's dress, she would resume men's dress immediately and do what is commanded of her by our Lord]; see also *Pc* 1: 67, 181, 209–10.

39. Perceval de Cagny, *Chroniques de Perceval de Cagny*, ed. H. Moranvillé (Paris: Renouard, 1902), 140; Guillaume Cousinot, *Chronique de la Pucelle*, ed. Vallet de Viriville (Paris: Delahays, 1864), 276.

40. See also *Pc* 1: 227, 344.

41. Nullification testimony responded to articles asserting that Joan's female clothing was stolen or that she otherwise did not wish to take men's clothes after her abjuration, illustrating the difficulty even her supporters had with her commitment to cross-dress: *Procès en nullité*, 1: 121, 137–38, 178 (articles), 1: 181–82, 186–88 (testimony); *Pc* 3: 151–59; *Documents et recherches relatifs à Jeanne la Pucelle*, vol. 3, *La Réhabilitation de Jeanne la Pucelle: l'enquête ordonnée par Charles VII* . . . , pp. 36–37, 40–45, 51, 54. Jean Toutmouillé recalls Joan saying she was virginal at her death, pp. 40–41.

42. For example, Cousinot, *Chronique*, pp. 276–77: "quand je seroie entre les hommes, estant en habit d'homme, ils n'auront pas concupiscence charnelle de moi; et me semble qu'en cest estat je conserveray mieulx ma virginié de pensée et de faict" [when I am among men, dressed as a man, they will not have carnal desire for me; and it seems to me that in this manner I will better maintain my virginity in thought and deed].

43. *Procès en nullité*, 1: 350, 387, in testimony friendly to her cause; in contrast,

Joan testifies that she slept "vestue et armee" [dressed and in armor] when in the field (*Pc* 1: 263).

44. Doctors of theology who were consulted about the charges at the end of the trial concede that if God had commanded cross-dressing it would be justified, but they conclude that the command is not believable in Joan's case (*Pc* 2: 257, 283).

45. *Procès de condamnation et de réhabilitation*, 4: 509.

46. Courcelles obscures Joan's statement by deleting the phrase "se ainsi est . . . qu'il la faile desvestir en jugement" [if it is necessary to undress her for judgment], which imagines that the court may tolerate physical coercion to change her way of dressing. See also *Pc* 1: 210, 227 where Joan again refers to death in relation to her cross-dressing. Testimony at the nullification trial (e.g., *Procès en nullité*, 1: 184) discredited the original sentence by declaring that Joan was executed only for wearing men's clothing, an offense not grave enough to warrant death. Penances of one to three years are prescribed for cross-dressing in contemporary manuals: Vern L. Bullough and Bonnie Bullough, *Cross Dressing, Sex, and Gender* (Philadelphia: University of Pennsylvania Press, 1993), p. 61; *Pc* 3: 87. Modern scholars also occasionally attribute Joan's execution to cross-dressing, but the first emphasis throughout the trial is on the validity of Joan's claim to hear voices; in the Courcelles trial record, Joan's declaration after her relapse that she continues to hear her voices carries the marginal annotation "responsio mortifera" [the fatal reply: *Pc* 1: 397, n. 1].

47. On the chemise as an undergarment see Piponnier and Mane, *Se vêtir*, pp. 53–54; examples of the man's shirt as the costume of the guilty or condemned: Ruth Mellinkoff, *Outcasts: Signs of Otherness in Northern European Art of the Middle Ages*, 2 vols. (Berkeley: University of California Press, 1993), pl. 1: 63 (men at execution, c. 1470–75); Jean Froissart, *Chroniques: Début du premier livre. Edition du manuscrit de Rome Reg. lat. 869*, ed. George T. Diller (Geneva: Droz, 1972), p. 841: the burgesses of Calais must surrender themselves "nus piés et nus chiefs, en lors lignes draps tant seullement." Alceste urges that a man should be shown mercy if he "profereth him, ryght in his bare sherte, / To ben ryght at your owen jugement": Geoffrey Chaucer, *Legend of Good Women*, in *The Riverside Chaucer*, 3rd ed., ed. Larry Benson (Boston: Houghton Mifflin, 1987), ll. F 405–6.

48. Stella Mary Newton, *Fashion in the Age of the Black Prince* (Woodbridge, Suffolk: Boydell, 1980), pp. 57–58, 127–28; Piponnier and Mane, *Se vêtir*, pp. 107–8.

49. On the expression of holiness through clothing, see Dyan Elliott, "Dress as Mediator Between Inner and Outer Self: The Pious Matron of the High and Later Middle Ages," *Mediaeval Studies* 53 (1991): 279–308; Gábor Klaniczay, *The Uses of Supernatural Power: The Transformation of Popular Religion in Medieval and Early-Modern Europe*, trans. Susan Singerman, ed. Karen Margolis (Princeton, N.J.: Princeton University Press, 1990), pp. 51–78.

50. Examples are *Pc* 1: 156–58, 182–83, 208.

51. *Procès en nullité*, 1: 384.

52. For example, *Pc* 1: 95, 153–54, 344.

53. *Pc* 1: 149, 244; see also 1: 174–75, where Joan is asked if she would still hear her voices if she were married or were not a virgin.

54. Caroline Walker Bynum, *Fragmentation and Redemption: Essays on Gender and the Human Body* (New York: Zone Books, 1992), pp. 183, 222; see also

Marie-Christine Pouchelle, "Représentations du corps dans la *Légende dorée*," *Ethnologie française* n.s. 5 (1975): 293–308.

55. Bynum, *Fragmentation*, p. 182.

56. For these and further examples see Miri Rubin, *Corpus Christi: The Eucharist in Late Medieval Culture* (Cambridge: Cambridge University Press, 1991), pp. 334–37, et passim; Bynum, *Holy Feast and Holy Fast*, pp. 113–49.

57. René Descartes, *The Philosophical Writings of Descartes*, vol. 2, *Meditations on First Philosophy*, trans. John Cottingham, Robert Stoothoff, and Dugald Murdoch (Cambridge: Cambridge University Press, 1984), pp. 17–18. For the Latin and French versions of this passage, see *Oeuvres de Descartes*, ed. Charles Adam and Paul Tannery (1897; reprint, Paris: Vrin, 1996), 7: 25–27, 9: 20–21.

58. Michel Foucault, *Discipline and Punish: The Birth of the Prison*, trans. Alan Sheridan (New York: Pantheon, 1977), p. 30.

59. Judith Butler, *Bodies That Matter: On the Discursive Limits of "Sex"* (London: Routledge, 1993).

60. Marina Warner, *Joan of Arc: The Image of Female Heroism* (New York: Knopf, 1981), pp. 22–24; Joan testifies that her voices call her "Jehanne la Pucelle," *Pc* 1: 126.

61. Kirsten Hastrup, "The Semantics of Biology: Virginity," in *Defining Females: The Nature of Women in Society*, ed. Shirley Ardener (New York: Wiley, 1978), pp. 58–59. On virginity as a modification of sexuality, see Sarah Salih, *Versions of Virginity in Late Medieval England* (Woodbridge, Suffolk: Boydell and Brewer, 2001).

62. *Pc* 1: 78, 114. Payment is recorded "à Hauves Poulnoir, paintre, demourant à Tours, pour avoir paint et baillié estoffes pour ung grant estandart et ung petit pour la Pucelle, 25 livres tournois" [to Hauves Poulnoir, painter, living in Tours, for painting and delivering cloth for a large standard and a small one for the Pucelle, 25 livres tournois]: *Procès de condamnation et de réhabilitation*, 5: 258.

63. *Procès en nullité*, 1: 320; see also 1: 332 (testimony of Jean Luillier).

64. *Procès de condamnation et de réhabilitation*, 2: 42, 3: 440–41; Warner, *Joan of Arc*, pp. 135, 151–55; Marie Delcourt, "Le Complexe de Diane dans l'hagiographie chrétienne," *Revue de l'histoire des religions* 153, no.1 (1958): 1–33; Valerie R. Hotchkiss, *Clothes Make the Man: Female Cross Dressing in Medieval Europe* (New York: Garland, 1996), pp. 49–68.

65. Hotchkiss, *Clothes Make the Man*, pp. 131–41.

66. C. H. Talbot, ed. and trans., *The Life of Christina of Markyate, a Twelfth Century Recluse* (Oxford: Clarendon Press, 1959), pp. 90–93; for all other examples see Jacobus de Voragine, *La Légende dorée: Edition critique, dans la révision de 1476 par Jean Batailler, d'après la traduction de Jean de Vignay (1333–1348) de la "Legenda Aurea" (c. 1261–1266)*, ed. Brenda Dunn-Lardeau (Paris: Champion, 1997), pp. 543–44, 601–5, 865–69 (quotation at p. 866).

67. *Légende dorée*, pp. 87–88; see pp. 9–43 for an overview of the many French translations and early printed editions of the *Legenda aurea*; and *Le Moyen français* 32 (1993) on the topic *Legenda aurea-la Légende dorée*. The many surviving manuscripts of Jean de Mailly's abridged legends indicate the importance of preaching in disseminating these plots: *Abrégé des gestes et miracles des saints*, trans. A. Dondaine, Bibliothèque d'Histoire Dominicaine 1 (Paris: Cerf, 1947), pp. 11–23. Jean de Mailly transmits the legends of Natalia, Pelagia, Thecla, and Eugenia.

68. *Légende dorée*, p. 868. I translate *cotte* as *tunic* following Piponnier and Mane, in *Se vêtir*, who define *cotte* as "une tunique portée sur la chemise, soit seule, soit sous la robe" (p. 190).

69. Perhaps the assumption in this plot that a woman could not be guilty of sexual aggression against another woman reinforces Eugenia's sexual normalcy and thereby reduces the potential transgressiveness of her sexual transformation.

70. *Pc* 1: 361, 377; for the argument that "idolatry" in this article refers to an absence of spirituality, see Susan Schibanoff, "True Lies: Transvestism and Idolatry in the Trial of Joan of Arc," in *Fresh Verdicts on Joan of Arc*, pp. 31–60. The *Sibylla francica* (1429) cites particular heathen rites in which women wore men's clothing ("virorum induviis") and carried weapons to honor Mars, but this work concludes that Joan wears men's clothing for legitimate reasons: *Procès de condamnation et de réhabilitation*, pp. 422–68 (quotation at p. 440).

71. Simon Gaunt, "Straight Minds / 'Queer' Wishes in Old French Hagiography: *La Vie de Sainte Euphrosine*," *GLQ: A Journal of Gay and Lesbian Studies* 1 (1995): 439.

72. *Pc* 1: 64, 3: 31 n. 1.

73. Cross-dress itself, according to Marjorie Garber, confuses categories: "this interruption, this disruptive act of putting into question, is ... precisely the place, and the role, of the transvestite": *Vested Interests: Cross-Dressing and Cultural Anxiety* (London: Routledge, 1992), p. 13.

74. Joan Cadden, *Meanings of Sex Difference in the Middle Ages: Medicine, Science, and Culture* (Cambridge: Cambridge University Press, 1993); Miri Rubin, "The Person in the Form: Medieval Challenges to Bodily 'Order,'" in *Framing Medieval Bodies*, ed. Sarah Kay and Miri Rubin (Manchester: Manchester University Press, 1994), pp. 100–122.

75. Cited (in a context apposite to my argument) by Barbara Newman, *From Virile Woman to WomanChrist: Studies in Medieval Religion and Literature* (Philadelphia: University of Pennsylvania Press, 1995), p. 4; see pp. 19–46.

76. Jacobus de Voragine, *Legenda aurea*, ed. Th. Graesse (1850; reprint Osnabrück: Otto Zeller, 1969), 603. The *Légende dorée* loses the persuasive pun on *vir* (p. 866).

77. Hotchkiss, *Clothes Make the Man*, pp. 23, 151; Herbert Musurillo, ed. and trans., *The Acts of the Christian Martyrs* (Oxford: Clarendon Press, 1972), pp. 118–19.

78. *Légende dorée*, p. 968, translating *Legenda aurea*, p. 677; compare the graceful translation of this passage in Jacobus de Voragine, *The Golden Legend*, trans. William Granger Ryan, 2 vols. (Princeton, N.J.: Princeton University Press, 1993), 2: 233: "It was not for purposes of deception that I allowed myself to be taken for a man, as I have shown by my deeds."

79. William Caxton, *The Golden Legend*, ed. F. S. Ellis, 7 vols. (London: Dent, 1900), 5: 240: "I am a man. I have not lived for to deceive, but I have showed that I have the virtue of a man."

80. Bynum, *Holy Feast and Holy Fast*, p. 291.

81. The vernacular intrusions in the Latin record deserve an article of their own. Steven Justice, "Inquisition, Speech, and Writing: A Case from Late-Medieval Norwich," *Representations* 48 (Fall 1994): 1–29, treats this topic for heresy trials in

Norwich, but his explanation that vernacular intrusions should be attributed to the notary's boredom because they "possessed no evidentiary advantage *as* vernacular phrases—no more than they would in Latin" (p. 3, his emphasis)—is belied by two of the three examples he cites, which make their arguments in verbal puns that would be lost if translated into Latin: every *Friday* is *fre* day and the stinging *bee* of oaths *by* God (pp. 2–3). These puns would have been more evident before long *i* diphthongized in the later fifteenth century.

82. *Procès de condamnation et de réhabilitation*, 4: 4, n. 1; Cagny, *Chroniques*, p. 141.

83. *Pc* 1: 82, 221, 262. On positive depictions of women warriors that may have historical basis in the Crusades, see Helen Solterer, "Figures of Female Militancy in Medieval France," *Signs* 16 (1990–91): 522–49. In contrast, chronicler Henry Knighton condemns women who cross-dressed at tournaments in 1348: *Knighton's Chronicle, 1337–1396*, ed. and trans. G. H. Martin (Oxford: Clarendon Press, 1995), pp. 92–95.

84. *Ditié de Jehanne d'Arc*, ll. 199, 222, 188–91.

85. Ibid., ll. 192, 274, 277.

86. Ibid., ll. 265–66.

87. *Habitus* is also the pivotal term in the passage quoted above from *De quadam puella* on Joan's shifting dress and behavior. See Karen Sullivan, *The Interrogation of Joan of Arc* (Minneapolis: University of Minnesota Press, 1999), pp. 50–54, on the language the court chooses for Joan's dress.

88. Pierre Bourdieu, *The Logic of Practice*, trans. Richard Nice (Cambridge: Polity Press, 1990), 52–65 (quotation at p. 56).

89. "*Esclarmonde, Clarisse et Florent, Yde et Olive*," ed. Max Schweigel, *Ausgaben und Abhandlungen aus dem Gebiete der romanischen Philologie* 83 (1889): 152–73; *Tristan de Nanteuil*, ed. Keith V. Sinclair (Assen: Van Gorcum, 1971); Michèle Perret, "Travesties et transsexuelles: Yde, Silence, Grisandole, Blanchandine," *Romance Notes* 25 (1984–85): 328–40.

90. *Tristan de Nanteuil*, ll. 15298–16423 (marriage and sex change); the change is forecast as an important sign of God's *courtoisie* (ll. 12783–92), as a miracle of the saints (ll. 13697–706), and as "certaine histoire sans mensonge conter. . . . On la pourroit moult bien ou moustier preescher" [a true story without lies . . . One could very well preach it in church (ll. 15772, 15775)]: Blanchandine becomes the father of St. Gilles.

91. *Yde et Olive*, l. 7066.

92. *Ovide moralisé*, ed. C. de Boer et al., vol. 3 (Amsterdam: Noord-Hollandsche Uitgeversmaatschappij, 1931), bk. 9, ll. 2913–17.

93. Christine de Pizan, *Le Livre de la mutacion de Fortune*, ed. Suzanne Solente, 4 vols. (Paris: Picard, 1959–66), bk. 1, lines 1156–58. Renate Blumenfeld-Kosinski comments on Christine's adaptation of the Iphis story: *Reading Myth: Classical Mythology and Its Interpretations in Medieval French Literature* (Stanford, Calif.: Stanford University Press, 1997), pp. 180–84.

94. Solente's note to these lines, *Livre de la mutacion*, 1: 158–59, identifies Vestis as the goddess Vesta. This is plausible, but Christine's alteration of the name Vesta to Vestis still needs an explanation; my proposal is that Christine altered Vesta's

name to recall the verb *vestir*. In the *Ovide moralisé*, Isis is named repeatedly: bk. 9, ll. 2812, 2840, 2856, 3041, 3045, 3048, 3072. "Vestis" appears in *Livre de la mutacion* at ll. 1133 and 1157.

95. On historical condemnations of female homoeroticism, see Cadden, *Meanings of Sex Difference*, pp. 223–24; Louis Crompton, "The Myth of Lesbian Impunity: Capital Laws from 1270 to 1791," *Journal of Homosexuality* 6 (1980–81): 11–25; Bennett, "'Lesbian-Like.'" The *Ovide moralisé* comments that such eroticism is "contre droit et contre nature" [against law and nature (l. 3133)].

96. *The Vulgate Version of the Arthurian Romances*, ed. H. Oskar Sommer, vol. 2: *Lestoire de Merlin* (Washington: Riverside, 1908), pp. 281–92; Heldris of Cornwall, *Silence*, ed. and trans. Sarah Roche-Mahdi (East Lansing, Mich.: Colleagues, 1992). On the circulation of this plot and analogues, see Keith V. Sinclair, *Tristan de Nanteuil: Thematic Infrastructure and Literary Creation* (Tübingen: Max Niemeyer, 1983), pp. 38–42, 98–105; Lucy Allen Paton, "The Story of Grisandole: A Study in the Legend of Merlin," *PMLA* 22 (1907): 234–76.

97. Heldris, *Silence*, ll. 2480, 2829–30, 6536–37. I rely heavily on Sarah Roche-Mahdi's translation although I have altered a few words toward more literal constructions of the French.

98. Heldris, *Silence*, ll. 2646–47, 2650. In one episode there is a vestige of divine intervention in Silence's success at passing, during a battle in which she asks God to strengthen "cho qu'afoiblie en moi Nature" [that in me which Nature has made weak], but generally it is Silence's own effort that accomplishes her successes (l. 5607, see also ll. 4181, 5646–47).

99. Heldris, *Silence*, ll. 6672–74.

100. Ibid., l. 3824.

101. Ibid., ll. 3640–46; on chalking cloth and fur when new see A. Långfors, "Mots rares chez Gautier de Coinci," *Romania* 59 (1933): 491–92. In the cited examples, chalking is always metaphorically positive, a sign of newness, value, or purity.

102. At some points the narration attempts to relocate nature deeper within, to the heart which in turn wears the body like a garment of sackcloth (ll. 1842–45) But this heart within is also divided in Silence's case, divided between living as a man and returning to womanhood (ll. 2667–81).

103. *Pc* 1: 207; see also 1: 14, 339, 377; Deuteronomy 22: 5; 1 Corinthians 11: 5–6, 13.

104. *Procès en nullité*, 1: 389.

105. Hotchkiss, *Clothes Make the Man*, p. 67; Newman, *From Virile Woman*, p. 165.

106. Warner, *Joan of Arc*, pp. 139–58 (quotation at p. 146).

107. Marjorie Garber, *Vice Versa: Bisexuality and the Eroticism of Everyday Life* (New York: Simon and Schuster, 1995), pp. 214–19.

108. *Pc* 1: 293; *Minute française*, p. 257. Here the collator of the Orleans manuscript is translating from the Latin record, and the omission is consistent with earlier expressions of support for Joan in this manuscript.

109. *Journal d'un bourgeois de Paris, 1405–1449*, ed. Alexandre Tuetey (Paris: Champion, 1881), p. 269; *A Parisian Journal, 1405–1449*, trans. Janet Shirley (Oxford: Clarendon, 1968), pp. 263–64.

Chapter 4. Display and Incognito

1. Geoffrey Chaucer, *A Variorum Edition of the Works of Geoffrey Chaucer*, vol. 5, *The Minor Poems*, ed. George B. Pace and Alfred David (Norman: University of Oklahoma Press, 1982), pt. 1, pp. 67–76; Geoffroi de Charny, *The "Book of Chivalry" of Geoffroi de Charny: Text, Context, and Translation*, ed. and trans. Richard W. Kaeuper and Elspeth Kennedy (Philadelphia: University of Pennsylvania Press, 1996), pp. 140–41. Translation by Elspeth Kennedy. On honor's imbrication of inherited status and personal merit, see Julian Pitt-Rivers, "Honour and Social Status," in *Honour and Shame: The Values of Mediterranean Society*, ed. J. G. Peristiany (Chicago: University of Chicago Press, 1966), pp. 21–24, 31, 35–38.

2. Claes Heinen, *L'Armorial universel du heraut Gelre (1370–1395)*, ed. Paul Adam-Even (Neuchatel: Paul Attinger, 1971), pp. 5–13. Gelre visited England in 1390 when his patron, Duke William I of Guelders, was made a Knight of the Garter: W. van Anrooij, "Gelre Herald and Late Medieval Chivalric Culture," *Coat of Arms* n.s. 9, no. 160 (1992): 337–44. Adam-Even identifies the eight men represented on this leaf, after Edward and his sons, beginning with the middle tier at the left, as John Holland, duke of Huntingdon (d. 1400), Thomas Beauchamp, earl of Warwick (d. 1401), Roger Mortimer, earl of March (d. 1398), Richard Fitz Alan, earl of Arundel (d. 1397), William Montague, earl of Salisbury (d. 1397), Robert de Vere, earl of Oxford (d. 1392), Henry Percy, earl of Northumberland (d. 1408), Edward de Courtenay, earl of Devonshire (d 1419): Heinen, *Armorial universel*, p. 47.

3. La Curne de Sainte-Palaye, *Dictionnaire historique de l'ancien langue françois* (Niort: Favre, 1876), *bande, faisse*.

4. Anthony Richard Wagner, *Heralds and Heraldry in the Middle Ages*, 2nd ed. (Oxford: Oxford University Press, 1956), pp. 12–20; Maurice Keen, *Chivalry* (New Haven, Conn.: Yale University Press, 1984), pp. 125–32; Richard Marks and Ann Payne, *British Heraldry from Its Origins to c. 1800* (London: British Museum, 1978).

5. Winifred Hall, *Canting and Allusive Arms of England and Wales* (Canterbury: Achievements, 1966); Michel Pastoureau, *Traité d'héraldique*, 3rd ed. (Paris: Picard, 1997), pp. 251–55.

6. See, e.g., Christiane Klapisch-Zuber, *L'Ombre des ancêtres: Essai sur l'imaginaire médiéval de la parenté* (Paris: Fayard, 2000); Lee Patterson, "On the Margin: Postmodernism, Ironic History, and Medieval Studies," *Speculum* 65 (1990): 87–108.

7. On Thomas and Geoffrey Chaucer's coats, see *Chaucer Life-Records*, ed. Martin M. Crow and Clair C. Olson (Oxford: Oxford University Press, 1966), pp. 542–43, 549: the 1409 seal may show a bend overall instead of the bend counterchanged shown in later records.

8. *Annales Ricardi Secundi*, in *Chronica monasterii S. Albani*, ed. Henry Thomas Riley, Rolls Series 28, vol. 3 (London: Longmans, 1866), p. 223; Rodney Dennys, *Heraldry and the Heralds* (London: Jonathan Cape, 1982), pp. 106–8.

9. Gerard J. Brault, *Early Blazon: Heraldic Terminology in the Twelfth and Thirteenth Centuries with Special Reference to Arthurian Literature* (Oxford: Clarendon Press, 1972), pp. 36, 54 (Ermenie); Max Prinet, "Armoiries familiales et armoiries de roman au XVe siècle," *Romania* 58 (1932): 569–73 (Regnier Pot). For further

examples, see Léon Jéquier, *Manuel du blason*, new ed. (Lausanne: David Perret, 1977), pp. 278–80; Dennys, *Heraldry and the Heralds*, pp. 19–20.

10. England's lion passant guardant (positioned horizontally, looking toward viewer) is called a leopard in medieval heraldry: Pastoureau, *Traité*, pp. 143–46. In *Wynnere and Wastoure*, the royal crest is described as "ane hattfull beste, / A lighte lebarde and a longe, lokande full kene, / 3arked alle of 3alowe golde in full 3ape wyse": ed. Stephanie Trigg, EETS, o.s., 297 (Oxford: Oxford University Press, 1990), ll. 73–75. In 1352 Edward III had a crested helmet "topped by a gold leopard, and with a crown of gold and silver decorated with sapphires and pastes set in silver": Kay Staniland, "Medieval Courtly Spendour," *Costume* 14 (1980): 20.

11. Max Prinet, "Cimiers et supports parlants d'armoiries françaises," *Archives héraldiques suisses* 30 (1916): 12–21.

12. On changes in the Montague arms during the Middle Ages, see Charles Boutell, *Boutell's Heraldry*, rev. J. P. Brooke-Little (London: Frederick Warne, 1973), pp. 81, 137, 161.

13. Keen, *Chivalry*, p. 128. Dissociating arms from military practice probably facilitated women's use of arms in their ceremonial dress: see Chapter 1, n. 72; Joan Evans, *Dress in Mediaeval France* (Oxford: Clarendon, 1952), p. 12, n.7. Tomb effigies offer late medieval examples of women's heraldic dress; the Luttrell Psalter shows Geoffrey Luttrell's wife and daughter so clothed: London, British Library, Additional MS 42130, fol. 202, verso.

14. *Medieval Heraldry: Some Fourteenth Century Heraldic Works*, ed. and trans. Evan John Jones (Cardiff: William Lewis, 1943), p. 215 (*Tretis on Armes*, c. 1400).

15. Household servants akin to minstrels in the twelfth century, heralds later gained status by standardizing a science of heraldry, celebrating chivalric deeds and ideals, and attributing meanings to heraldic devices. Several wrote biographies and lyrics: Anrooij, "Gelre Herald"; Wagner, *Heralds and Heraldry*; Michel Stanesco, *Jeux d'errance du chevalier médiéval: Aspects ludiques de la fonction guerrière dans la littérature du Moyen Age flamboyant* (Leiden: Brill, 1988), pp. 183–97.

16. Honoré Bonet, *L'Arbre des batailles*, ed. Ernest Nys (Brussels: Muquardt, 1883), p. 243; *Medieval Heraldry*, ed. Jones, pp. 11, 215–16.

17. *Medieval Heraldry*, ed. Jones, pp. 40–43, 121, 169–70; this *Tractatus de armis* by Johannes de Bado Aureo was written around 1394 at the request of Anne of Bohemia (p. xvii). Pastoureau, *Traité*, p. 255, notes that the significances attributed to arms from about 1350 are "sans aucun rapport avec l'héraldique primitive."

18. Keen, *Chivalry*, p. 131.

19. Michel Pastoureau, "Désigner ou dissimuler? Le Rôle du cimier dans l'imaginaire médiéval," in *Masques et déguisements dans la littérature médiévale*, ed. Marie-Louise Ollier (Montreal: University of Montreal, 1988), pp. 127–40 (at 136–39). Supporting Pastoureau's hypothesis that the Luxembourg line took Melusine as a mystical ancestor is Louis de Luxembourg's staging of "Melusine and her children" at a feast he sponsored: Mathieu d'Escouchy, *Chronique de Mathieu d'Escouchy*, ed. G. du Fresne de Beaucourt, 3 vols. (Paris: Renouard, 1863–64), 2: 241.

20. On these framing issues, see J. Christopher Crocker, "My Brother the Parrot," in *Animal Myths and Metaphors in South America*, ed. Gary Urton (Salt Lake City: University of Utah Press, 1985), pp. 13–47; S. J. Tambiah, "Animals Are Good to Think and Good to Prohibit," *Ethnology* 8 (1969): 423–59; Claude Lévi-Strauss,

Totemism, trans. Rodney Needham (Boston: Beacon, 1963). Late medieval totemism was fragmentary, with only a few families claiming animal ancestors. For an argument that some heraldic emblems such as the French fleur-de-lis, the German eagle, the English lion, and the Norman winged dragon began as clan totems, see Robert Viel, *Les Origines symboliques du blason* (Paris: Berg, 1972).

21. Crocker, "My Brother the Parrot," pp. 16, 20.

22. Tambiah, "Animals Are Good to Think," p. 454; Crocker, "My Brother the Parrot," pp. 16–18.

23. John Borneman, "Race, Ethnicity, Species, Breed: Totemism and Horse-Breed Classification in America," *Comparative Studies in Society and History* 30 (1988): 38–39.

24. "All totemism is initially a kind of reverse totemism. The animal and plant world does not order itself in a way that is immediately recognizable from a pancultural or universal-human perspective. The ordering that humans perceive to exist in the animal world is not initially an inference, it is a projection": Borneman, "Race, Ethnicity," p. 28.

25. *The Old French Crusade Cycle*, vol. 1, *La Naissance du Chevalier au Cygne*, ed. Emanuel J. Mickel, Jr. and Jan A. Nelson, intro. Geoffrey M. Myers (Tuscaloosa: University of Alabama Press, 1977), pp. lxxxi–lxxxix.

26. Anthony R. Wagner, "The Swan Badge and the Swan Knight," *Archaeologia* 97 (1959): 127–38; Pastoureau, "Désigner ou dissimuler?" p. 139. Berthault de Villebresmes, *Geste du Chevalier au Cygne* puts into prose an older verse text belonging to Marie de Clèves, widow of Charles d'Orléans, because "elle et ses predecesseurs, ducs et seigneurs de Clevez, sont issus, partiz et dessenduz d'un tres noble et tres victorieulx chevallier, filz de roy, nommé Helyas—et par merveilleuse adventure cy aprés descripte et recitee, denommé le chevallier au cigne" [she and her forebears, dukes and lords of Cleves, began, issued, and descended from a most noble and victorious knight, son of a king, named Elias—and by the marvelous adventure here to be described and recounted, called the Knight of the Swan]: *The Old French Crusade Cycle*, vol. 9, *La Geste du Chevalier au Cygne*, ed. Edmond A. Emplaincourt (Tuscaloosa: University of Alabama Press, 1989), p. 1. The lords of Cleves were claiming descent from the swan as early as 1287: Wagner, "Swan Badge," p. 132. Lineal commemoration also informs John Talbot's gift to Margaret of Anjou of a compound manuscript, London, British Library, MS Royal 15 E.vi, containing the "Ystoire du Chevalier au Signe." Margaret was the new wife of Henry VI, who claimed descent from the Swan Knight through his grandfather's marriage with Mary de Bohun; from that marriage onward the Lancastrians had used a swan badge, and Margaret adopted the device as well: George F. Warner and Julius P. Gilson, *Catalogue of Western Manuscripts in the Old Royal and King's Collections*, 4 vols. (London: Longmans, 1921), 2: 177–79; Wagner, "Swan Badge," pl. 40. As late as 1512, Edward Stafford commissions Robert Copland's translation because he "lynyally is dyscended" from "Helyas the knyght of the swanne": *The History of Helyas, Knight of the Swan*, trans. Copland (New York: Grolier Club, 1901), prologue, no pagination. On the Staffords' heraldic use of swans, see Dennys, *Heraldry*, pp. 24, 109. Thomas Cramer provides a bibliography of the medieval swan texts in *Lohengrin, Edition und Untersuchungen* (Munich: Wilhelm Fink, 1971), pp. 584–86.

27. I quote from the *Beatrix* version in *The Old French Crusade Cycle*, vol. 1; and from *The Romance of the Cheuelere Assigne*, ed. Henry H. Gibbs, EETS, e.s. 6 (London: Oxford University Press, 1868). Line numbers for quotations from these texts are given in parentheses following the quotations; *B* identifies the *Beatrix* version and *CA* the Middle English version.

28. Keen, *Chivalry*, p. 57. On the persistent subordination of religious to secular values in chivalry, see Richard Kaeuper, *War, Justice and Public Order: England and France in the Later Middle Ages* (Oxford: Clarendon Press, 1988), pp. 184–211.

29. John Rous, *The Rous Roll, with an Historical Introduction on John Rous and the Warwick Roll by Charles Ross* (Gloucester: Alan Sutton, 1980), no pagination, nos. 18, 19 and note. This edition reprints most of John Rows, *This rol was laburd & finished by Master John Rows of Warrewyk*, ed. William Courthope (London: Pickering, 1859).

30. Guy Beauchamp (d. 1316) married Alice de Tony around 1310, but bore the arms *gules, a fess between six cross crosslets or* at the siege of Carlaverok in 1300: *The Siege of Carlaverock*, ed. and trans. Nicholas Harris Nicolas (London: Nichols, 1828), pp. 18–19, 157–59. Walter Beauchamp of Alcester (d. 1303) continued to use six martlets, not crosses, after his marriage to another Alice de Tony: *Siege of Carlaverock*, ed. Nicolas, pp. 30–31, 200–201.

31. *Rous Roll*, no. 18 and note; in 1400 "the cup of the Swan" was bequeathed by Thomas Beauchamp to his son Richard: Wagner, "Swan Badge," p. 129.

32. Crocker, "My Brother the Parrot," pp. 16, 20. One implication of metonymy that I cannot follow out here, since it deals with social organization as a whole rather than self-presentation, is the connection between totemic and linguistic thought. Lévi-Strauss argued that totemism is an instance of the metonymic thought process that is also fundamental to language, whereby signs stand in relation to things as totems stand in relation to people. Stéphane Breton and Pierre Legendre focus on the ethical implications of the two systems' similarities. They argue that totemic and linguistic systems share a foundational capacity to appear natural and given, not under anyone's control. Elites rely on these systems to create the illusion of intransigence in social organization and naturalness in hierarchies. Those who are most in control of totemic and linguistic representation are most in control of society, since representation is what brings society into being. Breton concludes, "Que la société apparaisse comme cause et comme garant, sous la figure de la généalogie et de l'interdit, serait une conséquence imparable de l'entrée dans le langage. Dès lors qu'elles parlent, les sociétés s'élèvent sur des fictions" [That society appears to be an instigator and guarantor, through the figuration of genealogy and prohibition, is the unavoidable consequence of the entry into language. From the moment they speak, societies raise themselves on fictions]. His emphasis on fiction and spectacle as sites of social formation would be highly relevant to considering how family myths work beyond self-presentation, at the levels of national, class, or civic behavior: Breton, "De l'illusion totémique à la fiction sociale," *L'Homme* 151 (July–September 1999): 147; Legendre, *L'Inestimable objet de la transmission: Etude sur le principe généalogique en Occident* (Paris: Fayard, 1985).

33. *Political Poems and Songs Relating to English History*, 2 vols., ed. Thomas Wright, Rerum Britanicarum Medii Aevi Scriptores 14 (London: Longman, 1859, 1861) 2: 221. Similarly, the epitaph on the tomb of Edward III calls him "the

invincible leopard" ("invictus pardus"): Philip Lindley, "Absolutism and Regal Image in Ricardian Sculpture," in *The Regal Image of Richard II and the Wilton Diptych*, ed. Dillian Gordon, Lisa Monnas, and Caroline Elam (London: Miller, 1997), pp. 73, 292, n. 50.

34. See notes 20, 23 above and J. Christopher Crocker, "Being an Essence: Totemic Representation Among the Eastern Bororo," in *The Power of Symbols: Masks and Masquerade in the Americas*, ed. N. Ross Crumrine and Marjorie Halpin (Vancouver: University of British Columbia, 1983), pp. 157–76.

35. Crocker, "My Brother the Parrot," p. 16.

36. "Ele a fait contre Dieu et contre toute jent, / Ele n'est pas loiaus" [she has acted against God and all people, she is not loyal: *B* 220–21]; cf. *CA* 234–35 and *B* 923–24. She is imprisoned without comforts, on straw, "con une beste mue" [like a dumb beast: *B* 288], the simile indicating her mistreatment and abasement.

37. On wild men and women, see Chapter 5. On Elias, see Joan B. Williamson, "Elyas as a Wild Man in *Li Estoire del Chevalier au Cisne*," in *Essays in Honor of Louis Francis Solano*, ed. Raymond J. Cormier and Urban T. Holmes, University of North Carolina Studies in the Romance Languages and Literatures 92 (Chapel Hill: University of North Carolina Press, 1970), pp. 193–202.

38. See Donald Maddox and Sara Sturm-Maddox, eds., *Melusine of Lusignan: Founding Fiction in Late Medieval France* (Athens: University of Georgia Press, 1996).

39. Cf. "tolu m'avés mon frere" (*B* 2522).

40. Tambiah, "Animals Are Good to Think," p. 455.

41. Enyas receives his Christian name at *CA* 265–71, but he is called only "chevelere assigne" thereafter: ll. 328, 333, 369. In French he is called "Cevalier au Cisne" at the outset (*B* 7, 29), but "Elias" after his baptism.

42. Some fifteenth-century heralds say that crests were required in tournaments; heralds reviewed the tourneyers' crests and arms in preliminary ceremonies: Juliet R.V. Barker, *The Tournament in England, 1100–1400* (Woodbridge, Suffolk: Boydell, 1986), pp. 180–81; Arthur Charles Fox-Davies, *Heraldic Badges* (London: John Lane, 1907), pp. 50, 64. Ten crests from the stall-plates of the original twenty-four Garter knights are described in George F. Beltz, *Memorials of the Order of the Garter from Its Foundation to the Present Time* (London: Pickering, 1841), pp. 19–95.

43. Jonathan Alexander and Paul Binski, *Age of Chivalry: Art in Plantagenet England, 1200–1400* (London: Royal Academy of Arts, 1987), p. 480. On the heraldic "leopard" see note 10, above. On women's use of crests, see Pastoureau, "Désigner ou dissimuler?" p. 129, and Ann Payne, "The Salisbury Roll of Arms, c. 1463," in *England in the Fifteenth Century: Proceedings of the 1986 Harlaxton Symposium*, ed. Daniel Williams (Woodbridge, Suffolk: Boydell, 1987), pp. 187–98.

44. Fox-Davies, *Heraldic Badges*, pp. 17–18; Pastoureau, "Désigner ou dissimuler?" p. 136.

45. Pastoureau finds transgression in the choice of inferior animals such as dogs and serpents that do not have a high place in traditional heraldry ("Désigner ou dissimuler?" p. 133). Both animals and growling human heads suggest ferocity suitable to chivalric encounters. In addition, crests can express title to land or simply repeat a heraldic charge. All these possibilities could explain why crests were favored targets of attack in tournaments. Gelre Herald's armorial narrates a few

chivalric careers, and he twice mentions that crests suffer attack. "Jet-black bull's head," he addresses one crest, "you have often suffered blows between your golden horns"; a woman's torso dressed in the arms of Rudolph van Nydou "is often cut into bits by arms, and does not stay unbroken": Léon Jéquier, "Les Louanges des preux chevaliers de l'armorial du héraut Gelre," *Archives héraldiques suisses* 106, no. 1 (1992): 33, 37. Gelre notes of another crest that it was often seen at tournaments and jousts, p. 39. Perhaps adversaries in tournaments and jousts took crests to be concretized boasts that should be answered, just as concretely, with blows.

46. Ronald L. Grimes, "Masking: Toward a Phenomenology of Exteriorization," *Journal of the American Academy of Religion* 43 (1975): 508–16; N. Ross Crumrine, "Masks, Participants, and Audience" and Elisabeth Tooker, "The Many Faces of Masks and Masking: Discussion," in *The Power of Symbols*, ed. Crumrine and Halpin, pp. 1–11, 12–18; A. David Napier, *Masks, Transformation, and Paradox* (Berkeley: University of California Press, 1986).

47. Malcolm Vale, *War and Chivalry: Warfare and Aristocratic Culture in England, France and Burgundy at the End of the Middle Ages* (London: Duckworth, 1981); Juliet Vale, *Edward III and Chivalry: Chivalric Society and its Context, 1270–1350* (Woodbridge, Suffolk: Boydell, 1982); Keen, *Chivalry*; Stanesco, *Jeux d'errance*. Louise O. Fradenberg points out that war itself tends to be theatrical in its opportunities for display, its rules, and its expectations for performance: *City, Marriage, Tournament: Arts of Rule in Late Medieval Scotland* (Madison: University of Wisconsin Press, 1991), pp. 192–224. See also Johan Huizinga, *Homo Ludens: A Study of the Play-Element in Culture* (London: Routledge, 1949), and *The Autumn of the Middle Ages*, trans. Rodney J. Payton and Ulrich Mammitzsch (Chicago: University of Chicago Press, 1996).

48. Sally F. Moore and Barbara G. Myerhoff, "Secular Ritual: Forms and Meanings," intro. to *Secular Ritual*, ed. Sally F. Moore and Barbara G. Myerhoff (Assen: Van Gorcum, 1977), p. 18. See also John J. MacAloon, "Olympic Games and the Theory of Spectacle in Modern Societies," in *Rite, Drama, Festival, Spectacle: Rehearsals Toward a Theory of Cultural Performance*, ed. John J. MacAloon (Philadelphia: Institute for the Study of Human Issues, 1984), pp. 241–80; Don Handelman, *Models and Mirrors: Towards an Anthropology of Public Events* (Cambridge: Cambridge University Press, 1990).

49. Pastoureau, "Déguiser ou dissimuler?"

50. Marcel Mauss, "A Category of the Human Mind: The Notion of Person; the Notion of Self," trans. W. D. Halls, in *The Category of the Person: Anthropology, Philosophy, History*, ed. Michael Carrithers, Steven Collins, and Steven Lukes (Cambridge: Cambridge University Press, 1985), pp. 13–19; Grimes, "Masking," pp. 509–11.

51. Grimes, "Masking," pp. 509, 510.

52. *Siege of Carlaverock*, ed. Nicolas, p. 42.

53. Ibid., p. 43.

54. The dramatic moment of the swan's self-wounding is probably the source of Jean de Berry's swan badge, which shows a wound in the breast. On this badge, see James Hamilton Wylie, *The Reign of Henry the Fifth*, 3 vols. (New York: Greenwood, 1968), 2: 425–29. On the Tony family's claims to descent from the Swan Knight, see Brault, *Early Blazon*, pp. 43, 54, 146–47.

55. Disguise and recognition are configured quite differently in romance, epic, and fabliau. Since romances are the clear referent for late medieval tournaments and orders of chivalry, exploring the contrasts with other genres is beyond my purview.

56. Donald Maddox, *Fictions of Identity in Medieval France* (Cambridge: Cambridge University Press, 2000), makes an intriguingly analogous argument for "specular encounters" in which characters receive crucial information about themselves from others; here too identity is exterior, even more available to others than to oneself. On chivalric disguise in relation to public scrutiny, see Stanesco, *Jeux d'errance*, pp. 88–102.

57. Stephen Greenblatt, *Renaissance Self-Fashioning* (Chicago: University of Chicago Press, 1980), p. 2.

58. Jacob Burckhardt, *The Civilization of the Renaissance in Italy*, trans. S. G. O. Middlemore (London: Phaidon Books, 1965), p. 81, quoted in Lee Patterson, *Chaucer and the Subject of History* (Madison: University of Wisconsin Press, 1991), p. 7. See Patterson's discussion of subjectivity in relation to Chaucer and his work, pp. 3–46; and David Aers, "A Whisper in the Ear of Early Modernists; or, Reflections on Literary Critics Writing the 'History of the Subject,'" in *Culture and History, 1350–1600: Essays on English Communities, Identities, and Writing*, ed. David Aers (Detroit: Wayne State University Press, 1992), pp. 177–202.

59. Robert W. Hanning, *The Individual in Twelfth-Century Romance* (New Haven, Conn.: Yale University Press, 1977), p. 4, his emphasis; Colin Morris, *The Discovery of the Individual, 1050–1200* (London: SPCK, 1972) holds a similar view although he finds that the "self" is a more accurately medieval concept than the "individual" (e.g., pp. 64–95).

60. Peter Haidu, "Temps, histoire, subjectivité aux XIᵉ et XIIᵉ siècles," in *Le Nombre du temps: En hommage à Paul Zumthor*, ed. Emmanuèle Baumgartner et al. (Paris: Champion, 1988), p. 120. For similar views see Douglas Kelly, *The Art of Medieval French Romance* (Madison: University of Wisconsin Press, 1992), pp. 54–58, tracing rhetorical and philosophical pressures against individuality; and Paul Zumthor, *Essai de poétique médiévale* (Paris: Seuil, 1972), p. 351: "une exigence profonde de la mentalité de ce temps et de la société courtoise en particulier" determines that "les valeurs de l'individu n'ont d'existence que reconnues et visiblement manifestées par la collectivité" [a deeply rooted conviction in the mentality of this period and of courtly society in particular (determines that) the values of an individual exist only insofar as they are recognized and visibly manifested by the community].

61. John Locke, *An Essay Concerning Human Understanding*, ed. Peter H. Nidditch (Oxford: Clarendon Press, 1975), pp. 718–19.

62. Locke, *Human Understanding*, p. 711.

63. Ian Watt, *The Rise of the Novel: Studies in Defoe, Richardson, and Fielding* (Berkeley: University of California Press, 1957); Michael McKeon urges the continuing indebtedness of the novel to romance in *The Origins of the English Novel, 1600–1740* (Baltimore: Johns Hopkins University Press, 1987).

64. Fradenberg, *City, Marriage, Tournament*, pp. 201–11 (quotation at p. 209).

65. Patterson, *Chaucer and the Subject of History*, pp. 165–79 (quotation at p. 168).

66. Sarrazin, *Roman de Ham*, in *Histoire des ducs de Normandie et des rois d'Angleterre*, ed. Francisque Michel (Paris: Renouard, 1840), pp. 213–384 (entry of Yvain, pp. 315–16); on thirteenth-century engagements with literary models see J. Vale, *Edward III and Chivalry*, pp. 4–24.

67. Chrétien de Troyes, *Le Chevalier au Lion (Yvain)*, ed. Mario Roques, CFMA 89 (Paris: Champion, 1960), ll. 4810–12; *Ywain and Gawain*, ed. Albert B. Friedman and Norman T. Harrington, EETS o.s. 254 (London: Oxford University Press, 1964), ll. 2804–6. In order to concentrate on the Hundred Years War, I will cite primarily romance texts composed between 1300 and 1450.

68. J. Vale, *Edward III and Chivalry*, pp. 64, 68–69.

69. Nicholas Harris Nicolas, "Observations on the Institution of the Most Noble Order of the Garter," *Archaeologia* 31 (1846): 40, 121; Adam Murimuth, *Continuatio chronicarum Robertus de Avesbury*, ed. E. M. Thompson, Rolls Series 93 (London: Eyre and Spottiswood, 1889), pp. 123–24.

70. Brault, *Early Blazon*, pp. 31–32, 35–36.

71. *Ipomadon*, in *Ipomedon in drei englischen Bearbeitungen*, ed. Eugen Kölbing (Breslau: Koebner, 1889), ll. 5044–45.

72. *Ipomadon*, ll. 5189, 5200–201. J. A. Burrow, "The Uses of Incognito: *Ipomadon A*," in *Readings in Medieval English Romance*, ed. Carol M. Meale (Cambridge: D.S. Brewer, 1994), pp. 25–34, argues that Ipomadon engages in a "curious honorific calculus" whereby unclaimed glory continues to accrue to his merit (p. 30).

73. *The Middle-English Versions of Partonope of Blois*, ed. A. Trampe Bödtker, EETS e.s. 109 (London: Kegan Paul, 1912), ll. 9868–69. A courtier in *Ipomadon* similarly subsumes the protagonist into his disguise by announcing to his lady, "the blake baner hathe brought you blis" (l. 8682). On the moral implications of colors chosen for heraldic incognito see Michel Pastoureau, *Figures et couleurs: Etudes sur la symbolique et la sensibilité médiévales* (Paris: Léopard d'Or, 1986), pp. 193–207.

74. *Ywain and Gawain*, ll. 1611–12, 1621–23; cf. *Yvain*, ll. 2718–75.

75. *Ywain and Gawain*, ll. 1627, 2096, 2116.

76. Long versions by Froissart are *Chroniques*, ed. Simeon Luce et al., Société de l'Histoire de France, vol. 4 (Paris: Renouard, 1873), pp. 70–84; and *Chroniques: Dernière rédaction du premier livre. Edition du manuscrit de Rome Reg. lat. 869*, ed. George T. Diller (Geneva: Droz, 1972), pp. 861–76; corresponding to these more recent editions is Froissart, *Oeuvres de Froissart*, ed. Kervyn de Lettenhove, 25 vols. (Brussels: Victor Devaux, 1867–77), 5: 229–51. Another long account is Geoffrey le Baker, *Chronicon*, ed. E. M. Thompson (Oxford: Clarendon, 1889), pp. 103–8. The episode is briefly mentioned in William Worcestre, *Itineraries*, ed. John H. Harvey (Oxford: Clarendon Press, 1969), pp. 346–49; Thomas Walsingham, *Historia anglicana*, ed. H. T. Riley, 2 vols., Rolls Series 28 (London: Longman Green, 1863–64), 1: 273–74; and Robert de Avesbury's *De gestis mirabilibus Regis Edwardi Tertii*, ed. E. M. Thompson, Rolls Series 93 (London: Longmans, 1889), pp. 408–10.

77. Froissart, *Chroniques*, ed. Luce, 4 : 79.

78. Froissart, *Chroniques: Dernière rédaction*, ed. Diller, p. 870. Peter F. Ainsworth comments on revisions to this episode in *Jean Froissart and the Fabric of History: Truth, Myth, and Fiction in the "Chroniques"* (Oxford: Clarendon Press, 1990), p. 299–300.

79. Froissart, *Chroniques: Dernière rédaction*, ed. Diller, p. 870; compare the

briefer version in *Chroniques*, ed. Luce, 4: 80: "non qu'il le cognuist, ne il ne savoit à qui il avoit à faire" [not that he (Eustace) recognized him (Edward), or knew with whom he was dealing].

80. Froissart, *Chroniques*, ed. Luce, 4: 83.

81. Richard Kaeuper has pointed out to me that Edward's use of the terms "dedens" and "dehors" contributes to the analogy with tournaments. See J. Vale, *Edward III and Chivalry*, p. 6: "The notion of two teams, *dedens* and *dehors* is, of course, common in the late thirteenth and the fourteenth centuries."

82. Froissart, *Chroniques: Dernière rédaction*, p. 875, further emphasizes the renown accrued by Edward's strategy: Eustace tells the French king and lords "sen aventure" and his wearing of the chaplet produces "grandes nouvelles en France et en aultres pais."

83. *Ywain and Gawain*, ll. 4020–22.

84. J. Vale, *Edward III and Chivalry*, pp. 86–91; Keen, *Chivalry*, pp. 196–97.

85. J. Vale, *Edward III and Chivalry*, p. 91; Keen, *Chivalry*, pp. 185–86; D'Arcy Jonathan Dacre Boulton, *The Knights of the Crown: The Monarchical Orders of Knighthood in Later Medieval Europe, 1325–1520* (New York: St. Martin's Press, 1987), p. 109.

86. Charny, *Book of Chivalry*, pp. 166–71; Charny's probable source for this passage is *L'Ordene de chevalerie*, ed. Keith Busby, in *Raoul de Houdenc: Le Roman des eles; The Anonymous Ordene de chevalerie* (Amsterdam: Benjamins, 1983), ll. 137–88.

87. Léopold Pannier, *La Noble maison de Saint-Ouen, la villa Clippiacum, et l'Ordre de l'Etoile d'après les documents originaux* (Paris: Aubry, 1872), pp. 90, 93, n.; M. Vale, *War and Chivalry*, p. 54. Several orders (the Knot, Golden Fleece, Croissant, and Star) make provisions for returning the deeds of their members to literature in records of the order : Keen, *Chivalry*, p. 192.

88. Charny, *Book of Chivalry*, pp. 84–99, 166–91.

89. *Sir Gawain and the Green Knight*, ed. J. R. R. Tolkien and E. V. Gordon, 2nd ed., rev. Norman Davis (Oxford: Clarendon Press, 1967), ll. 919, 2364–65. Subsequent line references appear in parentheses in the text.

90. Charny, *Book of Chivalry*, pp. 152–55.

91. On the pentangle and girdle in relation to identity, see Geraldine Heng, "Feminine Knots and the Other *Sir Gawain and the Green Knight*," *PMLA* 106 (1991): 500–514; on chivalric identity as a performance in *Sir Gawain*, see Carolyn Dinshaw, "A Kiss Is Just a Kiss: Heterosexuality and Its Consolations in *Sir Gawain and the Green Knight*," *diacritics* 24 (1994): 205–26.

92. *Ipomadon* uses "conusaunce" in this sense when a young knight recognizes an adversary by his coat of arms: "Jasone wold no lengur byde, / To the knyght can he ryde, / He knewe his conusaunce" (ll. 4417–19).

93. The effigy on the Black Prince's tomb and the Luttrell Psalter's image of Sir Geoffrey Luttrell are familiar examples. Compare "þe pentangle nwe / He ber in schelde and cote" [on his shield and surcoat: *Sir Gawain*, 636–37]. The shorter, tighter *cote* of the later fourteenth century is sometimes called a *jupon*.

94. On heraldic revisions to indicate allegiance, commemorate feats of arms, and distinguish among family members, see Barker, *Tournament*, p. 87; A. C. Fox-Davies, *A Complete Guide to Heraldry*, rev. J. P. Brooke-Little (London: Nelson, 1969), pp. 366–88; 456–64.

95. Marjorie Garber, *Vested Interests: Cross-Dressing and Cultural Anxiety* (London: Routledge, 1992), e.g., pp. 36–37.

96. The slightly altered motto "hony soyt qui mal pence" at the end of the manuscript is "possibly by a later scribe," according to Israel Gollancz, *Sir Gawain and the Green Knight*, EETS o.s. 210 (London: Oxford University Press, 1940), p. 132, n.; other scholars tend to assume the hand is not that of the scribe, although of the same period.

97. Like the order sketched in *Sir Gawain*, 2515–18, the Order of the Garter included women members, "lordes and ladis," though it was always understood as a "broþerhede": James L. Gillespie, "Ladies of the Fraternity of Saint George and of the Society of the Garter," *Albion* 17 (1985): 259–78. Exchequer documents not cited by Gillespie or others on this subject are edited by Léon Mirot and E. Deprez: *Les Ambassades anglaises pendant la guerre de cent ans: catalogue chronologique, 1327–1450* (Paris: Picard, 1900), pp. 64–65: Richard II sent garter regalia to the French court in 1396 as part of his marriage negotiations; Isabel received a garter to wear on her arm ["ad utendum super brachium suum"], as it was worn according to several fifteenth-century women's effigies (Gillespie, "Ladies of the Fraternity of St. George," pp. 263–64).

98. In this interpretation, the blue garter may appropriate the blue ground of the French royal arms, the French motto may recall Edward's lineal claim to the throne, and the garter's design as a small belt (rather than the knotted strips of cloth that both men and women used in the period as garters) may imitate the knight's sword belt, one of his insignia of rank: e.g., J. Vale, *Edward III and Chivalry*, pp. 79–85.

99. "May he be punished who thinks evil of this": Joanot Martorell and MartíJoan de Galba, *Tirant lo Blanc*, trans. David H. Rosenthal (New York: Schocken, 1984), pp. ix–x; 121–23. Michael Packe, *King Edward III*, ed. L. C. B. Seaman (London: Routledge, 1983), pp. 170–74, adduces evidence that may sustain the fallen garter story; the color blue would then indicate loyalty (to women or to sovereign), a significance much attested in the later fourteenth century: Stella Mary Newton, *Fashion in the Age of the Black Prince* (Woodbridge, Suffolk: Boydell, 1980), p. 46; Boulton, *Knights of the Crown*, p. 246 (use of blue by Order of the Sword, with motto "c'est pour loyauté maintenir").

100. Quoted in Richard Barber, *Edward, Prince of Wales and Aquitaine* (New York: Scribner, 1978), p. 85; Barber also quotes the 1463 comment of Mondonus Belvaleti that "many assert that this order took its beginning from the feminine sex, from a lewd and forbidden affection" (p. 86). Nicolas, "Observations," publishes a Tudor translation of this episode from Polydore Vergil's history, pp. 131–32.

101. Vern L. Bullough, "Transvestites in the Middle Ages," *Journal of Sociology* 79 (1974): 1381–94; Michèle Perret, "Travesties et transsexuelles: Yde, Silence, Grisandole, Blanchandine," *Romance Notes* 25 (1984–85): 328–40.

102. Quoted in Barber, *Edward*, p. 85.

103. C. Stephen Jaeger, "L'Amour des rois: Structure sociale d'une forme de sensibilité aristocratique," *Annales: Economies, Sociétés, Civilisations* 46 (1991): 547–71.

104. On appearances of the mottos see J. Vale, *Edward III and Chivalry*, pp. 57–91; Newton, *Fashion*, passim. Even as they assert control, these mottos preserve

the empowering enigma characteristic of mottos, as discussed in Chapter 1: what "it" and "y" refer to is unspecified. Shame unto him who thinks ill of this garter? of this gesture? of this order? of this claim to France?

Chapter 5: Wild Doubles

1. Mathieu d'Escouchy, *Chronique de Mathieu d'Escouchy*, ed. G. du Fresne de Beaucourt, 3 vols. (Paris: Renouard, 1863–64), 2: 141; P. W. Hammond, *Food and Feast in Medieval England* (Dover, N.H.: Sutton, 1993); Christopher Dyer, *Standards of Living in the Later Middle Ages: Social Change in England, c. 1200–1520* (Cambridge: Cambridge University Press, 1989), pp. 49–70. Middle English *soteltie* refers to food presented as spectacle, but not to performances; see Robert Withington, *English Pageantry: An Historical Outline*, 2 vols. (1918, reprint New York: Blom, 1963), 1: 82–84.

2. English terms *interlude, mumming, disguising* and French *entremets, momerie, esbatement* tend to be interchangeable and to merge in Latin *ludus*. *Interlude*, because it is used similarly to the capacious term *entremets* as well as *ludus*, appears the most inclusive English term, although Chambers is probably correct that *interlude* tended to designate speech or dialogue in contrast to mumming: see E. K. Chambers, *The Mediaeval Stage*, 2 vols. (Oxford: Clarendon Press, 1903), 2: 179–98; Glynne Wickham, *Early English Stages, 1300–1660*, 2nd ed., 2 vols. (London: Routledge, 1980), 1: 191–228.

3. Nicholas H. Nicolas, "Observations on the Institution of the Most Noble Order of the Garter," *Archaeologia* 31 (1846): 37–38, 43.

4. On the wolf's skins and other disguisings see Françoise Piponnier, *Costume et vie sociale: La Cour d'Anjou, XIVe–XVe siècle* (Paris: Mouton, 1970), p. 235. Adrastus encounters Polynices in Statius, *Thebaid*, ed. and trans. J. H. Mozley, 2 vols. (Cambridge, Mass.: Harvard University Press, 1928), 1: 371–77; Polynices again dresses in the lion's skin, 1: 512–13.

5. Charles d'Orléans, *Poésies*, ed. Pierre Champion, 2 vols., CFMA 34, 56 (Paris: Champion, 1923, 1927), 1: 128–29; on James IV's robes for masking and his other disguises see Louise Olga Fradenberg, *City, Marriage, Tournament: Arts of Rule in Late Medieval Scotland* (Madison: University of Wisconsin Press, 1991), p. 175, *passim*.

6. Reading that accompanies a silent performance also characterizes Lydgate's mummings for the royal court. In his "Mumming at Hertford," overmatched husbands complain to the king through a proxy speaker, but the wives reply in the first person plural, as if one of them is speaking aloud: *The Minor Poems of John Lydgate*, ed. Henry Noble MacCracken, 2 vols., EETS o.s. 107, 192 (London: Oxford University Press, 1911, 1934), 2: 675–82.

7. Malcolm Vale, "The World of the Courts: Content and Context of the *Fauvel* Manuscript," in *Fauvel Studies: Allegory, Chronicle, Music, and Image in Paris, Bibliothèque Nationale de France, MS français 146*, ed. Margaret Bent and Andrew Wathey (Oxford: Clarendon Press, 1998), pp. 591–98.

8. E.g., Juliet Vale, *Edward III and Chivalry: Chivalric Society and Its Context 1270–1350* (Woodbridge, Suffolk: Boydell, 1982), pp. 70–71; Reyher, *Les Masques*

anglais: Etude sur les ballets et la vie de cour en Angleterre (1512–1640) (Paris: Hachette, 1909), p. 500 (knights and squires masked at a wedding banquet in 1433); Escouchy, *Chronique*, 2: 139 (disguised guests at a banquet in 1454).

9. Meg Twycross notes that even the more scripted hall plays of the Tudor period "were written to be performed by members of a closely-knit in-group for their fellows. Even if the group was highly stratified, nonetheless they were all part of this 'family' and shared the same private jokes": "The Theatricality of Medieval English Plays," in *The Cambridge Companion to Medieval English Theatre*, ed. Richard Beadle (Cambridge: Cambridge University Press, 1994), p. 79.

10. "The said mummers saluted them, shewing a peyr of dice upon a table to play with the prince, which dice were subtilly made so that when the prince shold cast he shold winne": Paul Reyher, *Masques anglais*, p. 499; *The Anonimalle Chronicle, 1333 to 1381*, ed. V. H. Galbraith (Manchester: Manchester University Press, 1927), pp. 102–3. A similar conjunction of mumming and dice playing occurs in 1405 according to the *Chronique de Jean de Stavelot*, ed. A. Borgnet (Brussels: Hayez, 1861), p. 95: "adonc une vesprée les barons, prinches, contes et dus s'avisont qu'ilh yroient momeir et joweir aux dées al hosteit monsangneur de Lige" [then one evening the barons, princes, counts, and dukes decided they would go mumming and play dice at the lodgings of the Bishop of Liège].

11. Richard Schechner, *The Future of Ritual: Writings on Culture and Performance* (London: Routledge, 1993), p. 74; Joseph Roach, "Kinship, Intelligence, and Memory as Improvisation: Culture and Performance in New Orleans," in *Performance and Cultural Politics*, ed. Elin Diamond (London: Routledge, 1996), p. 223. In contrast, Aron Gurevich argues that Christianity's inclusiveness as well as medieval society's relatively slight stratification are responsible for elite participation in the carnivalesque: *Medieval Popular Culture: Problems of Belief and Perception*, trans. János M. Bak and Paul A. Hollingsworth (Cambridge: Cambridge University Press, 1988), pp. 176–210.

12. Roberto DaMatta, *Carnivals, Rogues, and Heroes: An Interpretation of the Brazilian Dilemma*, trans. John Drury (Notre Dame, Ind.: University of Notre Dame Press, 1991), pp. 116–36. Paul Strohm discusses carnival appropriations by both commons and elites around the Rising of 1381: *Hochon's Arrow: The Social Imagination of Fourteenth-Century Texts* (Princeton, N.J.: Princeton University Press, 1992), pp. 33–56.

13. Emmanuel Le Roy Ladurie, *Carnival in Romans*, trans. Mary Feeney (New York: Braziller, 1979).

14. Stuart Hall, "The Emergence of Cultural Studies and the Crisis of the Humanities," *october* 53 (1990): 18.

15. Pierre Bourdieu, *Outline of a Theory of Practice*, trans. Richard Nice (Cambridge: Cambridge University Press, 1977), p. 110; *The Logic of Practice*, trans. Richard Nice (Cambridge: Polity Press, 1990), pp. 271–83.

16. Roger Vaultier, *Le folklore pendant la guerre de Cent Ans d'après les Lettres de Rémission du Trésor des Chartes* (Paris: Guénégaud, 1965), pp. 29–36 (quotation at p. 30).

17. A good overview is François Lebrun, "Le charivari à travers les condamnations des autorités ecclésiastiques en France du XIVe au XVIIIe siècle," in *Le*

Charivari: Actes de la table ronde organisée à Paris (25-27 avril 1977), ed. Jacques le Goff and Jean-Claude Schmitt (Paris: Mouton, 1981), pp. 221–28.

18. Lebrun, "Charivari," p. 224.

19. L. Sainéan, *Les Sources indigènes de l'étymologie française*, vol. 1 (Paris: Boccard, 1925): 282; Lebrun, "Charivari," p. 224; Vaultier, *Folklore*, p. 33; Arnold van Gennep, *Manuel de folklore français contemporain*, vol. 1 (Paris, 1946), pt. 2, pp. 614–28.

20. Vaultier, *Folklore*, pp. 31, *passim*.

21. Lebrun, "Charivari," p. 225; Vaultier, *Folklore*, pp. 31–32; Claude Gauvard and Altan Gokalp, "Les Conduites de bruit et leur signification à la fin du Moyen Age: Le Charivari," *Annales: Economies, Sociétés, Civilisations* 29 (1974): 698–99.

22. Especially comprehensive studies are Roger Pinon, "Qu'est-ce qu'un charivari?" in *Kontakte und Grenzen: Probleme der Volks-, Kultur- und Sozialforschung* (Göttingen: Otto Schwartz, 1969), pp. 393–405; and E. P. Thompson, "'Rough Music': Le Charivari anglais," *Annales: Economies, Sociétés, Civilisations* 27 (1972): 285–312.

23. Claude Lévi-Strauss, *The Raw and the Cooked: Introduction to a Science of Mythology: I*, trans. John and Doreen Weightman (New York: Harper and Row, 1969), p. 289.

24. Thompson, "'Rough Music,'" p. 301.

25. Violet Alford, "Rough Music or Charivari," *Folklore* 70 (1959): 505; Natalie Zemon Davis, "Charivari, Honor, and Community in Seventeenth-Century Lyon and Geneva," in *Rite, Drama, Festival, Spectacle: Rehearsals Toward a Theory of Cultural Performance*, ed. John J. MacAloon (Philadelphia: Institute for the Study of Human Issues, 1984), pp. 45, 49; see also Natalie Zemon Davis, *Society and Culture in Early Modern France* (Stanford, Calif.: Stanford University Press, 1965), pp. 97–123.

26. Davis, *Society and Culture*, p. 107.

27. The English term "skimmington," for the large ladle with which overweening wives were said to beat their husbands, reflects the tendency of charivari to take female rather than male transgressions as its pretext. Thompson's "'Rough Music'" notes charivari's patriarchal affinities.

28. Noting this feature of charivari, Claude Karnoouh proposes that its noisy aggression is directed against the couple's previous marriage(s) and normalizes the new marriage by annihilating the earlier ones: "Le Charivari ou l'hypothèse de la monogamie," in *Charivari*, pp. 38–39. This explanation is counterintuitive, to say the least, because the ritual's violence is pointed straight at the present couple, as the judicial records show. But Karnoouh's point is well taken that charivari fails if its purpose is to register genuine objections to the new marriage.

29. Introduction to Emile Durkheim and Marcel Mauss, *Primitive Classification*, ed. and trans. Rodney Needham (Chicago: University of Chicago Press, 1963), p. xl.

30. My position is closest to that of van Gennep, *Manuel de folklore*, vol. 1, pt. 2, pp. 621–22, who concludes that the much reduced celebration typical of second marriages generates the charivari's extortion of celebration in the demand for drinking money.

31. Peter Burke's thesis in *Popular Culture in Early Modern Europe* (New York: New York University Press, 1978), p. 25, that the carnivalesque is common to all social groups in early Europe because all social groups shared one culture, is surprisingly ignorant of the period's social differences and tensions, its disparities in wealth and entitlement, and its contending clerical and courtly elites. When these elites drew on the rich popular culture beyond their courts, there is ample evidence that they were aware of complicating their claim to difference and superiority.

32. Gervais du Bus and Chaillou de Pesstain, *Le Roman de Fauvel*, ed. Arthur Långfors, SATF 64 (Paris: Firmin Didot, 1914–19). On Fauvel's name see lines 181–260. The text of Chaillou's additions appears at the end of this edition, the line numbers preceded by "E" to designate BNF 146. Quotations are from this edition, with line numbers in parentheses in the text.

33. *Roman de Fauvel*, ed. Långfors, pp. 135–38; Jean-Claude Mühlethaler, *Fauvel au pouvoir: Lire la satire médiévale* (Paris: Champion, 1994), pp. 17–29.

34. The manuscript's other contents are contemporary court poems and chronicles; the atelier that executed its illuminations worked primarily for the high nobility and the royal family; and its musical selections represent court genres more fully than any other collection: see the new facsimile edition, *Le Roman de Fauvel in the Edition of Mesire Chaillou de Pesstain*, ed. Edward H. Roesner, François Avril, and Nancy Freeman Regalado (New York: Broude, 1990).

35. Mühlethaler, *Fauvel au pouvoir*, pp. 396–400; *Roman de Fauvel*, ed. Roesner et al., pp. 4–7, 48–53; Elizabeth A. R. Brown, "*Rex ioians, ionnes, iolis*: Louis X, Philip V, and the *Livres de Fauvel*," in *Fauvel Studies*, ed. Bent and Wathey, pp. 53–72.

36. Hellekin appears "trop forment braiant" [howling extremely loudly: E 748] just after the revelers' own predilection for "la chançon au deable" is noted (E 744). Some readers of *Fauvel*, most recently Henri Rey-Flaud, argue that Hellekin is crucial to the charivari, which then becomes a ritual of remembering/evoking the dead, especially the dead spouses of remarrying widows and widowers: *Le Charivari: Les Rituels fondamentaux de la sexualité* (Paris: Payot, 1985). For most scholars, however, Hellekin is a secondary accretion evoking disorderly violence and nothing more: for example, van Gennep, *Manuel de folklore français*, vol. 1, pt. 2, pp. 618–20, 627–28; Nancy F. Regalado, "Masques réels dans le monde de l'imaginaire. Le Rite et l'écrit dans le charivari du *Roman de Fauvel*, MS. B.N. fr. 146," in *Masques et déguisements dans la littérature médiévale*, ed. Marie-Louise Ollier (Montreal: Montreal University Press, 1988), pp. 111–26.

37. Scholars tend to identify *Fauvel*'s charivari with "la fête populaire," "[les] juges populaires des villages," "le peuple": Regalado, "Masques réels," p. 119; Vaultier, *Folklore*, p. 34; Paul Fortier-Beaulieu, "Le Charivari dans le Roman de Fauvel," *Revue de folklore français* 11 (1940): 1–16.

38. The early facsimile edition is very rare (Gervais du Bus and Chaillou de Pesstain, *Le Roman de Fauvel, reproduction photographique du manuscrit français 146 de la Bibliothèque nationale de Paris*, ed. Pierre Aubry [Paris: Geuthner, 1907]); Långfors edits the text only; the standard edition of the musical texts is *L'Hérésie de Fauvel*, ed. Emilie Dahnk, Leipziger romanistische Studien, no. 4 (Leipzig: Romanischen Seminars, 1935); for the music, see "*Le Premier et le secont livre de fauvel*" *in the version preserved in B.N. f. fr. 146*, ed. Paul Helmer (Ottawa: Institute of

Mediaeval Music, 1997). The new facsimile edition of Roesner, Avril, and Regalado reassembles all the manuscript's contents.

39. Jean-Claude Schmitt, "Les Masques, le diable, les morts dans l'occident médiéval," *Razo: Cahiers du centre d'études médiévales de Nice* 6 (1986): 87–119, calls the figures watching the charivari clerics ("sans doute clercs," p. 94), but they lack the obvious tonsures marking clerics in other illuminations. The charivari's onlookers are dressed approximately like men and women in the banqueting and court settings of other illuminations. Mühlethaler, *Fauvel au pouvoir*, p. 135, reads the sides of these two larger illuminations as buildings along a street and the rectangular central spaces as exterior to the buildings, but the bedroom scene in the top rectangle of the first illumination confuses this otherwise plausible reading.

40. Michael Camille, *Image on the Edge: The Margins of Medieval Art* (Cambridge, Mass.: Harvard University Press, 1992), p. 145.

41. See Vaultier, *Folklore*, pp. 29–36; Gauvard and Gokalp, "Conduites de bruit," p. 699. For historical mumming, soot and flour were the inexpensive alternatives to masks : Henry Prunières, *Le Ballet de cour en France avant Benserade et Lully* (Paris: Laurens, 1914), p. 8 ; Meg Twycross and Sarah Carpenter, "Masks in Medieval English Theatre : The Mystery Plays," *Medieval English Theatre* 3, no. 2 (1981): 15.

42. DaMatta contrasts the orderly movements of normal life to carnival's "inverted movement that has no sure direction or destination": *Carnivals, Rogues, and Heroes*, p. 83.

43. Mühlethaler, *Fauvel au pouvoir*, pp. 131–38, argues that the most pejorative of these biformations is the animal head on the human body, because it suggests a loss of reason, the defining human attribute. The editors of the facsimile *Roman de Fauvel* propose that "Fauvel bears a horse's head whenever his true nature is in evidence," p. 44. Michael Camille argues for influences from beast fables and stresses the hybridity of Chaillou's entire project as context for the illuminations, "Hybridity, Monstrosity, and Bestiality in the *Roman de Fauvel*," in *Fauvel Studies*, ed. Bent and Wathey, pp. 161–74.

44. The face mask is the illuminator's deliberate choice for this contrast with Fauvel's profiled head, since full head masks ["testes," "hedes"] were as current as face masks ["viseres"] in court revels and drama: on mask technology in general see Twycross and Carpenter, "Masks in Medieval English Theatre."

45. See *Roman de Fauvel*, ed. Långfors, pp. 136–37; *Roman de Fauvel*, ed. Roesner et al., pp. 21–42; the editors hazard that these songs "were composed (if that is the correct word) by Chaillou or his musical editor" (p. 25).

46. See *L'Hérésie de Fauvel*, ed. Dahnk, pp. 184–86, 191–92 for the texts: for instance, "Trente-quatre pez moysis" [thirty-four moist farts], "Vostre bele bouche besera mon cul" [your (polite form) lovely mouth will kiss my ass], "Dame, se vos fours est chaut" [Lady, if your (polite form) oven is hot].

47. Patrice Uhl, "Les 'Sotes chançons' du *Roman de Fauvel* (MS E): La Symptomatique indécision du rubricateur," *French Studies* 45 (1991): 389.

48. Ernest Hoepffner, "Chanson française du XIIIᵉ siècle (*Ay Dex! ou porrey jen trouver*)," *Romania* 47 (1921): 367–80.

49. Hans Tischler, "A Lai from the *Roman de Fauvel*," in *Essays on the Music of J. S. Bach and Other Divers Subjects: A Tribute to Gerhard Herz*, ed. Robert L. Weaver et al. (Louisville, Ky.: University of Louisville, 1981), pp. 146, 149.

50. *L'Hérésie de Fauvel*, ed. Dahnk, pp. 187–91.

51. For Gaston Paris, the motet is simply out of place: "Le *Roman de Fauvel*," *Histoire littéraire de la France* 32 (Paris, 1898): 148. Regalado agrees it is incongruous, but argues that the motet as well as the figure of Hellekin are not part of the charivari proper; they are additional entertainments that Chaillou groups after the royal wedding to imitate the diverse *entremets* that celebrated state occasions of his time: "Masques," pp. 123–25. Mühlethaler proposes in contrast that the evening's elements are all allegories of the evil that Fauvel's rule is perpetrating throughout his realm: *Fauvel au pouvoir*, pp.136–38. Mühlethaler's premise is that *Fauvel's* narrative point of view remains consistently moralizing when its authorship shifts from Gervais du Bus to Chaillou, but in my view, Chaillou is not so faithful to the didactic program of his original. Long passages on the various dishes at his wedding (E 388–445), the glorious twittering dawn of the next day (E 771–99), and I would add the charivari here, necessitate Chaillou's warning that once the tournament of Vices and Virtues begins, "en clerjais en parleré" [I will be speaking in clerical terms: E 988]. Regalado is sensitive to Chaillou's largely secular aesthetic when she proposes that the Maytime motet is one of several entertainments celebrating Fauvel's wedding. I disagree, however, with Regalado's conclusion that the charivari is a toothless imitation of ritual, staged only to entertain.

52. On aristocratic violence see Richard W. Kaeuper, *War, Justice, and Public Order: England and France in the Later Middle Ages* (Oxford: Clarendon Press, 1988), pp. 184–268; for rhetoric associating lowness and violence see Strohm, *Hochon's Arrow*, pp. 33–56.

53. *Barboeres* are among the disguises ordered for Edward III's Christmas at Guildford ("xiiij. similitudines facierum hominum cum barbis"): Nicolas, "Observations," p. 37.

54. On the iconography of the hats see Mühlethaler, *Fauvel au pouvoir*, pp. 133–35, 360–61.

55. *L'Hérésie de Fauvel*, ed. Dahnk, p. 191.

56. Mikhail Bakhtin, *Rabelais and His World*, trans. Hélène Iswolsky (Cambridge, Mass.: MIT Press, 1968); the most suggestive reconsideration of Bakhtin remains Peter Stallybrass and Allon White, *The Politics and Poetics of Transgression* (Ithaca, N.Y.: Cornell University Press, 1986).

57. Historical charivaris sometimes featured a reveler impersonating the husband or wife to enhance their ridicule: see Jacques Le Goff and Jean-Claude Schmitt, eds., *Le Charivari: Actes de la table ronde organisée à Paris (25–27 avril 1977)* (Paris: Mouton, 1981), *passim*.

58. J. C. Crocker, "Ceremonial Masks," in *Celebration: Studies in Festivity and Ritual*, ed. Victor Turner (Washington, D.C.: Smithsonian Institution Press, 1982), p. 83.

59. Gervais du Bus shields the church from complicity in Fauvel's marriage by noting that he married Vaine Gloire "a la main senestre: / Sans bans et sans clerc et sans prestre" [with the left hand, without banns or cleric or priest]: *Roman de Fauvel*, ed. Långfors, ll. 3191–92.

60. A. David Napier, *Masks, Transformation, and Paradox* (Berkeley: University of California Press, 1986), pp. 4–15; Ronald L. Grimes, "Masking: Toward a Phenomenology of Exteriorization," *Journal of the American Academy of Religion* 43 (1975): 508–16.

61. Twycross and Carpenter, "Masks in Medieval English Theatre," pp. 24–29; Enid Welsford, *The Court Masque: A Study in the Relationship Between Poetry and the Revels* (New York: Russell, 1962), pp. 94–97; Schmitt, "Les Masques, le diable, les morts."

62. François Timoléon de Choisy, *Histoire de Charles VI* (Paris: Coignard, 1695), p. 132; Otto Driesen, *Der Ursprung des Harlekin: Ein kulturgeschichtliches Problem* (1904; reprint Hildesheim: Gerstenberg, 1977), p. 121. Driesen located two other manuscripts "de Monsieur Rousseau, Auditeur des Comptes" in the collections of the BNF, but not the manuscript Choisy cites. Richard Famiglietti, in correspondence, suspects that Choisy has confused the tumultuous entry of Queen Isabeau into Paris (1389) with the charivari of 1393.

63. Eustache Deschamps, *Oeuvres complètes de Eustache Deschamps*, ed. Le Marquis de Queux de Saint-Hilaire, SATF 9, 11 vols. (Paris : Firmin Didot, 1878–1903), 8: 44–49 (quotations at lines 92, 94–95, 161–62); 11: 285.

64. Yann Grandeau, "De Quelques dames qui ont servi la reine Isabeau de Bavière," *Bulletin philologique et historique du comité des travaux historiques et scientifiques* (Paris: Bibliothèque Nationale, 1975), pp. 153–56.

65. Jean Froissart, *Oeuvres de Froissart*, ed. Kervyn de Lettenhove, 25 vols. (Brussels: Victor Devaux, 1867–77), 15: 84–92; Michel Pintoin, *Chronique du Religieux de Saint-Denys*, ed. and trans. M. L. Bellaguet (1842), intro. Bernard Guenée, 6 vols. in 3 (Paris: Comité des Travaux Historiques et Scientifiques, 1994), 2: 64–71. According to Froissart and Pintoin, the participants were Charles VI, Hugh de Guisay, Yvain de Galles, Nantouillet (the lord of or son of the lord of), the Count of Joigny, and Aymeri or Charles or Jacques de Poitiers.

66. London, British Library, Harley 4380: see Froissart, *Oeuvres*, vol. 1, pt. 3, pp. 323–25; Lorraine Kochanske Stock, "Froissart's *Chroniques* and Its Illustrators: Historicity and Fictivity in the Verbal and Visual Imaging of Charles VI's Bal des Ardents," *Studies in Iconography* 21 (2000): 123–80.

67. The illuminator may be following Froissart's detail that the men were stitched into their costumes ["ils furent dedens enjoinds et cousus"], *Oeuvres*, 15: 85.

68. *Le Livre et la vraye hystoire du bon roy Alixandre*, London, British Library, MS Royal 20 B.xx, fol. 64: Alexander's men offer the naked woman to the wild man, then take him before Alexander, "et pour ce qu'il lui sembloit qu'il estoit homme sans point d'entendement, il le fist incontinent prendre et lier et puis fist faire un feu et le fist ardoir dedans" [and because it seemed to him that the man was without any understanding, he had him seized and bound immediately and then had a fire made and had him burned in it].

69. See the introduction by Guenée, in *Chronique du Religieux*, pp. xci–xvii; Froissart, *Oeuvres*, vol. 1, pt. 2, pp. 117–19, 122–23, 167–70. The *Chronique des quatre premiers Valois (1327–1393)*, ed. Siméon Luce (Paris: Renouard, 1862), pp. 327–29, provides a short contemporary corroboration of the event's outlines (the wedding context, the costumes, the fire).

70. *Chronique du Religieux*, 1: li–liii.

71. *Chronique du Religieux*, 2: 66.

72. *Chronique du Religieux*, 2: 68–71.

73. *Chronique du Religieux*, 2: 68.

74. Froissart, *Oeuvres*, 15: 87–90. The *Chronique des quatre premiers Valois*,

written independently in Rouen, pleonastically terms the event an "esbatement" performed "par druerie et sot esbatement" [for flirting and foolish amusement], p. 328.

75. Peter F. Ainsworth, *Jean Froissart and the Fabric of History: Truth, Myth, and Fiction in the "Chroniques"* (Oxford: Clarendon Press, 1990), pp. 151–69 (quotation at p. 167); 180–92.

76. Froissart, *Oeuvres*, 15: 85, 87; *Chronique du Religieux*, 2: 66.

77. Froissart, *Oeuvres*, 15: 85; *Chronique du Religieux*, 2: 64.

78. The *moresque* was "a favourite dance at Court theatricals, but never as a purely social dance. As a rule it was danced by people of one sex and usually by men": Welsford, *Court Masque*, p. 25. The terms *moresque* and *momerie* appear often together or interchangeably, suggesting the dance tended to involve impersonations: ibid., pp. 25–30; see also Chambers, *Mediaeval Stage*, 1: 198–201. The courtly *moresque* was probably taken over from popular local dancing, but it sustained "a strong and persistent tradition that it was a dance of Moorish origin": Welsford, *Court Masque*, p. 28.

79. *Chronique du Religieux*, 2: 66.

80. *Chronique du Religieux*, 2: 66: "penes eos tanta immodestia inolevit, quod se in larvis et inordinatis vestibus turpiter transfigurantes, in amborum conjugium displicenciam ignominiosa verba soleant publice divulgare."

81. The fifteenth-century chronicle of Jean Juvénal des Ursins represents the performance as a dance of chained, hairy wild men ["hommes sauvages enchaisnez, tous velus . . . vinrent comme pour danser"]: *Histoire de Charles VI*, in *Nouvelle collection des mémoires pour servir à l'histoire de France*, ed. Michaud and Poujoulat, vol. 2 (Paris: Guyot, 1850), p. 390.

82. Pintoin does not use the term *charivari*, although he describes the practice in detail. Pierre Cochon calls the event a "quallivally de gens desguysés" [charivari of disguised men]: *Chronique normande de Pierre Cochon*, ed. Charles de Beaurepaire (Rouen: Le Brument, 1870), p. 192. I am grateful to Richard Famiglietti for this reference.

83. See Richard Schechner, *Performance Theory*, 2nd ed. (London: Routledge, 1988), pp. 120–24; John J. MacAloon, "Introduction: Cultural Performances, Culture Theory," in *Rite, Drama, Festival, Spectacle*, pp. 1–15.

84. Richard Bernheimer, *Wild Men in the Middle Ages: A Study in Art, Sentiment, and Demonology* (Cambridge, Mass.: Harvard University Press, 1952); John Block Friedman, *The Monstrous Races in Medieval Art and Thought* (Cambridge, Mass.: Harvard University Press, 1981); Hayden White, "The Forms of Wildness: Archaeology of an Idea," in *The Wild Man Within: An Image in Western Thought from the Renaissance to Romanticism*, ed. Edward Dudley and Maximillian E. Novak (Pittsburgh: University of Pittsburgh Press, 1972), pp. 3–38; Dorothy Yamamoto, *The Boundaries of the Human in Medieval English Literature* (Oxford: Oxford University Press, 2000), pp. 144–96.

85. A few of the revelers disguise themselves as wild men in *Fauvel*'s illuminations, but they wear some item of clothing along with their fur, echoing Fauvel's hybrid appearance. Samuel Kinser sees seven wild men in the *Fauvel* illuminations, and provides context: "Wildmen in Festival, 1300–1550," in *Oral*

Tradition in the Middle Ages, ed. W. F. H. Nicolaisen (Binghamton, N.Y.: Medieval and Renaissance Texts and Studies, 1995), pp. 145–60.

86. For a survey of wild children, see Arthur Dickson, *Valentine and Orson: A Study in Late Medieval Romance* (New York: Columbia University Press, 1929), pp. 97–127. I discuss the Swan Knight, Elias, in Chapter 4.

87. Fradenberg, *City, Marriage, Tournament*, pp. 164, 240.

88. White, "Forms of Wildness," p. 21; Bernheimer, *Wild Man in the Middle Ages*, pp. 121–75 ("The Erotic Connotations"). Bernheimer conflates wild women's with wild men's sexuality, but in his data the women's involves deception and is not so recuperable as the men's.

89. Bernheimer, *Wild Men in the Middle Ages*, pp. 121, 136–41.

90. Ursins, *Histoire de Charles VI*, p. 390, concurs that a woman rescues Charles, though most of his chronicle draws on the *Chronique du Religieux*; at a later point, the *Chronique du Religieux* records the version that a woman rescued Charles (3: 762–63).

91. Penelope Doob, *Nebuchadnezzar's Children: Conventions of Madness in Middle English Literature* (New Haven. Conn.: Yale University Press, 1974); V. A. Kolve, "God-Denying Fools and the Medieval 'Religion of Love,'" *Studies in the Age of Chaucer*, 19 (1997): 3–59; Danielle Régnier-Bohler, "Le corps mis à nu: Perception et valeur symbolique de la nudité dans les récits du Moyen Age," *Europe* 654 (October 1983): 51–62.

92. Auguste Brachet, *Pathologie mentale des rois de France* (Paris: Hachette, 1903), pp. 621–50. Brachet counts 42 further episodes of madness after June 1393.

93. Alford, "Rough Music," p. 512; Bernheimer, *Wild Men in the Middle Ages*, p. 67; Welsford, *Court Masque*, p. 43; Brachet refutes the connection, *Pathologie mentale*, pp. 629–31. Froissart overtly disconnects the dance from Charles's illness by opining that the dance's sad end was a *second* sign from God that Charles should mend his ways (the first sign apparently having been his illness several months earlier). The link between the two episodes is God's repeated warning that Charles "trop jeunement se maintenoit" [was acting too youthfully], not that his madness was recurring: Froissart, *Oeuvres*, 15: 90.

94. Bernheimer, *Wild Men in the Middle Ages*, p. 143; Fradenberg, *City, Marriage, Tournament*, pp. 235–36. Around 1400, but especially in the later fifteenth century, wild men and women came also to be regarded nostalgically as uncorrupted, admirable ancestors: Bernheimer, *Wild Men in the Middle Ages*, pp. 143–49; White, "Forms of Wildness," pp. 23–28. Such "primitivism" is not evoked in any of the chronicle accounts of Charles VI's disguise.

95. Froissart, *Oeuvres*, 15: 87.

96. Don Handelman, *Models and Mirrors: Towards an Anthropology of Public Events* (Cambridge: Cambridge University Press, 1990), p. 151. To be sure, there are many differences between the Newfoundland mummers and the dancers of January 1393, but they share a pleasure in appearing hostile to their audience and in breaking free of normal constraints. Both performances end when an onlooker guesses identity. Handelman argues that the Newfoundland mummers compensate for the austerity, constraint, and responsibilities of their daily lives with the threatening, amoral, disconnected persona of mumming.

97. *Sir Gawain and the Green Knight*, ed. J. R. R. Tolkein and E. V. Gordon, 2nd ed., rev. Norman Davis (Oxford: Clarendon Press, 1967), ll. 467, 471–73. Subsequent references to this edition are given by line number in the text.

98. Escouchy, *Chronique*, 2: 149; he also records a horse that runs around the hall backwards carrying two trumpeters, a white stag that sings with a man's voice while carrying a girl and a child, and twenty-eight musicians inside a pie who pop out at intervals to perform songs (3: 133–34, 142–43, 146–47).

99. For information on the manuscript, see Anne D. Hedeman, *The Royal Image: Illustrations of the "Grandes Chroniques de France," 1274–1422* (Berkeley: University of California Press, 1991). On the event, see Laura Hibbard Loomis, "Secular Dramatics in the Royal Palace, Paris, 1378, 1389, and Chaucer's 'Tregetoures,'" *Speculum* 33 (1958): 242–55; the chronicler calls the boat and the castle "entremés" and the enactment an "esbatement" (p. 246). See also Wickham, *Early English Stages*, 1: 212–14; Victoria L. Weiss, "The 'laykyng of enterludez' at King Arthur's Court: The Beheading Scene in *Sir Gawain and the Green Knight*," in *The Medieval Court in Europe*, ed. Edward R. Haymes (Munich: Fink, 1986), pp. 189–99.

100. Loomis, "Secular Dramatics," pp. 246–47.

101. Escouchy, *Chronique*, 2: 160–222; Agathe Lafortune-Martel, *Fête noble en Bourgogne au XVᵉ siècle. Le banquet du Faisan (1454): Aspects politiques, sociaux et culturels* (Montreal: Bellarmin, 1984).

102. "The Vows of the Heron," ed. and trans. Thomas Wright, in *Political Poems and Songs Relating to English History*, vol. 1 (London: Longman, 1859), 1–25; on similar vows see John L. Grigsby, "L'Intertextualité interrompue par l'histoire: Le Cas des *Voeux du Héron*," in *Courtly Literature: Culture and Context*, ed. Keith Busby and Erik Kooper (Amsterdam: Benjamins, 1990), pp. 239–48; B. J. Whiting, "The Vows of the Heron," *Speculum* 20 (1945): 261–78.

103. Constance Bullock-Davies, *Menestrellorum Multitudo: Minstrels at a Royal Feast* (Cardiff: University of Wales Press, 1978).

104. G. Huet, "Les Traditions arturiennes chez le chroniqueur Louis de Velthem," *Le Moyen Age* 26 (1913): 173–97; Lodewijk van Velthem, *Voortzetting van den Spiegel historiael (1248–1316)*, ed. Herman vander Linden and Willem de Vreese, vol. 1 (Brussels: Hayez, 1906): 305–12. Victoria L. Weiss argues for taking Velthem's account seriously: "*Sir Gawain and the Green Knight* and the Fourteenth-Century Interlude," in *Text and Matter: New Critical Perspectives of the "Pearl"-Poet*, ed. Robert J. Blanch, Miriam Youngerman Miller, and Julian N. Wasserman (Troy, N.Y.: Whitston, 1991), pp. 229–41.

105. Weiss, "*Sir Gawain and the Green Knight* and the Fourteenth-Century Interlude"; Carl Lindahl, "*Sir Gawain and the Green Knight* and Myth in Its Time," in *Telling Tales: Medieval Narratives and the Folk Tradition*, ed. Francesca Canadé Sautman, Diana Conchado, and Giuseppe Carlo Di Scipio (New York: St. Martin's Press, 1998), pp. 249–67; see also Frederick B. Jonassen, "Elements from the Traditional Drama of England in Sir Gawain and the Green Knight," *Viator* 17 (1986): 221–54.

106. Larry Dean Benson, *Art and Tradition in Sir Gawain and the Green Knight* (New Brunswick, N.J.: Rutgers University Press, 1965), p. 59.

107. Derek Brewer, "The Colour Green," in *A Companion to the "Gawain"-Poet*,

ed. Derek Brewer and Jonathan Gibson (Cambridge: D.S. Brewer, 1997), pp. 181–95; Lindahl, "Myth in Its Time."

108. Benson, *Art and Tradition*, pp. 56–95; Kathleen Basford, *The Green Man* (Cambridge: D.S. Brewer, 1978).

109. Wickham, *Early English Stages*, 1: 24–28; Withington, *English Pageantry*, 1: 75–77; Prunières, *Ballet de cour*, p. 9; Dauphin's cape: Louis Claude Douët-d'Arcq, *Comptes de l'argenterie des rois de France au XIVe siècle* (Paris: Renouard, 1851), p. 146; Edward's robe: Nicolas, "Observations," pp. 41, 122.

110. *Wynnere and Wastoure*, ed. Stephanie Trigg, EETS o.s. 297 (Oxford: Oxford University Press, 1990), ll. 70–82. Juliet Vale points out resemblances between *Wynnere and Wastoure* and court interludes: *Edward III and Chivalry*, pp. 73–75.

111. Robert Levine, "Aspects of Grotesque Realism in *Sir Gawain and the Green Knight*," *Chaucer Review* 17, no. 1 (1982): 65–75; Arthur Lindley, "'Ther he watz dispoyled, with spechez of myerthe': Carnival and the Undoing of Sir Gawain," *Exemplaria* 6 (1994): 67–86.

112. Handelman, *Models and Mirrors*, p. 71.

113. *Chronique du Religieux*, 1: 132–35 (an eyewitness account, but written some fifteen years later); see also Jeffrey J. Cohen, "Decapitation and Coming of Age: Constructing Masculinity and the Monstrous," *Arthurian Yearbook* 3 (1993): 173–92. The Gawain manuscript has an illumination of the interlude scene with the headless knight, but it is so awkwardly executed that nothing certain can be said about its design. For example, Cohen (p. 183) finds it significant that Gawain's head is turned away from the beheaded knight, but the illuminator seems hardly able to draw a head except in this three-quarter profile: see *Pearl, Cleanness, Patience and Sir Gawain Reproduced in Facsimile from the Unique MS. Cotton Nero A.x in the British Museum*, intro. Israel Gollancz, EETS o.s. 162 (London: Milford, 1923).

114. Elizabeth D. Kirk, "'Wel Bycommes Such Craft upon Cristmasse': The Festive and the Hermeneutic in *Sir Gawain and the Green Knight*," *Arthuriana* 4 (1994): 95–96.

115. Nicholas Watson, "The *Gawain*-Poet as Vernacular Theologian," in *Companion to the "Gawain"-Poet*, ed. Brewer and Gibson, p. 311; David Aers makes an analogous argument about the poems' secular commitments: "Christianity for Courtly Subjects: Reflections on the *Gawain*-Poet," in *Companion to the "Gawain"-Poet*, pp. 91–101.

116. Helen Cooper, "The Supernatural," in *Companion to the "Gawain"-Poet*, pp. 288–89.

117. Brewer, "The Colour Green"; Robert J. Blanch, "Games Poets Play: The Ambiguous Use of Color Symbolism in *Sir Gawain and the Green Knight*," *Nottingham Medieval Studies* 20 (1976): 64–85.

118. *Sir Gawain*, l. 150; Chaucer, *Franklin's Tale*, 5.1125. Bertilak's and Morgan's attendance at religious functions further implies that their magic is natural rather than devilish. For an image of a wild man surviving his beheading, see *The Sherborne Missal*, ed. Janet Backhouse (Toronto: University of Toronto Press, 1999), p. 22: two wild men joust, one brandishing his own severed leg and the other holding a sword in one hand and his own severed head in the other. The

image decorates the page for Easter Sunday, along with more conventional images of the Resurrection, such as Elijah carried up to heaven and a lion breathing life into his cubs.

119. William P. Marvin, "Slaughter and Romance: Hunting Reserves in Late Medieval England," in *Medieval Crime and Social Control*, ed. Barbara A. Hanawalt and David Wallace (Minneapolis: University of Minnesota Press, 1999), pp. 224–52; Yamamoto, *Boundaries of the Human*, pp. 99–131.

120. As in lines 2366–68, it seems possible to read one phrase, "þen grene aumayl on golde," as the complement for both "grener" and "bry3ter."

Bibliography

PRIMARY SOURCES

Brussels, Bibliothèque royale de Belgique, MS 15652–56
London, British Library, Additional MS 5141
London, British Library, Additonal MS 42130
London, British Library, MS Harley 4380
London, British Library, MS Harley 4866
London, British Library, MS Royal 15 E.vi
London, British Library, MS Royal 20 B.xx
Paris, Archives nationales, MS KK 24
Paris, Archives nationales, MS X1A 1481
Paris, Bibliothèque nationale de France, MS français 146
Paris, Bibliothèque nationale de France, MS français 836
Paris, Bibliothèque nationale de France, MS français 2813
Paris, Bibliothèque nationale de France, MS français 23279

The Acts of the Christian Martyrs. Ed. and trans. Herbert Musurillo. Oxford: Claren-
don Press, 1972.
*Les Ambassades anglaises pendant la guerre de cent ans: Catalogue chronologique,
1327–1450.* Ed. Léon Mirot and E. Deprez. Paris: Picard, 1900.
Annales Ricardi Secundi. Vol. 3 of *Chronica monasterii S. Albani,* ed. Henry Thomas
Riley. Rolls Series 28. London: Longmans, 1866.
The Anonimalle Chronicle, 1333 to 1381. Ed. V. H. Galbraith. Manchester: Manchester
University Press, 1927.
The Antient Kalendars and Inventories of the Treasury of His Majesty's Exchequer. Ed.
Francis Palgrave. 3 vols. London: PRO, 1836.
Beatrix. Ed. Jan A. Nelson. Vol. 1 of *The Old French Crusade Cycle.* Tuscaloosa: Uni-
versity of Alabama Press, 1977. Pp. 130–355.
Berthault de Villebresmes. *Geste du Chevalier au Cygne.* Ed. Edmond A. Emplain-
court. Vol. 9 of *The Old French Crusade Cycle.* Tuscaloosa: University of
Alabama Press, 1989.
The Brut, or the Chronicles of England. Ed. Friedrich W. D. Brie. EETS o.s. 131, 136.
London: Oxford University Press, 1906, 1908.
Cagny, Perceval de. *Chroniques de Perceval de Cagny.* Ed. H. Moranvillé. Paris:
Renouard, 1902.
Caxton, William. *The Golden Legend.* Ed. F. S. Ellis. 7 vols. London: Dent, 1900.

Charles d'Orléans. *Fortunes Stabilnes: Charles of Orleans's English Book of Love. A Critical Edition.* Ed. Mary-Jo Arn. Binghamton, N.Y.: Medieval and Renaissance Texts and Studies, 1994.
_____. *Poésies.* Ed. Pierre Champion. 2 vols. CFMA 34, 56. Paris, 1923, 1927.
Charny, Geoffroi de. *The "Book of Chivalry" of Geoffroi de Charny: Text, Context, and Translation.* Ed. and trans. Richard W. Kaeuper and Elspeth Kennedy. Philadelphia : University of Pennsylvania Press, 1996.
Chaucer, Geoffrey. *The Riverside Chaucer.* 3rd ed. Ed. Larry Benson. Boston: Houghton Mifflin, 1987.
_____. *A Variorum Edition of the Works of Geoffrey Chaucer.* Vol. 5, *The Minor Poems.* Ed. George B. Pace and Alfred David. Norman: University of Oklahoma Press, 1982.
Chaucer Life-Records. Ed. Martin M. Crow and Clair C. Olson. Oxford: Oxford University Press, 1966.
Chaucerian and Other Pieces. Ed. Walter W. Skeat. Oxford: Clarendon Press, 1897.
Chrétien de Troyes. *Le Chevalier au Lion (Yvain).* Ed. Mario Roques. CFMA, 89. Paris: Champion, 1960.
Christine de Pizan. *Ditié de Jehanne d'Arc.* Ed. Angus J. Kennedy and Kenneth Varty. Medium Aevum Monographs n.s. 9. Oxford: Society for the Study of Mediaeval Languages and Literature, 1977.
_____. *Le Livre de la mutacion de Fortune.* Ed. Suzanne Solente. 4 vols. Paris: Picard, 1959–66.
_____. *Oeuvres poétiques de Christine de Pisan.* Ed. Maurice Roy. SATF 22. 3 vols. Paris: Firmin Didot, 1886–96.
Chronica Johannis de Reading et anonymi Cantuariensis, 1346–1367. Ed. James Tait. Manchester: Manchester University Press, 1914.
Chronique des quatre premiers Valois (1327–1393). Ed. Siméon Luce. Paris: Renouard, 1862.
Chronique du Religieux de Saint-Denys [Michel Pintoin]. Ed. and trans. M. L. Bellaguet (1842), intro. Bernard Guenée. 6 vols. in 3. N.p.: Comité des Travaux Historiques et Scientifiques, 1994.
Clanvowe, John. "The Cuckoo and the Nightingale." In *Chaucerian and Other Pieces,* ed. Walter W. Skeat. Oxford: Clarendon Press, 1897. Pp. 347–58.
Clément de Fauquembergue. *Journal de Clément de Fauquembergue.* Ed. Alexandre Tuetey. 3 vols. Paris: Renouard, 1903–15.
Cochon, Pierre. *Chronique normande de Pierre Cochon.* Ed. Charles de Robillard de Beaurepaire. Rouen: Le Brument, 1870.
Cousinot, Guillaume. *Chronique de la Pucelle.* Ed. Vallet de Viriville. Paris: Delahays, 1864.
Deschamps, Eustache. *Oeuvres complètes de Eustache Deschamps.* Ed. Le Marquis de Queux de Saint-Hilaire. 11 vols. SATF 9. Paris: Firmin Didot, 1878–1903.
Documents et recherches relatifs à Jeanne la Pucelle. Ed. Paul Doncoeur and Yvonne Lanhers. Vol. 2, *Instrument public des sentences . . .* Paris: Argences, 1954. Vol. 3, *La Réhabilitation de Jeanne la Pucelle: L'Enquête ordonnée par Charles VII . . .* Paris: Argences, 1956.
Douët-d'Arcq, Louis Claude. *Choix de pièces inédites relatives au règne de Charles VI.* 2 vols. Paris: Renouard, 1863–64.

_____. *Comptes de l'argenterie des rois de France au XIVe siècle.* Paris: Renouard, 1851.

_____. *Nouveau recueil de comptes de l'argenterie des rois de France.* Paris: Renouard, 1874.

"L'Entrevue d'Ardres." Ed. Paul Meyer. *Annuaire-Bulletin de la société de l'histoire de France* 18 (1881): 209–15.

"*Esclarmonde, Clarisse et Florent, Yde et Olive.*" Ed. Max Schweigel. *Ausgaben und Abhandlungen aus dem Gebiete der romanischen Philologie* 83 (1889): 152–73.

Escouchy, Mathieu d'. *Chronique de Mathieu d'Escouchy.* Ed. G. du Fresne de Beaucourt. 3 vols. Paris: Renouard, 1863–64.

L'estoire de Griseldis en rimes et par personnages (1395). Ed. Mario Roques. Geneva: Droz, 1957.

The Floure and the Leafe and The Assembly of Ladies. Ed. Derek Pearsall. 1962. Reprint Manchester: Manchester University Press, 1980.

Froissart, Jean. *Chroniques.* Ed. Simeon Luce et al. 15 vols. Société de l'Histoire de France. Paris: Renouard, 1869–.

_____. *Chroniques: Début du premier livre. Edition du manuscrit de Rome Reg. lat. 869.* Ed. George T. Diller. Geneva: Droz, 1972.

_____. *Chroniques: Dernière rédaction du premier livre. Edition du manuscrit de Rome Reg. lat. 869.* Ed. George T. Diller. Geneva: Droz, 1972.

_____. "*Dits*" *et* "*débats*". Ed. Anthime Fourrier. Geneva: Droz, 1979.

_____. *Oeuvres de Froissart.* Ed. Kervyn de Lettenhove. 25 vols. Brussels: Victor Devaux, 1867–77.

_____. *Oeuvres de Froissart: Poésies.* Ed. Auguste Scheler. 3 vols. Brussels: Victor Devaux, 1870–72.

_____. *Le Paradis d'amour, L'Orloge amoureus.* Ed. Peter F. Dembowski. Geneva : Droz, 1986.

Geoffrey le Baker. *Chronicon.* Ed. E. M. Thompson. Oxford: Clarendon Press, 1889.

Gervais du Bus and Chaillou de Pesstain. *Le Roman de Fauvel.* Ed. Arthur Långfors. SATF 64. Paris: Firmin Didot, 1914–19.

_____. *Le Roman de Fauvel in the Edition of Mesire Chaillou de Pesstain.* Ed. Edward H. Roesner, François Avril, and Nancy Freeman Regalado. New York: Broude, 1990.

_____. *Le Roman de Fauvel, reproduction photographique du manuscrit français 146 de la Bibliothèque nationale de Paris.* Ed. Pierre Aubry. Paris: Geuthner, 1907.

Gower, John. *Confessio Amantis.* Vols. 2–3 of *The Complete Works of John Gower.* Ed. G. C. Macaulay. Vols. 2–3. Oxford: Clarendon Press, 1901.

Guillaume de Lorris and Jean de Meun. *Le Roman de la Rose.* Ed. Félix Lecoy. 3 vols. CFMA 92, 95, 98. Paris: Champion, 1973, 1975, 1976.

The Harley Lyrics. Ed. G. L. Brooke. Manchester: Manchester University Press, 1956.

Heinen, Claes. *L'Armorial universel du heraut Gelre (1370–1395).* Ed. Paul Adam-Even. Neuchatel: Paul Attinger, 1971.

Heldris of Cornwall. *Silence.* Ed. and trans. Sarah Roche-Mahdi. East Lansing, Mich.: Colleagues Press, 1992.

L'Hérésie de Fauvel. Ed. Emilie Dahnk. Leipziger romanistische Studien, no. 4. Leipzig: Romanischen Seminars, 1935.

Heures de Turin: Quarante-cinq feuillets à peintures provenant des "Très Belles Heures" de Jean de France, duc de Berry. Intro. Albert Chatelet and Paul Durrieu. Turin: Erasmo, 1967.

The History of Helyas, Knight of the Swan. Trans. Robert Copland. New York: Grolier Club, 1901.

Household Accounts from Medieval England. Ed. C. M. Woolgar. 2 vols. Oxford: Oxford University Press, 1992–93.

Ipomadon. In *Ipomedon in drei englischen Bearbeitungen.* Ed. Eugen Kölbing. Breslau: Koebner, 1889.

Itinéraires de Philippe le Hardi et de Jean sans Peur, ducs de Bourgogne (1363–1419). Ed. Ernest Petit. Paris: Imprimerie Nationale, 1888.

Jacobus de Voragine. *The Golden Legend.* Trans. William Granger Ryan. 2 vols. Princeton, N.J.: Princeton University Press, 1993.

————. *Legenda aurea.* Ed. Th. Graesse. 1850. Reprint Osnabrück: Otto Zeller, 1969.

————. *La Légende dorée, édition critique, dans la révision de 1476 par Jean Batail- lier, d'après la traduction de Jean de Vignay (1333–1348) de la "Legenda Aurea" (c. 1261–1266).* Ed. Brenda Dunn-Lardeau. Paris: Champion, 1997.

Jean de Mailly. *Abrégé des gestes et miracles des saints.* Trans. A. Dondaine. Biblio- thèque d'Histoire Dominicaine, 1. Paris: Cerf, 1947.

Journal d'un bourgeois de Paris, 1405–1449. Ed. Alexandre Tuetey. Paris: Champion, 1881.

Juvénal des Ursins, Jean. *Histoire de Charles VI.* In *Nouvelle collection des mémoires pour servir à l'histoire de France,* vol 2. Ed. Michaud and Poujoulat. Paris: Guyot, 1850. Pp. 333–356.

Knighton, Henry. *Knighton's Chronicle, 1337–1396.* Ed. and trans. G. H. Martin. Oxford: Clarendon Press, 1995.

Laborde, Léon de. *Les Ducs de Bourgogne: Etudes sur les lettres, les arts et l'industrie pendant le XVᵉ siècle.* Pt. 2: *Preuves.* 3 vols. Paris: Plon, 1849, 1851, 1852.

The Life of Christina of Markyate, a Twelfth Century Recluse. Ed. and trans. C. H. Talbot. Oxford: Clarendon Press, 1959.

Lodewijk van Velthem. *Voortzetting van den Spiegel historiael (1248–1316).* Ed. Herman vander Linden and Willem de Vreese. Vol. 1. Brussels: Hayez, 1906.

Lydgate, John. *The Minor Poems of John Lydgate.* Ed. Henry Noble MacCracken. 2 vols. EETS o.s. 107, 192. London: Oxford University Press, 1911, 1934.

Machaut, Guillaume de. *Oeuvres.* Ed. Prosper Tarbé. 1849. Reprint Geneva: Slatkine, 1977.

Malory, Thomas. *The Works of Sir Thomas Malory.* 3rd ed. Ed. Eugène Vinaver rev. P. J. C. Field. 3 vols. Oxford: Clarendon Press, 1990.

Marie de France. *Eliduc.* In *Les Lais de Marie de France,* ed. Jean Rychner. CFMA 93. Paris: Champion, 1983. Pp. 155–91.

Martin le Franc. *Le Champion des Dames.* Ed. Robert Deschaux. 5 vols. CFMA 127–31. Paris: Champion, 1999.

Martorell, Joanot, and Martí Joan de Galba. *Tirant lo Blanc.* Trans. David H. Rosenthal. New York: Schocken, 1984.

Mathieu d'Escouchy. *Chronique de Mathieu d'Escouchy.* Ed. G. du Fresne de Beau- court. 3 vols. Paris: Renouard, 1863–64.

Medieval Heraldry: Some Fourteenth Century Heraldic Works. Ed. and trans. Evan John Jones. Cardiff: William Lewis, 1943.
The Middle-English Versions of Partonope of Blois. Ed. A. Trampe Bödtker. EETS e.s. 109. London: Kegan Paul, 1912.
La Minute française des interrogatoires de Jeanne la Pucelle. Ed. Paul Doncoeur. Melun: Argences, 1952.
Monstrelet, Enguerrand de. *La Chronique d'Enguerran de Monstrelet*. Ed. Louis Douët-d'Arcq. 6 vols. Paris: Renouard, 1857–62.
Murimuth, Adam. *Continuatio chronicarum Robertus de Avesbury*. Ed. E. M. Thompson. Rolls Series 93. London: Eyre and Spottiswood, 1889.
La Naissance du Chevalier au Cygne. Vol. 1 of *The Old French Crusade Cycle*, ed. Emanuel J. Mickel, Jr., and Jan A. Nelson, intro. Geoffrey M. Myers. Tuscaloosa: University of Alabama Press, 1977.
L'Ordene de chevalerie. In *Raoul de Houdenc: Le Roman des eles; The Anonymous Ordene de chevalerie*. Ed. Keith Busby. Amsterdam: Benjamins, 1983.
Ovid. *Metamorphoses*. Ed. Frank J. Miller. 2nd ed. Rev. G. P. Goold. 2 vols. Cambridge, Mass.: Harvard University Press, 1921.
————. *Ovide moralisé*. Ed. C. de Boer et al. Vol. 2. Amsterdam: Müller, 1920. Vol. 3, Amsterdam: Noord-Hollandsche Uitgeversmaatschappij, 1931.
A Parisian Journal, 1405–1449. Trans. Janet Shirley. Oxford: Clarendon Press, 1968.
Pearl, Cleanness, Patience and Sir Gawain, Reproduced in Facsimile from the Unique MS. Cotton Nero A.x in the British Museum. Ed. Israel Gollancz. EETS o.s. 162. London: Milford, 1923.
Philippe de Mézières. *Le Livre de la vertu du sacrement de mariage*. Ed. Joan B. Williamson. Washington, D.C.: Catholic University of America Press, 1993.
————. *Letter to King Richard II*. Ed. and trans. G. W. Coopland. New York: Barnes and Noble, 1976.
Political Poems and Songs Relating to English History. Ed. Thomas Wright. 2 vols. Rerum Britannicarum Medii Aevi Scriptores, 14. London: Longman, 1859, 1861.
"Le Premier et le secont livre de fauvel" in the version preserved in B.N. f. fr. 146. Ed. Paul Helmer. Ottawa: Institute of Mediaeval Music, 1997.
Procès de condamnation de Jeanne d'Arc. Ed. Pierre Tisset with the assistance of Yvonne Lanhers. 3 vols. Paris: Klincksieck, 1960–71.
Procès de condamnation et de réhabilitation de Jeanne d'Arc, dite la Pucelle. Ed. Jules Quicherat. 5 vols. Paris: Renouard, 1841–49.
Procès en nullité de la condamnation de Jeanne d'Arc. Ed. Pierre Duparc. 5 vols. Paris: Klincksieck, 1977–88.
Register of Edward the Black Prince. 4 vols. Ed. M. C. B. Dawes. London: HMSO, 1930–33.
Robert de Avesbury. *De gestis mirabilibus Regis Edwardi Tertii*. Ed. E. M. Thompson. Rolls Series 93. London: Eyre and Spottiswood, 1889.
The Romance of the Cheuelere Assigne. Ed. Henry H. Gibbs. EETS e.s. 6. London: Oxford University Press, 1868.
Rous, John. *The Rous Roll, with an Historical Introduction on John Rous and the Warwick Roll by Charles Ross*. Gloucester: Alan Sutton, 1980.
————. *This rol was laburd & finished by Master John Rows of Warrewyk*. Ed. William Courthope. London: Pickering, 1859.

Salmon, Pierre. *Les Demandes faites par le roi Charles VI, touchant son état et le gouvernement de sa personne, avec les réponses de Pierre Salmon, son secrétaire et familier.* Ed. G.-A. Crapelet. Paris: Crapelet, 1833.

Sarrazin. *Le Roman de Ham.* In *Histoire des ducs de Normandie et des rois d'Angleterre,* ed. Francisque Michel. Paris: Renouard, 1840. Pp. 213–384.

The Sherborne Missal. Ed. Janet Backhouse. Toronto: University of Toronto Press, 1999.

The Siege of Carlaverock. Ed. and trans. Nicholas Harris Nicolas. London: Nichols, 1828.

Sir Gawain and the Green Knight. Ed. Israel Gollancz. EETS o.s. 210. London: Oxford University Press, 1940.

Sir Gawain and the Green Knight. Ed. J. R. R. Tolkien and E. V. Gordon. 2nd ed. Rev. Norman Davis. Oxford: Clarendon Press, 1967.

Sources and Analogues of Chaucer's Canterbury Tales. Ed. W. F. Bryan and Germaine Dempster. 1941. Reprint Atlantic Highlands, N.J.: Humanities Press, 1958.

Statius. *Thebaid.* Ed. and trans. J. H. Mozley. 2 vols. Cambridge, Mass.: Harvard University Press, 1928.

Stavelot, Jean de. *Chronique de Jean de Stavelot.* Ed. A. Borgnet. Brussels: Hayez, 1861.

The Trial of Joan of Arc, Being the Verbatim Report of the Proceedings from the Orleans Manuscript. Trans. W. S. Scott. Westport, Conn.: Associated Booksellers, 1956.

Tristan de Nanteuil. Ed. Keith V. Sinclair. Assen, Neth.: Van Gorcum, 1971.

Valentine and Orson. Trans. Henry Watson, ed. Arthur Dickson. EETS o.s. 204. London: Milford, 1937.

"The Vows of the Heron." In *Political Poems and Songs Relating to English History,* ed. and trans. Thomas Wright. Vol. 1. London: Longman, 1859. Pp. 1–25.

The Vulgate Version of the Arthurian Romances. Vol. 2, *Lestoire de Merlin.* Ed. H. Oskar Sommer. Washington, D.C.: Riverside, 1908.

Walsingham, Thomas. *Historia anglicana.* Ed. Henry Thomas Riley. 2 vols. Rolls Series 28. London: Longman, Green, 1863–64.

The Westminster Chronicle, 1381–1394. Ed. and trans. L. C. Hector and Barbara F. Harvey. Oxford: Clarendon, 1982.

William Worcestre. *Itineraries.* Ed. John H. Harvey. Oxford: Clarendon Press, 1969.

Wynnere and Wastoure. Ed. Stephanie Trigg. EETS o.s. 297. Oxford: Oxford University Press, 1990.

Ywain and Gawain. Ed. Albert B. Friedman and Norman T. Harrington. EETS o.s. 254. London: Oxford University Press, 1964.

SECONDARY SOURCES

Aers, David. "Christianity for Courtly Subjects: Reflections on the *Gawain*-Poet." In *A Companion to the "Gawain"-Poet,* ed. Derek Brewer and Jonathan Gibson. Cambridge: D.S. Brewer, 1997. Pp. 91–101.

———. "A Whisper in the Ear of Early Modernists; or, Reflections on Literary Critics Writing the 'History of the Subject.'" In *Culture and History, 1350–1600: Essays on English Communities, Identities, and Writing,* ed. David Aers. Detroit: Wayne State University Press, 1992. Pp. 177–202.

Ainsworth, Peter. "Heralds, Heraldry and the Colour Blue in the Chronicles of Jean Froissart." In *The Medieval Chronicle: Proceedings of the 1st International Conference on the Medieval Chronicle, Driebergen/Utrecht, 13–16 July 1996*, ed. Erik Kooper. Amsterdam: Rodopi, 1999. Pp. 40–55.

————. *Jean Froissart and the Fabric of History: Truth, Myth, and Fiction in the "Chroniques"*. Oxford: Clarendon Press, 1990.

Alexander, Jonathan J. G. "The Portrait of Richard II in Westminster Abbey." In *The Regal Image of Richard II and the Wilton Diptych*, ed. Dillian Gordon, Lisa Monnas, and Caroline Elam. London: Miller, 1997. Pp. 197–206.

Alexander, Jonathan, and Paul Binski. *Age of Chivalry: Art in Plantagenet England, 1200–1400*. London: Royal Academy of Arts, 1987.

Alford, Violet. "Rough Music or Charivari." *Folklore* 70 (1959): 505–18.

Allmand, Christopher. *The Hundred Years War: England and France at War, c. 1300–c. 1450*. Cambridge: Cambridge University Press, 1988.

Anrooij, W. van. "Gelre Herald and Late Medieval Chivalric Culture." *Coat of Arms* n.s. 9, no. 160 (1992): 337–44.

Appadurai, Arjun. "Introduction: Commodities and the Politics of Value," in *The Social Life of Things: Commodities in Cultural Perspective*, ed. Arjun Appadurai. Cambridge: Cambridge University Press, 1986.

————, ed. *The Social Life of Things: Commodities in Cultural Perspective*. Cambridge: Cambridge University Press, 1986.

Apter, Emily S. *Feminizing the Fetish: Psychoanalysis and Narrative Obsession in Turn-of-the-Century France*. Ithaca, N.Y.: Cornell University Press, 1991.

Arn, Mary-Jo. *Charles d'Orléans in England (1415–1440)*. Woodbridge, Suffolk: D.S. Brewer, 2000.

Arnade, Peter J. *Realms of Ritual: Burgundian Ceremony and Civic Life in Late Medieval Ghent*. Ithaca, N.Y.: Cornell University Press, 1996.

Asad, Talal. *Genealogies of Religion: Discipline and Reasons of Power in Christianity and Islam*. Baltimore: Johns Hopkins University Press, 1993.

Austin, J. L. *How to Do Things with Words*. Cambridge, Mass.: Harvard University Press, 1962.

L'Aveu: Antiquité et Moyen-Age. Rome: Ecole Française de Rome, 1986.

Badel, Pierre-Yves. *Le Roman de la Rose au XIVᵉ siècle: Etude de la réception de l'oeuvre*. Geneva: Droz, 1980.

Baildon, W. Paley. "A Wardrobe Account of 16–17 Richard II, 1393–4." *Archaeologia* 62 (1911): 497–514.

Bakhtin, Mikhail. *Rabelais and His World*. Trans. Hélène Iswolsky. Cambridge, Mass.: MIT Press, 1968.

Barber, Richard. *Edward, Prince of Wales and Aquitaine*. New York: Scribner, 1978.

Barker, Juliet R. V. *The Tournament in England, 1100–1400*. Woodbridge, Suffolk: Boydell, 1986.

Barstow, Anne Llewellyn. *Joan of Arc: Heretic, Mystic, Shaman*. Lewiston, N.Y.: Edwin Mellen, 1986.

Barthes, Roland. *The Fashion System*. Trans. Matthew Ward and Richard Howard. Berkeley : University of California Press, 1983 [1967].

Basford, Kathleen. *The Green Man*. Cambridge: D.S. Brewer, 1978.

Baskins, Cristelle L. "Griselda, or the Renaissance Bride Stripped Bare by Her
   Bachelor in Tuscan *Cassone* Painting." *Stanford Italian Review* 10 (1991): 153–75.
Baudrillard, Jean. *For a Critique of the Political Economy of the Sign.* Trans. Charles
   Levin. St. Louis: Telos, 1981.
————. *Simulations.* Trans. Paul Foss, Paul Patton, and Philip Beitchman. New
   York: Semiotext(e), 1983.
Beaune, Colette. "Costume et pouvoir en France à la fin du Moyen Age: Les
   Devises royales vers 1400." *Revue des sciences humaines* n.s. 55, no. 183 (July–
   September 1981): 125–46.
Bech, M. "Quellen und Plan der 'Legende of Good Women' und ihr Verhältniss zur
   'Confessio Amantis.'" *Anglia* 5 (1882): 313–82.
Beckwith, Sarah. "Ritual, Theater, and Social Space in the York Corpus Christi
   Cycle." In *Bodies and Disciplines: Intersections of Literature and History in
   Fifteenth-Century England,* ed. David Wallace and Barbara A. Hanawalt. Min-
   neapolis: University of Minnesota Press, 1996. Pp. 63–86.
————. *Signifying God: Social Relation and Symbolic Act in the York Corpus Christi
   Plays.* Chicago: University of Chicago Press, 2001.
Bédier, Joseph. "Les Fêtes de mai et les commencemens de la poésie lyrique au
   Moyen Age." *Revue des deux mondes* 4th ser. 135 (1896): 146–72.
————. "Les Plus anciennes danses françaises." *Revue des deux mondes* 5th ser. 31
   (1906): 398–424.
Bell, Catherine. *Ritual Theory, Ritual Practice.* Oxford: Oxford University Press,
   1992.
Bellaguet, M. L., trans. *Chronique du Religieux de Saint-Denys.* 6 vols. in 3. 1842.
   Reprint Paris: Comité des Travaux Historiques et Scientifiques, 1994.
Beltz, George F. *Memorials of the Order of the Garter from Its Foundation to the Pre-
   sent Time.* London : Pickering, 1841.
Bennett, Judith M. "'Lesbian-like' and the Social History of Medieval Lesbian-
   isms." *Journal of the History of Sexuality* 9 (2000): 1–24.
Benson, Larry Dean. *Art and Tradition in Sir Gawain and the Green Knight.* New
   Brunswick, N.J.: Rutgers University Press, 1965.
Benton, John F. "Consciousness of Self and Perceptions of Individuality." In *Renais-
   sance and Renewal in the Twelfth Century,* ed. Robert L. Benson and Giles
   Constable. Cambridge, Mass.: Harvard University Press, 1982. Pp. 263–95.
Bernheimer, Richard. *Wild Men in the Middle Ages: A Study in Art, Sentiment, and
   Demonology.* Cambridge, Mass.: Harvard University Press, 1952.
Berthelot, Anne. *Figures et fonction de l'écrivain au XIIIe siècle.* Montreal: Institut
   d'Etudes Médiévales, 1991.
Bestor, Jane Fair. "Marriage Transactions in Renaissance Italy and Mauss's *Essay on
   the Gift.*" *Past and Present* 164 (August 1999): 6–46.
Blanc, Odile. "Historiographie du vêtement: Un Bilan." In *Le Vêtement: Histoire,
   archéologie et symbolique vestimentaires au Moyen Age,* ed. Michel Pastoureau.
   Paris: Léopard d'Or, 1989. Pp. 7–33.
————. "Vêtement féminin, vêtement masculin à la fin du Moyen Age: le point
   de vue des moralistes." In *Le Vêtement: Histoire, archéologie et symbolique vestimentaires au Moyen Age,* ed. Michel Pastoureau. Paris: Léopard d'Or, 1989. Pp.
   243–51.

Blanch, Robert J. "Games Poets Play: The Ambiguous Use of Color Symbolism in *Sir Gawain and the Green Knight.*" *Nottingham Medieval Studies* 20 (1976): 64–85.

Blau, Herbert. *Nothing in Itself: Complexions of Fashion.* Bloomington: Indiana University Press, 1999.

Blumenfeld-Kosinski, Renate. *Reading Myth: Classical Mythology and Its Interpretations in Medieval French Literature.* Stanford, Calif.: Stanford University Press, 1997.

Boffey, Julia. "English Dream Poems and Their French Connections." In *Literary Aspects of Courtly Culture*, ed. Donald Maddox and Sara Sturm-Maddox. Cambridge: D.S. Brewer, 1994. Pp. 113–21.

Bond, Gerald A. *The Loving Subject: Desire, Eloquence, and Power in Romanesque France.* Philadelphia: University of Pennsylvania Press, 1995.

Borneman, John. "Race, Ethnicity, Species, Breed: Totemism and Horse-Breed Classification in America." *Comparative Studies in Society and History* 30 (1988): 25–51.

Boulton, D'Arcy Jonathan Dacre. *The Knights of the Crown: The Monarchical Orders of Knighthood in Later Medieval Europe, 1325–1520.* New York: St. Martin's Press, 1987.

Bourdieu, Pierre. *Distinction: A Social Critique of the Judgement of Taste.* Trans. Richard Nice. Cambridge, Mass.: Harvard University Press, 1984.

———. "L'Illusion biographique." *Actes de la recherche en sciences sociales* 12, no. 62–63 (June 1986): 69–72.

———. *The Logic of Practice.* Trans. Richard Nice. Cambridge: Polity Press, 1990.

———. *Outline of a Theory of Practice.* Trans. Richard Nice. Cambridge: Cambridge University Press, 1977.

Boutell, Charles. *Boutell's Heraldry.* Rev. J. P. Brooke-Little. London: Frederick Warne, 1973.

Brachet, Auguste. *Pathologie mentale des rois de France.* Paris: Hachette, 1903.

Brault, Gerald. *Early Blazon: Heraldic Terminology in the Twelfth and Thirteenth Centuries with Special Reference to Arthurian Literature.* Oxford: Clarendon Press, 1972.

Breton, Stéphane. "De l'illusion totémique à la fiction sociale." *L'Homme* 151 (July–September 1999): 123–50.

Brewer, Derek. "The Colour Green." In *A Companion to the "Gawain"-Poet*, ed. Derek Brewer and Jonathan Gibson. Cambridge: D.S. Brewer, 1997. Pp. 181–95.

Brooke, Christopher N. L. *The Medieval Idea of Marriage.* Oxford: Oxford University Press, 1989.

Brown, Elizabeth A. R. "*Rex ioians, ionnes, iolis*: Louis X, Philip V, and the *Livres de Fauvel.*" In *Fauvel Studies: Allegory, Chronicle, Music, and Image in Paris, Bibliothèque Nationale de France, MS français 146*, ed. Margaret Bent and Andrew Wathey. Oxford: Clarendon Press, 1998. Pp. 53–72.

Brownlee, Kevin. *Poetic Identity in Guillaume de Machaut.* Madison: University of Wisconsin Press, 1984.

Brundage, James A. *Law, Sex, and Christian Society in Medieval Europe.* Chicago: University of Chicago Press, 1987.

Bugge, John. *Virginitas: An Essay in the History of a Medieval Ideal.* The Hague: Nijhoff, 1975.

Bullock-Davies, Constance. *Menestrellorum Multitudo: Minstrels at a Royal Feast.* Cardiff: University of Wales Press, 1978.

Bullough, Vern L. "Cross Dressing and Gender Role Change in the Middle Ages." In *Handbook of Medieval Sexuality*, ed. Vern L. Bullough and James A. Brundage. New York: Garland, 1996. Pp. 223–42.

————. "Transvestism in the Middle Ages." In *Sexual Practices and the Medieval Church*, ed. Vern L. Bullough and James A. Brundage. Buffalo, N.Y.: Prometheus, 1982. Pp. 43–54.

————. "Transvestites in the Middle Ages." *Journal of Sociology* 79 (1974): 1381–94.

Bullough, Vern L. and Bonnie Bullough. *Cross Dressing, Sex, and Gender.* Philadelphia: University of Pennsylvania Press, 1993.

Burckhardt, Jacob. *The Civilization of the Renaissance in Italy: An Essay.* Trans. S. G. O. Middlemore. London: Phaidon Books, 1965 [1860].

Burke, Peter. *Popular Culture in Early Modern Europe.* New York: New York University Press, 1978.

Burns, E. Jane. *Courtly Love Undressed: Reading Through Clothes in Medieval French Culture.* Philadelphia: University of Pennsylvania Press, 2002.

Burrow, J. A. "The Uses of Incognito: *Ipomadon A.*" In *Readings in Medieval English Romance*, ed. Carol M. Meale. Cambridge: D.S. Brewer, 1994. Pp. 25–34.

Butler, Judith. *Bodies That Matter: On the Discursive Limits of "Sex".* London: Routledge, 1993.

————. *Gender Trouble: Feminism and the Subversion of Identity.* London: Routledge, 1990.

Bynum, Caroline Walker. "Did the Twelfth Century Discover the Individual?" *Journal of Ecclesiastical History* 31 (1980): 1–12.

————. *Fragmentation and Redemption: Essays on Gender and the Human Body.* New York: Zone Books, 1992.

————. *Holy Feast and Holy Fast: The Religious Significance of Food to Medieval Women.* Berkeley: University of California Press, 1987.

Cadden, Joan. *Meanings of Sex Difference in the Middle Ages: Medicine, Science, and Culture.* Cambridge: Cambridge University Press, 1993.

Camille, Michael. "Hybridity, Monstrosity, and Bestiality in the *Roman de Fauvel.*" In *Fauvel Studies: Allegory, Chronicle, Music, and Image in Paris, Bibliothèque Nationale de France, MS français 146*, ed. Margaret Bent and Andrew Wathey. Oxford: Clarendon Press, 1998. Pp. 161–74.

————. *Image on the Edge: The Margins of Medieval Art.* Cambridge, Mass.: Harvard University Press, 1992.

Campbell, Marian. "'White Harts and Coronets': The Jewellery and Plate of Richard II." In *The Regal Image of Richard II and the Wilton Diptych*, ed. Dillian Gordon, Lisa Monnas, and Caroline Elam. London: Miller, 1997. Pp. 95–114.

Cazenave, Annie. "Aveu et contrition. Manuels de confesseurs et interrogatoires d'inquisition en Languedoc et en Catalogne (XIIIᵉ–XIVᵉ siècles)." In *Actes du 99ᵉ Congrès national des Sociétés savantes, Besançon, 1974, Philologie et histoire*, vol. 1. Paris: Bibliothèque Nationale, 1977. Pp. 333–52.

Certeau, Michel de. *The Practice of Everyday Life*. Trans. Steven Rendall. Berkeley: University of California Press, 1984.

Chambers, E. K. *The Mediaeval Stage*. 2 vols. Oxford: Clarendon Press, 1903.

Champion, Pierre. *Vie de Charles d'Orléans*. Paris: Champion, 1911.

Chiffoleau, Jacques. "Sur la pratique et la conjoncture de l'aveu judicaire en France du XIIᵉ au XVᵉ siècle." In *L'Aveu: Antiquité et Moyen-Age*. Rome: Ecole Française de Rome, 1986. Pp. 341–80.

Choisy, François Timoléon de. *Histoire de Charles VI*. Paris: Coignard, 1695.

Chojnacki, Stanley. "Dowries and Kinsmen in Early Renaissance Venice." *Journal of Interdisciplinary History* 5 (1975): 571–600.

———. "The Power of Love: Wives and Husbands in Late Medieval Venice." In *Women and Power in the Middle Ages*, ed. Mary Erler and Maryanne Kowaleski. Athens: University of Georgia Press, 1988. Pp. 126–48.

Clark, Cecily. "Charles d'Orléans: Some English Perspectives." *Medium Aevum* 40 (1971): 254–61.

Clarke, M. V. *Fourteenth Century Studies*. Ed. L. S. Sutherland and M. McKisack. Oxford: Clarendon Press, 1937.

Clifford, James. "On Ethnographic Self-Fashioning: Conrad and Malinowski." In *Reconstructing Individualism: Autonomy, Individuality, and the Self in Western Thought*, ed. Thomas C. Heller, Morton Sosna, and David E. Wellbery. Stanford, Calif.: Stanford University Press, 1986. Pp. 140–62.

Cohen, Jeffrey J. "Decapitation and Coming of Age: Constructing Masculinity and the Monstrous." *Arthurian Yearbook* 3 (1993): 173–92.

Coleman, Joyce. *Public Reading and the Reading Public in Late Medieval England and France*. Cambridge: Cambridge University Press, 1996.

Contamine, Philippe. "Naissance d'une historiographie. Le Souvenir de Jeanne d'Arc, en France et hors de France, depuis le 'procès de son innocence' (1455–1456) jusqu'au début du XVIᵉ siècle." *Francia* 15 (1987): 233–56.

Contamine, Philippe, Charles Giry-Deloison, and Maurice H. Keen, eds. *Guerre et société en France, en Angleterre et en Bourgogne, XIVᵉ–XVᵉ siècle*. Villeneuve d'Ascq: Centre d'Histoire de la Région du Nord et de l'Europe du Nord-Ouest, 1991.

Cooper, Helen. "The Supernatural." In *A Companion to the "Gawain"-Poet*, ed. Derek Brewer and Jonathan Gibson. Cambridge: D.S. Brewer, 1997. Pp. 277–91.

Courtemanche, Andrée. *La Richesse des femmes: Patrimoines et gestion à Manosque au XIVᵉ siècle*. Cahiers d'Etudes Médiévales 11. Montreal: Bellarmin, 1993.

Cox, John D., and David Scott Kastan. "Demanding History." Introduction to *A New History of Early English Drama*, ed. John D. Cox and David Scott Kastan. New York: Columbia University Press, 1997. Pp. 1–5.

Coxe, Henry O. *Catalogus codicum MSS. qui in collegeiis aulisque Oxoniensibus*. Vol. 1. Oxford: Typographeo Academico, 1852.

Cramer, Thomas. *Lohengrin, Edition und Untersuchungen*. Munich: Wilhelm Fink, 1971.

Crane, Susan. "Clothing and Gender Definition: Joan of Arc." *Journal of Medieval and Early Modern Studies* 26 (Spring 1996): 297–320.

Crocker, J. Christopher. "Being an Essence: Totemic Representation Among the Eastern Bororo." In *The Power of Symbols: Masks and Masquerade in the*

Americas, ed. N. Ross Crumrine and Marjorie Halpin. Vancouver: University of British Columbia Press, 1983. Pp. 157–76.

_____. "Ceremonial Masks." In *Celebration: Studies in Festivity and Ritual*, ed. Victor Turner. Washington, D.C.: Smithsonian Institution Press, 1982. Pp. 77–88.

_____. "My Brother the Parrot." In *Animal Myths and Metaphors in South America*, ed. Gary Urton. Salt Lake City: University of Utah Press, 1985. Pp. 13–47.

Crompton, Louis. "The Myth of Lesbian Impunity: Capital Laws from 1270 to 1791." *Journal of Homosexuality* 6 (1980–81): 11–25.

Crowfoot, Elisabeth, Frances Pritchard, and Kay Staniland. *Medieval Finds from Excavations in London, 4: Textiles and Clothing c. 1150–c. 1450*. London: HMSO, 1992.

Crumrine, N. Ross. "Masks, Participants, and Audience." In *The Power of Symbols: Masks and Masquerade in the Americas*, ed. N. Ross Crumrine and Marjorie Halpin. Vancouver: University of British Columbia Press, 1983. Pp. 1–11.

Culler, Jonathan D. *Structuralist Poetics: Structuralism, Linguistics, and the Study of Literature*. Ithaca, N.Y.: Cornell University Press, 1975.

Cunnington, Phillis and Catherine Lucas. *Costume for Births, Marriages and Deaths*. New York: Barnes and Noble, 1972.

DaMatta, Roberto. *Carnivals, Rogues, and Heroes: An Interpretation of the Brazilian Dilemma*. Trans. John Drury. Notre Dame, Ind.: University of Notre Dame Press, 1991.

Davis, Fred. *Fashion, Culture, and Identity*. Chicago: University of Chicago Press, 1992.

Davis, Kathleen. "Limit of the Nation: The Hymen and Griselda's Smock." Paper given at the Modern Language Association, Toronto, December 1997.

Davis, Natalie Zemon. "Charivari, Honor, and Community in Seventeenth-Century Lyon and Geneva." In *Rite, Drama, Festival, Spectacle: Rehearsals Toward a Theory of Cultural Performance*, ed. John J. MacAloon. Philadelphia: Institute for the Study of Human Issues, 1984. Pp. 42–57.

_____. *Society and Culture in Early Modern France*. Stanford, Calif.: Stanford University Press, 1965.

De Grazia, Margreta. "World Pictures, Modern Periods, and the Early Stage." In *A New History of Early English Drama*, ed. John D. Cox and David Scott Kastan. New York: Columbia University Press, 1997. Pp. 7–21.

Delaruelle, Etienne. *La Piété populaire au Moyen Age*. Turin: Erasmo, 1975.

Delcourt, Marie. "Le Complèxe de Diane dans l'hagiographie chrétienne." *Revue de l'histoire des religions* 153, no. 1 (1958): 1–33.

Delumeau, Jean. *Sin and Fear: The Emergence of a Western Guilt Culture, 13th–18th Centuries*. Trans. Eric Nicholson. New York: St. Martin's Press, 1990.

Dennys, Rodney. *Heraldry and the Heralds*. London : Jonathan Cape, 1982.

Derrida, Jacques. *Of Grammatology*. Trans. Gayatri Chakravorty Spivak. Baltimore: Johns Hopkins University Press, 1974 [1967].

_____. *Margins of Philosophy*. Trans. Alan Bass. Chicago: University of Chicago Press, 1982.

Descartes, René. *Meditations on First Philosophy*. 1641. In *The Philosophical Writings of Descartes*, vol. 2, trans. John Cottingham, Robert Stoothoff, and Dugald Murdoch. Cambridge: Cambridge University Press, 1984. Pp. 1–62.

_____. *Oeuvres de Descartes*. Ed. Charles Adam and Paul Tannery. 11 vols. 1897. Reprint Paris: Vrin, 1996.

de Vaivre, Jean-Bernard. "A propos des devises de Charles VI." *Bulletin monumental* 141 (1983): 92–95.

_____. "Troisième note sur le sceau du comté de Charolais au temps de Jean Sans Peur." *Archivum heraldicum* 3–4 (1982): 34–36.

Diamond, Elin, ed. *Performance and Cultural Politics*. London: Routledge, 1996.

Dickson, Arthur. *Valentine and Orson: A Study in Late Medieval Romance*. New York: Columbia University Press, 1929.

Dinshaw, Carolyn. *Chaucer's Sexual Poetics*. Madison: University of Wisconsin Press, 1989.

_____. "A Kiss Is Just a Kiss: Heterosexuality and Its Consolations in *Sir Gawain and the Green Knight*." *diacritics* 24 (1994): 205–26.

Dondaine, A. "Le Manuel de l'inquisiteur." *Archivum fratrum predicatorum* 17 (1947): 85–194.

Doob, Penelope. *Nebuchadnezzar's Children: Conventions of Madness in Middle English Literature*. New Haven, Conn.: Yale University Press, 1974.

Douglas, Mary, and Baron Isherwood. *The World of Goods*. New York: Basic Books, 1979.

Driesen, Otto. *Der Ursprung des Harlekin: Ein kulturgeschichtliches Problem*. 1904. Reprint Hildesheim: Gerstenberg, 1977.

Dronke, Peter. *Medieval Latin and the Rise of European Love-Lyric*. 2nd ed. 2 vols. Oxford: Clarendon, 1968.

Durkheim, Emile. *The Elementary Forms of the Religious Life*. Trans. Joseph Ward Swain. London: Allen and Unwin, 1915.

Durkheim, Emile and Marcel Mauss. *Primitive Classification*. Ed. and trans. Rodney Needham. Chicago: University of Chicago Press, 1963 [1903].

Dyer, Christopher. *Standards of Living in the Later Middle Ages: Social Change in England, c. 1200–1520*. Cambridge: Cambridge University Press, 1989.

Eberle, Patricia J. "The Politics of Courtly Style at the Court of Richard II." In *The Spirit of the Court: Selected Proceedings of the Fourth Congress of the International Courtly Literature Society (Toronto 1983)*. Cambridge: D.S. Brewer, 1985. Pp. 168–78.

Egan, Geoff, Frances Pritchard, et al. *Dress Accessories c 1150–c 1450*. Medieval Finds from Excavations in London: 3. London: HMSO, 1991.

Elias, Norbert. *The Civilizing Process*. Vol. 1, *The History of Manners*. Trans. Edmund Jephcott. New York: Urizen, 1978 [1939].

Elliott, Dyan. "Dress as Mediator Between Inner and Outer Self: The Pious Matron of the High and Later Middle Ages." *Mediaeval Studies* 53 (1991): 279–308.

Enders, Jody. *The Medieval Theater of Cruelty: Rhetoric, Memory, Violence*. Ithaca, N.Y.: Cornell University Press, 1999.

Evans, Joan. *Dress in Mediaeval France*. Oxford: Clarendon Press, 1952.

Famiglietti, R. C. *Royal Intrigue: Crisis at the Court of Charles VI, 1392–1420*. New York: AMS Press, 1986.

_____. *Tales of the Marriage Bed from Medieval France (1300–1500)*. Providence, R.I.: Picardy, 1992.

248

Fernandez, James W. "The Performance of Ritual Metaphors." In *The Social Use of Metaphor: Essays on the Anthropology of Rhetoric*, ed. J. David Sapir and J. Christopher Crocker. Philadelphia: University of Pennsylvania Press, 1977. Pp. 100–131.

Flugel, J. C. *The Psychology of Clothes*. New York: International Universities Press, 1969 [1930].

Fortier-Beaulieu, Paul. "Le Charivari dans le Roman de Fauvel." *Revue de folklore français* 11 (1940): 1–16.

Foucault, Michel. "About the Beginning of the Hermeneutics of the Self: Two Lectures at Dartmouth." *Political Theory* 21 (1993): 198–227.

―――. *Discipline and Punish: The Birth of the Prison*. Trans. Alan Sheridan. New York: Pantheon, 1977.

Fowler, Elizabeth. "Civil Death and the Maiden: Agency and the Conditions of Contract in *Piers Plowman*." *Speculum* 70 (1995): 760–92.

Fox-Davies, Arthur Charles. *A Complete Guide to Heraldry*. Rev. J. P. Brooke-Little. London: Nelson, 1969.

―――. *Heraldic Badges*. London: John Lane, 1907.

Fradenberg, Louise O. *City, Marriage, Tournament: Arts of Rule in Late Medieval Scotland*. Madison: University of Wisconsin Press, 1991.

Fraioli, Deborah. "The Literary Image of Joan of Arc: Prior Influences." *Speculum* 56 (1981): 811–30.

―――. "Why Joan of Arc Never Became an Amazon." In *Fresh Verdicts on Joan of Arc*, ed. Bonnie Wheeler and Charles T. Wood. New York: Garland, 1996. Pp. 189–204.

La "France anglaise" au Moyen Age: Actes du IIIᵉ congrès national des sociétés savantes (Poitiers, 1986). Paris: CTHS, 1988.

Frank, Robert W., Jr. *Chaucer and "The Legend of Good Women"*. Cambridge, Mass.: Harvard University Press, 1972.

French, Robert Dudley. *A Chaucer Handbook*. 2nd ed. New York: Appleton-Century-Crofts, 1947.

Friedman, John Block. *The Monstrous Races in Medieval Art and Thought*. Cambridge, Mass.: Harvard University Press, 1981.

Galderisi, Claudio. "Personnifications, réifications et métaphores créatives dans le système rhétorique de Charles d'Orléans." *Romania* 114 (1996): 385–412.

Garber, Marjorie. *Vested Interests: Cross-Dressing and Cultural Anxiety*. London: Routledge, 1992.

―――. *Vice Versa: Bisexuality and the Eroticism of Everyday Life*. New York: Simon and Schuster, 1995.

Gaunt, Simon. "Straight Minds/'Queer' Wishes in Old French Hagiography: *La Vie de Sainte Euphrosine*." *GLQ: A Journal of Gay and Lesbian Studies* 1 (1995): 155–73.

Gauvard, Claude, and Altan Gokalp. "Les Conduites de bruit et leur signification à la fin du Moyen Age: Le Charivari." *Annales: Economies, Sociétés, Civilisations* 29 (1974): 693–704.

Gay, Victor. *Glossaire archéologique du Moyen Âge et de la renaissance*. 2 vols. 1887. Reprint, Paris: Picard, 1928.

Gell, Alfred. "Newcomers to the World of Goods: Consumption Among the

Muria Gonds." In *The Social Life of Things: Commodities in Cultural Perspective*, ed. Arjun Appadurai. Cambridge: Cambridge University Press, 1986. Pp. 110–138.

Giddens, Anthony. *Central Problems in Social Theory*. Berkeley: University of California Press, 1979.

Gillespie, James L. "Ladies of the Fraternity of Saint George and of the Society of the Garter." *Albion* 17 (1985): 259–78.

Given, James B. *Inquisition and Medieval Society: Power, Discipline, and Resistance in Languedoc*. Ithaca, N.Y.: Cornell University Press, 1997.

Goffman, Erving. *Interaction Ritual: Essays in Face-to-Face Behavior*. Chicago: Aldine, 1967.

————. *The Presentation of Self in Everyday Life*. Garden City, N.Y.: Doubleday, 1959.

Goldberg, Jonathan. *Sodometries: Renaissance Texts, Modern Sexualities*. Stanford, Calif.: Stanford University Press, 1992.

Golenistcheff-Koutouzoff, Elie. *L'Histoire de Griseldis en France au XIVᵉ et au XVᵉ siècle*. Paris: Droz, 1933.

Goodwin, Amy W. "The Griselda Story in France." In *Sources and Analogues of Chaucer's "Canterbury Tales"*, ed. Robert Correale and Mary Hamel. Cambridge: Boydell and Brewer, forthcoming.

Goody, Jack. "Against 'Ritual': Loosely Structured Thoughts on a Loosely Defined Topic." In *Secular Ritual*, ed. Sally F. Moore and Barbara G. Myerhoff. Amsterdam: Van Gorcum, 1977. Pp. 25–35.

————. *The Culture of Flowers*. Cambridge: Cambridge University Press, 1993.

————. *The Development of the Family and Marriage in Europe*. Cambridge: Cambridge University Press, 1983.

Gordon, Stewart, ed. *Robes and Honor: The Medieval World of Investiture*. New York: Palgrave, 2001.

Gosden, Chris and Yvonne Marshall, eds. *The Cultural Biography of Objects. World Archaeology* 31, no. 2 (1999).

Grandeau, Yann. "De quelques dames qui ont servi la reine Isabeau de Bavière." *Bulletin philologique et historique du comité des travaux historiques et scientifiques*. Paris: Bibliothèque Nationale, 1975. Pp. 129–238.

Green, Richard Firth. *Poets and Princepleasers: Literature and the English Court in the Late Middle Ages*. Toronto: University of Toronto Press, 1980.

Greenblatt, Stephen. *Renaissance Self-Fashioning*. Chicago: University of Chicago Press, 1980.

Grigsby, John L. "L'Intertextualité interrompue par l'histoire: Le Cas des *Voeux du Héron*." In *Courtly Literature: Culture and Context*, ed. Keith Busby and Erik Kooper. Amsterdam: Benjamins, 1990. Pp. 239–49.

Grimes, Ronald L. "Masking: Toward a Phenomenology of Exteriorization." *Journal of the American Academy of Religion* 43 (1975): 508–16.

Gurevich, Aaron. *Medieval Popular Culture: Problems of Belief and Perception*. Trans. János M. Bak and Paul A. Hollingsworth. Cambridge: Cambridge University Press, 1988.

————. *The Origins of European Individualism*. Trans. Katharine Judelson. Oxford: Blackwell, 1995.

Haidu, Peter. "Temps, histoire, subjectivité aux XIᵉ et XIIᵉ siècles." In *Le Nombre du temps: En hommage à Paul Zumthor*, ed. Emmanuèle Baumgartner et al. Paris: Champion, 1988. Pp. 105–22.

Hall, Stuart. "The Emergence of Cultural Studies and the Crisis of the Humanities." *october* 53 (1990): 11–23.

Hall, Stuart and Tony Jefferson, eds. *Resistance Through Rituals: Youth Subcultures in Post-War Britain*. London: Hutchinson, 1976.

Hall, Winifred. *Canting and Allusive Arms of England and Wales*. Canterbury: Achievements, 1966.

Hammond, P. W. *Food and Feast in Medieval England*. Dover, N.H.: Sutton, 1993.

Handelman, Don. *Models and Mirrors: Towards an Anthropology of Public Events*. Cambridge: Cambridge University Press, 1990.

Hanna, Ralph, III. *Pursuing History: Middle English Manuscripts and Their Texts*. Stanford, Calif.: Stanford University Press, 1996.

Hanning, Robert W. *The Individual in Twelfth-Century Romance*. New Haven, Conn.: Yale University Press, 1977.

Harmand, Adrien. *Jeanne d'Arc: ses costumes, son armure*. Paris: Leroux, 1929.

Harris, Jennifer. "'Estroit vestu et menu cosu': Evidence for the Construction of Twelfth-Century Dress." In *Medieval Art: Recent Perspectives: A Memorial Tribute to C. R. Dodwell*, ed. Gale R. Owen-Crocker and Timothy Graham. Manchester: Manchester University Press, 1998. Pp. 89–103.

Harvey, John H. "The Wilton Diptych—A Re-examination." *Archaeologia* 98 (1961): 1–28.

Hastrup, Kirsten. "The Semantics of Biology: Virginity." In *Defining Females: The Nature of Women in Society*, ed. Shirley Ardener. New York: Wiley, 1978. Pp. 49–65.

Hedeman, Anne D. *The Royal Image: Illustrations of the "Grandes Chroniques de France," 1274–1422*. Berkeley: University of California Press, 1991.

Helmholz, R. H. *Marriage Litigation in Medieval England*. Cambridge: Cambridge University Press, 1974.

Heng, Geraldine. "Feminine Knots and the Other *Sir Gawain and the Green Knight*." *PMLA* 106 (1991): 500–514.

Hindman, Sandra L. *Christine de Pisan's "Epistre Othea": Painting and Politics at the Court of Charles VI*. Toronto: Pontifical Institute of Mediaeval Studies, 1986.

Hodges, Laura F. *Chaucer and Costume: The Secular Pilgrims in the General Prologue*. Cambridge: D.S. Brewer, 2000.

Hoepffner, Ernest. "Chanson française du XIIIᵉ siècle (*Ay Dex! ou porrey jen trouver*)." *Romania* 47 (1921): 367–80.

Hollander, Anne. *Sex and Suits*. New York: Knopf, 1995.

Hotchkiss, Valerie R. *Clothes Make the Man: Female Cross Dressing in Medieval Europe*. New York: Garland, 1996.

Howell, Martha. *The Marriage Exchange: Property, Social Place, and Gender in Cities of the Low Countries, 1300–1550*. Berkeley: University of California Press, 1998.

Huet, G. "Les Traditions arturiennes chez le chroniqueur Louis de Velthem." *Le Moyen Age* 26 (1913): 173–97.

Hughes, Diane Owen. "Regulating Women's Fashion." In *A History of Women in the West*, vol. 2, *Silences of the Middle Ages*, ed. Christiane Klapisch-Zuber. Cambridge, Mass.: Belknap Press, 1992. Pp. 136–58.

Huizinga, Johan. *The Autumn of the Middle Ages*. Trans. Rodney J. Payton and Ulrich Mammitzsch. Chicago: University of Chicago Press, 1996 [1921].

———. *Homo Ludens: A Study of the Play-Element in Culture*. London: Routledge, 1949.

Hunt, Alan. *Governance of the Consuming Passions: A History of Sumptuary Law*. New York: St. Martin's Press, 1996.

Hutton, Ronald. *The Rise and Fall of Merry England: The Ritual Year, 1400–1700*. Oxford: Oxford University Press, 1994.

Irigaray, Luce. *This Sex Which Is Not One*. Trans. Catherine Porter with Carolyn Burke. Ithaca, N.Y.: Cornell University Press, 1985.

Jaeger, C. Stephen. "L'Amour des rois: Structure sociale d'une forme de sensibilité aristocratique." *Annales: Economies, Sociétés, Civilisations* 46 (1991): 547–71.

———. *Ennobling Love: In Search of a Lost Sensibility*. Philadelphia: University of Pennsylvania Press, 1999.

———. *The Origins of Courtliness: Civilizing Trends and the Formation of Courtly Ideals, 939–1210*. Philadelphia: University of Pennsylvania Press, 1985.

Jéquier, Léon. "Les Louanges des preux chevaliers de l'armorial du héraut Gelre." *Archives héraldiques suisses* 106, no. 1 (1992): 28–42.

———. *Manuel du blason*. New ed. Lausanne: David Perret, 1977.

Jonassen, Frederick B. "Elements from the Traditional Drama of England in Sir Gawain and the Green Knight." *Viator* 17 (1986): 221–54.

Justice, Steven. "Inquisition, Speech, and Writing: A Case from Late-Medieval Norwich." *Representations* 48 (Fall 1994): 1–29.

Kaeuper, Richard W. *War, Justice, and Public Order: England and France in the Later Middle Ages*. Oxford: Clarendon Press, 1988.

Karnoouh, Claude. "Le Charivari ou l'hypothèse de la monogamie." In *Le Charivari: Actes de la table ronde organisée à Paris (25–27 avril 1977)*, ed. Jacques le Goff and Jean-Claude Schmitt. Paris: Mouton, 1981. Pp. 33–43.

Kay, Sarah. *The "Chansons de geste" in the Age of Romance: Political Fictions*. Oxford: Clarendon Press, 1995.

Keen, Maurice. *Chivalry*. New Haven, Conn: Yale University Press, 1984.

Kelly, Douglas. *The Art of Medieval French Romance*. Madison: University of Wisconsin Press, 1992.

Kelly, Henry Ansgar. "Joan of Arc's Last Trial: The Attack of the Devil's Advocates." In *Fresh Verdicts on Joan of Arc*, ed. Bonnie Wheeler and Charles T. Wood. New York: Garland, 1996. Pp. 205–36.

———. "The Right to Remain Silent: Before and After Joan of Arc." *Speculum* 68 (1993): 992–1026.

Kelly, John D. and Martha Kaplan. "History, Structure, and Ritual." *Annual Review of Anthropology* 19 (1990): 119–50.

Kinser, Samuel. "Wildmen in Festival, 1300–1550." In *Oral Tradition in the Middle Ages*, ed. W. F. H. Nicolaisen. Binghamton, N.Y.: Medieval and Renaissance Texts and Studies, 1995. Pp. 145–60.

Kipling, Gordon. *Enter the King: Theater, Liturgy, and Ritual in the Medieval Civic Triumph*. Oxford: Clarendon Press, 1998.

Kirk, Elizabeth D. "'Wel Bycommes Such Craft Upon Cristmasse': The Festive and the Hermeneutic in *Sir Gawain and the Green Knight.*" *Arthuriana* 4 (1994): 93–137.

Kiser, Lisa. *Telling Classical Tales: Chaucer and the "Legend of Good Women".* Ithaca, N.Y.: Cornell University Press, 1983.

Kittredge, G. L. "Chaucer and Some of His Friends." *Modern Philology* 1 (1903): 1–18.

Klaniczay, Gábor. *The Uses of Supernatural Power: The Transformation of Popular Religion in Medieval and Early-Modern Europe.* Trans. Susan Singerman. Ed. Karen Margolis. Princeton, N.J.: Princeton University Press, 1990.

Klapisch-Zuber, Christiane. "The Griselda Complex: Dowry and Marriage Gifts in the Quattrocento." In *Women, Family, and Ritual in Renaissance Italy*, trans. Lydia Cochrane. Chicago: University of Chicago Press, 1985. Pp. 213–46.

———. *L'Ombre des ancêtres: Essai sur l'imaginaire médiéval de la parenté.* Paris: Fayard, 2000.

Kolve, V. A. "From Cleopatra to Alceste: An Iconographic Study of *The Legend of Good Women.*" In *Signs and Symbols in Chaucer's Poetry*, ed. John P. Hermann and John J. Burke, Jr. University: University of Alabama Press, 1981. Pp. 130–78.

———. "God-Denying Fools and the Medieval 'Religion of Love.' " *Studies in the Age of Chaucer* 19 (1997): 3–59.

Laborde, Léon de. *Glossaire français du Moyen Age à l'usage de l'archéologue et de l'amateur des arts.* 1872. Reprint Paris: Laget, 1994.

Lachaud, Frédérique. "Liveries of Robes in England, c. 1200–c. 1330." *English Historical Review* 111 (1996): 279–98.

Lafortune-Martel, Agathe. *Fête noble en Bourgogne au XVᵉ siècle: Le Banquet du Faisan (1454): Aspects politiques, sociaux et culturels.* Montreal: Bellarmin, 1984.

Landsberg, Sylvia. *The Medieval Garden.* London: British Museum, 1996.

Langbein, John H. *Torture and the Law of Proof: Europe and England in the Ancien Régime.* Chicago: University of Chicago Press, 1976.

Långfors, A. "Mots rares chez Gautier de Coinci." *Romania* 59 (1933): 491–92.

Lawton, David. *Chaucer's Narrators.* Cambridge: D.S. Brewer, 1985.

Le Goff, Jacques and Jean-Claude Schmitt, eds. *Le Charivari: Actes de la table ronde organisée à Paris (25–27 avril 1977).* Paris: Mouton, 1981.

Le Nordez, [Albert]. *Jeanne d'Arc racontée par l'image.* Paris: Hachette, 1898.

Le Roy Ladurie, Emmanuel. *Carnival in Romans.* Trans. Mary Feeney. New York: Braziller, 1979.

Lebrun, François. "Le Charivari à travers les condamnations des autorités ecclésiastiques en France du XIVᵉ au XVIIIᵉ siècle." In *Le Charivari: Actes de la table ronde organisée à Paris (25–27 avril 1977)*, ed. Jacques le Goff and Jean-Claude Schmitt. Paris: Mouton, 1981. Pp. 221–28.

Legenda aurea–la Légende dorée. Special issue of *Le Moyen Français* 32 (1993).

Legendre, Pierre. *L'Inestimable objet de la transmission: Etude sur le principe généalogique en Occident.* Paris: Fayard, 1985.

Levine, Robert. "Aspects of Grotesque Realism in *Sir Gawain and the Green Knight.*" *Chaucer Review* 17, no. 1 (1982): 65–75.

Lévi-Strauss, Claude. *The Elementary Structures of Kinship.* Trans. James Harle Bell,

John Richard von Sturmer, and Rodney Needham. Boston: Beacon Press, 1969.

_____. *The Raw and the Cooked*. Introduction to a Science of Mythology 1. Trans. John and Doreen Weightman. New York: Harper and Row, 1969.

_____. *Totemism*. Trans. Rodney Needham. Boston: Beacon, 1963.

Lindahl, Carl. *Earnest Games: Folkloric Patterns in the Canterbury Tales*. Bloomington: Indiana University Press, 1987.

_____. "*Sir Gawain and the Green Knight* and Myth in Its Time." In *Telling Tales: Medieval Narratives and the Folk Tradition*, ed. Francesca Canadé Sautman, Diana Conchado, and Giuseppe Carlo Di Scipio. New York: St. Martin's Press, 1998. Pp. 249–67.

Lindley, Arthur. "'Ther he watz dispoyled, with spechez of myerthe': Carnival and the Undoing of Sir Gawain." *Exemplaria* 6 (1994): 67–86.

Lindley, Philip. "Absolutism and Regal Image in Ricardian Sculpture." In *The Regal Image of Richard II and the Wilton Diptych*, ed. Dillian Gordon, Lisa Monnas, and Caroline Elam. London: Miller, 1997. Pp. 61–83.

Little, Lester K. "Les Techniques de la confession et la confession comme technique." In *Faire croire: Modalités de la diffusion et de la réception des messages religieux du XIIe au XVe siècle*, ed. G. Barone, J. Berlioz, J. Chiffoleau, and A. Vauchez. Rome: Ecole Française de Rome, 1981. Pp. 87–99.

Lock, Margaret. "Cultivating the Body: Anthropology and Epistemologies of Bodily Practice and Knowledge." *Annual Review of Anthropology* 22 (1993): 133–55.

Locke, John. *An Essay Concerning Human Understanding*. 1689. Ed. Peter H. Nidditch. Oxford: Clarendon Press, 1975.

London, H. Stanford. *Royal Beasts*. East Knoyle, Wilts: Heraldry Society, 1956.

Loomis, Laura Hibbard. "Secular Dramatics in the Royal Palace, Paris, 1378, 1389, and Chaucer's 'Tregetoures.'" *Speculum* 33 (1958): 242–55.

Lossing, Marian. "The Prologue to the Legend of Good Women and the *Lai de Franchise*." *Studies in Philology* 39 (1942): 15–35.

Lowes, John L. "The Prologue to the *Legend of Good Women* as Related to the French *Marguerite* Poems and the *Filostrato*." *PMLA* 19 (1904): 593–683.

MacAloon, John J. "Introduction: Cultural Performances, Culture Theory." In *Rite, Drama, Festival, Spectacle: Rehearsals toward a Theory of Cultural Performance*, ed. John J. MacAloon. Philadelphia: Institute for the Study of Human Issues, 1984. Pp. 1–15.

_____. "Olympic Games and the Theory of Spectacle in Modern Societies." In *Rite, Drama, Festival, Spectacle: Rehearsals Toward a Theory of Cultural Performance*, ed. John J. MacAloon. Philadelphia: Institute for the Study of Human Issues, 1984. Pp. 241–80.

MacAloon, John J., ed. *Rite, Drama, Festival, Spectacle: Rehearsals Toward a Theory of Cultural Performance*. Philadelphia: Institute for the Study of Human Issues, 1984.

Maddox, Donald. *Fictions of Identity in Medieval France*. Cambridge: Cambridge University Press, 2000.

Maddox, Donald, and Sara Sturm-Maddox, eds. *Melusine of Lusignan: Founding Fiction in Late Medieval France*. Athens: University of Georgia Press, 1996.

Marks, Richard, and Ann Payne. *British Heraldry from Its Origins to c. 1800*. London: British Museum, 1978.

Marsh, George L. "Sources and Analogues of 'The Flower and the Leaf.'" *Modern Philology* 4 (1906–7): 121–67, 281–327.

Marvin, William P. "Slaughter and Romance: Hunting Reserves in Late Medieval England." In *Medieval Crime and Social Control*, ed. Barbara A. Hanawalt and David Wallace. Minneapolis: University of Minnesota Press, 1999. Pp. 224–52.

Mathew, Gervase. *The Court of Richard II*. London: Murray, 1968.

Mauss, Marcel. "A Category of the Human Mind: The Notion of Person; the Notion of Self." 1938. Trans. W. D. Halls in *The Category of the Person: Anthropology, Philosophy, History*, ed. Michael Carrithers, Steven Collins, and Steven Lukes. Cambridge: Cambridge University Press, 1985. Pp. 1–25.

——. "Body Techniques." 1935. In *Sociology and Psychology: Essays*, trans. Ben Brewster. London: Routledge, 1979.

McCracken, Grant. "Clothing as Language: An Object Lesson in the Study of the Expressive Properties of Material Culture." In *Material Anthropology: Contemporary Approaches to Material Culture*, ed. Barrie Reynolds and Margaret A. Stott. Lanham, Md.: University Press of America, 1987. Pp. 103–28.

McKeon, Michael. *The Origins of the English Novel, 1600–1740*. Baltimore: Johns Hopkins University Press, 1987.

McNeill, John T., and Helena M. Gamer. *Medieval Handbooks of Penance*. New York: Columbia University Press, 1938.

McSheffrey, Shannon. "'I Will Never Have None Ayenst My Faders Will': Consent and the Making of Marriage in the Late Medieval Diocese of London." In *Women, Marriage, and Family in Medieval Christendom: Essays in Memory of Michael M. Sheehan, C.S.B.*, ed. Constance M. Rousseau and Joel T. Rosenthal. Kalamazoo, Mich.: Medieval Institute Publications, 1998. Pp. 153–74.

Meiss, Millard. *French Painting in the Time of Jean de Berry: The Boucicaut Master*. London: Phaidon, 1968.

Mellinkoff, Ruth. *Outcasts: Signs of Otherness in Northern European Art of the Middle Ages*. 2 vols. Berkeley: University of California Press, 1993.

Middle English Dictionary. Ed. Hans Kurath et al. Ann Arbor: University of Michigan Press, 1952– .

Mirot, Léon. "Un Trousseau royal à la fin du XIVe siècle," *Mémoires de la Société de l'histoire de Paris et de l'Ile-de-France* 29 (1902): 125–58.

Monnas, Lisa. "Fit for a King: Figured Silks Shown in the Wilton Diptych." In *The Regal Image of Richard II and the Wilton Diptych*, ed. Dillian Gordon, Lisa Monnas, and Caroline Elam. London: Miller, 1997. Pp. 165–77.

Moore, Sally F., and Barbara G. Myerhoff. "Introduction: Secular Ritual: Forms and Meanings." In *Secular Ritual*, ed. Sally F. Moore and Barbara G. Myerhoff. Assen: Van Gorcum, 1977. Pp. 3–15.

Morris, Colin. *The Discovery of the Individual, 1050–1200*. London: SPCK, 1972.

Morris, Rosalind C. "All Made Up: Performance Theory and the New Anthropology of Sex and Gender." *Annual Review of Anthropology* 24 (1995): 574–79.

Morse, Charlotte Cook. "What to Call Petrarch's Griselda." In *The Uses of Manuscripts in Literary Studies: Essays in Memory of Judson Boyce Allen*, ed. Charlotte

Cook Morse, Penelope Reed Doob, and Marjorie Curry Woods. Kalamazoo, Mich.: Medieval Institute Publications, 1992. Pp. 263–303.

Mühlethaler, Jean-Claude. *Fauvel au pouvoir: Lire la satire médiévale*. Paris: Champion, 1994.

Mulvey, Laura. "Some Thoughts on Theories of Fetishism in the Context of Contemporary Culture." *october* 65 (Summer 1993): 3–20.

Murray, Jacqueline. "Individualism and Consensual Marriage: Some Evidence from Medieval England." In *Women, Marriage, and Family in Medieval Christendom: Essays in Memory of Michael M. Sheehan, C.S.B.*, ed. Constance M. Rousseau and Joel T. Rosenthal. Kalamazoo, Mich.: Medieval Institute Publications, 1998. Pp. 121–51.

Napier, A. David. *Masks, Transformation, and Paradox*. Berkeley: University of California Press, 1986.

Newman, Barbara. *From Virile Woman to WomanChrist: Studies in Medieval Religion and Literature*. Philadelphia: University of Pennsylvania Press, 1995.

Newton, Stella Mary. *Fashion in the Age of the Black Prince*. Woodbridge, Suffolk: Boydell, 1980.

Nichols, John Gough. "Observations on the Heraldic Devices Discovered on the Effigies of Richard the Second and His Queen in Westminster Abbey." *Archaeologia* 29 (1842): 32–59.

Nichols, Stephen G. "Prophetic Discourse: St. Augustine to Christine de Pizan." In *The Bible in the Middle Ages: Its Influence on Literature and Art*, ed. Bernard S. Levy. Binghamton, N.Y.: Medieval and Renaissance Texts and Studies, 1992. Pp. 51–76.

Nicolas, Nicholas Harris. "Observations on the Institution of the Most Noble Order of the Garter." *Archaeologia* 31 (1846): 1–163.

————. "Observations on the Origin and History of the Badge and Mottoes of Edward Prince of Wales." *Archaeologia* 31 (1846): 350–84.

————. *The Scrope and Grosvenor Controversy*. 2 vols. London: Samuel Bentley, 1832.

Norris, Malcolm. *Monumental Brasses: The Craft*. London: Faber and Faber, 1978.

————. *Monumental Brasses: The Memorials*. 2 vols. London: Phillips and Page, 1977.

Nouvet, Claire. "The 'Marguerite': A Distinctive Signature." In *Chaucer's French Contemporaries: The Poetry/Poetics of Self and Tradition*, ed. R. Barton Palmer. New York: AMS Press, 1999. Pp. 251–76.

Owst, G. R. *Literature and Pulpit in Medieval England*. Oxford: Blackwell, 1961.

Packe, Michael. *King Edward III*. Ed. L. C. B. Seaman. London: Routledge, 1983.

Pannier, Léopold. *La Noble maison de Saint-Ouen, la villa Clippiacum, et l'Ordre de l'Etoile d'après les documents originaux*. Paris: Aubry, 1872.

Paris, Gaston. "Le *Roman de Fauvel*." *Histoire littéraire de la France* 32 (Paris, 1898): 108–53.

Parker, Andrew, and Eve Kosofsky Sedgwick, eds. *Performativity and Performance*. London: Routledge, 1995.

Pastoureau, Michel. "Désigner ou dissimuler? Le Rôle du cimier dans l'imaginaire médiéval." In *Masques et déguisements dans la littérature médiévale*, ed. Marie-Louise Ollier. Montreal: Presses de l'Université de Montréal, 1988.

_____. *Figures et couleurs: Etudes sur la symbolique et la sensibilité médiévales*. Paris: Léopard d'Or, 1986.

_____. *Traité d'héraldique*. 3rd ed. Paris: Picard, 1997.

Paton, Lucy Allen. "The Story of Grisandole: A Study in the Legend of Merlin." *PMLA* 22 (1907): 234–76.

Patterson, Lee. *Chaucer and the Subject of History*. Madison: University of Wisconsin Press, 1991.

_____. "Making Identities in Fifteenth-Century England: Henry V and John Lydgate." In *New Historical Literary Study*, ed. Jeffrey N. Cox and Larry J. Reynolds. Princeton, N.J.: Princeton University Press, 1993. Pp. 69–107.

_____. "On the Margin: Postmodernism, Ironic History, and Medieval Studies." *Speculum* 65 (1990): 87–108.

Payne, Ann. "The Salisbury Roll of Arms, c. 1463." In *England in the Fifteenth Century: Proceedings of the 1986 Harlaxton Symposium*, ed. Daniel Williams. Woodbridge, Suffolk: Boydell, 1987. Pp. 187–98.

Pearsall, Derek, and Elizabeth Salter. *Landscapes and Seasons of the Medieval World*. Toronto: University of Toronto Press, 1973.

Pernoud, Régine. *Joan of Arc by Herself and Her Witnesses*. Trans. Edward Hyams. New York: Stein and Day, 1966.

_____. *The Retrial of Joan of Arc*. Trans. J. M. Cohen. New York: Harcourt, Brace, 1955.

Perret, Michèle. "Travesties et transsexuelles: Yde, Silence, Grisandole, Blanchandine." *Romance Notes* 25 (1984–85): 328–40.

Peters, Edward. "Destruction of the Flesh—Salvation of the Spirit: The Paradoxes of Torture in Medieval Christian Society." In *The Devil, Heresy and Witchcraft in the Middle Ages: Essays in Honor of Jeffrey B. Russell*, ed. Alberto Ferreiro. Leiden: Brill, 1998. Pp. 131–48.

_____. *Inquisition*. New York: Macmillan, 1988.

_____. *Torture*. Oxford: Blackwell, 1985.

Peyronnet, Georges. "Gerson, Charles VII et Jeanne d'Arc: La Propagande au service de la guerre." *Revue d'histoire ecclesiastique* 84 (1989): 334–70.

Pietz, William. "The Problem of the Fetish, I." *Res* 9 (Spring 1985): 5–17.

_____. "The Problem of the Fetish, II." *Res* 13 (Spring 1987): 23–45.

Pinon, Roger. "Qu'est-ce qu'un charivari?" In *Kontakte und Grenzen: Probleme der Volks-, Kultur- und Sozialforschung*. Göttingen: Otto Schwartz, 1969. Pp. 393–405.

Piponnier, Françoise. *Costume et vie sociale: La Cour d'Anjou, XIVe–XVe siècle*. Paris: Mouton, 1970.

_____. "Une Révolution dans le costume masculin au XIVe siècle." In *Le Vêtement: Histoire, archéologie et symbolique vestimentaires au Moyen Age*, ed. Michel Pastoureau. Paris: Léopard d'Or, 1989. Pp. 225–42.

Piponnier, Françoise, and Perrine Mane. *Se vêtir au Moyen Age*. Paris: Adam Biro, 1995.

Pitt-Rivers, Julian. "Honour and Social Status." In *Honour and Shame: The Values of Mediterranean Society*, ed. J. G. Peristiany. Chicago: University of Chicago Press, 1966. Pp. 21–137.

Planche, Alice. *Charles d'Orléans ou la recherche d'un langage*. Paris: Champion, 1975.

Poirion, Daniel. *Le Poète et le prince: L'Evolution du lyrisme courtois de Guillaume de Machaut à Charles d'Orléans*. Paris: Presses Universitaires de France, 1965.

Porter, Roy. Introduction to *Rewriting the Self: Histories from the Renaissance to the Present*, ed. Roy Porter. London: Routledge, 1993.

Pouchelle, Marie-Christine. "Représentations du corps dans la *Légende dorée*." *Ethnologie française* n.s. 5 (1975): 293–308.

Prinet, Max. "Armoiries familiales et armoiries de roman au XVᵉ siècle." *Romania* 58 (1932): 569–73.

———. "Cimiers et supports parlants d'armoiries françaises." *Archives héraldiques suisses* 30 (1916): 12–21.

Prunières, Henry. *Le Ballet de cour en France avant Benserade et Lully*. Paris: Laurens, 1914.

Quicherat, Jules. "Relation inédite sur Jeanne d'Arc." *Revue historique* 4 (1877): 327–44.

Quinn, William A. *Chaucer's Rehersyngs: The Performability of the "Legend of Good Women"*. Washington, D.C.: Catholic University Press, 1994.

Regalado, Nancy F. "Masques réels dans le monde de l'imaginaire. Le Rite et l'écrit dans le charivari du *Roman de Fauvel*, MS. B.N. fr. 146." In *Masques et déguisements dans la littérature médiévale*, ed. Marie-Louise Ollier. Montreal: Montreal University Press, 1988. Pp. 111–26.

Régnier-Bohler, Danielle. "Le Corps mis à nu: Perception et valeur symbolique de la nudité dans les récits du Moyen Age." *Europe*, no. 654 (October 1983): 51–62.

Renfrew, Colin. "Varna and the Emergence of Wealth in Prehistoric Europe." In *The Social Life of Things: Commodities in Cultural Perspective*, ed. Arjun Appadurai. Cambridge: Cambridge University Press, 1986. Pp. 141–68.

Rey-Flaud, Henri. *Le Charivari: Les Rituels fondamentaux de la sexualité*. Paris: Payot, 1985.

Reyher, Paul. *Les Masques anglais: Etude sur les ballets et la vie de cour en Angleterre (1512–1640)*. Paris: Hachette, 1909.

Roach, Joseph. *Cities of the Dead: Circum-Atlantic Performance*. New York: Columbia University Press, 1996.

———. "Kinship, Intelligence, and Memory as Improvisation: Culture and Performance in New Orleans." In *Performance and Cultural Politics*, ed. Elin Diamond. London: Routledge, 1996. Pp. 217–36.

Roach, Mary Ellen, and Joanne Bubolz Eicher. "The Language of Personal Adornment." In *The Fabrics of Culture: The Anthropology of Clothing and Adornment*, ed. Justine M. Cordwell and Ronald A. Schwartz. The Hague: Mouton, 1979. Pp. 7–21.

Rubin, Gayle. "The Traffic in Women: Notes on the 'Political Economy' of Sex." In *Toward an Anthropology of Women*, ed. Rayna R. Reiter. New York: Monthly Review Press, 1975. Pp. 157–210.

Rubin, Miri. *Corpus Christi: The Eucharist in Late Medieval Culture*. Cambridge: Cambridge University Press, 1991.

———. "The Person in the Form: Medieval Challenges to Bodily 'Order.' " In *Framing Medieval Bodies*, ed. Sarah Kay and Miri Rubin. Manchester: Manchester University Press, 1994. Pp. 100–122.

Sahlins, Marshall. *Culture and Practical Reason*. Chicago: University of Chicago Press, 1976.

———. "The Sadness of Sweetness: The Native Anthropology of Western Cosmology." *Current Anthropology* 37 (1996): 395–415.

Saineanu, Lazar. *Les Sources indigènes de l'étymologie française*. Vol. 1. Paris: Boccard, 1925.

Sainte-Palaye, La Curne de. *Dictionnaire historique de l'ancien langue françois*. Niort: Favre, 1876.

Salih, Sarah. *Versions of Virginity in Late Medieval England*. Woodbridge, Suffolk: Boydell and Brewer, 2001.

Salter, Elizabeth. "The Timeliness of *Wynnere and Wastoure*." *Medium Aevum* 47 (1978): 40–65.

Sapir, J. David, and J. Christopher Crocker, eds. *The Social Use of Metaphor*. Philadelphia: University of Pennsylvania Press, 1977.

Saul, Nigel. *Richard II*. New Haven, Conn.: Yale University Press, 1997.

Scanlon, Larry. "What's the Pope Got to Do with It? Forgery, Didacticism and Desire in the Clerk's Tale." *New Medieval Literatures* 6 (2002).

Schechner, Richard. *Between Theater and Anthropology*. Philadelphia: University of Pennsylvania Press, 1985.

———. *The Future of Ritual: Writings on Culture and Performance*. London: Routledge, 1993.

———. *Performance Theory*. 2nd ed. London: Routledge, 1988.

Schibanoff, Susan. "True Lies: Transvestism and Idolatry in the Trial of Joan of Arc." In *Fresh Verdicts on Joan of Arc*, ed. Bonnie Wheeler and Charles T. Wood. New York: Garland, 1996. Pp. 31–60.

Schmitt, Jean-Claude. "Les Masques, le diable, les morts dans l'occident médiéval." *Razo: Cahiers du centre d'études médiévales de Nice* 6 (1986): 87–119.

Schneider, Jane. "Peacocks and Penguins: The Political Economy of European Cloth and Colors." *American Ethnologist* 5 (1978): 413–47.

Scott, Margaret. *A Visual History of Costume: The Fourteenth and Fifteenth Centuries*. London: Batsford, 1986.

Severs, J. Burke. *The Literary Relationships of Chaucer's "Clerkes Tale"*. New Haven, Conn.: Yale University Press, 1942.

Sheehan, Michael M. *Marriage, Family, and Law in Medieval Europe: Collected Studies*. Ed. James K. Farge. Toronto: University of Toronto Press, 1996.

Simpson, James. "Ethics and Interpretation: Reading Wills in Chaucer's *Legend of Good Women*." *Studies in the Age of Chaucer* 20 (1998): 73–100.

Sinclair, Keith V. *Tristan de Nanteuil: Thematic Infrastructure and Literary Creation*. Tübingen: Max Niemeyer, 1983.

Smith, C. E. J. "The Livery Collar." *Coat of Arms* n.s. 3, no. 151 (Autumn 1990): 238–53.

Smith, Jonathan Z. "The Domestication of Sacrifice." In *Violent Origins: Walter Burkert, René Girard, and Jonathan Z. Smith on Ritual Killing and Cultural Formation*, ed. Robert G. Hamerton-Kelly et al. Stanford, Calif.: Stanford Univ. Press, 1987. Pp. 191–205.

———. *Imagining Religion: From Babylon to Jonestown*. Chicago: University of Chicago Press, 1982.

Solterer, Helen. "Figures of Female Militancy in Medieval France." *Signs* 16 (1990–91): 522–49.

Sombart, Werner. *Luxury and Capitalism*. Trans. W. R. Dittmar, intro. Philip Siegelman. Ann Arbor: University of Michigan Press, 1967 [1913].

Sponsler, Claire. *Drama and Resistance: Bodies, Goods, and Theatricality in Late Medieval England*. Minneapolis: University of Minnesota Press, 1997.

Stallybrass, Peter and Ann Rosalind Jones. *Renaissance Clothing and the Materials of Memory*. Cambridge: Cambridge University Press, 2000.

Stallybrass, Peter and Allon White. *The Politics and Poetics of Transgression*. Ithaca, N.Y.: Cornell University Press, 1986.

Stanesco, Michel. *Jeux d'errance du chevalier médiéval: Aspects ludiques de la fonction guerrière dans la littérature du Moyen Age flamboyant*. Leiden: Brill, 1998.

Staniland, Kay. "Court Style, Painters, and the Great Wardrobe." In *England in the Fourteenth Century: Proceedings of the 1985 Harlaxton Symposium*, ed. W. M. Ormrod. Woodbridge, Suffolk: Boydell, 1986. Pp. 236–46.

————. "The Great Wardrobe Accounts as a Source for Historians of Fourteenth-Century Clothing and Textiles." *Textile History* 20 (1989): 275–81.

————. "Medieval Courtly Splendour." *Costume* 14 (1980): 7–23.

Steele, Valerie. *Fetish: Fashion, Sex, and Power*. New York: Oxford University Press, 1996.

Stock, Brian. "Reading, Writing, and the Self: Petrarch and His Forerunners." *New Literary History* 26 (1995): 717–30.

Stock, Lorraine Kochanske. "Froissart's *Chroniques* and Its Illustrators: Historicity and Ficticity in the Verbal and Visual Imaging of Charles VI's Bal des Ardents." *Studies in Iconography* 21 (2000): 123–80.

————. "The Two Mayings in Chaucer's *Knight's Tale*: Convention and Invention." *Journal of English and Germanic Philology* 85 (1986): 206–21.

Stoller, Robert J. *Observing the Erotic Imagination*. New Haven, Conn.: Yale University Press, 1985.

Strathern, Marilyn. *The Gender of the Gift: Problems with Women and Problems with Society in Melanesia*. Berkeley: University of California Press, 1988.

————. "No Nature, No Culture: The Hagen Case." In *Nature, Culture and Gender*, ed. Carol P. MacCormack and Marilyn Strathern. Cambridge: Cambridge University Press, 1980. Pp. 174–222.

Strohm, Paul. *Hochon's Arrow: The Social Imagination of Fourteenth-Century Texts*. Princeton, N.J.: Princeton University Press, 1992.

Sullivan, Karen. *The Interrogation of Joan of Arc*. Minneapolis: University of Minnesota Press, 1999.

Tambiah, Stanley J. "Animals Are Good to Think and Good to Prohibit." *Ethnology* 8 (1969): 423–59.

————. *Culture, Thought, and Social Action: An Anthropological Perspective*. Cambridge, Mass.: Harvard University Press, 1985.

Taylor, Charles. *Sources of the Self: The Making of Modern Identity*. Cambridge, Mass.: Harvard University Press, 1989.

Tentler, Thomas N. *Sin and Confession on the Eve of the Reformation*. Princeton, N.J.: Princeton University Press, 1977.

Thiselton-Dyer, T. F. *British Popular Customs*. London : G. Bell. 1876.

Thompson, E. P. "'Rough Music': Le Charivari anglais." *Annales: Economies, Sociétés, Civilisations* 27 (1972): 285–312.

Tischler, Hans. "A Lai from the *Roman de Fauvel.*" In *Essays on the Music of J. S. Bach and Other Divers Subjects: A Tribute to Gerhard Herz*, ed. Robert L. Weaver et al. Louisville, Ky.: University of Louisville, 1981. Pp. 145–155.

Tooker, Elisabeth. "The Many Faces of Masks and Masking: Discussion." In *The Power of Symbols: Masks and Masquerade in the Americas*, ed. N. Ross Crumrine and Marjorie Halpin. Vancouver: University of British Columbia Press, 1983. Pp. 12–18.

Travis, Peter W. "Chaucer's Heliotropes and the Poetics of Metaphor." *Speculum* 72 (1997): 399–427.

The "Très Riches Heures" of Jean, Duke of Berry, Musée Condé, Chantilly. Intros. Raymond Cazelles, Jean Longnon, and Millard Meiss. New York: Brazillier, 1969.

Turner, Victor W. *The Forest of Symbols: Aspects of Ndembu Ritual*. Ithaca, N.Y.: Cornell University Press, 1967.

—————. *From Ritual to Theatre: The Human Seriousness of Play*. New York: PAJ Publications, 1982.

—————. *The Ritual Process: Structure and Anti-Structure*. Chicago: Aldine, 1969.

Twycross, Meg. "The Theatricality of Medieval English Plays." In *The Cambridge Companion to Medieval English Theatre*, ed. Richard Beadle. Cambridge: Cambridge University Press, 1994. Pp. 37–84.

Twycross, Meg, and Sarah Carpenter. "Masks in Medieval English Theatre: The Mystery Plays." *Medieval English Theatre* 3, no. 2 (1981): 7–44.

Uhl, Patrice. "Les 'Sotes chançons' du *Roman de Fauvel* (MS E): La Symptomatique indécision du rubricateur." *French Studies* 45 (1991): 385–402.

Vale, Juliet. *Edward III and Chivalry: Chivalric Society and Its Context, 1270–1350*. Woodbridge, Suffolk: Boydell, 1982.

Vale, Malcolm. *War and Chivalry: Warfare and Aristocratic Culture in England, France and Burgundy at the End of the Middle Ages*. London: Duckworth, 1981.

—————. "The World of the Courts: Content and Context of the *Fauvel* Manuscript." In *Fauvel Studies: Allegory, Chronicle, Music, and Image in Paris, Bibliothèque Nationale de France, MS français 146*, ed. Margaret Bent and Andrew Wathey. Oxford: Clarendon Press, 1998. Pp. 591–98.

van Gennep, Arnold. *Manuel de folklore français contemporain*. 4 vols. Paris: Picard, 1946.

—————. *The Rites of Passage*. Trans. Monika B. Vizedom and Gabrielle L. Caffee. Chicago: University of Chicago Press, 1960 [1909].

Vaultier, Roger. *Le Folklore pendant la guerre de Cent Ans d'après les Lettres de Rémission du Trésor des Chartes*. Paris: Guénégaud, 1965.

Viel, Robert. *Les Origines symboliques du blason*. Paris: Berg, 1972.

Wagner, Anthony Richard. *Heralds and Heraldry in the Middle Ages*. 2nd ed. Oxford: Oxford University Press, 1956.

—————. "The Swan Badge and the Swan Knight." *Archaeologia* 97 (1959): 127–38.

Wallace, David. *Chaucerian Polity: Absolutist Lineages and Associational Forms in England and Italy*. Stanford, Calif.: Stanford University Press, 1997.

Warner, George F., and Julius P. Gilson. *Catalogue of Western Manuscripts in the Old Royal and King's Collections*. 4 vols. London: Longmans, 1921.

Warner, Marina. *Joan of Arc: The Image of Female Heroism*. New York: Knopf, 1981.

Wathey, Andrew. "The Marriage of Edward III and the Transmission of French Motets to England." *Journal of the American Musicological Society* 45 (1992): 1–29.

Watson, Nicholas. "The *Gawain*-Poet as Vernacular Theologian." In *A Companion to the "Gawain"-Poet*, ed. Derek Brewer and Jonathan Gibson. Cambridge: D.S. Brewer, 1997. Pp. 293–313.

Watt, Ian. *The Rise of the Novel: Studies in Defoe, Richardson and Fielding*. Berkeley: University of California Press, 1957.

Waugh, Christina Frieder. "'Well-Cut Through the Body': Fitted Clothing in Twelfth-Century Europe." *Dress* 26 (1999): 3–16.

Weiner, Annette B. *Inalienable Possessions: The Paradox of Keeping-While-Giving*. Berkeley: University of California Press, 1992.

Weiner, Annette B., and Jane Schneider, eds. *Cloth and Human Experience*. Washington, D.C.: Smithsonian Institution Press, 1989.

Weiskopf, Steven. "Readers of the Lost Arc: Secrecy, Specularity, and Speculation in the Trial of Joan of Arc." In *Fresh Verdicts on Joan of Arc*, ed. Bonnie Wheeler and Charles T. Wood. New York: Garland, 1996. Pp. 113–29.

Weiss, Victoria L. "The 'laykyng of enterludez' at King Arthur's Court: The Beheading Scene in *Sir Gawain and the Green Knight*." In *The Medieval Court in Europe*, ed. Edward R. Haymes. Munich: Fink, 1986. Pp. 189–199.

————. "*Sir Gawain and the Green Knight* and the Fourteenth-Century Interlude." In *Text and Matter: New Critical Perspectives of the "Pearl"-Poet*, ed. Robert J. Blanch, Miriam Youngerman Miller, and Julian N. Wasserman. Troy, N.Y.: Whitston, 1991. Pp. 227–42.

Welsford, Enid. *The Court Masque: A Study in the Relationship Between Poetry and the Revels*. New York: Russell, 1962.

White, Hayden. "The Forms of Wildness: Archaeology of an Idea." In *The Wild Man Within: An Image in Western Thought from the Renaissance to Romanticism*, ed. Edward Dudley and Maximillian E. Novak. Pittsburgh: University of Pittsburgh Press, 1972. Pp. 3–38.

Whiting, B. J. "The Vows of the Heron." *Speculum* 20 (1945): 261–78.

Wickham, Glynne. *Early English Stages, 1300–1660*. 2nd ed. 2 vols. London: Routledge, 1980.

Williamson, Joan B. "Elyas as a Wild Man in *Li Estoire del Chevalier au Cisne*." In *Essays in Honor of Louis Francis Solano*, ed. Raymond J. Cormier and Urban T. Holmes. University of North Carolina Studies in the Romance Languages and Literatures 92. Chapel Hill: University of North Carolina Press, 1970. Pp. 193–202.

Wimsatt, James I. *The Marguerite Poetry of Guillaume de Machaut*. University of North Carolina Studies in the Romance Languages and Literatures 87. Chapel Hill: University of North Carolina Press, 1970.

Withington, Robert. *English Pageantry: An Historical Outline*. 2 vols. 1918. Reprint, New York: Blom, 1963.

Wylie, James Hamilton. *The Reign of Henry the Fifth*. 3 vols. New York: Greenwood, 1968.

Yamamoto, Dorothy. *The Boundaries of the Human in Medieval English Literature*. Oxford: Oxford University Press, 2000.

Yeager, Robert F. "British Library Additional MS. 5141: An Unnoticed Chaucer Vita." *Journal of Medieval and Renaissance Studies* 14 (1984): 261–81.

Zijlstra-Zweens, H. M. *Of His Array Telle I No Lenger Tale: Aspects of Costume, Arms and Armour in Western Europe, 1200–1400*. Amsterdam: Rodolpi, 1988.

Zink, Michel. *The Invention of Literary Subjectivity*. Trans. David Sices. Baltimore: Johns Hopkins University Press, 1999.

Zumthor, Paul. *Essai de poétique médiévale*. Paris: Seuil, 1972.

———. *La Lettre et la voix: De la "littérature" médiévale*. Paris: Seuil, 1987.

Index

Page numbers in italics indicate illustrations.

Acknowledgments

For extensive comments on sections and chapters I am grateful to Kathleen Davis, Susan Gal, Simon Gaunt, David Lawton, and Paul Strohm. Astute listeners at lectures have enlightened me at every stage: David Aers, Sarah Beckwith, Judith Bennett, Christine Chism, Karma Lochrie, Larry Scanlon, Sylvia Tomasch, and David Wallace are responsible for many improvements. An Andrew W. Mellon Foundation fellowship at the Huntington Library (1996) and a National Endowment for the Humanities fellowship at the National Humanities Center (1999–2000) facilitated my research; in particular I owe thanks to Karen Carroll, Jean Houston, and Eliza Robertson of the NHC for their expert assistance. My research assistant at Rutgers, Nicole Smith, was resourceful and reliable at every turn.

An earlier version of part of Chapter 2 appeared as "Maytime in Late Medieval Courts," *New Medieval Literatures* 2 (1998): 159–79. An earlier version of part of Chapter 3 appeared as "Clothing and Gender Definition: Joan of Arc," *Journal of Medieval and Early Modern Studies* 26 (1996): 297–320. An earlier version of part of the last section of Chapter 4 appeared as "Knights in Disguise: Identity and Incognito in Fourteenth-Century Chivalry," in *The Stranger in Medieval Society*, ed. F. R. P. Akehurst and Stephanie Cain Van D'Elden (Minneapolis: University of Minnesota Press, 1997), pp. 63–79. Permission to reprint these materials is acknowledged.

CPSIA information can be obtained at www.ICGtesting.com
Printed in the USA
BVOW07s2104260814

364354BV00003B/187/P